NOW WE ARE CITIZENS

Now We Are Citizens

INDIGENOUS POLITICS IN
POSTMULTICULTURAL BOLIVIA

Nancy Grey Postero

STANFORD UNIVERSITY PRESS

STANFORD, CALIFORNIA

Stanford University Press
Stanford, California
© 2007 by the Board of Trustees of the Leland Stanford Junior University.
All rights reserved.

Printed in the United States of America on acid-free, archival-quality paper

Library of Congress Cataloging-in-Publication Data
Postero, Nancy Grey.
    Now we are citizens : indigenous politics in postmulticultural Bolivia /
Nancy Grey Postero.
        p.   cm.
    Includes bibliographical references and index.
    ISBN-13: 978-0-8047-5519-1 (cloth : alk. paper)
    ISBN-13: 978-0-8047-5520-7 (pbk. : alk. paper)
        1. Guarani Indians—Bolivia—Santa Cruz (Dept.)—Politics and govern-
ment.   2. Guarani Indians—Bolivia—Santa Cruz (Dept.)—Government
relations.   3. Multiculturalism—Political aspects—Bolivia—Santa Cruz
(Dept.)   4. Santa Cruz (Bolivia : Dept.)—Ethnic relations—Political aspects.
5. Santa Cruz (Bolivia : Dept.)—Politics and government.   I. Title.
F2230.2.G72P67   2007
323.1198'38220843—dc22   2006017975

Typeset by BookMatters in 10/12.5 Sabon
Original Printing 2006
Last figure below indicates year of this printing:
15   14   13   12   11   10   09   08   07   06

For Cissie

Contents

Acknowledgments

The writing of this book was made possible by funding from the University of California–San Diego (UCSD) Academic Senate Committee on Research, the UCSD Faculty Career Development Program, and the University of California Humanities Research Institute (UCHRI), where I was a faculty fellow in the fall of 2004. Earlier funding for field research and writing was provided by a Fulbright IIE Fellowship, the Inter-American Foundation, the Tinker Foundation, the Lowie/Olson Foundation, and the Simpson Foundation.

I am most indebted to the Guaraní people of Zona Cruz, whose openness and generosity made this book possible. I am particularly grateful to the leaders of the Capitanía Zona Cruz (CZC), who authorized and collaborated in my research. The capitán grande, whom I call Don Álvaro Montero throughout this work, allowed me to accompany him almost everywhere during my first six months in Santa Cruz. I thank him and the other members of the CZC for their patience and their friendship. The members of the Equipo Técnico Zonal (ETZ, the technical team of the CZC) cheerfully allowed me to attend all their meetings and follow the business of the organization through them. I also thank the leaders and workers of Confederación Indígena del Oriente de Bolivia (CIDOB), the national indigenous federation in Santa Cruz, for all their help.

I could not have carried out my research in Bella Flor without the hospitality of the family I call here the Taperas. Their invitation to live with them opened the way to Bella Flor and gave me a warm home during my stay. Samuel Tapera was a regular companion and became a great friend. His deep commitment to his people is inspiring. More than any other person in Bella Flor, Samuel's father, Don Jesús, taught me about Guaraní life, history, and sensibilities. Despite the great conflicts they were living through, the people of Bella Flor graciously shared their time, their memories, their anguish, and their thoughtful reflections with me.

I would also like to express my gratitude to the many other people in Bolivia who opened their lives and homes to me and helped me understand Bolivia's many realities. Julio Calla, my "adopted father" and dear friend, shared his La Paz home with me, nursed me through all my illnesses, and serenaded me with music and memories. An organic intellectual if there ever was one, Julio taught me a great deal about Bolivia past and present. I thank the whole Calla family in La Paz for their friendship, Sunday lunches, and stimulating discussions: Ricardo Calla Ortega, Jenny Cárdenas, and Hernando Calla Ortega. I give special thanks to Pamela Calla Ortega and Tom Kruse; their son, Benjamin; and their daughter, Julia Elena. They became my family away from home. I am grateful for all the contacts they provided, the open invitation to come visit, their great libraries, the music and the parties, and their intellectual solidarity. Ben Kohl was an important colleague and friend during our overlapping fieldwork periods. Our discussions continue to influence my thinking about Bolivian politics and popular participation. I also thank José de la Fuente, Juan Carlos Guzmán, and Luis Bredow for their friendship over these years.

In Santa Cruz, I thank Wendy Townsend, a great colleague and friend. Her commitment to indigenous people continues to be an inspiration to me. Juan León Corajes shared his deep understanding of campesino life and the ecology of the tropics. I am lucky to have had such a dear friend and teacher. Jordi Benería-Surkin was a wonderful colleague. His work with the Izozeño Guaraní was an extremely helpful counterpoint to my work in the urban context. I thank José Mirtenbaum and his wife, Gaby, for their friendship and for institutional support. Marta Medina, my housemate, gave me a warm introduction into *cambalandia*. Finally, I thank anthropologist Enrique Herrera for sharing with me his many years of experience with the indigenous people of Bolivia and for accompanying me to the Bolivian Amazon in the summer of 1999. Our discussions over the years about anthropology, the role of activism, and indigenous politics in Bolivia have deeply affected this book.

My understanding of Bolivian politics has benefited from ten years of discussions, coffees, conferences, and late-night talk with Bolivia's many brilliant social scientists. On this point, I thank Xavier Albó, Alejandro Almaraz, Iván Arias, Diego Ayo Saucedo, Rossanna Barragán Romano, Luis Bredow, Ricardo Calla Ortega, Pamela Calla Ortega, Luz María Calvo, Isabelle Combes, José de la Fuente, Rosario León, Álvaro García Linera, Javier Gómez, José M. Gordillo, George Gray-Molina, Enrique Herrera Sarmiento, Thomas A. Kruse, Zulema Lehm Ardaya, Ana María Lema, Luis Enrique López, Javier Medina, Adolfo Mendoza, José Mirtenbaum, Ramiro Molina,

René Orellana Halkyer, Sarela Paz, Mamerto Pérez Luna, José Enrique Pinelo, Pablo Regalsky, Jürgen Riester, Gonzalo Rojas, Carlos Romero, José Ros, Inge Sichra, and Luis Tapia.

Several institutions' libraries were critical to my research in Bolivia: in Santa Cruz, Apoyo Para el Campesino–Indígena del Oriente Boliviano (APCOB, Support for the Peasants–Indigenous People of Eastern Bolivia) and CIDOB; and in La Paz, Centro de Estudios Para el Desarrollo Laboral y Agrario (CEDLA, Center for Studies of Labor and Agrarian Development) and la Universidad de la Cordillera. I especially appreciate the collaboration of their librarians, who work under such difficult conditions.

At the University of California–Berkeley, I thank my adviser, Nancy Scheper-Hughes, whose courageous political anthropology is an inspiration. Allan Pred's seminars were a place of both intellectual stretching and human connection. Donald Moore's intellectual clarity as well as his commitment to students and humanity make me glad to have him as a friend and mentor. Thanks also to Michael Watts and Gillian Hart.

I am grateful for the comments and careful readings many colleagues have given this book in its various stages of development. I especially thank Robert Albro, Jody Blanco, Charles Briggs, Elizabeth Dougherty, Daniel Goldstein, Karen Greene, Charles R. Hale, James Holston, Ben Kohl, Misha Kokotovic, Thomas A. Kruse, Miguel La Serna, Sian Lazar, José Antonio Lucero, Keith McNeal, Donald S. Moore, Esra Ozyürek, Joel Robbins, Susana Wappenstein, Elana Zilberg, and Leon Zamosc. I am especially grateful to María Elena García and Shannon Speed for their enormously helpful readings of the manuscript, which helped me clarify my argument. My cohort at the UCHRI in Irvine was very helpful at an important moment in my thinking.

At UCSD, I thank the members of the Department of Anthropology, who have provided a collegial atmosphere for the writing of this book. The Center for Iberian and Latin American Studies (CILAS) and its directors, Charles Briggs and Christine Hunefeldt, have been especially supportive. I am also lucky to have such wonderful graduate students at UCSD. Our work together continues to expand my thinking.

I am most grateful to my family and friends for their continued support and love. Thanks to Steve and Nikki Postero, Parker Postero, and especially to my mother, Cissie Postero, my favorite intellectual and traveling companion and an endless source of encouragement. The Pomegranates have made these years in San Diego so much fun — thanks. Elizabeth, Susana, and Elana have been true friends through it all. To Mike, whose support has been unwavering, I give my deepest thanks and all my love.

Parts of the introduction and chapter 6 originally appeared in "Indigenous Responses to Neoliberalism: A Look at the Bolivian Uprising of 2003," in the journal *Political and Legal Anthropology Review* 28 (1): 73–92. Parts of chapter 1 appeared in "Commentary on Douglas Hertzler's Essay: 'Campesinos and Originarios,'" in the *Journal of Latin American Anthropology* 10 (1): 72–77. Parts of chapter 4 appeared in "Articulations and Fragmentations: Indigenous Politics in Bolivia," in *The Struggle for Indian Rights in Latin America*, which I edited with Leon Zamosc (Brighton: Sussex Academic Press, 2004). Parts of chapter 6 appeared in "Neoliberal Restructuring in Bolivia," in the online journal *A Contracorrientes* 2 (5).

List of Abbreviations

ADN   Acción Democrática Nacional (Nacional Democratic Action), the Bolivian political party formerly led by General Hugo Suárez Banzer.

APCOB   Apoyo Para el Campesino–Indígena del Oriente Boliviano (Support for the Peasants–Indigenous People of Eastern Bolivia), a small NGO based in Santa Cruz.

APG   Asociación del Pueblo Guaraní (Association of Guaraní People), the national Guaraní association.

CABI   Capitanía del Alto y Bajo Izozog, the Guaraní federation from the Izozog region.

CBF   Corporación Bolivian de Fomento (Bolivian Development Corporation).

CDD   Community-driven development.

CEAAL   Consejo de Educación de Adultos de América Latina (Council for Adult Education in Latin America).

CEADES   Colectivo de Estudios Aplicados y Desarrollo Social (Collective for Applied Studies and Social Development), a small Bolivian NGO based in Santa Cruz.

CEDLA   Centro de Estudios Para el Desarrollo Laboral y Agrario (Center for Studies of Labor and Agrarian Development), a small NGO based in La Paz.

CEJIS   Centro de Estudios Jurídicos y Sociedad (Center for Juridical and Societal Studies), an NGO and law collective based in Santa Cruz.

CEPAC   Centro de Promoción Agropecuaria Campesina (Center for the Promotion of Peasant Agriculture).

CEPB   Confederación de Empresarios Privados de Bolivia
                (Bolivian Confederation of Private Entrepreneurs).

CIDOB   Confederación Indígena del Oriente de Bolivia (Indige-
                nous Federation of Eastern Bolivia), the Santa Cruz–
                based national federation of indigenous people.

CIPCA   Centro de Investigación y Promoción del Campesinado
                (Center for the Investigation and Promotion of the
                Peasantry), a Jesuit-based NGO in Bolivia.

COMIBOL   Corporación Minera de Bolivia (Bolivian Mining
                Corporation).

CONDEPA   Conciencia de la Patria (Conscience of the Fatherland),
                a La Paz–based political party formerly led by Carlos
                Palenque.

CPESC   Cordinadora de Pueblos Étnicos de Santa Cruz (Coun-
                cil of Ethnic Peoples of Santa Cruz), a Santa Cruz–
                based regional indigenous federation.

CSUTCB   Confederación Sindical Única de Trabajadores Cam-
                pesinos de Bolivia (United Confederation of Peasant
                Workers of Bolivia).

CZC   Capitanía Zona Cruz, the Guaraní federation based in
                Santa Cruz.

DMI   Distrito municipal indígena (indigenous municipal
                district).

ETZ   Equipo Técnico Zonal, the technical team of the CZC.

FEJUVE   Federación de Juntas Vecinales (Federation of Neigh-
                borhood Associations), based in El Alto.

FSE   Fondo Social de Emergencia (Social Emergency Fund),
                established to moderate poverty caused by structural
                adjustment.

IBIS-Dinamarka A Danish foreign aid agency.

ILO   International Labor Organization, part of the United
                Nations.

IMF   International Monetary Fund, based in Washington,
                D.C.

INRA   Instituto Nacional de Reforma Agraria (National Insti-
                tute of Agrarian Reform), also the name of the political
                reform granting collective territorial titling to indige-
                nous groups.

IWGIA	International Working Group on Indigenous Affairs, based in Geneva.
JV	Junta vecinal (neighborhood association).
LPP	Ley de Partícipación Popular (Law of Popular Participation).
MAS	Movimiento al Socialismo (Movement Toward Socialism), the Bolivian political party led by Evo Morales.
MBL	Movimiento Bolivia Libre (Free Bolivia Movement), a Bolivian political party.
MIP	Movimiento Indígena Pachakuti.
MITKA	Movimiento Indio Túpac Katari (Túpac Katari Indian Movement).
MNC	Multinational corporation.
MNR	Movimiento Nacional Revolucionario (National Revolutionary Movement), the Bolivian political party that led the 1952 revolution.
MRTK	Movimiento Revolucionario Túpac Katari (Túpac Katari Revolutionary Movement), later called the Movimiento Revolucionario Túpac Katari de Liberación (MRTKL, Túpac Katari Revolutionary Movement for Liberation).
MST	Movimiento Sin Tierra (Movement of People Without Land).
NEP	New Economic Policy.
NGO	Nongovernmental organization.
OC	Oversight committee.
OTBs	Organizaciones territoriales de base (territorial grassroots organizations, defined by the LPP).
PLI	Proyecto de Ley Indígena (Indigenous Law Project), proposed by CIDOB.
POA	Plan anual operativa (the annual operating plan of a municipal budget).
PROCESO	A Bolivian NGO.
RPGIs	Responsables de planificación y gestión indígena (people in charge of indigenous planning and management).

SAE   Subsecretaría de Asuntos Étnicos (Subsecretariat of Ethnic Affairs).

SEAPAS   Secretaríado Ejecutivo de Pastoral Social (Executive Secretariat of Social Pastoral Work), a local NGO run by the archbishop of the Catholic Church in Santa Cruz.

SNPP   Secretaría Nacional de Participación Popular (Secretariat of Popular Participation).

TCOs   Tierras comunitarias de origen (original communal lands, lands given in collective title to indigenous groups).

USAID   U.S. Agency for International Development.

VAIPO   Vice Ministerio de Asuntos Indígenas y Pueblos Originarios (Vice Ministry of Indigenous and Original Peoples Affairs).

YPBF   Yacimientos Petrolíferos Fiscales de Bolivia (the national oil and gas corporation of Bolivia).

NOW WE ARE CITIZENS

Bolivia

Introduction: Neoliberal Multiculturalism in Bolivia

The reforms [of the 1990s] just changed a few things, but it wasn't enough. It was a change in name only. They, the politicians, made the changes among themselves, the authorities. They never consulted with the people [*el pueblo*]. . . . So, the people arose, they got mad, they kicked out Goni [the president, Gonzalo Sánchez de Lozada].

— Anacleto Supayabe, secretary of land and territory, Cordinadora de Pueblos Étnicos de Santa Cruz (CPESC, Council of Ethnic Peoples of Santa Cruz)

The third millennium is the epoch of the original peoples, no longer that of the empire; it is the epoch of the struggle against the [neoliberal] economic model.

— Evo Morales, president-elect of Bolivia

On December 18, 2005, Evo Morales was elected president of Bolivia, the first indigenous person to lead the country since the arrival of the Spaniards more than five hundred years ago. On the night of his victory, Morales, who is Aymara, proclaimed, "Indigenous comrades, for the first time we are presidents!" ("Compañeros indígenas, por primera vez somos presidentes!") (La Razón 2005e). The nearly delirious crowd burst into even louder applause. "Next year," he promised, "begins the new history of Bolivia" (ibid.).

Indigenous people and social movements have been organizing for decades, seeking cultural recognition and more inclusive representation. Yet Morales's election is the culmination of a striking new kind of activism in Bolivia. Born out of a history of resistance to colonial racism, and developed in collective struggles against the postrevolutionary state since 1952, this kind of activism has crystallized over the past decade, as poor and Indian Bolivian citizens have engaged with the democratic promises and exclusions of neoliberal multiculturalism. Now, armed with the language of citizenship and the expectations of the rights it implies, this emerging public is demanding radical changes in the traditional relationship between state and civil society, calling for an end to the structured inequalities that mark Bolivian society. I call this form of social engagement "postmulticultural citizenship." The social convulsions of the tumultuous period from 2000 to the present — during which popular protests have toppled two presidents and paralyzed the country on numerous occasions — intimated how strong this new social formation might be. The 2005 election of Morales, who campaigned against the neoliberal economic model and promised instead to nationalize the country's natural resources for the benefit of all Bolivians, demonstrates that Bolivia's most marginalized people can challenge fundamental ideas about the nation, multiculturalism, neoliberalism, and democracy.

The "Gas War"

The shift to this postmulticultural social formation became particularly evident during the so-called gas war of October 2003, which forced the resignation of then president Gonzalo Sánchez de Lozada. Poor, urban Aymara Indians, who make up the majority of the population in the satellite city of El Alto, above the capital city of La Paz, began the demonstrations. They objected to the president's proposal to allow foreign corporations to export natural gas from Bolivia's eastern lowlands via a pipeline through Chile to processing plants and markets in the United States and Mexico. They were soon joined by peasants, students, the unemployed, teachers, and miners from around the highlands. Carrying signs claiming *"el gas es nuestro"* ("the gas is ours"), protesters demanded the nationalization of transnational gas concessions and an end to *"el modelo"* ("the model," referring to the neoliberal or free-market economic model that had been dominant in Bolivia since the mid-1980s).

After six weeks of violence and popular outrage, and more than eighty deaths, the president fled to Miami. The insurrection had powerful results. The new president, former vice president Carlos Mesa, promised novel forms of direct democracy, including a referendum on gas export policies (held in July 2004) and an assembly to rewrite the constitution. The constitutional assembly had been a long-held demand of indigenous and labor sectors, who argued that the state's current model denied representation to the people, allowing politics to be run by the traditional elite. This demand became more salient as a result of the uprising, when debates about the effects of neoliberal economic and political restructurings, especially the privatization of public decision making, filled the public sphere.

These activists were essentially arguing for a different vision of development for their country. Perhaps the most important result of the insurrection, however, is the growing political power of indigenous and popular social movements whose continuing mass mobilizations have forced the rest of

Bolivia to reckon with them as important political actors.[1] If the power of these social movements was still in doubt after the gas war, however, it was publicly acknowledged in June 2005. While the parliament dragged its feet in setting dates for the *asamblea constituyente* (the constitutional assembly), two months of strikes forced a second popular impeachment and President Mesa resigned to make way for new elections.

An Indian Uprising?

Was the 2003 gas war an "Indian Revolution," as the international media has portrayed it? Was the 2005 election of Morales as president evidence that the Indians of Bolivia have finally risen? Commentators have suggested that given the conditions under which many Bolivian Indians live, such a revolution would certainly be understandable. In a country that is considered the poorest in Latin America, the approximately 60 percent of Bolivians who consider themselves to be native peoples are significantly poorer than the rest of the population (Psacharopoulos and Patrinos 1994).[2] A World Bank 2005 study showed that 52 percent of Bolivian indigenous people live in extreme poverty. Their condition appears relatively untouched by efforts to combat poverty. For example, between 1997 and 2002, extreme poverty rates began to fall for nonindigenous people (from 31 percent to 27 percent), but they remained constant for indigenous people. Even more stunning was the finding that in rural areas, poverty actually increased for indigenous peoples (from 65 percent to 72 percent) while decreasing slightly for nonindigenous people (ibid.).

The economic status of Bolivian Indians reflects a historical fact: native populations in Bolivia have been dominated and exploited since the Spanish conquest in the 1500s. In the colonial era, native Andean peoples (the Aymara in the highlands around Lake Titicaca and the Quechua-speaking peoples in the valleys to the east) were lumped together as "Indians," put to work in the silver mines, and forced to pay tribute to the Crown. The many smaller groups of Indians in the Amazonian basin were treated as dangerous savages and killed or forced into servitude during the rubber boom. The Guaraní peoples of the southern mountains and Chaco desert area were gradually overrun by the expansion of the cattle-ranching frontier. Across the country, Indian resistance was eventually put down through several centuries of military force, religious indoctrination, and economic exploitation.

In the eighteenth century, after independence from Spain, liberal Republican governments instituted legal reforms that made communal property — the central organizing structure of indigenous communities — illegal. This paved the way for massive expropriation of Indian lands and the creation of the *latifundio* system, in which Indians served as labor for white or mestizo landowners. The 1952 revolution addressed some of these injustices, with an agrarian reform program that gave land to Indian peasants. Nevertheless, Indians continued to suffer widespread economic and political discrimination. In the 1970s and 1980s, Indians began organizing, and by the 1990s a powerful national indigenous movement had emerged, mounting demonstrations demanding cultural recognition and territorial rights. In the mid-1990s, the government of Sánchez de Lozada instituted a series of constitutional and legislative reforms that purported to expand citizenship to all Bolivians, especially its indigenous population.

Despite these "multicultural" reforms, however, the faces on the front lines of the 2003 demonstrations were overwhelmingly indigenous, especially in El Alto, where most of the violence occurred. Indian pride in the results of the gas war was palpable. One Aymara protester in El Alto described his participation in the demonstrations. Flexing his biceps muscles, he said: "That's what I felt like . . . I feel the Aymara nation has exerted itself finally and stood up for its rights. I feel that we are strong now and can never go back to being pushed around and ignored and neglected" (Hispanicvista 2003). Such assertions and their representations in the media resonated with centuries of Indian domination and resistance. Many white and mestizo residents of La Paz perceived the blockade of the city by indigenous peoples from the highlands and El Alto as a reenactment of the Indian insurrections of 1781, when Aymara leader Túpac Katari laid siege to La Paz, leaving half the urban population dead.[3]

Yet a closer look shows that characterizing the October uprising as simply an "Indian" uprising misses the complexity of the situation. Although many of the protesters identified themselves as Indians, this was not a protest on behalf of Indian rights and recognition like those protests that made history in the 1990s. Rather, this was a strikingly new social formation by which the protesters made objections on behalf of "the Bolivian people." Besides a resolution of the gas issue, the protesters also demanded clarity in coca eradication laws, rejection of the Latin American Free Trade agreement, rejection of harsh national security laws, and a raise in basic wages.[4] Thus, although racism and marginalization continue to be central issues for Bolivian Indians, these demands were about development and distribution of national resources, commonly referred to as the *patrimonio* (patrimony) of the Bolivian people. This is because neoliberal reforms have reinforced the racialized inequalities long existing in Bolivia, laying bare the continued monopoly of power held by dominant classes and transnational corporations (Rivera Cusicanqui 2004: 22). This combination laid the stage for the uprising and for the new forms of politics that are currently emerging in Bolivia.

Thus the 2003 gas war marked an important new stage in Bolivian politics. Its protagonists blended indigenous activism with a renewed populist notion of the nation, reflecting the fact that the majority of Bolivians are both indigenous and poor. Since the 1952 revolution, indigenous people and the poor have organized their demands against the state primarily on the basis of class. Even when there was a strong cultural or ethnic component to these demands, such as the Aymara-led Katarista movement, they tended to be articulated through class-based corporate organizations, such as workers and peasants unions. Over the past several decades, however, indigenous social movements have characterized their demands more on the basis of ethnic difference and recognition.

This process was shaped, in part, by international nongovernmental organization (NGO) funding and a global discourse that made "indigenousness" and indigenous rights central tropes of social movement organizing in the 1990s. The multicultural reforms passed under the Sánchez de Lozada administration reflected this transition, as the Bolivian state specifically recognized ethnic difference. The October uprising showed that social movements have begun to integrate ethnic difference with issues of class. In the process of the contests over gas and neoliberalism, a new Bolivian public was being formed that presented the state with demands based on experiences of race *and* class discrimination.[5] Yet, as this book shows, this is not just a return to the class-centered politics of the previous era. Instead, this emerging public is raising its demands in the language of citizenship, rights, and democracy, reflecting both Bolivians' positive experiences and their frustrations with the neoliberal and multicultural reforms of the 1990s.

How and why did this transition occur? And why is this important? Most analyses of the October uprising and the social chaos surrounding it point to the terrible costs neoliberal restructuring has imposed on Indians and the poor in Bolivia. Although this is certainly an essential proximate cause of the unrest (as I detail in chapter 7), a critical contribution of this book is to point out that the new social activism is not just a response to increased poverty under neoliberalism. These costs have been borne by the poor of many countries, including Bolivia, for years without this kind of response. Why is this moment in Bolivia different? I argue that this novel protagonism was formed in relation to the regime of citizenship that I call neoliberal multiculturalism. Under Sánchez de Lozada's administration (1993–97), the constitution was changed to recognize Bolivia as a "multiethnic" and "pluricultural" nation, and a whole series of legal reforms were passed that promised to alter radically the position of the country's indigenous peoples. The three most important were the Ley de Partícipación Popular (LPP, Law of Popular Participation), a form of political decentralization that named indigenous peoples as actors in municipal development decisions; the Ley INRA, an agrarian reform that instituted collective titling for indigenous territories; and the Intercultural Bilingual Education Law, which promoted the teaching of indigenous languages and culture in schools.

These multicultural reforms were an integral part of Sánchez de Lozada's implementation of neoliberalism, the form of government that proposed to minimize and streamline the state to allow the unfettered operation of the market. As indigenous actors embraced the democratic potentials of the reforms and contested the exclusions inherent in them, they forged alternative repertoires of representation, participation, and leadership that they are now putting into effect at the national level. Thus this case goes beyond the simple explanations found in the international media in which Indians are acclaimed as "dragon slayers" resisting all forms of neoliberalism (Hispanicvista 2003). I argue instead that the current forms of challenge combine historical struggles against racism with new indigenous subjectivities and rationalities forged precisely through contested engagements with neoliberal multiculturalism.

What does this mean for Bolivian democracy? Can the Bolivian case be seen as a forerunner for other emerging democracies where questions of multiethnicity are central? Politicians, activists, and academics in the 1990s hailed "indigenous politics" as the key to a new phase in democracy across Latin America. This book shows that although the politics of difference was an important step in the democratizing process, the particular version of multiculturalism enacted by the neoliberal Bolivian state proved insufficient for real democratic participation in Bolivia. It did not sufficiently alter the structural inequalities that continue to plague the country, especially as they pertain to race. In fact, neoliberal reforms often reinforced the structures of exclusion that keep Indians poor and powerless. My argument is that because of this failure, poor and indigenous Bolivians are moving past neoliberal forms of multiculturalism — and indeed "indigenous politics" — to a new era of citizenship practices and contestation focused on redefining the state and popular access to it.

This new stage of political activism is forcing radical changes in the meaning of citizenship, what we can think of as the relation between the state and its members. First, new protagonists are drawing attention to the ways Indians and the poor have been excluded from political participation in Bolivia's multiethnic society. Although the political reforms of the 1990s promised to make access to political institutions easier for all Bolivian citizens, this book demonstrates how the legacy of racism was recontextualized but not erased by those reforms. Racism continues to structure and limit participation, making it impossible for many Bolivians to exercise their political rights. Second, Bolivia's new activists are pushing beyond traditional notions of substantive rights to rethink what they consider their rights to be. Central to this is an understanding that the political arena must be redefined to include not only questions of access to power, but also contestations over cultural meanings embedded in the unequal and hierarchical organization of social relations (Dagnino 2003: 4). Bolivian activism has already had significant effects on Bolivian democracy: popular claims for change have led to profound questioning of neoliberalism as the appropriate model for Bolivia's development, to rethinking political representation (as Morales's election showed), and to a reformulation of the very role of the state (as the 2006–7 constitutional assembly shows).

Indigenous peoples across Latin America eagerly watched the Bolivian multicultural reforms of the 1990s, hailed as a revolutionary reversal of centuries of exclusion and domination. The lesson this book tells is that Bolivia's neoliberal multiculturalism was no panacea. Instead, it was a site of articulation and contestation with unexpected results: postmulticultural citizenship. As other countries with multiethnic populations experiment with forms of multiculturalism and neoliberalism, they might do well to ask whether Bolivia is a bellwether for changes in other parts of the world.

The Guaraní Indians of Zona Cruz

To tell the story of the Bolivian experience of neoliberal multiculturalism, I focus on one group of Bolivian indigenous people, the Guaraní of Santa Cruz, and their leaders. In doing so, this book highlights the importance of the eastern lowlands, called the Oriente. Most literature focuses on Bolivia as an Andean country, yet since the early 1970s, the Oriente has become a center of economic development through massive colonization projects for the poor from the highlands, the development of agribusiness, and the exploitation of rich natural gas reserves. In the 1980s, responding to the invasions of their lands and the devastating impacts on their livelihoods, lowland indigenous people began to organize. In 1990, indigenous activists marched from the tropical lowlands over the Andes to La Paz to demand recognition of their culture and territories. The highly publicized March for Territory and Dignity pushed the issue of indigenous rights onto the national agenda and provided a sudden urgency for the multicultural reforms of the 1990s. Although the struggle for Indian rights has a long history in the Bolivian highlands, the tensions between race, nation, and neoliberal development are being played out in a specific way in the Oriente.

Neoliberal market-led strategies have had especially harsh impacts on indigenous groups in the Oriente. Many of the oil and gas exploration and development zones overlap with indigenous territories, bringing environmental damage and political battles. The experience of the Guaraní of Santa Cruz, migrants to the large boomtown, shows another side of the effects of

export-led growth. As the city expands, it has engulfed many rural communities like the Guaraní village I call Bella Flor in this book (the subject of
chapter 3). What does multiculturalism mean when "traditional indigenous"
lifestyles are recognized by the constitution but swallowed up by the economic realities of rapid urbanization or resource exploitation? The Guaraní
case, then, offers a unique perspective, far from the well-studied Andean highlands, in the heart of Bolivia's most dynamic growth zone.

Indian leaders, as anthropologist and historian Thomas Abercrombie has
shown, are often guardians of tradition, but they are also important agents
of change. Indians' cultural survival is the result of their active engagement
with the power-infused cultural programs of the state, and Indian leaders
are critical mediators in this process (Abercrombie 1998: 23, 85). The meanings and functions of indigenous leadership have also undergone tremendous change over time. Leadership is a contested relationship between
authorities and their followers, in which leaders win, maintain, and lose the
right to represent their followers in material and symbolic struggles. Such
struggles respond to and produce tensions within communities and render
visible the differing interests among community members. Thus this ethnography of Guaraní leadership is based on a study of both individual leaders
and the people in the communities and organizations they lead. Steering a
course through profound discursive shifts in "multicultural" Bolivia of the
1990s, Guaraní leaders negotiated a complex cultural politics that involved
them and their people in national indigenous activism, neoliberal political
reforms, internationally funded development projects, and radical economic
change.

This book focuses on Guaraní leaders at several institutional levels. In
chapter 2, I introduce the leaders of the regional federation, the Capitanía
Zona Cruz (CZC), an organization born and developed during the height of
the multicultural 1990s. Chapter 3 describes the local leaders of one Guaraní
village, Bella Flor, which faced a terrible crisis of leadership and representation as urban Santa Cruz encroached on the community. In chapter 4, we
see local Guaraní leaders engaged with the most important of the political
reforms, the LPP. Under this new legal structure, community leaders represented their people in municipal budget meetings and negotiated with powerful political elite. Finally, in chapter 5, I follow a group of young Guaraní
activists as they received training from an NGO about how to develop leadership skills necessary to exercise their new citizenship rights under the LPP.

The struggles and frustrations of Guaraní leaders at the local, municipal,
and regional levels are at the heart of this book. Their lives and work — as
they participated in the national Indian federation, as they lobbied local
politicians for resources for their communities, as they negotiated with NGOs
for development projects, and as they tried to enact traditional leadership

roles in changing contexts and community conflicts — provide a lens onto the multicultural reforms and the neoliberal logics underlying them.

Indians, Race, and Nation: The Sediments of History

> This [national identity] card, and the registration papers for
> the federation, are like birth certificates. Before we had
> them, we were savages, we were like animals, not people.
> Now we are citizens. [*Ahora somos ciudadanos.*]
> — Pablo, a Guaraní resident of Bella Flor

For Pablo, citizenship in multicultural Bolivia — evidenced by possessing a new national identification card — promised a radical break with the past and a wholly new relation with the state. His diachronic framing of indigenous citizenship (*before* we were animals, *now* we are citizens) points out the hold that history has on the present. Conflict between Indians and the state is not new; it has been at the center of Bolivian politics since colonial times. To understand current struggles for Indian rights, it is therefore critical to understand the historical sediments, the outcomes of past conflicts that determine current distributions of power and influence. Bolivian historian Ana María Lema has called this sedimentation the *huella* (the footprint or traces) of the past, which she sees as the starting point for understanding the present (Lema 2001).

In Bolivia, as elsewhere in the Americas, ruling classes have debated the "Indian Question" since the conquest: how best to control and use the labor, land, and resources of the native populations. In each era, there have been different answers to this question relying on specific discourses of Otherness and corresponding forms of contestation that troubled the answers. Following the work of Italian Marxist writer Antonio Gramsci (1971), we can describe this as a process of hegemony in which interlocking political, economic, and cultural forces operate to order society and subordinate certain social classes. As literary critic Raymond Williams has made clear, however, hegemony is carried out not just through coercion, but rather through "a whole lived social process as practically organized by specific and dominant meanings and values" (Williams 1977: 109). The result is that domination and subordination are experienced through "a saturation of the whole process of living — not only of political and economic activity, nor only of manifest social activity, but of the whole substance of lived identities and relationships," which ultimately come to be felt as "simple experience and common sense" (ibid.: 110).

I begin this book by examining the historical struggles through which meanings and values about race and Indianness have saturated Bolivian life.

Chapter 1 traces the status of Indians since the colonial period, through the Republic and the 1952 revolution, to the neoliberal reforms of the 1990s. Central to this account are the ways in which Indians have been included and excluded by the state through various regimes of race and belonging. Whether it be the dual republics of the colonial order, the liberal Republican regime engaged in nation building, or the 1990's neoliberal multicultural project, such regimes provided a framework for Indian-state relations. It is important to note, of course, as the history of Bolivian Indian struggles amply underscores, that hegemonic processes are characterized by contention and argument. What these regimes construct, as historical anthropologist William Roseberry so elegantly put it, is "not a shared ideology, but a common material and meaningful framework for living through, talking about, and acting upon social orders characterized by domination" (Roseberry 1996: 80).

Such "languages of contention" are the foundation for state policies and institutions, but they are also the basis for identity formation. Race and ethnicity are not natural categories of difference that precede social relations. Rather, they are formed precisely by and in contested and historically contingent relations of power. Thus they are part of technologies of domination, especially within the context of state formation (Wilmsen 1996; Comaroff 1996). State practices are enormously important in the construction of such subject positions, by defining acceptable cultural forms and images of social activity and individual and collective identity (Corrigan and Sayer 1985: 3).

In Bolivia, the category of "Indian" reflects and constitutes these historically constructed and power-laden political relations. In colonial times, for instance, the *casta* system classified and ranked colonial subjects by blood purity: Spaniards, Indians, mestizos, Blacks, mulattos, and so on. Even then, however, such categories were manipulated, modified, and sometimes resisted. The same person might be classified differently depending on whether she lived in the city or the country, how she dressed, whom she married, and what kind of work she did (Cope 1994). Despite the slippage in the categories, though, colonial authorities maintained this system of social control through a combination of economic and cultural policies. Ultimately, as anthropologist Olivia Harris has pointed out, "Indian" became fundamentally a fiscal category by which the obligations of the native population to the colonial state were defined. Thus those who lived in native communities, paid tribute, and provided labor to the Crown were considered Indians (Harris 1995: 354).

Both highland and lowland native peoples in Bolivia were called *indios*, or Indians, until the 1952 revolution. Then, through the agrarian reform advocated by the newly organized *sindicatos campesinos* (peasant unions), the state tried to assimilate Indians into the national economy as farmers rather than Indians (Gordillo 2000). In the process, highland peoples were

referred to by the term campesinos (peasants), and the term indio was abandoned as a vestige of the past. Campesino identity and membership in class-
based peasant unions became a central part of the lived experience of rural
highland people. Nevertheless, many campesinos continued to practice
their native customs, languages, and religion. This reflects what sociologist
Leon Zamosc and I have argued is the continuing ambiguity between class
and ethnicity. For many Bolivians, being indigenous and being peasants may
simply be two aspects of a lived identity (Postero and Zamosc 2004: 12). For
many others, however, Indian identity was blurred, and in some cases
erased, through assimilation, *mestizaje* (the emergence of non-Indian sectors
from miscegenation and cultural syncretism), and integration into national
markets.

For these people, ethnicity was encompassed by class as the most salient
basis for political organizing. It is important to note that the significance of
ethnicity tends to differ widely between the highlands and lowlands as a
result of differing historical trajectories. Highland people have been engaged
with colonizing religious, political, and economic institutions for centuries.
Beginning with Spanish silver mining, the large highland populations were
forced to provide labor, food, and resources for state and private exploitation schemes. In the lowlands, where populations were smaller and fewer
mineral riches were found, indigenous groups escaped these forms of assimilation for much longer (although many people suffered violence in missionary reductions or rubber boom plantations). Consequently, contemporary lowland people tend to have more a homogenous ethnic identification
(ibid.: 13).

This brief genealogy of ethnic categories demonstrates that the frameworks giving meaning to Indianness are in constant evolution. That is
because indigenousness — like any identity — is not an uncontested category
of domination, but a contingent category negotiated by individual and collective subjects. Bolivian social scientist Álvaro García Linera (who is now
vice president under Evo Morales) has suggested that identity formations are
"enunciations of meaning that demarcate social boundaries and that invent
a sense of authenticity and otherness, with the practical effect of developing
the subject thus constructed. But they are also discursive constructions that
work on the basis of material supports, on facts, and in the tracks of practical action" (García Linera 2004: 78).

This was clearly demonstrated in the 1980s and 1990s, as the discourse
of multiculturalism linked citizenship and political representation to ethnicity
rather than just to class. This articulation produced a new lexicon. Previously,
the terms *indio* and *indígena* had derogatory connotations. One common
insult, for instance, is to say "Te salió el indio," meaning roughly, "Your
Indianness is showing." As the discourse of multiculturalism and indigenous

rights gained ground, however, many lowland and Amazonian Indians began to identify as *pueblos indígenas* (indigenous peoples), and highland groups began using the term *pueblos originarios* (original peoples). These terms were also adopted as part of the state-sponsored multicultural reforms; a government vice ministry was created called the Vice Ministro de Asuntos Indígenas y Pueblos Originarios (VAIPO, Vice Ministry of Indigenous and Original Peoples Affairs). Thus "indigenous" took on a specific meaning in the context of the times.

Yet one example illustrates how complex and contested these categories remain. During my first summer's research with the Guaraní in 1996, I interviewed two teenaged brothers in an urban neighborhood of Santa Cruz where about ten Guaraní families lived. Seventeen-year-old Esteban kicked his soccer ball around as we talked. "Are you Guaraní?" I asked. "Are you kidding?" he replied, shaking his head vehemently. "No, I am a Cruceño [someone from Santa Cruz]. Just because I was born there [in a rural village in the Cordillera region] doesn't mean I am Guaraní. I don't speak the language, and I have never been back there. I don't know anything about it, and I don't want to, either. I am from here." His younger brother, Jaime, sixteen, looked on. "And you?" I asked him. "Oh yes, I am Guaraní. I was born there [in the Cordillera], and my family is all Guaraní. It is in my blood and my flesh, I can't run away from it. I don't speak the language very well but I am Guaraní and always will be."

Obviously for these two brothers, being a Guaraní was not something to be taken for granted. I argue that "Guaraní-ness," like "indigenousness," is a category that can only be understood in the context of the political, economic, and social relations that produce it — where these young men lived and what it meant for them at that moment. When I recounted this conversation to the leaders of the Guaraní federation, the CZC, they frowned and shook their heads. Don Álvaro Montero, the capitán grande, said, "What a shame [*Qué vergüenza*]. Whether they like it or not, both of those boys are *indígenas*. They should both be proud of their identity!"

Don Álvaro also made it clear that in multicultural Bolivia of the 1990s, being "indigenous" carried enormous material consequences. International NGOs gave funding to indigenous people for *etnodesarrollo* (ethnic development projects). In rural areas, membership in indigenous groups could mean access to land and the resources on it. In the cities, indigenous organizations had the right to make demands on municipal funds under the new popular participation law. So, for Don Álvaro and the leaders of the federation, cultural identity was both a set of strongly held feelings about being Guaraní as well as a set of strategic representations and practices.

But because these terms of identification have such important political and material consequences, there exists wide variation in terms for native people in Bolivia, depending in part on the claims being made by their users. Besides *indígena* and *pueblo originario*, some groups prefer to use *nativo*, while still others use *indio*. Some highland groups and scholars now use the term "indigenous campesinos" to point out the polyvalent nature of their identities or to emphasize the class basis of their organization (see Albó 2000). Others eschew such terms and identify themselves simply as Aymara, or Quechua speakers. In this book, where possible, I use the terms that the people I am discussing use to describe themselves. The Guaranís with whom I worked in Santa Cruz usually refer to themselves as either Guaraní or indígena. Otherwise, I use the general terms "Indian" and "indigenous" to describe those people who self-identify as indigenous.[6] I use these terms interchangeably, although I follow the tendency to refer to lowland people as indigenous and highland people as Indians.

Multiculturalism: Recognition or Redistribution?

In the previous sections, I have referred to discourse of multiculturalism as well as a series of multicultural reforms passed by the government. Here let me explain what I mean by the term "multiculturalism" and lay out what is at stake. "Multiculturalism" is used in many ways. It can refer to the multiethnic makeup of a place or a society — that is, the "hybrid co-existence of diverse cultural life-worlds" (Zizek 1997: 46). More often the term refers to the efforts of liberal democratic governments to accept and embrace these ethnic differences (Kymlicka 1995a, 1995b; Bennett 1998; Povinelli 2002). There are various phrases for these efforts: "multicultural constitutionalism" (Van Cott 2000), "liberal multiculturalism," "pluralism," or the term widely used in Latin America, "interculturality" (García 2005; Rappaport 2005). While "multiculturalism" implies recognition and respect of numerous cultures, "interculturality" signals a more interactive process of mutual influence among bearers of cultural and especially linguistic difference. Thus this term has been used to describe the goals of programs of bilingual bicultural education that accompanied the other reforms described in this chapter. Although it might have been better to use here the phrase commonly used by Bolivians, NGOs, and indigenous people, I prefer to use the more precise term "state-sponsored multiculturalism," which calls attention to the fact that I am not studying a utopian goal but a project promulgated by the government. Thus I use this phrase to describe the constitutional and legislative reforms directed by the state with the intention of granting cultural and political rights to Bolivia's indigenous populations. I use a second term, "neoliberal multiculturalism," to draw attention to the relation between those state-sponsored political reforms and the neoliberal philosophies that underlie them.[7]

Most forms of multiculturalism specifically recognize formerly marginalized groups, ensuring their individual rights as citizens, and in some cases
granting collective rights as groups. In Latin America, eight states have
adopted various forms of multiculturalism since the mid-1980s in an effort
to expand the participation of indigenous people and to remedy past histories of ethnic and racial domination (Seider 2002: 4; see also Maybury Lewis
2002; Van Cott 2002; Postero and Zamosc 2004).[8] Nevertheless, there is a
wide-ranging debate about how such protection should best be afforded. Is
this a wrong that can be remedied through state intervention? That is, can
minority cultures or ways of life be sufficiently protected by legal structures
that ensure individual rights, or do they need special group protection or
rights (Goldberg 1994; Bennett 1998; Okin 1999)?

One axis of difference in this debate is between those advocating a politics of recognition and those arguing for a politics of redistribution. The first
group focuses on the cultural or symbolic nature of injustice, arguing that
injustice is "rooted in social patterns of representation, interpretation, and
communication" (Fraser 1997: 14). In this view, cultural domination, non-
recognition, and disrespect are forms of oppression that require state intervention (Honneth 1992; Taylor 1992). Such views favor identity politics and
urge the state to privilege diversity and grant special treatment for disadvantaged groups (what legal philosopher Iris Marion Young has called "differentiated citizenship") (Young 1996). Critics of this position, like political scientist Seyla Benhabib, argue that it is based on static and bounded
notions of culture, which end up balkanizing social groups and making true
deliberative democracy impossible (Benhabib 2002). Other scholars point out
the danger of invoking culture to solve problems previously in the province
of economic and politics (Yúdice 2003: 1). A second perspective focuses on
injustice as socioeconomic, rooted in the political economic structure of society (Fraser 1997: 13). These critics argue for a politics of redistribution, suggesting that true equality can only be found in transforming the political economic structure of society (Rawls 1971; Dworkin 1981). For this group, a
focus on cultural rights rather than economics is a dangerous trap that dimin-
ishes the ability to resist the status quo (Almeida Vinueza 2005).

Of course, such analytical oppositions do not accurately reflect reality. In
practice, as political philosopher Nancy Fraser has forcefully argued, economic and cultural injustice are fundamentally related: discursive categories
and practices are underpinned by material supports, and economic institutions operate through culturally meaningful frameworks (Fraser 1997: 15).
The Bolivian case described in this book shows that efforts to bring about
social justice in a multiethnic society must take into account the ways cultural and economic forms of domination and resistance are co-constituted
and mutually reinforcing. Simply recognizing cultural pluralism or promoting

tolerance of difference in a managed multiculturalism is insufficient if there is little lasting change for the dominated group (see Bennett 1998; Goldberg 1994; Hale 2002).

This becomes clear from my analysis of the LPP, which established new forms of idigenous participation at the municipal level. The LPP fulfilled some of the functions of a policy of recognition in that it addressed centuries of discrimination by naming indigenous people as citizens and in the process fueled their expectations of participation. This remained mostly symbolic, however, because the LPP did not produce a meaningful redistribution of resources or radically challenge the structured inequalities of power. As chapter 4 demonstrates, the law was not part of a democraticizing effort intended to benefit the poor. Rather, it was part of an overarching strategy on the part of a neoliberal government that intended the reforms as a palliative for the larger structural adjustments it imposed. I argue that frustrations with the failures to make substantial changes in the distributive structures of Bolivian society are a key component to the current social upheavals in Bolivia.

Neoliberal Multiculturalism

If, as I contend, Bolivia's multiculturalism was not sufficiently transformative, why not? This cannot be understood without analyzing the relation between multiculturalism and neoliberalism, the form of government that gained dominance in Bolivia since the mid-1980s. Where neoliberalism is the key organizing principle of government, it acts to define citizen participation in accordance with its logic.

I take neoliberalism to be a philosophy about the relation between the state, the market, and individuals. Neoliberalism, like its classical ancestor, liberalism, privileges the individual and holds the market to be the guarantor of social good. Unlike liberalism, which saw some state interventions as necessary to facilitate citizens' freedoms, neoliberalism (reflecting its central critique of the post–World War II welfare state) characterizes the state as an inefficient, often corrupt actor that only encumbers the market's neutral and unselfish actions (Gill 2000: 3). Proponents of neoliberal philosophies criticize state entitlements, saying they weaken political participation by making citizens dependent on the state. In essence, this argument questions the "passive" nature of citizenship rights and urges citizens to take more individual responsibility for their own welfare. In this view, the state's functions should be minimized and its role as guarantor of rights abandoned.[9] Governments following this rationale often made radical cuts in state spending, privatized state-run enterprises, and encouraged foreign capital investments. In this context, the market is posited as an efficient bearer of liberty for responsible individual citizens, and citizenship is increasingly understood as individual integration into the market (Ignatieff 1995: 29; Dagnino 2003: 4–7).

As neoliberal economic strategies promoted by powerful multilateral financial institutions took hold across Latin America, these notions of state-citizen relations also gained ground, profoundly changing what it means to be a citizen. My analysis of the Bolivian political reforms of the 1990s demonstrates a corollary to this neoliberal turn: at the same time that the state offered fewer services and funding, it also passed on the responsibility for much of governance from the state to private individuals and groups (see Yashar 1999, 2005). "A sustainable government," said Fernando Romero Moreno, Bolivia's minister of human development, must foster "shared responsibility," which is "the essence of citizen participation" (Romero Moreno 1996: 30). This sort of reorganization of responsibility (discussed further below) is not the same thing as a policy of redistribution, despite the rhetoric to the contrary. Instead, the LPP encouraged a specific form of civil society participation intended to make the economic system run more efficiently and with less conflict. Rather than fighting the national government over large issues of resource allocation, civil society organizations were encouraged to engage in decisions over small development projects at the local level, with limited or shared funding.

This point echoes what anthropologist Charles Hale has argued: that neoliberalism includes a seductive cultural project. It does not merely encourage individualism; rather, it urges citizens — be they individuals or organized into collective groups — to take on the role of solving the problems in which they are immersed in collaboration with nonstate civil society entities like NGOs (Hale 2002: 496). This valuing of civil society can be compatible with some facets of indigenous cultural rights — but only as long as there are no fundamental threats to the productive regime or to state power. The bottom line is that successful neoliberal subjects must govern themselves in accordance with the logic of globalized capitalism. The result — what Hale has termed the "menace" of neoliberal multiculturalism — is that those Indians who conduct themselves within this logic and are appropriately "modern" and "rational" are rewarded and empowered. He calls these individuals "*indios permitidos*" ("authorized Indians"). Unruly, conflict-prone Indians, however, are condemned to the racialized spaces of poverty and social exclusion (Hale 2004).

But the Bolivian case is quite different from that in Guatemala, where Hale does his research. Although the role of the indio permitido can certainly be alluring, as my analysis in chapter 5 demonstrates, Bolivian Indians and their allies in civil society have pushed beyond the limitations of such roles. Many Indians are vigorously contesting neoliberal notions of multiculturalism as well as the model of the state. Throughout *Now We Are Citizens*, I show how indigenous citizens in Bolivia have taken advantage of political openings that the LPP offered, in many cases by assuming many of the rationalities of neoliberalism. In an interesting turnabout, however — and this is the crux of my book — these indigenous citizens are using them to pose important challenges to the workings of global capitalism. National Indian leaders, neighborhood associations, and workers organizations — strengthened in part through the institutions created by the neoliberal reforms — have questioned the framework on which those reforms are based. For instance, chapter 6 describes how neighborhood groups organized according to the LPP formed the backbone of the October 2003 uprisings in El Alto, which ultimately deposed the president. Political organizing for municipal elections, also made possible by the LPP, was key to the growth of the Movimiento al Socialismo party (MAS, Movement Toward Socialism), which in 2005 won the presidency with the election of Morales. These social movements have used institutional channels to demand that decisions about energy be taken out of the privatized realm of the market and reinserted into the public arena, where the citizenry can participate. They are also demanding a constitutional assembly to rethink the model of the state in public deliberations. Morales's election is evidence that these demands may bear fruit.

Here I offer a contrast to most characterizations of the effects of neoliberalism, which tend to generalize about its negative or positive effects without examining the complexity of how subjects engage with it. On the one hand, many critics of neoliberalism argue that its institutions and practices frame subjects more and more as consumers, forcing a coerced (or enchanted) compliance with neoliberal agendas (Comaroff and Comaroff 2000; Schild 2000). On the other hand, advocates of neoliberalism promote free trade and political decentralization as the most efficient mechanisms for delivering the economic and social development desperately needed by the poor. They argue that local community groups with strong social capital are able to pressure the state and the private sector to deliver goods and services, contributing to good governance (Putnam 1993, 1995; World Bank 2004). I find more compelling those analyses that note the strength of neoliberal discourses while also documenting the often surprising responses its subjects produce. Hale's 2002 and 2004 analysis is one example. Anthropologist Suzana Sawyer's analysis of indigenous activism in Ecuador's Oriente is another. She has argued that the neoliberal reforms which sought to create economic and political stability "backfired," jeopardizing the little credibility the state held and producing transgressive political subjects who were able to mount challenges to the state's oil and lending policies (Sawyer 2004: 15). Anthropologist Daniel Goldstein's excellent study of an urban barrio in Cochabamba, Bolivia, describes how neoliberal reforms prompted "spectacular" actions by barrio residents, such as attempted lynchings of thieves. He characterizes lynchings as ritual expressions of belonging that act to render the actors visible to the state and call attention to the neoliberal state's neglect of their rights as citizens (Goldstein 2004).

Like these authors, I seek to show that the subjects of neoliberalism find in it a number of resources and tools. This is because neoliberalism is not an all-encompassing or hegemonic paradigm that dominates society but rather a philosophy that is expressed in various policies, practices, and institutions that are constantly being conserved and/or contested. In *Now We Are Citizens*, I focus on three aspects — or moments — of neoliberalism in Bolivia: the political reforms of the 1990s, the diffusion of neoliberal rationalities, and the policies and costs of economic restructuring. Each of these aspects competes with other discourses and interests and engenders articulations and resistance. That is, Indian and popular actors actively engaged with each of these sites of neoliberal practice, taking advantage of the potentials and contesting their exclusionary or negative sides. The result was a new form of protagonism that both incorporates and challenges the underlying philosophies of neoliberalism. Thus, although this analysis shares much with such authors as Goldstein and Sawyer, who focus on the agency of neoliberal subjects, this book describes a new stage in the study of neoliberalism: the shift to postmulticultural citizenship.

I argue that postmulticultural citizenship will be pivotal to Bolivia's developing democracy. Furthermore, its development and continuing enactment may offer insights to scholars and activists in other multiethnic societies. To help readers understand this new phenomenon, I describe its history, its political and economic context, and the discursive formations that give it meaning. But the heart of this account is an analysis of how the political and cultural formations of the past — from the colonial era to the multicultural 1990s — have contributed to create current social relations. As an anthropologist, I begin with the words and practices of the indigenous people I work with and know. Thus this book is about the Guaraní's experience with neoliberal multiculturalism. Yet the work of anthropology is to compile a social history, by building on the stories of the people we study with our own analyses. To that end, I also provide readers with data and analytical tools to interpret the social history of contemporary Bolivia.

A Word about the Author

My interest in Bolivia's neoliberal multiculturalism was informed by my previous occupations: ten years as a lawyer and four as a radio journalist. I spent the 1980s practicing criminal defense and immigration law in

Tucson, Arizona, an hour north of the United States–Mexico border. In the 1990s, I left law to find a different perspective (and methodology) on the questions of human rights, politics, and justice. From 1990 to 1994, I was part of a team of radio journalists producing documentaries that were aired on National Public Radio. From our base in Costa Rica, we traveled across Latin America, covering the relations between development, environment, and culture for our series, *Vanishing Homelands* and *Searching for Solutions*.[10] It was in this context that I first worked in Bolivia. My partner and I reported about one of the last nomadic indigenous groups to be contacted, the Yuquí Indians of the Chapare region, and the New Tribes Missionaries who persuaded the Yuquí to come live in their settlement (Tolan and Postero 1992). During that trip, we first met the *cocalero* (coca growers) leader Evo Morales as part of our investigation into the effects of neoliberal reforms and the growth of the informal market.

My experiences as a journalist in Latin America, and especially in Bolivia and Ecuador, brought me back to the questions of cultural differences and human rights that I had confronted as a lawyer on the border. In both of those countries in the early 1990s, indigenous groups were becoming important political forces pushing the state to recognize them. What role would they assume? With such questions in mind, I returned to graduate school in anthropology and to Bolivia for my fieldwork. Bolivia had just embarked on its experiment in multiculturalism, and the nation's indigenous people were among the most organized on the continent. I began the research for this book in the summer of 1995 and returned again in 1996 to work with the CZC doing a survey of urban Guaraní communities. Then in 1997 and 1998, I carried out long-term fieldwork in Santa Cruz and the surrounding communities. I continued research during the summers of 1999, 2000, 2002, and the spring of 2003. In 2004, I expanded my research to the highlands to better understand the events of October 2003.

I describe my methodology throughout the following chapters, but let me note here how grateful I am to the Guaraní leaders who authorized and collaborated in my research. From the beginning, I sought to do an investigation that would prove helpful to the organization and the community in which I lived. I developed my research topics through multiple discussions with the Guaraní. I reported my results to the organization, translating sections of my data and dissertation into Spanish for them, and holding community meetings to discuss the implications. That said, I want to be clear about my own motivations in this research and to draw the connections between my previous work and the ethnographic project that *Now We Are Citizens* represents. Part of the reason that I left law was because I grew tired of the dualisms inherent to it. Although I respect the merits of the adversary system, I do not feel it is the best way to think about such complex issues as race and politics. I changed my career to journalism and then to anthropology precisely to find more nuanced ways of thinking about these issues.

Yet trading the role of advocate for that of scholar is not an easy solution. As has been amply demonstrated elsewhere, anthropologists do not inhabit a neutral or objective place outside the power relations we study (Clifford 1986; Nelson 1999; Warren and Jackson 2002). I could not avoid the privileges and limitations that my identities as a white, female, and (relative to my Guaraní friends) rich North American provided. I do not deny my sympathies and affection for the Indians I worked with, nor for the indigenous movement as a whole. But I do not consider my work advocacy in the standard definition of the word. Understanding that all identities (including the observer's) are mutually constituted, I believe that critiques of power must go beyond binaries (good-bad, Indian-white, leaders-followers, observer-observed, and so on) to examine the processes by which those binaries are produced (Nelson 1999). Thus this is not a romantic picture of Bolivian Indians; rather, it is an attempt to recount the ways Indianness and neoliberal citizenship are constructed, experienced, and used strategically by all involved. This book documents the complex and dynamic manner in which Bolivian Indians advocate and represent themselves. I believe that the best contribution I can make to Bolivia is my analysis about how and why this is occurring.

Names

Throughout this book, I use pseudonyms for individual indigenous people as well as for the villages in which they live. This is not for fear that the individuals will face any danger should their identities be exposed, but to protect their privacy. All the people I interviewed were advised of the purposes of my research and gave me their permission to interview them and to use their words in my writing. Nevertheless, the Human Subjects Protection program of the University of California required that I keep all my notes hidden and my sources confidential. I have therefore invented names for all of the Guaranís of Zona Cruz and the urban leaders in El Alto. The names of the Guaraní villages are also invented, although the organization name, the Capitanía Zona Cruz, is real. The name of the NGOs with whom the Guaraní worked are also real, but the names of the individual NGO workers are pseudonyms. Finally, I include information from interviews with several indigenous congress members. Because they are public figures, I use their real names.

Part 1

THE INDIAN QUESTION

1 Regimes of Race and Citizenship

> The tradition of all the dead generations weighs like a
> nightmare on the brain of the living.
> — Karl Marx

An Old Grief

One warm night in 1998, the leader of the Capitanía Zona Cruz
(CZC), Don Álvaro Montero, took me with him to the community of La
Cañada, about ten kilometers north of the city of Santa Cruz. Several of the
young leaders of the capitanía's technical team, Equipo Técnico Zonal (ETZ),
had just returned from a national Guaraní youth meeting and they wanted
to share their experiences. There was also a birthday among the group, so
we were invited to a small party at the home of Rosana Moreno, one of the
ETZ members. The capitán grande drove his car, a run-down Toyota sedan
of the kind Cruceños ironically call "transformers," after the children's toys.
These used cars with the steering wheels originally on the right side have been
imported from Japan and brought across the border illegally. Somewhere
along its way, the steering wheel had been switched to the left side, leaving
a gaping hole on the right. Don Álvaro filled the gap with cassettes, one of
which he played at full volume during our drive.[1]

We drove out of the crowded city, through the surrounding agricultural
country. Vast cattle ranches owned by the elite stretched away from the highway, alternating with fields of tall sugarcane. Guaranís migrated here to work
the *zafras* (sugarcane harvests) in the 1950s and 1960s and stayed to work
on the large haciendas as peons for the local *patrones* (ranchers). The nearly
twenty-five communities that made up the capitanía were scattered all
around the city's periphery, especially near the cane fields and the large farming zones. The community of La Cañada had grown up around the sugar
refinery of the same name and had a small Guaraní neighborhood for the
workers. Rosana's father had worked at the refinery for nearly twenty years.

Rosana's house was in the town center, right in front of a large park under
construction. It looked like any other home in the neighborhood, made of
adobe and block, with a small backyard containing a latrine and washing

post. Rosana proudly showed off her pig, which she had bought as a suckling and was raising for sale. Her mother had added on a small store to the front, where she sold sodas, bread, beer, and other essentials. We sat under the palm roof of the patio, listening to popular Bolivian dance music called *chicha*, and enjoyed a cold beer — always welcome in Santa Cruz's tropical climate. Rosana and fellow ETZ member Samuel Tapera told us about the youth meeting they had attended in Camiri, in the south, organized by the national Guaraní federation, the Asociación del Pueblo Guaraní (APG). The meeting marked the anniversary of the January 1892 massacre in Kuruyuki, where the Bolivian army had put down a massive Guaraní rebellion, ending a century of revolts and insurrections.[2] (This history is discussed in more detail throughout the chapter.) Samuel, a young man in his early thirties, recounted the meeting and the ritual dances on the last night. "It was so moving to be with so many other Guaranís," he said. "It made me remember the warrior side of our people, the strength of being together. It was something I can't measure, just the feeling of being Guaraní. We danced for hours, listening to the Guaraní music, feeling the drums inside of us."

Don Álvaro retrieved a cassette from his car and popped it in Rosana's boom box. It was traditional Guaraní music and everyone got up to dance. "This is our music," he said. "My father played the violin, and whenever I hear it, I remember the old ones, the old ways." He arranged us in a circle and we all held onto each other's arms, moving slowly and rhythmically to the mournful violin and drum tune. The young folk, Samuel, Rosana, and the others who had joined us, eagerly followed his lead. As we danced and talked that night, Don Álvaro told them stories about the Guaraní past, especially about the *queremba reta* (warriors) who had fought their enemies so valiantly. They remembered their forebears' reputation for ferocity: only the Mapuche of Chile had resisted pacification by the Spaniards longer than the Chiriguano had. "Imagine," said Samuel, "this massacre was only a hundred years ago." For these young Guaraní leaders, raised in the suburbs of a large city, the tragedy — and the challenge — of Kuruyuki are not altogether in the past. "We are still forced to be queremba reta," said Rosana at the end of the evening, "but now it is in a different kind of struggle."

The bittersweet pride the Guaraní of Zona Cruz hold for their bellicose past reflects the long history of domination and subjugation of Indians in Bolivia. This struggle, which began more than five hundred years ago with the arrival of the Europeans in the Americas, continues to affect the lives of Indians today in numerous ways. The evening at Rosana's house made clear that the long-lasting impact of such a devastating event is experienced at an emotional or psychic level: the pain and losses are seared into the memories of its victims' descendants, like the Guaraní. But this history also continues to affect Indians as contemporary members of Bolivian society. Domination of Indians did not only happen through massacres, but also through the establishment of regimes of social order that naturalized such domination. These regimes laid out categories of belonging and Otherness that continue to operate today. These governing systems and their accompanying "languages of contention" (Roseberry 1996) have changed since the colonial period, but each regime has left its cumulative traces in the culture and social relations of Bolivian society. This chapter examines regimes of the past, rendering visible the political and discursive techniques by which Indians have been included and excluded. Readers will note the troubling echoes between the present and the past.[3]

The Guaraní and the Spaniards

According to historians, the ancestors of the people we now know as the Guaraní apparently migrated from Brazil to the Chaco area between what is now Santa Cruz and Paraguay (called the Cordillera) sometime in the 1400s.[4] Part of the Tupi-Guaraní family, they had come in search of La Tierra Sin Mal (the land without evil), the mythical land where they could live in peace and find bountiful sustenance for their families. The Tupi-Guaraní intermarried with the Chané people who already lived in the zone, and the resulting blend of these two groups was called the Chiriguano (Saignes and Combes 1995). They formed communities throughout the zone, farming, hunting, and engaging in battles with other lowland tribes as well as occasionally with the far frontiers of the Inca empire (Pifarré 1989). The descendants of the Chiriguano are known today as the Guaraní.

After the conquest of the Inca empire in the Peruvian highlands, Spaniards set up colonial administration of the former Inca empire, which included what is now Bolivia.[5] From the 1540s on, the rich silver veins of Cerro Rico in Potosí were exploited with the labor of the well-organized highland Indian population, and La Paz was established as a commercial and trans-shipment center (Klein 1992: 35). This silver-mining boom lasted late into the 1600s, and a *criollo* (Creole) class of settlers developed on large haciendas, especially in the Cochabamba valley, to support the mining project (ibid.).

The eastern lowlands, however, had no silver, so this region was left mainly to missionaries and rubber producers. Spanish explorers from Paraguay seeking paths to the silver mines from the Atlantic side arrived in the late 1500s and, not finding a way up the mountains, settled in the area. The city of Santa Cruz was founded in 1561 by explorer Ñuflo de Chavez and slowly grew into a sugar- and cotton-producing zone (Gill 1987; Pifarré 1989). For several centuries the Chiriguano forcefully resisted the Spanish invasions and settlements. Jesuit and Franciscan missionaries established numerous missions, bringing dispersed Guaranís into *reducciones* (mission towns), in which they were forced to participate in mission agricultural schemes. These invariably lasted a short period, as Guaranís revolted and often killed the missionaries. As Spanish settlers increased in numbers, establishing large farms and cattle-ranching haciendas in the area, military invasions attacked the "savage" and "dangerous" Guaranís, driving them off their lands and farther into the Cordillera. The histories of this period are filled with accounts of insurrections and brutal repression, followed by short periods of peace and then additional cycles of uprisings.

The years between 1727 to 1735 were an especially violent period. Apparently, one explosive incident involved the Chiriguano, who were frustrated about missionary control and the penetration of their lands. A Spanish officer in the Tariquea valley brutally whipped a Chiriguano who had been going from community to community, encouraging resistance. As a result of the whipping, Chiriguanos across the region began preparing for war. In a short time, nearly seven thousand warriors gathered and began a new cycle of war, in which missions were burned, missionaries killed, and haciendas taken over or destroyed by the Indians. These uprisings led to swift and brutal repression, as the Crown sent out army expeditions to punish and subdue the insurrectionists (Pifarré 1989: 232ff). As in the rest of Latin America, this repeated process of extermination and subordination resulted in a sharp drop in the Guaraní population — a result of massacres, epidemics, warfare, and the loss of farmland and means of subsistence. Meanwhile, inevitable processes of *mestizaje* began, as the Chiriguano began to be *españolizado* ("Spanish-ized") (ibid.: 140).

Despite these processes, however, the Chiriguano remained a determined and rebellious force. The last uprising of the Guaraní, who were desperate to protect their lands, occurred in January 1892. In the years immediately before the uprising, a young *ipaje* (healer or shaman) named Chapiaguasu had gained the reputation for extraordinary powers of healing and vision. The people called him Tumpa Hapiaoeki, a term of divinity, and flocked to hear his oracular pronouncements. He told them that they should not fear the guns of the soldiers, which would "only spit out water" (cited in ibid.: 376). Instead, Chapiaguasu told them, those who waged war against the soldiers would have a new life. His presence among the people would guarantee the Chiriguanos' victory and the combatants' invulnerability.

This rhetoric, which combined several features of Guaraní myth, mobilized thousands of Indians from across the Cordillera region. The Spanish army responded to the growing "warlike euphoria" and sent a brigade of soldiers, which engaged several groups of rebels in small actions, defeating and dispersing them. In the final battle on January 28, 1892, the Guaraní insurgents were brutally defeated by the military. Historian Francisco Pifarré has estimated the dead at six hundred to nine hundred and the wounded, most of whom perished later, at eight hundred (ibid.: 385; see also Sanabria Fernandez 1972: 159–69). After the rebellion was put down, the Chiriguano people were dispersed, some escaping to the mountains. The communities that remained came under the economic and political dominance of the regional elites. Many other Chiriguanos were sent off to the Amazon, where captive native people were employed in rubber tapping. There the near-slavery conditions in the rubber boom (which lasted from the late 1880s to the early 1900s) decimated the Amazon populations already greatly affected by missionary reductions. The remaining Indians, far from their homelands, gradually became part of the region's mestizo poor (Herrera Sarmiento 2002).

The Dual Republics

Colonial domination in the highlands took a different path. There the Indian population was much greater, and the Inca empire had left a preexisting system of indirect rule. The Spanish assumed control over this system, leaving land in the hands of the native peasants and the local governing power in the hands of caciques, local elites whose authority was inherited from their Incan nobility forebears. Indian communities were divided up into districts called *encomiendas*, large extensions of lands given to Spanish grantees (*encomenderos*). In exchange for religious education of the Indians, the encomendero was given rights to the Indians' yearly tribute payments, which could be paid in crops (Klein 1992: 37; see also Service 1954 and Thomson 2002).[6]

Although the encomenderos were officially prohibited from extracting Indian labor, they had enormous power over their charges and used their labor for their own interests. In response, in the mid-1500s the Spanish Crown attempted to break the feudal power of the encomenderos, to control Indian labor needed for the growing silver mines. Through the reforms administered by Viceroy Francisco de Toledo, the Crown set up two separate legal and institutional systems: the *república de los españoles* for Spaniards and the *república de indios* for Indians. Indians became a separate juridical and political category of subjects from Spanish, criollos, or mestizos, with separate rights and obligations. Indians were allowed to hold and use communal property in what were called *comunidades indígenas* (indigenous communities), and they maintained the right to local self-governance under the *cacicazgo* system. In exchange, in what anthropologist Tristan Platt has called the "tributary pact" (Platt 1982), Indians contributed their labor to the Crown and were required to pay tribute taxes, which provided an important source of revenue to the Crown. The caciques collected the tax and delivered it to the Crown. Indians were entitled to royal protection on the basis of their "inferior condition" and their fulfillment of their tributary obligations (Barragán Romano 1999: 52).

Despite the semblance of protection offered to Indians, however, the relation between the two republics was essentially exploitative. The centerpiece of the labor system was the *mita*, based on the pre-Columbian collective labor system. Sixteen mita districts from Cuzco to Potosí were established, from which one-seventh of the adult males were subject to one year's service at the mines (Klein 1992: 39–42). In a century and a half, the forced service of these laborers, called the *mitayos*, produced enough silver to triple the total European reserves and turned Potosí into the richest city in the Americas. As historian Eduardo Galeano has chronicled, the silver from the "open veins" of the Americas passed through Spanish coffers to the rest of Europe, stimulating economic development. Yet the natives of the Americas paid the enormous cost of this economic transformation. More than eight million Indian lives were lost to brutal servitude, mercury poisoning, and freezing temperatures in the mines (Galeano 1973).[7]

The colonial tribute system was paired with and justified by a biological discourse about race, which established categories based on purity of blood. This system, called the *sistema de castas*, ranked Spaniards (considered to be people of pure blood) at the top, *castas* (mixed-blood people) in the middle, and Indians and Africans on the bottom (Cope 1994: 4). Of course, such artificially created categories quickly became impossible to police, as intermarrying between groups produced new racial categories, such as *mulattos*, *mestizos*, and *zambos*. Cultural and spatial mixtures also resulted as native people migrated to the cities and Spaniards moved into the lands that were supposedly Indian (Larson 2004: 40). Racial identity quickly became a matter determined more by social markers than biology. People could pass from one category to another by changing their dress, place of residence, language, or working conditions. Historian Douglas Cope has argued that subordinate groups were not passive recipients of this elite ideology; rather, they often resisted the definitions to promote social mobility, group solidarity, and self-definition (Cope 1994: 5).[8]

Despite the difficulties in administering this socio-racial stratification between whites and Indians, however, colonial powers maintained this system because it was the legal mechanism necessary to maintain the economic basis of the colonies: Indian labor and tribute. Thus, as anthropologist Olivia Harris has argued, the term "Indian" became "fundamentally a fiscal category by which the obligations of the native population to the colonial state were defined" (Harris 1995: 354). That is, an Indian was one who lived in an Indian community and paid tribute, in labor or goods. Anthropologist Peter Wade has noted that it was also a census category, as colonial administrators needed to keep track of Indians as a working and tributary population (Wade 1997: 28). The caste system, like all hegemonic forms of sub-ordination, operated on multiple levels. Exploitative economic practices were enabled by the juridical definitions and, in turn, reinforced the result-ing discursive racial categories, naturalizing particular forms of domination. Political historian Adolfo Gilly has argued, however, that the domination that was based in and justified by purely racial differences to start with developed into what he calls a "racial subalternity" (Gilly 2003: 19). Regardless of its arbitrariness and imprecision, he suggests, the color line impregnated all social relations, naturalizing the imagined inherited right to dominate.

Critical to this was one feature: an intrinsic ingredient of humiliation in social treatment of the subaltern classes. Domination was not sustained through some fiction of juridical equality between dominators and subal-terns, but rather "in convictions deeply rooted in the conscience of the dom-inators of the existence of a genetic inequality between the parts" (ibid.: 20). The resulting need to humiliate in order to control, made into a habit and routine by those who exercised control, was one of the constitutive elements of colonial rule. Gilly suggests that this was materialized through such prac-tices as corporal punishment or threat thereof; paternalistic treatment toward subordinates and domestic servants, including the *tuteo* (use of the familiar *tú* form of address); the separation of living and working spaces; the visual difference in clothing; and the notion that education was the privilege of some and not the right of all. These external and corporal marks of infe-riority were reproduced and naturalized through daily life practices that con-tinued long past the colonial period (ibid.: 21).

This did not preclude contestation, however. As historian Brooke Larson has argued, following the work of historical anthropologist William Roseberry (1996), this colonial policy of legal-political separation created a legal-discursive medium through which Indians could negotiate or contest colonial policy or local transgressions (Larson 2004: 40). Historian Steve Stern's now classic research in Huamanga, Peru, showed how native Andean peoples and their *kuraka* leaders used the colonial legal system to challenge the land expropriations and labor demands of criollo landholders. By hid-ing many of their tributaries, and petitioning for lengthy and time-consuming *revisitas* (reinspections) of their populations to demonstrate demographic declines, kurakas substantially lowered their tribute and mita quotas. This affected the state's extractive institutions, causing disruptions in colonial min-ing and other enterprises (Stern 1993 [1982]: 114–37).[9] Nevertheless, despite these creative and strategic interventions into the legal system, native peo-ples continued to bear the brunt of the colonial economic system. As a result, peasants (particularly in Upper Peru) were relentlessly involved in popular risings to contest the mita throughout the entire eighteenth century (O'Phelan Godoy 1985).

The End of Cacicazgo and the Age of Insurrection

By the end of the eighteenth century, the system of indirect rule by local Indian elites came under increasing pressures. Spanish extraction systems, notably the *repartimiento* (forced sale of commodities), squeezed native populations more and more, as royal officials (*corregidores*) administering the sales profited. Historian Jürgen Golte's study of the *reparto* system showed a direct link between repartimiento exigencies and popular uprisings in the late-eighteenth-century Andes. He even found evidence of corregidores requiring Indians to purchase goods as useless as multicolored silk stockings (Golte 1980: 89).[10] Moreover, the caciques — mediators between their communities and the Crown — sometimes failed to protect their communities from criollo exploitation, instead using their connections to the Crown to shore up their own power and private benefits. This created a divisive class dynamic among Indians and weakened their ability to mount a united assault on their common enemy — the colonial extractive system (ibid.: 132). In addition, access to the colonial justice system exacerbated rivalries among communities and ethnic groups over lands, as native groups relied on colonial authorities to settle disputes.

Historian Sinclair Thomson (2002) has argued that in La Paz, at least, the cacicazgo system began to fall apart as local populations resisted both the abuses of corrupt caciques and the increasingly painful demands of colonial domination. Legal actions against such caciques mounted, and communities began to demand the right to choose their own authorities who would be better and more just mediators, fairly administering the tribute taxes and the repartimiento. Thomson documented one lawsuit filed by the community of Calacoto, on the altiplano of Pacajes, against the cacique and his brother, the alcalde. According to the legal papers, the Canqui brothers forced community members to carry out such unlawful and uncompensated services as house service, supplying firewood, carrying mail, and work in their private commercial interests. The brothers also took over the best lands, leaving Indians with infertile plots, where the Canquis' animals foraged. The suit also alleged brutal physical abuse at the brothers' hands, including battering one man in front of a crowd as he sought refuge in a church cemetery (ibid.: 84ff). Growing frustration often broke out as small Indian uprisings demanded an end to this bad government.

This came to a head in the late 1700s, when Andean natives waged a series of violent insurrections across the region from Cuzco to La Paz. The insurrections of 1780 and 1781 — led by Tomás Katari, Túpac Amaru, and Túpac Katari (Julian Apaza) — attempted to break with the colonial order and establish Indian sovereignty. Historians have extensively analyzed the motivations of these leaders, from the return of local political power to millenarianism and utopianism.[11] As historian Herbert S. Klein has noted, however, it was essentially an independence movement led by the kuraka class of Upper Peru (Klein 1992: 75). At the height of the insurrections, more than a hundred thousand Indians followed these leaders, capturing Spanish cities and killing many thousands of residents. During the final stage, rebels led by Tomás Katari and Túpac Katari encircled and besieged La Paz for months. The uprisings were finally put down, the leaders executed, and their properties confiscated. Klein has argued that this was the deathblow for the kuraka class, as all the rebel kurakas were removed from office, their positions taken by Spaniards and mestizos.

In the sweeping changes following the insurrections, the Crown officially retained the cacique system, but by the time of independence in the 1820s, its institutional strength had faded. Thomson has argued that this had already happened before the insurrections, as the caciques' dual accountability to the Crown and to their tributaries proved untenable. Andean communities had gradually shifted to a more democratic system of representation, in which authority was not based on nobility or state regulation, but rather on accountability to the community. The power that had been centralized at the apex of the political system was dispersed to a number of sites in the community, particularly through the civil *cargo* system, a rotating system in which community elders do temporary community service (Thomson 2002: 273). This system, which has a firm basis in the community assembly, is still recognizable in the highlands today (Ticona et al. 1995; Platt 1999).[12]

Anthropologist Roger Rasnake's 1988 study of the Yura in Potosí is an excellent description of the historical development of the role of local authorities. After the insurrectionary period, Yura authorities no longer acted as the intermediary between the state and communities. Instead, the job of imposing state demands was given to colonial officials (corregidores), while local authorities (*kuraqkunas*) took on such cultural and social roles as maintaining cohesive group identity. When Rasnake studied the Yura's community in the 1970s, their leaders continued to exercise this role, which he characterized as ritualistic and symbolic rather than economic. Through carefully ordered rituals and repeated symbolic enunciations of the social order, the kuraqkunas act to bind the community together (Rasnake 1988).

Republican Transitions

Despite these important changes in the structure of local governments after the insurrections, colonial racial hierarchies remained in place. In fact, the terror of the "barbarous" Indians increased in the aftermath of the uprisings. In the early 1800s, however, criollo independence movements began to reconsider the colonial order and with it, the special status of Indians. As political scientist Mahmood Mamdani has shown in his studies of colonial rule in Africa, colonial domination not only defines social relations at the time of the rule, but it also greatly affects the forms of resistance and reforms that follow it (Mamdani 1996). Thus when Creole elites began to push for independence from Spain, one of the justifications they used was the degraded condition of the Indians, which they claimed to be proof of the cruel despotism of the Spanish rule (see Thurner 1997: 11). Under European "civilizing" models of democracy, and the liberal ideals of universal equality, the separate treatment of Indians — especially their right to communally held lands — was seen as a sort of aberration (Larson 2004: 41).

Instead, along with political self-rule, the followers of Simón Bolivar proposed the abolition of Indian tribute and the creation of nations of small holders, all citizens under the same rule of law. After independence in 1825, republicans engaged in the work of nation building waged long and bitterly fought struggles to impose these liberal political and economic reforms in Bolivia. Many in the ruling class rejected these notions, seeking to hold onto their privileges and the values of the colonial periods. Nevertheless, despite the liberal trend, criollo leaders of the new Bolivian republic reinstated the tribute because they badly needed revenue for the economy that had been crippled by the independence war. Haunted by the insurrections of the previous century, they were also leery of radical changes to the status quo (Klein 1992: 105).

By the mid-nineteenth century, however, capitalist demands for land, labor, and raw materials pushed liberal reforms back onto the criollo agenda. As Larson put it, "Modernization's material mandates thus required the ideological work of nation-making" (Larson 2004: 49). The big paradox for liberals, she has argued, was how to impose universal definitions of free labor and citizenship and to mold national cultures into homogenous wholes while at the same time creating symbols and categories of innate difference that would set limits on those universal ideals — this would allow continued domination over the Indian Other (ibid.: 13).

The solution to this dilemma was the land reform of 1874, which ended the Indian tribute and made the holding of communal property illegal, paving the way for the commercial use of Indian lands and the foundation of the *latifundio* (estate) system of landholding. This would resolve the pressing Indian Question by erasing colonial forms of servitude, turning Indians into Bolivians. Bolivian historian Marta Irurozqui Victoriano's fascinating 2000 study of the language of Bolivian legislators during this period reveals a nation-making process underlain by a dual discourse about Indian culture and nature. One position argued that Indians were barbarous savages unable to participate with reason in the state's affairs. This could only be remedied, if at all, by transforming their near-slavery status and by providing universal public education. The other position suggested that the main problem was Indian communal organizations that tied them to local and ethnic-based power relations rather than the state. This left them outside the liberal notion of the individual citizen. By destroying the juridical base of communal property, and dissolving the communities as collective entities, Bolivian legislators believed they were opening the path to modernity and civilization (Irurozqui Victoriano 2000: 70).

This then was the first offer of "citizenship" to Indians, who were to become part of the rural proletariat, either as *colonos* (laborers) on the haciendas or as small landholders. It must be said that this offer did not really include the right to vote, because the constitutions continued to require voters to be able to read and write in Spanish, to be landed or have rents, and to not be a domestic servant. As few Indians were literate, the land reform's greatest result was to deprive Indians of their lands (ibid.).[13] The 1874 reform made all communally held lands state property, which could be purchased in what was to be a reformulation of the country's land titling system. Naturally, most Indians did not have the money to buy back their lands, which were scooped up by the large landholders. This left the peasants little option but to become colonos, which automatically excluded them from voting. Many other Indians left their lands and fled into the racially mixed urban zones, to make up the new *cholo* (mixed-race) class, where they worked as servants or laborers. Many Indian communities, however, mounted sharp defenses of their communal lands, filing legal cases much like those of the colonial period and organizing violent protests. In many places, Indian resistance was so fierce that the revisita (title survey process) became all but impossible. Finally, the impoverished state cancelled the process.

Platt has argued that the resistance to these reforms demonstrated that Indians did not want the "tributary pact" (which had protected their lands throughout the colonial period) rescinded. He documents how ayllu members in Chayanta, in Northern Potosí, filed legal petitions asking to continue paying the tribute and serving in mitas, thus demonstrating a deep Indian "ambiguity about liberalism and citizenship" (Platt 1993, cited in Larson 2004: 211). Instead, they sought a hybrid status, known as "tributary citizenship," in which they received the benefits of citizenship, such as education and individual legal protection from the state/judiciary, but also the protections of tributaries, most important of which was state recognition of colonial titles to ethnically controlled communal lands (ibid.). This desire has not evaporated. In Northern Potosí, for example, some ayllus continue ritualized payment of the tribute to this day (Platt 1999: 46). Ultimately, in the face of Indian opposition and intransigence, the congress changed the law to allow for communities to hold collective titles called *proindiviso*, but this too was revoked. The result was a confused legal system contested at every level by Indians who tried to defend their colonial titles and livelihoods (Irurozqui Victoriano 2000; Larson 2004).

Historians have also noted a strong contradictory effect during the republican period. On the one hand, Indians demanded the state provide education through which they could learn to read and write, so that they could meet suffrage requirements. On the other hand, the radical social and juridical transformations resulted in a revitalized sense of common identity and ethnic memory, which grew into a national movement by the end of the nineteenth century (Larson 2004: 228). Bolivian sociologist Silvia Rivera Cusicanqui has contended that this abolition of communities and the rapacious process of land seizures was key to the revitalization of traditional systems of communal authority (Rivera Cusicanqui 1987: 26). The caciques who had retained cultural and religious functions during the early part of the century began to take on political roles transcending the community. The most notable example was Aymara Indian leader Pablo Zárate Willka, who mobilized an army of insurgent Indians frustrated by the loss of land and continued oppression. He formed a temporary alliance with Liberals in the 1899 war between Conservatives and Liberals, but his activism on behalf of Indians threatened white supremacy. After his army killed a number of whites, Zárate Willka and his army were captured, tried, and executed (Larson 2004: 229–42; see also Rivera Cusicanqui 1987).

Liberal Exclusions

The overall result of republican liberalism for the majority of Indians in the Andean region was a stunning loss of communal lands and deep cultural incursions, as Indians became subjects of law and liberal bureaucratic regimes controlled by whites and mestizos (Larson 2004). Although there was never a unitary discourse about race, race continued to play a central part in oligarchic debates about the formation of the nation, the role of Indians in the modern society, and the fitness of nonwhite subalterns for national inclusion (ibid.: 65). In Bolivia, particularly after the Zárate Willka trials, it was clearer than ever that the Indian Question had not been resolved. In his 2000 work, literary scholar Fernando Unzueta described this period of active state formation and showed, following anthropologist Benedict Anderson, how the narrative practices of criollo newspapers and gazettes worked to construct a particular racialized vision of the nation (Anderson 1991). The papers articulated notions of Bolivian patriotism and citizenship, clearly contrasting the new *ciudadanos* (citizens) with the *indiada desestructurada y no reconocida* (unrecognized and destructured Indians) (Albó 1996).[14]

The new republican elites, echoing the social Darwinism that was popular at the time, argued that for the good of the nation, *"nuestros bárbaros"* ("our savages") had to be either civilized and assimilated or encouraged to disappear (Unzueta 2000: 44). The 1900 census, for example, argued that the "cause of backwardness in our civilization is the indigenous race, which is particularly unresponsive to innovation and progress" (cited in Rivera Cusicanqui 1987: 17). Yet because the Indian population was so large, assimilation was not a short-term possibility. Nor was the cultural mestizaje that had become the basis of revolutionary Mexican national identity. In Bolivia, the boundaries between "white" and "Indian" remained salient, and mestizos were seen as impure and degraded hybrids sharing none of the virtues of either race (Larson 2004: 66–68; see also Wade 1997).[15] Instead, Larson has argued, the practices and institutions of republican liberalism produced an informal system of apartheid based on the wholesale exclusion of Indians from the political sphere. Indians were removed from their lands and converted into disciplined manual laborers anchored to the countryside. The result of this modern race-thinking was to locate Indians and hybrid popular cultures "on the boundaries of national belonging" (Larson 2004: 242). Thus, as Bolivian sociologist Álvaro García Linera has suggested, "ethnic exclusion was converted into the articulating axis of state cohesion" (García Linera 2003: 13; see also Pérez Luna 2006).

What is clear from this account is that the transformations of the liberal republican period cannot be understood merely by an analysis of the political sphere. Rather, the process of nation making was carried out through complex linkages between political reforms promising universal inclusion and cultural understandings about race that produced profoundly exclusionary effects. Philosopher Uday Mehta has offered a compelling explanation for the gap between liberalism's doctrinal commitment to freedom, on the one hand, and the sustained political exclusionary practices it produces across the world, on the other hand. He argues that such liberal philosophers as Locke and Mill based their doctrine of equal rights on the notion of a set of rational capacities that all individuals share and that form the basis of political inclusion. Concealed behind these universal capacities, however, are culturally defined characteristics that the elite hold as preconditions for rational behavior (Mehta 1997: 61–62). So, for example, although all people have the potential for rational citizenship, uneducated or so-called savage Indians were not considered able to actualize that rationality, and thus were not granted full citizenship rights. Liberalism works by modulating the gap between abstract capacity and actual conditions, in essence determining acceptable boundaries between who is included and who is not. In every society, there is a tacit allegiance to a particular ordering of society and set of distinctions that act as specific cultural and psychological conditions for the actualization of universal capacities (ibid.). In republican Bolivia, the elite's assumptions about Indians' barbarous and communal natures therefore justified their exclusion from the nation.

The political move to exile Indians from the public sphere did not mean that they escaped control, however. Rather, their control took the form of patriarchal relations based on centuries-old practices of racial management. Historian Andrés Guerrero, who studies liberalism in Ecuadorian Andean communities, has explained that once the administration of Indian populations was no longer the state's concern, it was displaced onto the private sphere. Indians became invisible in official registers, and their management and control as laborers and subjects were left to the territorial power of propertied citizens who owned haciendas. These local patrones acted through what Guerrero calls "colonial knowledges," systems of habitus " 'made bodily' in the trans-generational socialization of a centuries-long experience of domination" (Guerrero 2003: 293–97). García Linera has explained that such hierarchies of knowledge "identified the Indian with those who are not trained, those who should be directed, educated, indoctrinated, guided, governed, and placated" (García Linera 2003: 12). Such prejudices naturalized and legitimated the accompanying economic exclusion and political monopolies. So although Indians were officially citizens of the republic, they continued to be subject to colonial forms of discrimination and exploitation by powerful local caudillos (Thurner 1997).

Bolivian historian Rossana Barragán Romano has provided a concrete example of how this worked. She describes the adoption of new criminal and civil codes in Bolivia during the nineteenth century, which were intended to rationalize and modernize legal systems. The new codes erased the formal legal colonial categories of Indians, making them subject to the same laws and obligations as all other citizens, but allowed a more subtle form of discrimination based on the social differentiations that coincided with the old colonial divisions. Thus people could lose their citizenship status and their right to give testimony in trials if found guilty of infamy or being a woman of ill repute. Moreover, the language of credibility and merit was based in social distinctions of class, honor, and superiority. This gave dominant groups the ability to invalidate the rights and the testimony of subalterns by attributing to them negative social characteristics, such as their roles as servants or their Indian identity. Lacking a juridical category of protection, Indian and women subalterns were subject to the authority and power of elite men and effectively silenced. Thus republican citizenship was based in, and reinforced by, hierarchy, racism, and patriarchy (Barragán Romano 1999: 56).

The 1952 Revolution

The new century brought continued resistance by highland Indians protesting republican forms of economic and political domination. In a cycle of rebellions from 1910 to 1930 that were ultimately put down, Aymara leaders articulated a series of political demands, including restitution of lands (based on colonial deeds and proof of hereditary leadership), access to the markets being taken over by large-scale agricultural production, and the presence of Indian representatives in congress (Rivera Cusicanqui 1987: 37). Some uprisings took on messianic overtones, echoing the insurrections of the previous century. More important, Indians were articulating a desire to return to the economic systems they had enjoyed before the colonial and liberal impositions (ibid.: 35–36). These demands were at odds with oligarchs who were expanding their private landholdings, as well as modernizers who saw the future of Bolivia as a unified nation of peasant farmers contributing to the national market.

The 1930s Chaco war between Bolivia and Paraguay brought Indians and mestizos together as never before and made clear the continuing colonial racial inequalities. The four-year Chaco war was tragic on all sides. Thousands of soldiers died in the harsh desert when broken supply lines left them stranded without water. More than a hundred thousand Bolivians and Paraguayans died in all. By the end of the conflict, Bolivia had lost not only a generation of its young men, but also a major part of the Chaco desert. In the chaotic years after the war, the oligarchy was replaced by emerging political actors who saw the Indian peasantry and the miners as allies for political change. Throughout the postwar years, new parties and organizations had sprung into life, particularly trade and peasant unions that sought fresh forms of representation, along with new political parties like the Movimiento Nacional Revolucionario (MNR), the National Revolutionary Movement, which was run mostly by the urban, white middle class (Klein 1992).

In 1945, highland Indians held their first national congress to articulate objections to ongoing Indian labor abuses, and Indians began organizing unions and militias to take over the large latifundios. Particularly in the Cochabamba valleys, peasants began to raise the possibility of destroying the hacienda system, employing the slogan "land for those who work it" (Albó 1987). In 1947, tensions rose and in several highland communities Indian rebellions were violently repressed (Dandler and Torrico 1987; Rivera Cusicanqui 1987: 53ff). The old political system began to fall apart, and Bolivia degenerated into what political scientist James Malloy has called an "invertebrate sociopolitical society" (Malloy 1977: 465). In 1952, the MNR party brought together the fragmented segments — labor, the miners, the middle class, and the Indian peasants — to institute a revolutionary republic under MNR leadership that promised to develop a national political economy based on economic development and modernization. The MNR platform had three prongs: (1) nationalization of the mines to reorganize the process of capitalist accumulation, (2) agrarian reform to eliminate the servile relationships in agriculture and to promote a domestic market, and (3) universal suffrage (Rivera Cusicanqui 1987: 3).

After the revolution, the populist MNR party established itself as the dominant inclusionary political organization to bring together three main social classes: the middle class, workers, and peasants. In essence, the MNR positioned itself as the vertebral column bringing structure to the unorganized, segmented society (Malloy 1977). To organize their cooperation, the MNR took advantage of the colonial legacy of corporatist social values and sectoral organizations that had persisted in Bolivia despite the liberal democratic modes of political organization. This was particularly important in the case of the Indian peasant population, which had become independent, militant, and armed in the period before the revolution and had taken over haciendas to redistribute land to their members (Lagos 1994).

The result was a corporatist party structure that organized the bulk of the populace into a "limited number of discrete, officially sanctioned organizations coordinated from the top by the central political committee" (Malloy 1977: 467).[16] Malloy suggests that over time the MNR lost the ability to control the multiple sectoral organizations it had mobilized and resorted to fashioning public policies designed to win support by buying it. This was possible in part, says Bolivian political scientist Roberto Laserna, because the state ran the most important sectors of the economy, including the mines, petroleum, airlines, railroads, and so on. Because the state controlled the country's natural resources, and the riches that flowed from them, the ruling MNR party could distribute benefits according to a "prebendal populism," run by local and national politicians with extensive patron-client networks (Laserna 2002: 26).

For Indians, this corporatist political system took the form of state-sponsored peasant unions, which integrated Indians into the state as producers and not as Indians per se. This meant the official codification of a new social and political category for them: campesinos (peasants). Like the previous categories defined by the Crown or the state, this set of practices and institutions created new subjects in a particular relation to the state with "acceptable forms and images of social activity and individual and collective identity" (Corrigan and Sayer 1985: 3). For the MNR, that meant instituting a unifying nationalist program that attempted to erase all ethnic references (Albó 1996: 7). Instead, Indians were called campesinos, their organizations were converted to sindicatos (peasant unions or leagues), and the government indigenous office was submerged into the peasant ministry. In the 1960s, ethnicity was seen as a form of racism, which had to be replaced by a vision of class or simply be seen as a "primitive form condemned to disappear with the rapid processes of modernization" (ibid.: 8). These policies were not unusual — throughout Latin America, as nation-states were being formed, governments were experimenting with novel forms of *indigenismo* policies to assimilate their indigenous populations.[17]

Here we see the legacy of the liberal period: the continued need for political technologies that would include Indians in "modern" Bolivia but would also ensure their control and continued subordination. Rivera Cusicanqui has suggested that the MNR's strategy of assimilation was intended to preclude the crystallization of the radical, anticolonial proposal against criollo domination that underlay peasant Indian activism (Rivera Cusicanqui 1987). The MNR's solution to this was a new offer of citizenship: universal suffrage, national education, and full membership in the national economy. Through such new mechanisms as the sindicato and the campesino ministry, Indians were to be assimilated into the state, their labor incorporated into the market, and their difference minimized and managed. This strategy also determined a particular form of representation and leadership as well as a secure, though contested, form of identity. Indian leaders held authority through their positions within the sindicato hierarchy, and the unions had direct relations with a patron state through national labor federations. Although this offer met one part of the demands of Indian peasants, it denied another fundamental demand: autonomy and self-government (Ticona et al. 1995: 102).

Analysts point out that the reforms and the sindicato movement had different effects in different areas of the highlands. First, the agrarian reform of 1953 was pushed by the campesino unions of the Cochabamba valley and adopted by the MNR, and it privileged the consolidation of individual parcels instead of the recognition or restitution of communally held ayllu land (Platt 1999: 43). In the Cochabamba area and in Achacachi, where Indian communities had long been broken up, Indians were in some cases small landholders or, more frequently, they worked on large haciendas. The peasant unions proved an effective means for land acquisition after the abolition of the feudal haciendas, and Indians there tended to feel included in the nation through their membership in the state-sponsored peasant federations. There, peasant unions were rewarded with agricultural credit, subsidized food coupons, and government attention (Albó 1987; Rivera Cusicanqui 1987; Ströbele-Gregor 1996; Larson 2004).

The result, says Bolivian historian José Gordillo, was that the Indian peasants of the Cochabamba valley were able to use the collectivist organizations to channel their demands directly to the state in a way that had never been possible. Through their base organizations, they were able to bring pressure against the local and regional elites, gain economic rights, and find some new spaces of political participation (Gordillo 2000: 209). Anthropologist Maria Lagos's study of peasant landholders in Cochabamba makes it clear, however, that neither acquiring land nor forming peasant unions resolved the unequal relations with hacendados or the merchant class, as poor peasants remained tied to these elite through economic relations of production as well as cultural and kinship practices. Nor did it resolve racial questions, as "Indian" and "campesino" became synonymous (Lagos 1994).

In the Aymara areas of the altiplano and in Northern Potosí, where people maintained strong cultural ties to collective landholding and traditional social organizations, however, the reforms were not as successful, mainly because they did not respond to the Indians' centuries-old claims for restitution of colonial communal titles. Moreover, the unions were perceived as externally imposed and in conflict with traditional ayllu forms of representations (Albó 2000: 84; Ticona et al. 1995: 102). This was aggravated by the fact that the sindicatos fell immediately into the hands of mestizo townfolk, reproducing already existing patriarchal and clientelistic relations (Platt 1999: 44). In those areas, Indians continued to feel excluded from the nation and resisted the state's domination, eventually allying with radical workers unions during the years of the military dictatorships in the 1970s (Rivera Cusicanqui 1987).

Thus, although the reforms after the revolution addressed some of the inequalities that had faced Bolivia's Indian peasants, they also provoked an ambiguity between class and ethnicity that has continued to the present. By renaming Indians as "peasants," a title that did not fit smoothly in all cases, the state attempted to find a way to incorporate the labor and political force of this sector. Although many Indians found this subject position strategic, others resisted its totalizing effects, holding onto other forms of representation. This tension, explored further throughout this book, continues to trouble Indians and their organizations.

Even in the areas where Indian peasants benefited from the state's attention, the sindicato movement did not amount to a radical empowerment of Indians. During the decades after the revolution, peasant unions were increasingly brought under state control. The state took advantage of the sectoral divisions and used peasant militias against the labor movement, particularly the miners, who were the most powerful force antagonistic to the state. More important, once the land redistribution was completed and the government-sponsored structures became consolidated, the sindicatos began to fragment, as the inconsistencies of the MNR's positions became obvious (ibid.). Worse, the MNR was able to co-opt many local-level leadership groups, tainting their image in the minds of their followers (Malloy 1977: 471).

By 1964, when the weakened MNR had been supplanted by the military, the dictator General René Barrientos took advantage of this polarization, gradually co-opting the sindicatos and their federations into a vertical, bureaucratic, and corrupt state structure that manipulated union policies through a combination of savvy patronage and brutal repression. Barrientos finally disarmed the militias in the so-called Military-Peasant Pact government, during which, Rivera Cusicanqui concluded, the formal or "parastatal" (Albó 2000: 96) peasant movement had become a docile supporter of the new power structure (Rivera Cusicanqui 1987: 3; but see Gordillo 2000).[18] By the General Hugo Banzer Suárez years, however, the authoritarian-dictatorial state had turned decidedly antilabor, defining labor federations as subversive internal enemies. They were outlawed and then finally violently repressed (Tapia 2002: 43; see also Klein 1992). Nevertheless, peasant unions continued to persist and to push for their constituencies' rights. Sindicatos were responsible for reestablishing peasant access to markets, previously controlled by haciendas and elites, and advocated on the national scene that Indians be taken seriously as producers and political actors.

When democratic rule returned in 1985, it was clear that corporatist models of representation, especially peasant sindicatos, remained the predominant forms of mediation with the state for most parts of the highlands. This extended from the highlands to the Chapare, where coca growers established important unions, and to the colonization projects in the Oriente. In these areas, peasant sindicatos were (and still are) key to land distribution and local government (Klein 1992: 268; Albó 2000). Although the sindicato was originally a foreign form of representation for Indian communities, Bolivian anthropologist Xavier Albó has noted that throughout much of the highlands, the sindicato has taken on many features of Andean culture, becoming in the end a traditional communal organization, "structured internally, the same as always, according to Indian uses and customs" (Albó 2000: 85; see also Rivera Cusicanqui 1987: 98). There, the boundary between the categories of "Indian" and "peasant" is blurred. In other areas, however, like in Northern Potosí, the ayllu form of government has remained more important and has in fact been in conflict with the union model, which is perceived as a means of colonial domination (ibid.).

Postrevolutionary Legacies

Many analysts argue that like the republican reforms, the postrevolutionary form of Indian integration only reinscribed discrimination in the new institutions of citizenship. Platt has argued that the 1952 agrarian reform proved to be little different from the first reforms of 1874 under the republican regime. In both reforms, there was an effort to consolidate a regime of small producers within a "modern" society, and a failure to meet the real demands of Andean peoples, by ratifying the Spanish treaties with the native societies of the Andes (Platt 1999). Ticona and his coauthors have suggested that the citizenship offer did not overcome racism but rather was a reflection of it. That is, Indians were offered citizenship if they abandoned their identity as Indians and incorporated themselves into the national society. Thus the saying, "One will no longer be discriminated against when one stops being an Indian" ("Se va a dejar de ser discriminado cuando uno deje de ser indio"). As a result of this flawed logic, they argued, the promises of revolutionary citizenship for Indians remained incomplete (Ticona et al. 1995: 190–91).

Other scholars have more extreme critiques. Aymara sociologist Félix Patzi has offered that rather than forming a citizenship of equality, the 1952 revolution resulted in a Bolivia "structured in the form of hierarchical colonial rings, that is, a social stratification overlaying an ethnic base" (Patzi 2002: 41). This is because the peasant movement chose to ally itself with the working class during the revolution. In the process, it gave up long-held demands for autonomy and control of lands, as expressed by Túpac Katari and Zárate Willka, and struggled instead for the interests of the new dominant mestizo/white class: private property and peasant participation in the government through the vote and education. As a result of this conformist logic, Patzi says, the peasant movement arrived at a "doxic submission," a naturalization of hegemonic ideas that ultimately frustrated indigenous dreams of citizenship (ibid.).

García Linera has noted that public education and universal suffrage after the revolution did open certain means to social ascent for Indians who accumulated the cultural capital of schooling. This was severely constrained, however, by the obligation to learn a foreign language (Spanish) and to adopt cultural norms produced and monopolized by the urban mestizo class. In the same way, Indian leaders were forced to assume new forms of authority through the sindicato system, which was foreign to the traditional models. The result was the construction of a "space of linguistic and organizational competencies regulated by the state, in which the indigenous, now converted into 'hermanos campesinos' [peasant brothers], were newly located in the bottom-most positions in the struggle for legitimate political and educational knowledges" (García Linera 2003: 14–15). These arguments reflect the continuing paradox of liberalism, in which inclusion and marginalization are always paired and in tension.

The frustrations revealed in these critiques provoked several different responses in the highlands. The most important was the Katarismo movement, which arose from Aymara intellectuals in the 1960s and which linked rural and urban Aymaras, calling for cultural recognition and Indian rights within a "multicultural" Bolivia (see generally Albó 1987, 1994; Rivera Cusicanqui 1987). Named after eighteenth-century insurrection leader Túpac Katari, this movement began as a cultural movement in the La Paz and Oruro areas and then developed into a strong trade-unionist movement that tied ethnic questions to the primary notion of class. Central to the Katarista project was the recuperation of the past, particularly in the figure of Túpac Katari. Literary scholar Javier C. Sanjinés has argued that Katarista ideology offered "a powerful tradition that is counterhegemonic to both liberal (ethnocidal) nation-building projects, and to Eurocentric ideals of cultural homogenization and citizenship under a reified form of cultural mestizaje" (Sanjinés 2004: 155).

In 1973, Aymara intellectuals published the Manifesto of Tiwanaku, declaring indigenous people to be "economically exploited and culturally and politically oppressed" (cited in Rivera Cusicanqui 1987: 118). In 1978, the movement split into two factions. The moderate group, Movimiento Revolucionario Túpac Katari de Liberación (MRTKL), led by Víctor Hugo Cárdenas, continued to work within the political system, urging that the problems of Bolivian society be analyzed through the "theory of two eyes": one eye focusing on the problem of exploited social classes, and the other seeing it as a problem of oppressed nations, peoples, and ethnic groups (Albó 1987: 402; Sanjinés 2004: 160). The more radical group, the Movimiento Indio Túpac Katari (MITKA), maintained a more radical outsider strategy, refusing to ally with mestizo political parties.

The Kataristas worked with other labor federations, gradually becoming key figures in peasant political organizations working against the Military-Peasant Pact. After repression and exile during the military years, the Kataristas and their charismatic leader, Jenaro Flores, formed the Confederación Sindical Única de Trabajadores Campesinos de Bolivia (CSUTCB, the Unified Federation of Peasant Workers of Bolivia). The CSUTCB was a central actor in the struggle against the military dictatorships, articulating the hopes of the working and popular sectors of civil society (Tapia 2002: 43; see also Zavaleta 1987) as well as reflecting the strength of Indian peasantry as a major social actor (Albó 2000). Kataristas also formed a political party, the MRTK (Movimiento Revolucionario Túpac Katari), which had little political success but was important in promoting Indian issues at the national level.

During the early 1980s, Katarismo continued to be an important political force in the trade movement, advocating for peasant rights and agrarian reform (Ströbele-Gregor 1996: 84). For instance, in 1983 under Katarista influence, the CSUTCB proposed the Fundamental Agrarian Law, which included the recognition of the identity, authorities, and jurisdiction of indigenous campesino communities (Van Cott 2000: 137). Since the late 1980s, however, Katarismo's power has declined. Although its followers continued to argue for indigenous participation in national politics, they were not able to push the Indian Question into the public arena, and the movement began to lose force and split into several parties. In the mid-1990s, however,

Katarista Víctor Hugo Cárdenas was elected vice president and brought a much diluted version of Katarismo to the MNR platform, urging an end to ethnic exclusion in the new multicultural Bolivia (Albó 1994: 69).

The more radical Katarismo proposals of Aymara nationalism and autonomy grew in the late 1980s, expressed most clearly by the guerrilla movement called the Ofensiva Roja de Ayllus Tupakataristas (Red Offensive of Tupakatarista Ayllus). In their 1988 political thesis, they asserted themselves as the owners and original people of the land, seeking self-determination and the right to form independent nations of Quechua and Aymara workers (Patzi 2002: 42). This group was repressed, and its leaders jailed, but its ideology continues to circulate, especially in Aymara areas. Aymara leader Felipe Quispe, called El Mallku (the prince, or condor), the present leader of the CSUTCB, is the most widely known spokesperson for this current. In a 2002 interview, former guerrilla Quispe said the Aymara Indians consider themselves to be an indigenous nation. They are in the process, he said, of creating the state of Kollasuyo (the original name of the Inca empire), with their own laws, codes, and authorities. Central to this task is the re-Indianization of many Indians who have accepted foreign ideology, who must "retake the essence of our ancestral culture" (Gómez and Giordano 2002).[19]

The Making of the Oriente

The preceding history has centered on the highlands, and on the particular ways the Bolivian state has attempted to assimilate and manage highland Indians. Lowland Indians came to national attention along a different trajectory. Indians in the Oriente were not part of "the tributary pact" colonial powers made with the Andean people of the former Incan empire. Instead, they were considered *bárbaros* (savages) and forced into labor on the haciendas or as rubber tappers. Indigenous lands were considered *tierras baldias* (empty lands), and colonization, ranching, and logging drove Indians into ever smaller territories. In the Amazonian forests along Bolivia's northeastern border, indigenous groups were small and disperse, with small local clan-centered forms of social organization. These nomadic or seminomadic groups were controlled by Catholic missionaries, who brought them into sedentary settlements in the seventeenth and eighteenth centuries.

In the twentieth century, this pattern was repeated, as evangelical groups such as the New Tribes Missions and the Summer Linguistics Institute established missions among the Indians (Stearman 1989; Tolan and Postero 1992; Herrera Sarmiento 2002). Many of these small groups have disappeared or gone "extinct." Today, twenty-two separate groups or *pueblos indígenas* (indigenous peoples) live in Bolivia's Amazon (Lema 1998). In the far east and south of the country along the borders with Paraguay and Argentina are dry forests and the Chaco desert. This part of the Oriente is home to the Chiquitano, Guarayo, and Ayoreo Indians, as well as the Guaraní people, the largest group in the Oriente. After the state's colonial and republican pacification programs, which ended in the Kuruyuki massacre in 1892, many Guaranís lived predominantly as subsistence farmers and ranchers in the Cordillera and Izozog regions, in long-term patron-client relations with the local hacienda owners. Others lived as slaves, even until very recently.

Although lowland Indians were not treated in the same ways as Andean native people, they were not isolated from Bolivian national events. The 1930s Chaco war brought highlanders to the eastern lowlands and began what has become the now permanent opening of the Oriente to national development. The war began as a dispute over borders and was exacerbated by the possibility of lucrative oil resources in the Chaco desert area between Paraguay and Bolivia. For the Guaraní people, the war was devastating. As the battles raged across their lands, they were forced to flee to Argentina and Paraguay. Some Guaranís gave their support to Paraguay, working as cattle herders for the army and then, labeled as traitors after the war, went to Paraguay. A large group of Guaranís from the Izozog region supported the Bolivians but was captured by the Paraguayan army and held in a fortress in Paraguay until the war ended. Pifarré has calculated that nearly fifteen thousand Guaranís left the Cordillera region or were killed as a result of the war (Pifarré 1989: 410).

After the war, one of the tenuous new governments nationalized U.S.-owned Standard Oil. As can be imagined, this set up a dispute with the United States, but it did not last long. The United States was just entering World War II and needed a reliable source of cheap tin. So the rift over Standard Oil was settled in an accord signed in Rio in 1942, in which Bolivia was given a grant for $25 million for economic development programs to be developed by U.S. economist Mervin Bohan. The resulting "Bohan Plan" recommended economic diversification, import substitution, and monetary stabilization. These were not unusual prescriptions, given the times, but what was distinctive was the plan's focus on the Oriente. It proposed starting import substitution of basic agricultural commodities in Santa Cruz, by totally overhauling the region's agrarian structure. It called for building a road network to link the production areas to the cities and for transforming the precapitalist and inefficient hacienda system into extensive commercial agricultural enterprises. The Bohan Plan saw the Oriente as Bolivia's new growth area (Thorn 1971).

This plan was not instituted until after the revolution, when the postrevolutionary government began to modernize its economy. The MNR's agrarian reform law cemented its support by the rural farmers, most of whom were highland Indians (Eckstein 1983: 107–8). The preamble of the Agrarian Reform Decree set forth six basic goals, the first three of which responded directly to the demands of the Indian peasants. First, the law was to provide adequate parcels of land to peasants with little or no land, providing they worked the parcels, expropriating for this purpose latifundios, the large land-holdings not personally worked by the owners. Second, the law was intended to restore to corporate Indian communities usurped lands and to cooperate in the modernization of their agriculture, respecting and building on col-lectivist traditions. Third, the agrarian reform was to free peasant laborers from their condition as servants, making gratuitous and obligatory personal service illegal.

The next three goals of the agrarian reform show the complexities the MNR had inherited, including the tensions between peasant farmers and agrarian capitalists. The fourth goal was to stimulate productivity and com-mercialization of agricultural goods, encouraging investment of new capi-tal, respecting small and medium-size landholdings, encouraging agrarian cooperativism, giving technical aid, and opening possibilities for credit. Fifth, the law was intended to protect natural resources through the adoption of modern technical and scientific means. Sixth, the reform was to promote internal rural migration from the overpopulated Inter-Andean zone, to advance rational population distribution and affirmation of national unity, so the Bolivian Oriente might be integrated with the rest of the country (Carter 1971: 243).

This new reform was signed into law in August 1953 in Ucureña, in the Cochabamba valley, before fifty thousand militant campesinos (Gordillo 2000). Within two years of the promulgation of the law, 49 percent of farm families received land, but because they got only what land they had been using, the size of their farms tended not to increase. Although the reforms did redistribute land, they did not do much for economic growth. In fact, the amount of produce going to market was sharply reduced, as the new farm-owners kept much of the income from their lands in the form of food. The reforms also failed to improve the productivity of farm labor or to end the fragmentation of land through inheritance and land sales (Sanabria 1993: 50). The law did, however, significantly damage the large landholding sys-tem of latifundio, by eliminating the key element that had sustained it: the rendering of personal service as payment for the land (Thorn 1971: 161–62).

But the land reform was never designed merely to benefit the peasants; it was also meant to encourage agrarian capitalism. Few farmers before the rev-olution had employed wage labor or focused on maximizing agricultural profits. To stimulate capitalist agriculture, therefore, the reform granted loans, technical assistance, and capital investments; ensured that big, capi-talized agricultural enterprises and medium-size farms were exempt from expropriation; and encouraged peasants in the densely populated parts of the country to migrate and acquire larger holdings in areas where land was abundant — meaning the Oriente (see Carter 1971: 243; Eckstein 1983: 108).

As a result, the 1960s brought dramatic growth to the Oriente. The Cochabamba–Santa Cruz highway, finished in 1954 with funds from the U.S. Export-Import Bank, linked the Oriente to the rest of the country. In 1963, the Plan Nacional de Colonización (National Colonization Plan) was organized to resettle tens of thousands of highland- and valley-based peasants to the sparsely populated eastern lands of Santa Cruz and the Chapare, as well as to the Yungas, the subtropical valleys east of La Paz. The "colonization" projects to settle the frontier were portrayed as a sincere attempt by the government to redistribute the population more evenly and to provide peasants with land. However, colonization also posed a way for the government to avoid dealing with the serious inequities that remained after the revolution, such as landlessness and growing poverty (Gill 1987: 38; Sanabria 1993: 51).

It was during these years that most of the Guaranís who currently live in the Santa Cruz area arrived. As the zone received more funding, sugarcane farms grew and more laborers were needed to harvest the cane. Guaranís had been following sugarcane harvests (*zafras*) in Argentina for years, and so when their labor was needed in Santa Cruz, closer to home, many thousands answered the call. They came, formed relationships with local ranchers and farmers, and began to stay year round, forming Guaraní communities throughout the agricultural areas. The Guaraní laborers were encouraged by MNR activists to form sindicatos and to make land claims under the new laws. Many did so. Chapter 3 details the history of one such community, which I call Bella Flor. The Guaranís found work in the zafra but also in the sugarcane refineries, the cattle ranches, and the farms springing up around the region. They also began to sell their own products in the growing market.

During the 1970s, the state invested much of its foreign aid into tin and petroleum exploitation, but the big push was into the Oriente, as the Bohan Plan was finally put into effect. Besides the colonization and highway projects that opened up Santa Cruz and the Chapare, and then to the Beni farther to the north, the government awarded large land concessions to individuals and agribusinesses — almost 10 million hectares in Santa Cruz alone (Sanabria 1993: 51). U.S. economic assistance focused on large-scale investment in agriculture and transportation, mainly in Santa Cruz. Agricultural programs supervised by the U.S. Agency for International Development (USAID) made credit, fertilizer, seed, and machinery available to the Santa Cruz oligarchy in agricultural import-substitution programs (Casanovas 1990). Ex-hacendados from the highlands whose lands had been appropriated in the agrarian reform, mining families with compensation money in hand from the nationalization of the mines, and all kinds of wealthy speculators made lucrative investments in sugar and cotton cultivation. Large-scale producers who received government subsidies often became enormously wealthy in a short time, and a new lowland elite formed. Sugar mill owners got loans to expand and modernize, and a state-owned mill was built (Gill 1987: 37).

The 1970s were a time of economic crisis. Many of the speculative loans in the Oriente defaulted, and this added to Bolivia's national debt. By the end of the decade, inflation soared, export revenues dropped, and commercial and multilateral loans began to dry up. Bolivia's situation was, lamentably, one part of the debt crisis that shook most of Latin America. Landlessness and unemployment were on the rise (Sanabria 1993: 56), and a steady drop in agricultural commodity prices produced by agribusinesses in Santa Cruz led to a steep drop in production (Stearman 1985: 35–38). This was part of the situation that forced the Hernán Siles Zuazo government in 1982 to adopt structural adjustment programs and begin the neoliberal economic restructuring that continued throughout the 1990s. (This history is discussed further in chapters 4 and 6.) In the late 1980s and early 1990s, this downturn was offset in part by revenues from the illegal cocaine and coca paste market. By 1992, it was estimated that coca/cocaine exports amounted to 37 percent of Bolivia's legitimate exports (Doria Medina 1986; Painter 1994). That revenue has dropped considerably as a result of U.S. drug eradication efforts in the 1990s.

Nevertheless, the boom in Santa Cruz continues, as poor people from the highlands continue to migrate to the city and the surrounding agricultural communities. In 1998, the population of the city of Santa Cruz reached one million, and all the cities and towns in the region are growing almost as fast. Also in the 1990s, new gas reserves were found in the departments of Santa Cruz, Tarija, and the Beni (the so-called Media Luna, or half moon, because of the crescent shape these departments form along the eastern frontier of the country). These natural gas resources represent a large proportion of state revenues and have brought the Oriente into the center of Bolivia's economic, political, and social agendas.

Indigenous Movements of the 1980s and 1990s

For lowland indigenous groups, the most immediate effect of the Oriente's intense growth was the endangerment of their lands. Like the republican period in the highlands, the 1970s began a period of massive land invasion in the Oriente. Lands that had been too remote or too difficult to farm or ranch suddenly began to be invaded by government colonization projects, Mennonite migrants, logging and petroleum companies, or agribusinesses.

Across the Oriente, indigenous people were forced to defend their lands. Lowland groups began organizing slowly throughout the 1980s, with the help of NGOs and anthropologists. In the late 1970s, an NGO called Apoyo Para el Campesino–Indígena del Oriente Boliviano (APCOB, Support for the Peasants–Indigenous People of Eastern Bolivia), run by German anthropologist Jürgen Riester, sponsored meetings between several lowland indigenous groups (the Chiquitano and Ayoreo Indians), and slowly these meetings grew to include other groups (the Guaraní, Guarayo, and Mataco Indians). In 1982, these groups met in Santa Cruz and founded a regional federation of indigenous people called the Confederación Indígena del Oriente de Bolivia (CIDOB).

Regional federations were forming in other areas as well, also with the help of NGOs. In the Beni, a multiethnic federation brought together various groups, including the Mojeño, Trinitario, Sirionó, and Chimane Indians (Lehm 1999). In Camiri, in the Cordillera region, Guaranís formed a federation called the Asamblea del Pueblo Guaraní (APG). Supported by a Jesuit NGO called the Centro de Investigación y Promoción del Campesinado (CIPCA), the APG started development and cultural projects throughout the Guaraní region (Hirsch 2003). These regional organizing efforts had important effects at the local level. For instance, the Guaraní of Santa Cruz were influenced by the APG projects, particularly the literacy and development campaigns. As I describe in chapter 2, these proved an important platform for local organizing that eventually led to the establishment of the Capitanía Zona Cruz (CZC).

Although the historical hostility between some of the groups was an initial obstacle to national organizing, one central issue unified them: the need to defend and control their own land from the increased settlement in lowland areas (Riester 1985). In 1990, indigenous groups overcame their differences and united to take their demand for territory public. Led by the well-organized Mojeños from the Beni and their charismatic leader Marcial Fabricano, they staged a massive (and well-publicized) march from the lowlands up the Andes to La Paz in what was called the Marcha por Territorio y Dignidad (March for Territory and Dignity).[20] The lowland groups were met at the summit by Andean groups, and together they marched into La Paz. Without a doubt, this march changed the face of Bolivia forever.[21] Indigenous people and their demands for territory and recognition as part of the nation caused an immediate response. President Paz Zamora met with the indigenous leaders, negotiated with them on their demands, and created seven indigenous territories by presidential decree. *Territorio* became an icon of indigenous-state relations.

Although the march was an impressive demonstration of the mobilizing force of lowland Indians, the reaction of the state reflected something else:

the emerging international discourse on indigenous rights. Bolivian indigenous activism of the 1980s and 1990s was part of a larger trend across Latin America. Since the 1960s, indigenous movements had begun to organize and to demand cultural recognition and political rights. The demands and strategies of indigenous groups vary widely from country to country (and even from region to region), depending on the particular histories of domination and assimilation, the political and cultural processes at work, and the majority or minority status Indians hold in their country (Postero and Zamosc 2004).[22] However, since the 1970s, with the help of international NGOs, indigenous people have begun to organize transnational indigenous federations and develop a network of allies to help legitimate their organizations and aspirations (Keck and Sikkink 1998; Brysk 2000). Indigenous groups began to identify themselves as *pueblos indígenas* or *pueblos originarios* (indigenous peoples or original peoples), rejecting previous deprecatory terms such as *indio* or *auca*, and to identify as native peoples facing the legacies of colonial oppression.

A crucial turning point was a 1977 United Nations conference on discrimination against indigenous peoples in the Americas. The conference helped forge communication among groups, which led to increased coordination of their demands (Anaya 1997). Indigenous representatives began to travel to international meetings, take part in international human rights tribunals, and make alliances with various other civil society sectors, most notably the human rights and environmental movements (Conklin and Graham 1995; Varese 1996).[23] The plight of native peoples began to be paired with that of the disappearing rainforest, and global rock stars like Sting rallied in their defense. In the process, a transnational indigenous movement was born that espoused a discourse linking indigenous identity, human rights, and democracy (Brysk 2000; Conklin 2002). This was crystallized in 1992, when Indians organized continentwide demonstrations rejecting the celebration of the "discovery of America," commemorating instead "five hundred years of popular and indigenous resistance" (Hale 1994; Assies 2000).

Also, as a result of the 1977 conference and the related commissions and ensuing reports, indigenous people began taking their demands to international intergovernmental institutions, which further justified the emerging discourse of indigenous rights by positioning it in terms of international law (Anaya 1997). In 1982, the United Nations established the U.N. Working Group of Indigenous Populations, which gathers information and develops standards on Indian-state relations as well as cultural and intellectual property. Probably the most important result of this international activity was the adoption of the International Labor Organization's Convention No. 169 in 1989. This convention recognizes "the aspirations of [indigenous] peoples to exercise control over their institutions, ways of life, and economic development and to maintain and develop their identities, languages, and religions, within the framework of the States in which they live" (ILO 1989, cited in Anaya 1997: 440). The ILO convention became a critical tool for indigenous activists across the world to use in demanding a revision of state-indigenous relations. They could now embarrass a government by exposing the distance between the government's discourse on human rights and its actual practices of exclusion (Van Cott 2000: 262, citing Keck and Sikkink 1998: 24).

Bolivia was one of the first Latin American countries to adopt ILO Convention 169.[24] President Zamora signed it in 1991, shortly after the 1990 March for Territory and Dignity. That did not mean that Bolivians unquestioningly adopted its contents, however. This was made clear in 1992, when CIDOB, the national indigenous organization, proposed a national indigenous law, the Proyecto de Ley Indígena (PLI, Indigenous Law Project), based in large part on the convention. It called for the recognition of the juridical personality of indigenous peoples and protected their collective rights, forms of government and social organization, and legal systems (Van Cott 2000: 136). There were two central themes to the demands: the right to collective territory and the demand for intercultural bilingual education, which implied respect for cultural identity and language (Lema 2001: 28). This proposed legislation was not taken seriously by the Paz government, but it did establish CIDOB as the national interlocutor on behalf of indigenous people (ibid.).

More important, the PLI began to articulate a coherent set of indigenous demands, which were frequently cited in public debates in the early 1990s. In essence, this was the basis of a radical multiculturalism that challenged the homogenizing nature of the republican and postrevolutionary regimes of citizenship. It called for a reevaluation of the naturalized notions of nation-state and territoriality that underlies those regimes. The recognition of Indians as special categories of citizens with such special rights as collective landownership implies rethinking liberal notions of individual citizenship. Once again, as in the republican period, questions arose as to whether Indian collective rights violate the twin bases of the modern nation-state: cultural homogeneity and universal rights. Doesn't giving Indians special rights like ownership to large and valuable tracts of land violate the notion of equal rights for all? Proponents of multiculturalism have argued that under limited conditions, such special rights do not violate liberal principles, because they are necessary for marginalized people to exercise their individual rights (Kymlicka 1995a; Kymlicka and Norman 1996; Young 1996).[25] Opponents considered such proposals a shameful use of identity politics to gain advantage, which they believed had no place in a modern democracy. Many other critics, of course, simply saw the PLI's proposals as a threat to their interests.

State-Sponsored Multiculturalism

Although the PLI was not adopted by the Bolivian congress, when Gonzalo Sánchez de Lozada ran for president two years later in 1992, issues of indigenous rights were very much present in the country's political agenda. His strategic choice of Aymara leader Víctor Hugo Cárdenas as vice president gained support from both highland indigenous groups allied with labor organizations and lowland indigenous groups who saw this as a benefit for all indigenous peoples (Albó 1994). Once again, MNR elites, this time with Aymara elites by their side, promised to incorporate indigenous demands into the new state. In fact, once elected, the Sánchez de Lozada administration passed major legal and constitutional reforms that radically altered the position of Bolivia's indigenous people. Article 1 of the Reformed Constitution of the State declares Bolivia to be a "multiethnic and pluri-cultural" nation.[26] More specifically, Article 171 declares: "The social, economic, and cultural rights of the indigenous peoples [*pueblos indígenas*] who inhabit the national territory are recognized, respected, and protected within the legal framework, especially rights to their communal lands of origin [*tierras comunitarias de origin*], guaranteeing the use and sustainable exploitation [*aprovechamiento*] of natural resources, and to their identity, values, languages, customs, and institutions."[27]

These articles were the foundational language for Bolivia's state-instituted multiculturalism, and they were followed by legislative acts that gave specific rights to indigenous people in all sorts of areas. After Sánchez de Lozada and Cárdenas were elected, they created a Subsecretariat of Ethnic Affairs (SAE), which managed indigenous issues and pushed indigenous interests in upcoming legislation reforms. It was staffed in part by anthropologists and social scientists who had spent their professional lives in NGOs working with indigenous and Andean peasants. This was the first chance these professionals had to work from within the government, and there was enormous desire to implement progressive changes in this fortunate political conjuncture. In April 1994, the SAE signed an agreement with CIDOB, in which they agreed to work together on the SAE's projects and legislation. Central to this agreement was the notion of indigenous participation in the decisions regarding their development at all levels, from the local to the national (Lema 2001: 7).[28]

Throughout the Goni years (the era of President Gonzalo Sánchez de Lozada), although the control of the SAE shifted to other parties, and the dedication to these revolutionary alliances diminished, the SAE was able to get indigenous issues incorporated into the upcoming legislation on energy, natural resources, forestry, protected areas, and so on.[29] Two of the most important new laws were the Ley de Partícipación Popular (LPP, Law of Popular

Participation), passed in 1994, and the new land reform law, La Ley INRA, passed in 1997. The INRA law was the result of massive pressure by indigenous groups on the Goni government, including the first march in 1990 and then a second large march in 1996. La Ley INRA established collective land titling for indigenous territories, making it possible for indigenous groups to make claims on large tracts of land. The law recognizes the "rights of indigenous and original peoples and communities to what are called their original communal lands [*tierras comunitarias de origen*, TCOs]" and grants them collective titles, with the right to "participate in the use and sustainable development of the renewable natural resources" on those lands.[30] Thus, although progress on implementation has been slow — and in many areas, blocked by corruption and interests of the local elite — for the most part, the law was seen as responding to the demands put forward by the indigenous people (Lema 1998; Herrera Sarmiento 2002).[31]

The LPP, though, was not primarily the project of the indigenous movement. Rather, as I describe more fully in chapter 4, it was a reform initiated by regional elites tired of centralized state control and pushed forward by the decentralizing trends that were a common part of neoliberal political restructurings. This dovetailed with indigenous demands for greater participation, and so the architects of the LPP included a limited version of multicultural participation in the political modernization reform. It must be clearly noted, however, that there was almost no participation by the national indigenous movement in the drafting of the law. Vice president Cárdenas undoubtedly provided his input, and certain members of the SAE team were also involved, but for the most part this was a top-down reform instituted by the ruling MNR party. Although it responded to internal demands, particularly those of the regional elites, it was most significantly a part of a larger strategy of economic and state restructuring based on neoliberal notions. Nevertheless, most indigenous leaders saw the LPP as a political opening in which to push for Indian rights. Many were worried that the law would fragment or supplant traditional leadership forms. Others complained about manipulation of indigenous issues for political gain. But as Marcial Fabricano, then president of CIDOB, said, participation was a permanent demand of the indigenous people, and it was at least partially expressed in the LPP. Although the law was insufficient, it was one part of the state response to indigenous proposals (cited in Lema 2001: 32).

The following chapters trace the effects of the neoliberal multiculturalism of the 1990s by focusing on the case of the Guaraní people of Santa Cruz. The citizen participation produced and enacted by the LPP is a far cry from the rights embodied in the ILO convention and proposed by indigenous groups in the PLI. Instead, the regime of citizenship offered by the LPP defines indigenous citizenship as participation in municipal administrations. This interpellates Indians through a series of new political practices and institutions that radically alter existing models of representation and leadership. Although some indigenous groups have managed to take advantage of these spaces, most groups, like the Guaraní of Santa Cruz, have encountered enormous obstacles, as power relations in municipalities are often controlled by clientelist politicians and traditional political parties operating under nearly unchanged racial discourses of exclusion and domination.

As in previous epochs, in the 1990s indigenous citizens had to bring to bear many resources to fight for their rights, merging traditional forms of social organization with new state-approved forms of political participation. The experiences of the Guaraní of Santa Cruz are illustrative of this creative strategizing. In chapter 2, I trace the development of their federation, the CZC, during the 1990s. Responding to the international discourse of indigenous rights as well as development projects of local NGOs, Guaranís from several communities formed a regional organization and then allied themselves with the national Indian movement. In chapter 3, I describe one Guaraní village, which I call Bella Flor, where a bitter struggle over land tenure has torn apart the community. By tracing the ways in which the Guaranís there have adopted different leadership models — sometimes incorporating traditional Guaraní notions of land and leadership, sometimes adopting corporatist models from postrevolutionary Bolivian politics, and, recently, balancing state land reform laws — I illustrate what the history recounted in this chapter has shown: that indigenous representation and participation have always been complex and contested constructions influenced by state institutions and conflicting discourses.

2 An Indigenous Federation in Boomtown Santa Cruz

> Latent in any discussion of an organization accommodated
> to the new challenges presently confronting the Guaraní-
> Chiriguano people is the theme of their own identity as a
> people — with their history, tradition, and culture.
> — Xavier Albó

Old Santa Cruz

The city center of Santa Cruz de la Sierra is the *plaza principal*, a lovely town square with huge flowering *tajibo* and *jacaranda* trees. Old men sit and talk and play checkers. On hot afternoons, waiters in sharp white shirts circulate with jars of cold lemonade for sale. Shoe-shine boys fight for business, usually convincing dusty-footed pedestrians to sit in the shade for a moment and watch the passersby or catch a glimpse of the sloths hanging in the boughs overhead. On one side of the plaza is the cathedral; facing it is the *alcaldía*, the mayor's office. The Casa de la Cultura (the cultural center), with its galleries and auditorium, attracts mainly tourists to the plaza. On the far corner is the social club, where the elite hold dinners and weddings. The blocks around the plaza show off traditional Santa Cruz architecture: covered walkways, with large wooden columns called *harcones* supporting the overhangs. These are more than decorative: in the rainy season, they make walking in the city possible. From the street, one sees only walls and gates. Enter the gates, however, and one finds lovely old houses, built around open patios, filled with birdcages, plants, and hanging hammocks.

This charming city center represents the legacy of old Santa Cruz, the slow-paced agricultural hinterlands famous for its relaxed *camba* lifestyle.[1] Today, however, Santa Cruz is the center of Bolivia's most fast-paced and dynamic growth zone. Colonization, agribusiness, and export enterprises have brought together people from all over the country in a new urban sphere. The 1960s and 1970s saw international development money flood the Santa Cruz area, and the Santa Cruz elites invested in sugar and cotton, opening large extensions of cultivated land. All of these new agricultural endeavors relied on labor, especially for harvesting. Thousands of Guaranís migrated to the zone to work in the *zafra*, or sugarcane harvest. In the 1970s and 1980s, Andean farmers and miners scratched small farms out of the forests in the colonization zones across the Santa Cruz department. Global capital was invested in land, agriculture, and natural gas, bringing oil men and transnational corporate executives to town. The old city center is now filled with Internet cafes, sports bars, and computer stores. The elites browse in the boutiques of the shopping centers on the plaza edge and compare prices from their recent trips to Miami. The growth has not only expanded the opportunities for the wealthy, however; the poor areas have grown equally quickly. As Santa Cruz has developed into Bolivia's major production zone, the poor from all over the country have flocked to the city. As a result, Santa Cruz is an exciting boomtown filled with migrants hoping to take part in Bolivia's national development.

Boomtown Life

As the city began to grow, it grew out from the colonial center in concentric circles, or *anillos* (rings). The newer neighborhoods are the farthest out. Now the city extends to the ninth or tenth anillo, and it keeps growing. The rich, for the most part, have left the city center and moved to exclusive neighborhoods with more space and more security. The poor live wherever they can. Guaraní migrants established their communities in the outlying rural areas, from twenty to a hundred kilometers from the city, on lands they obtained from local landowners or, in the 1960s, from the national agrarian reform project. There are about twenty of these villages now, surrounding the city, part of the regional boom. When Guaranís first began to migrate into the city, many found permanent work on ranches and farms in the area, entered into an informal relationship with a patron, or farmer, and settled permanently. Many lived in this way for years, away from other Guaranís. Gradually, these Guaranís began to form their own communities in the mid-1960s, taking advantage of the agrarian reform laws in the post-1952 revolution years.

Today, Guaranís live in a variety of kinds of communities around the area. Many settled north of the city, near the rural center of Warnes, where one of the largest sugar mills is located, in the village I call La Cañada. There are numerous Guaraní communities in the surrounding lands. Three of these are suburban communities whose residents primarily work at the mill. These communities have no farming land and are essentially Guaraní neighborhoods in mill towns. Outside Warnes, there are eight rural villages in the cane field areas. Some of the villages have small extensions of land where the people carry on subsistence agriculture; others are made up of landless sharecroppers. Another small group of rural communities is farther north, near the town of Minero. One large community is located several hundred kilometers northeast, in the colonization area. It has a large extension of land and is quite prosperous. There is another urban barrio, about fifteen years old, in the outmost southern edge of Santa Cruz. Its residents are mostly laborers and domestic workers in urban Santa Cruz. Five communities, including one I call Bella Flor, are just southeast of the city, in the fastest-growing area.

In the 1960s, a large *barrio popular* (lower-class neighborhood) was established in the southeast part of the city, called Villa Primero de Mayo (usually just referred to as "la Villa"). Throughout the 1970s and 1980s, it grew rapidly, providing a housing and market area for the large numbers of the city's poor migrants. In 1983, the Rio Piraí, the large river along which Santa Cruz was founded, overflowed. The poor populations living in the marginal neighborhoods on the city's west and northwest sides were inundated and their barrios destroyed. To alleviate the crisis, the city opened up a large area of land farther southeast for a new barrio. The new neighborhood was called Plan Tres Mil (Plan Three Thousand) because it originally intended to provide lots for three thousand families. That number was doubled in the first few years, however, and now the Plan, as it is called, is a sprawling city within the city. It continues to expand at an amazing rate in the direction of the cluster of the other five Guaraní communities, causing rapid changes there, as land values skyrocket and housing developments push up against their quickly blurring boundaries.

Across the city, emerging neighborhoods begin as dirt lots, with no houses or services. Often the land is inhabited as part of a land invasion. Soon families buy the lots and put up shacks made from pallets and plastic tarps. Large families might huddle into a tiny tentlike structure for months, until they can afford the bricks and roofing material to build a one-room house. Gradually the neighborhoods take form, and soon an enterprising *micro* (bus) line will begin service. Electric lines are next, and finally water piping is put in along the streets, so that each corner might have a faucet. The residents of these poor neighborhoods are the workers of Santa Cruz: the laborers, bus drivers, carpenters, cooks, and domestic servants. They are mostly highland people, come from Cochabamba and La Paz to find their fortune — *buscando oportunidad* (looking for opportunities). As a result of all this enterprise, there is a sense of the future in Plan Tres Mil that is palpable. The sound of pounding hammers gives rise to the feeling that new lives are being constructed before one's eyes.

I traveled frequently through the Plan to get out to the Guaraní villages where I was working, but many of the rich people of Santa Cruz have never been there. It is far out on the city's southeast side, away from the elite neighborhoods on the near northside. Indeed, the Plan is a center for the poor. It is chaotic, busy, dirty, noisy, and very much alive at all hours of the day. At the Plan center is a traffic circle called the Rotonda, a bustling meeting point always jammed with micros, taxis, and trucks, clouded by fumes from all of them. Passersby have to step aside for *cargadores* (carriers) unloading goods and street vendors hawking food and products. In the two or three blocks around the Rotonda, the market provides almost any service imaginable. There is a food market, where mostly highland women sell vegetables, fruit, yuca (cassava or manioc root), eggs, cooking oil, spices, cheap liquor, individual plastic ampoules of shampoo, and toilet paper. Next door are the butchers, displaying huge sides of beef, pigs' heads, and chickens swarming with flies in the tropical heat. The poor buy what is called *menudo*, the leftover parts of the meat — the cheapest and often toughest parts — to cook in soups or stews for large families. In the late afternoon, when Cruceños have their coffee break, vendors surround the Rotonda, selling hot bread, rice bread wrapped in banana leaves, and Santa Cruz's signature food, *cuñapés* (delicious cheese-filled buns). In the summer, the fruit sellers hawk ripe mangos, ten for one Boliviano (about two cents U.S. apiece), or pineapples from the lowland farms nearby. When it rains, the Rotonda is horrible: mud covers everything, the garbage rots, and the odors are overwhelming.

Regardless of the weather, though, the Plan is always busy. Sundays are especially crowded and festive, because people come in from all the surrounding farms and ranches to spend their paychecks for food and a little fun. All along one side of the Rotonda are the barbers and beauty shops, where laborers in from the country get the latest cuts and domestic servants on their days off get permanents and manicures. Along another side are the shoe repairmen, with their industrial-strength sewing machines that can fix anything. Bicycle repairs, watch repairs, TV repairs: whatever needs fixing, there is someone in the Plan who can do it. Used American clothes are for sale everywhere, and quite inexpensive.[2] Cheap food and beer are plentiful, and no matter how hot it is, you can always count on the beer to be cold. The most popular places are the *pollo a la broaster* (roasted chicken) restaurants, where large-screen kung-fu videos accompany a quarter chicken and french fries served with beer or a soft drink. Many who can't afford to eat at the restaurants come anyway, to hang on the wire fences and watch Bruce Lee in action.

Bella Flor: A Rural Village at the Edge of the City

As the Plan has grown and stretched out to touch their communities, the Guaranís of the region find themselves face-to-face with suburban life.

Since the early 1990s, there have been rapid and radical changes in the communities near the city, as the people have found their lands more valuable as housing developments than as farms. Yet when I first visited Bella Flor in 1996, the Guaranís who lived there made their livings as most of the Guaraní communities still do — through a combination of subsistence farming and manual labor.

I began my work with the Guaraní of Zona Cruz in 1995, when I met the leaders of the CZC and discussed the possibility of doing a long-term study in the area. On that trip, I visited several Guaraní communities, two in the urban area and one in Warnes. By the end of my stay, the leadership agreed that my research would be helpful to their own work, and we agreed that I would return the next summer to begin. In 1996, I began my investigation of the capitanía. That first summer, I concentrated on getting to know as much as possible about the capitanía, learned some basic Guaraní, and did a survey in one of the urban barrios. I worked with and became friends with Samuel Tapera, one of the young workers in the CZC (see photo). He worked in the capitanía's office in town during the week and lived with some of his siblings in the Plan. Every weekend, he went home to Bella Flor, where his large family lived. One weekend, he invited me to accompany him to see what the more rural villages were like. I met his family and neighbors, and talked to them about the grave crisis they were facing, as their lands were being sold. When I returned to Bolivia for a longer stay in 1997, I began visiting Bella Flor regularly, staying for short times with the Tapera family. In 1998, I spent the majority of my time there, conducting a house-to-house survey of Bella Flor and El Futuro.

From my first weekend in Bella Flor, the Tapera family opened their home to me with grace and generosity. Don Jesús Tapera, the head of the family, was born and raised in a small rural Guaraní community in the Cordillera region, the dry mountainous zone several hundred kilometers to the south. He left that community to study at an evangelical bible college, later becoming a pastor. In the late 1960s, he brought his family to Santa Cruz and accepted a position as Bella Flor's pastor. His wife, Susana, was from the same small community in the Cordillera region. As their family grew, Don Jesús supplemented his small income by working on the nearby farms and ranches. He also managed to study linguistics with the Guaraní federation and become an able Guaraní-Spanish translator, earning extra money this way.

Don Jesús is a small, slim man, with crinkled eyes and a clever sense of humor. He never tired of sitting with me on his patio, explaining his views on the village's land crisis or the politics of the day. He was a devout Christian, but by the time I met him, Don Jesús had given up his job as pastor. Rather, he earned his living by translating, by working the small plot of land he and his family cultivated, and by playing in a gospel mariachi band. He played the violin in the traditional Guaraní way. His faith influenced him greatly, though, and he and I talked endlessly about ethical questions. Don Jesús was extremely concerned about the greed that seemed to him to be pervading the Guaraní communities as the city encroached upon them. Chapter 3 further explores the struggles the people of Bella Flor endured as they fought over the meaning of land and leadership.

Don Jesús taught me right off the bat about the complex mixture of cultures at play in suburban Guaraní villages. The first weekend I spent at the Tapera's home, we stayed up late on Sunday night, watching television and talking. Little by little, all the children fell asleep or went off to bed in the back room with their mother, leaving me and Samuel and Don Jesús. We watched American television shows dubbed into Spanish — *Baywatch*, *Robocop*, *ER* — and then the movie *Forrest Gump*. During the movie, Don Jesús asked me if I believed in UFOs. I told him I did not really know, but it didn't seem out of the realm of the possible to me. I said that I thought it fairly arrogant of humans to believe we are the only sentient beings in the universe. What did he think? "Well," he said, "I am pretty much split fifty-fifty. One the one hand, I think it is likely to be a trick of the Devil, something to do with evil spirits." This made sense to me given his evangelical training. "On the other, I think it might also be a scheme of the United States government, to confuse people and to hide something they are doing." I must admit to being somewhat surprised at this answer. I had supposed Don Jesús would give me an answer based on his Christian faith or perhaps based on some traditional Guaraní ideas. Instead, he demonstrated the range of information and analysis he and the rest of the urban Guaranís were used to negotiating. Far from simple peasants, they watched TV, read newspapers, and were often abreast of national and international news. Over the years, I have come to trust Don Jesús's opinions about much of Guaraní life. Much of the ethnography below is infused by his influence.

Don Jesús's son Samuel Tapera was equally worldly, and equally curious. Samuel had also left his home village to go to a state-run boarding school in the Cordillera region. Only a few of the very smartest Guaraní students were accepted to this school, which was mostly for the children of the region's rich ranchers. Samuel excelled in the school but was miserable. He felt he had to hide his ethnicity and therefore never spoke his native Guaraní language. When he graduated, he moved to Santa Cruz to be with his family and enrolled in a computer technical school. When I met him, he was the office manager of the capitanía, doing all the computer and administration work. Samuel was my entrée into the life of the capitanía and Bella Flor specifically. His experience in the world of the *karai*, the white people with whom he had gone to school, had strengthened his urge to be and speak

Guaraní, to feel pride in his own people. As a result, he had gone to many NGO-sponsored workshops for indigenous people and was deeply involved in national indigenous politics.

When I first started visiting Bella Flor, Samuel and I often traveled there together. We would meet at the Rotonda to find transport out to the village. In my first years, there was no direct service, so we would take a micro to the end of the line and walk or bicycle the remaining six kilometers. Later, as the city expanded, and villagers had more cash, a direct taxi line was started. Each line had a particular loading place in the crowded market, so that customers knew where to find them. When a taxi came, we crammed in with the other passengers — people from Bella Flor returning from shopping trips to the Plan, students returning for the weekend, and so on. In the back, the drivers packed in all the plastic bags of food, big burlap sacks of rice, or whatever provisions they might have bought, along with whatever extra passengers who might fit.

In the late 1990s, the dirt road from the Plan to Bella Flor took a passenger from city to country in a half an hour of bumps and potholes, starting with the endless neighborhoods that make up the Plan. Today a micro line goes right to Bella Flor. The neighborhoods closest to the center are most established; the houses there are made of bricks with walls around them, and trees and large plants in their gardens. Schools, churches, and stores are stuck in between the houses. The farther one ventures out of the Plan, the neighborhoods begin to be less developed. The road passes through the community of Arroyitos, a farming community of *kollas*, Quechua-speaking people from the highlands. They have been here since the 1970s, farming their parcels in yuca, corn, and sugarcane. Their houses are set apart from each other and have the look of years of hard work. After Arroyitos, the land along the road is all sugarcane fields, tall and green, waving in the wind. Tall *motacú* palms dot the fields, and birds fly about, calling and singing. There are few vehicles; most people walk. Women carry large loads, sometimes on their heads, followed by kids playing in the dust or the mud, depending on the time of year. In a few more kilometers, the traveler arrives at El Mangal. This is the western edge of the land shared by the three Guaraní villages. A kilometer farther is Bella Flor, and another kilometer curving back south is El Futuro.

Community Village Life

These Guaraní villages are quiet places for the most part. Each village is designed in the same way, with a large grassy field, the *cancha* (soccer field), at the center. The only large buildings are the churches and the schoolhouses, with small living quarters for the teacher. These communities were founded by evangelical Guaranís, and most of the residents are *hermanos,* or believers. Evangelical missionaries have had great success in Guaraní lands since the mid-1970s, so the church is the center of each village. In Bella Flor, a new church of bricks replaced the old mud and wood church, which fell down during my stay. In neighboring El Futuro, the church is an open-air structure. In both villages, the houses are arranged in an even grid surrounding the church.

During the time I stayed with the Tapera family, Don Jesús was often gone during the daytime, to his translating jobs in the city, as were the adult male children, Samuel and his older brother. Doña Susana stayed at home, caring for the six children still at home and several grandchildren who live with the Taperas during the week (see photo). She worked in the family *chaco* (farm plot), where they grow yuca and corn; she cooked and hauled water and firewood to the house. Their house was built, like most houses in the village, in the traditional Guaraní style, called a *pahuichi.*[3] Pahuichis have long hardwood poles as vertical beams and walls made of mud that have been packed together from the ground up to about four or five feet. The roof is made of motacú palm fronds, bent double and layered tightly one on the other. The roofs are water-tight when new, but as they age, the palm dries and splinters off, so they must be replaced every four or five years. It is not uncommon to have major leaks during the furious rainstorms, before the roofs are replaced. One night during my stay, we had a *sur,* a cold storm from the south. The strong winds blew the brittle roofing aside, and water poured into the house. We all jumped up and stuck plastic bags, tarps, whatever we could find, into the breaches. Soon the storm tapered off, the drips lessened, and all was well. In the next few weeks, though, Don Jesús and his sons were busy with the hard work of making a new roof.

The ceilings of these one-room houses are tall, coming to a peak. There are typically no windows, so it is quite dark and cool inside, even during the heat of the dry season. The floors are swept dirt, hard-packed by constant use. The Taperas, like most Bella Flor families, had little furniture. There were a few chairs and single beds lining the walls, a table, and a television. (In the village survey I conducted, I found only two houses in the village without a TV, and those were newlyweds who watched TV at their parents' house.) Inside spaces were reserved for sleeping, private family discussions, eating when it was windy, and watching TV. A few clothes hung from the beams; sometimes clothes were folded together and used as pillows. Because the Taperas are a large family, they had added on a small second room behind the main room. The parents and the teenage girls slept there, while all the boys and any visitors slept in the main room (see photo).

Regardless of the style of house, though, Guaraní kitchens are generally a separate structure — sometimes an older pahuichi, sometimes just a lean-to of palm fronds. Doña Susana and her daughters did the cooking on wood fires in a lean-to next to their house. This produces a lot of smoke, so the kitchens are almost always separated from the main house. The women had to go out into the fields and remaining scraggly woods to find firewood, carrying it back on their heads. Finding firewood was becoming harder and harder, as the surrounding area became more urban. I saw only one propane stove in either village during my survey period, but such stoves have become more necessary. The women generally prepare food in an *olla* (a big pot) on a single fire. The food most commonly eaten was yuca, which most families grew in their chacos. Doña Susana went out to the chaco every other morning or so to dig up the yuca for the next days' meals. Her strong arms show the effects of many years of this hard task. Then she hauled the heavy bag of tubers onto her head for the kilometer-long walk home. As the city outskirts approached Bella Flor and more residents got jobs in the city, the people began to eat more purchased food. Don Jesús and his sons worked in the city and brought home money and groceries from the Plan. They ate foods like rice, pasta, and some meat.

Although there was electricity in Bella Flor, there were only a few refrigerators in the village. The few that did exist were a business investment, part of a small *ventas* (stores) from which women sell cold drinks and frozen treats. In other small villages, the ventas might also sell cold beer, but not in these evangelical communities. One woman, Doña Angelina, had a commercial-size propane oven in which she baked bread for sale in the village. Several other women made food to sell on Sundays, when the men were home, and especially for after soccer games, when visiting teams from other villages stayed to eat and relax with their friends and relatives.

When visiting a Guaraní village, it is courteous to bring food with you, because the communities are typically located far away from markets. I asked my friend Samuel what would be a good thing to bring, and he suggested meat, which is always a treat. I bought what I thought was a nice big piece of meat, which we could eat while I was there, then they would have some left over for the next day. I didn't think about how it would be preserved, however. Doña Susana graciously accepted my gift and made dinner with it, cutting little pieces of meat into the big olla of rice. Later that night, I went out to sit with her as she was finishing her chores and found her working on that big piece of meat. She was transforming a steak a couple of inches thick into a very thin piece, almost two feet long, by accordionning it into ever thinner slices. This was then salted and hung to dry on the barbed wire strung between the kitchen and house. The resulting *charque* (jerky) could be used for many meals.

Like most families in the many Guaraní villages I visited during my years of investigation, the Taperas spent a great deal of time outside, in the smoothed dirt yard between the house and the cookhouse. Almost all of the houses have large trees, mostly mango trees, that provide shade and protection from the rain. This was the main social space where the families sat, played, and talked. Whenever I or any other visitor arrived, the family would pull chairs into the constantly moving shady spots and offer a round of *yerba mate*, a bitter herbal tea. The women almost always had a fire going, or some embers they kept hot in a metal bucket or a small fire pit in the yard, over which they could boil some water. Hot water, sometimes flavored with cinnamon, was poured into a gourd (the *porro*), filled with mate, and then completed with spoonfuls of sugar. The porro is passed to each person, who sucks it out of a *bombilla* (silver straw). Then the hostess refills it, pours in more water, and passes it to the next person. I passed many afternoons this way, waiting out the heat of the tropical summers, talking with the Taperas and their neighbors. While the women sat outside and drank mate, feeding the chickens and doing the endless task of washing the clothes by hand, the children played in the dirt yards or watched cartoons or Mexican comedies on television. The men were mostly gone working on nearby farms and came home in the evenings for dinner. In the later afternoons, people took baths in the straw lean-tos in the backyards. Then, in the cool evenings, families sat outside talking, drinking mate, and visiting each other. Many of the families were related, so evenings were often filled with visits from neighboring cousins or adult siblings.

Family and Language

Although they lived only a few kilometers from the city, these Guaranís assured me that they lived in a different way from their non-Guaraní neighbors. Their houses, their porro-drinking customs — these were the signs of their unique and traditional way of life. Two other important parts of Guaraní identity, they said, were their family relations and their continued use of the Guaraní language. In 1998, I conducted a house-to-house survey in Bella Flor and El Futuro to study the rapid changes occurring in the communities. At that time, there were 364 residents of Bella Flor (186 adults and 178 children younger than sixteen years old) living in 64 houses, forming 46 households.[4] Households were made up of varying combinations. When a young couple formed, they could join by legal marriage or simply start living together. As Bella Flor residents were highly influenced by evangelical beliefs, many chose to be married by the church. This required a large investment, however, such as wedding clothes and a party for the community, so not all young couples or their families could afford this. Sometimes the young couple moved into a house of their own, but more often they moved in with one of their families. As they began to have children, the couple might move into their own house. My research showed that 54 percent of households were nuclear families made up of a couple, or one parent, and their children. Often this included a brother or sister of one of the couple and maybe that person's children. Another 43 percent were extended families in which adult children and their partners and children live with the parents.[5]

These arrangements were quite fluid, changing as more children were born, as people left for work elsewhere, and as couples broke up. In cases of break-ups, the children seemed to stay with their mothers rather than their fathers. Children's living arrangements were quite flexible, surrounded by relatives of all kinds. They might sleep one night with their parents and the next with their cousins. They often spent a great deal of time with their grandparents while their parents were off working. This was true of daily work as well as during the zafra, when young couples might go off to work together for some months and leave their children to be cared for by the extended family.

Women usually formed relationships quite early, in their teens. It was not uncommon to see fourteen- or fifteen-year-old girls already in unions, with children. They might marry boys their own age, or a few years older, but it was also common to see women married to men ten years older than they were. A common pattern was for men to go off to work in the zafra for a few years or to do their military service, and then come home more mature and ready for a family, and then find a younger woman. Most Guaranís in these villages married other Guaranís.

While I lived with the Taperas, I was struck by the fluidity of the language choice. Samuel and his father mostly spoke Spanish to each other as well as to the children. Samuel is fluent in Guaraní, but because he went to boarding school, he said, he feels more comfortable in Spanish. This worried him because he wants to marry a Guaraní woman, and he wondered if he would be able to woo anyone in Guaraní. Once he and I were walking from Bella Flor to the last bus stop one evening. We caught up with a young Guaraní couple and their small daughter also making the long walk. After we passed them, Samuel said, "Did you hear the way he talks? He was raised speaking Guaraní. Doesn't it sound so sweet? No Guaraní woman will want to marry me if I can't talk that way."

That may not be a problem for Samuel, however, because most of the young women in his generation are bilingual. Samuel's mother Doña Susana, on the other hand, had little schooling and spoke mostly Guaraní. She spoke Guaraní at home with the children and her husband as well as a small amount of Spanish, with guests like me and on her occasional shopping trips to the city. Doña Susana was far more comfortable speaking Guaraní. This is the case for many older women who grew up in the rural areas, where girls were rarely sent to school. In the current generation, all children go to the community's primary school, which goes up to fifth grade, where they learn Spanish. Those who want to continue on to middle school and high school must commute into the Plan. In the Tapera family, all the children continued on to school. While I was in Bella Flor, Samuel's brother Tuto graduated from high school, and all the family proudly attended Samuel's graduation ceremony. His sister Felicia had already graduated and was training to become a journalist. The teenage girls were in high school, living in the Plan with their oldest brother during the week and coming home on the weekends to live with their parents. This is a common arrangement, as it is too far and too expensive to commute to the Plan every day.

My survey showed that bilingualism was the norm for Bella Flor adults (85 percent), a constant percentage since the mid-1980s. British anthropologist C. P. P. Davison, who studied in Bella Flor and another neighboring community, El Mangal, in 1985, found much the same information.[6] Moreover, my survey confirmed what I observed in the Tapera family — that most families spoke Guaraní at home, especially to their children. This, too, had changed little from 1985 to 1998. One difference existed, however: in 1998, 77 percent of families reported speaking only Guaraní, and 2 percent reported speaking more Guaraní than Spanish. In 1985, only 55 percent said they spoke only Guaraní, and 23 percent said they spoke Guaraní more than Spanish. If we combine these categories into one — that is, if we ask what is the percentage of families that speak only Guaraní or more Guaraní than Spanish — we see that the 1998 data is almost exactly the same as the older data. I speculate that the difference can be accounted for by the new awareness of the value of indigenous identity in the multicultural 1990s. People were quite proud of their language abilities and said things to me like, "Of course we speak Guaraní; we are Guaraní and proud of it!"

Thus the Guaranís were articulating a sense of identity through language that perhaps was not popular when Davison carried out his survey. One important part of the 1990s multicultural reforms was the intercultural education program, which promised to teach children in their native languages. This was a long-held component of the movement for indigenous rights and recognition, dating back to the Katarista movement of the 1970s. The program received substantial funding throughout the 1990s, but it is a long-term project, training bilingual teachers, establishing curricula, and getting both out into the country (López 1995). When I lived in Bella Flor, there were no teachers teaching in Guaraní yet, and there was a fairly brisk debate about the need for one. Most parents told me that although they understood the need to preserve their language, and especially their pride in their language, they felt they could do that at home. They wanted their children to learn

Spanish in school, so they would not have a recognizable Indian accent that would stigmatize them when they went to look for work in the city. Anthropologist María Elena García has described similar sorts of attitudes among indigenous parents in Peru (García 2005).

Although most people speak Guaraní at home, one important part of village life happened in Spanish: religious meetings. Two nights a week, there were church services, called *culto*. The culto was a big draw for children, who went and sang evangelical hymns accompanied by an electric organ. During culto, the singing could be heard throughout the village. Culto was also well attended by teenagers, washed and dressed in clean clothes for the event, smiling and shyly talking among themselves before and after the service. There were few men at these services. The women held babies on their laps, chatted with friends, and sang along quietly. Then they rushed home to watch the *telenovelas* (TV soap operas from Mexico or Brazil), in which the beautiful and poor heroine typically undergoes terrible suffering but because of her good morals learned from her humble beginnings, she triumphs and marries the handsome rich man who finally sees her true values. Almost all of the girls and women watched these shows every night, as did I while I was in Bella Flor. The telenovelas are incredibly seductive and, of course, they are filled with commercials for soaps, cold remedies, refrigerators, electrodomestic appliances, and so on — all things that the Guaranís couldn't afford or use in the present village environment.

I have described Bella Flor in some detail because it is representative of the Guaraní communities near the cities. In the communities farther out into the country, village life is much the same, although the residents do not venture into the city as much nor do they work in urban pursuits. There most people work in agriculture, and although they attend public primary school, many fewer people are bilingual. These rural communities are more isolated, and several of them still do not have electricity. Bella Flor was one of the first Guaraní communities founded and, being close to the city, it has been one of the first to begin the transformations that are slowly happening across the region. In the early 1990s, Bella Flor's residents were also at the forefront of regional organizing as indigenous struggles began to be a topic of national debate. The following section describes how the Guaraní communities organized themselves into a federation called the Capitanía Zona Cruz (CZC), with its headquarters in Santa Cruz.

Formation of the Capitanía Zona Cruz

During the late 1980s and early 1990s, indigenous people began organizing across Bolivia. With the help of NGOs and anthropologists, various lowland indigenous groups began to meet and strategize about common problems. In Camiri, in the Cordillera region, Guaranís formed a federation called the Asamblea del Pueblo Guaraní (APG, Assembly of the Guaraní People). Supported by a Jesuit NGO called Centro de Investigación y Promoción del Campesinado (CIPCA, Center for the Investigation and Promotion of the Peasantry), the APG started development and cultural projects throughout the Guaraní region. In Santa Cruz, a federation of indigenous people from the Oriente called the Confederación de Indígenas del Oriente de Bolivia (CIDOB, Indigenous Federation of Eastern Bolivia) brought together all the lowland groups and began to act as a national representative for indigenous issues, meeting with government representatives, indigenous federations from other Latin American countries, and international NGOs.

All these events began to have repercussions on the Guaraní migrants to Santa Cruz in the early 1990s. Until then, the individual communities had not been organized as Guaranís in any formal way. There was substantial contact between the people in the villages because many of them were related, but besides family visits and meeting through work, there was no regional Guaraní organization. One reason was that almost all the communities were organized as *sindicatos*, the peasant unions pushed by the government during the land reform era after the 1952 revolution. Furthermore, many of the sindicatos were made up of both Guaranís and their non-Guaraní neighbors. For these Guaranís, their identity as peasants was as salient as their identity as Guaranís. That is, although they always considered themselves Guaraní, these people also felt their membership in the sindicato determined much of their economic standing.

In 1991 and 1992, the APG began a broad campaign to organize Guaraní communities throughout the region. An important part of the campaign was to reclaim the "traditional" form of social and political organization, the capitanía, which had been replaced by the sindicato in many parts of the country. This was part of the larger international trend validating indigenous customs and cultural formations by staking a claim to ethnic and cultural difference. Thus the APG encouraged groups of Guaranís to organize themselves as capitanías and to identify themselves as Guaranís. The APG campaign was effective because it used two means of communication. The first was Radio Santa Cruz, a powerful station whose radio signal reached all over the region and transmitted programs in the Guaraní language. Through these Guaraní programs, the APG preached the importance of organization. Samuel Tapera remembered that "there were always programs on Radio Santa Cruz, talking about how important it was to organize to develop ourselves, in terms of education, health, to promote our interests, to get infrastructure. They said since we don't have money, we can't fight individually, but as a mass, we can." The other critical organizing tool was a literacy campaign. Teko-Guaraní, a program of the APG, put out books as well as literacy manuals and trained and paid for literacy volunteers to go out to the communities (see Hirsch 2003). Like the push for intercultural education, this literacy campaign showed how important language and language education could be for the development of indigenous identity and organizations.

In the spring of 1992, the people of the five Guaraní communities southeast of Santa Cruz began to organize. In April, a first meeting was held in Barrio Libre, and the group made a decision to form a capitanía. They also delegated several of their members to get trained by Teko-Guaraní and bring the *alfabetización* (literacy) project to their villages. David Chávez, from Barrio Libre, was one of the volunteers who went to the two-week APG training in Santa Cruz. Trained as an evangelical pastor in his youth, he was a good choice for the position, as he was also outgoing and energetic. After his literacy training, David began to go around to the communities talking to the leaders and pastors. He talked about the importance of changing the attitudes the community itself had about poverty.

David recalled: "There had always been a tolerance for scarcity, so I told them we needed to train our young people to confront the problems of the day, to help the people, so as not to lose our dignity. . . . We have always been oppressed, marginalized, submissive. Why? Because we don't know our rights. All we know how to do is sing hymns and pray."[7] As he traveled from community to community, David pushed the idea of the capitanía and the importance of education. Another volunteer, Arturo López, remembered how they used political ideas in their literacy classes — for example, using the words for "potable water" and various health issues as they learned to spell. They also used familiar forest animals as examples to encourage organizing, like the *chancho de monte* (peccaries), who defend themselves in groups, always united.

In March 1992, a second meeting was held in Barrio Libre, and a Santa Cruz NGO called Centro de Promoción Agropecuaria Campesina (CEPAC, Center for the Promotion of Peasant Agriculture) was invited. CEPAC had been doing some rural development projects in some of the local mixed communities, and its *técnicos* (workers) had gotten to know the Guaranís in the process. They had also begun to do some of the literacy work that was so popular for NGOs at the time, so they agreed to work with the inchoate capitanía to help them get organized. David was made the point person and asked to continue his community organizing and coordinate with CEPAC. The result was that in August 1992, a first meeting was held with representatives from five communities, in which enthusiasm for forming a Guaraní organization gathered. Then, in November 1992, representatives from nearly all the twenty or so Guaraní communities gathered and officially formed the Capitanía Zona Cruz. They elected a *mburuvicha guasu*, the leader of the federation or "big captain" (*capitán grande*), as well as a board of directors.

The first capitán grande was Lorenzo Diego, from Bella Flor. Bella Flor had been organized by a charismatic leader from the Izozog region, whose vision of the community was as a "traditional" Guaraní village, with collectively held land and a strong local capitán. For the migrant Guaranís trying to form a traditional capitanía to replace the outwardly imposed sindicato model, it was important to have a leader from the most traditional of the migrant villages. (As I discuss in chapter 3, the definition of the term "traditional" is contingent and constructed.) Don Lorenzo had contacts with traditional-style leaders from the Izozog, and that gave him even greater appeal. David Chávez was chosen as the *segundo* capitán (second captain), because of his connections to the APG and because he had shown so much initiative in organizing the meetings and in working with CEPAC.

The fledgling organization was encouraged by the APG and by the capitán grande of Izozog, Bonifacio Barrientos. Boni, as he is called, is the best-known and most powerful Guaraní leader in Bolivia; he is the current leader of the Capitanía de Alto y Bajo Izozog (CABI), a strong and well-funded Guaraní organization. Boni is also the descendant of a long line of leaders and is seen almost as Guaraní royalty, so his support was essential to the new CZC. Boni attended the Zona Cruz elections and personally carried out the ceremony of *posesión* (swearing in) of the capitanes. Here we see a strategic choice of leaders who blended the two important dimensions of a multicultural indigenous organization: strong claims to cultural authenticity and good connections to NGO funding.

After this auspicious beginning, the hard work of fundraising began. In 1993, CEPAC got a small grant for "institutional strengthening" from the international NGO International Working Group on Indigenous Affairs (IWGIA). This NGO grant of about $13,000 provided two important foundations for the capitanía. First, it funded five general assemblies of the organization, paying for the transportation costs of all the delegates, the food during the meetings, overnight lodging, as well as all the invitations and communications. This was critical to the functioning of the organization, as most of the members could not afford the travel or food costs. Throughout 1994 and 1995, the group met fairly often, discussing their problems and making connections with other institutions and groups that could assist them. They were part of the APG, which continued to encourage them to act as a source of both political and cultural strength for its people. At one of the first meetings in 1994, a representative from Teko-Guaraní told the assembly, "We have to begin to rescue our roots or our origins as Guaranís. Where do we come from? Where are we going? Only knowing our origins and identity can we move ahead as a people."[8] This sentiment clearly followed the discourse popular in international circles that operated a politics of difference, grounding rights and citizenship in ethnic identity. Thus in those first assemblies there was much talk about the importance of organizing and acting as the true representatives of the Guaraní people.

Although the organization was trying to act as a source of pride for its people, however, the main problem confronting the small organization was money — for the institution as well as for the communities. Asserting indigenousness was also a helpful strategy on this level, it turned out. The second part of the IWGIA grant that CEPAC obtained helped them get funding for a diagnostic investigation of the communities and their resources and needs. CEPAC trained four young Guaranís to carry out the surveys, and with the information they gathered, they held meetings with leaders and developed a strategic plan for the region's development. The written strategic plan, with good basic information to back it up, would allow the capitanía to obtain financial help for the development of the capitanía.

Don Álvaro Montero and the Equipo Técnico Zonal (ETZ)

There is no doubt that the CEPAC grant was critical to getting the capitanía on its feet. Nevertheless, the relationship with CEPAC rankled the Guaranís from the start. The main objection was that CEPAC got $19,000 and then spent only $6,000 of it on the assemblies. The rest went for the salaries of the técnicos, for transportation, and for CEPAC administration. This made the Guaranís feel taken advantage of; it was an issue of debate among the membership for some time. "They got that money in our name," people grumbled, "and look who made the salaries and drove around in expensive trucks!" Another objection was that CEPAC carried out the project with little consultation with the whole group, dealing only with David Chávez, who became increasingly distanced from the people in the communities. According to many people I interviewed, David got quite wrapped up with CEPAC and the APG and began making promises to the people that were never fulfilled, saying that money and scholarships were available, for example. The organization's board of directors complained that he never gave them information, even when they specifically asked for it. At the same time, the capitán grande Don Lorenzo had all but faded out of sight. He had not been involved with the diagnostic, and many claimed he was drunk at meetings.

At the March 1995 assembly, Don Lorenzo made a proposal to make the position of capitán grande a lifelong post. The assembly rejected the proposal and instead held new elections. Diego lost nearly unanimously to a newcomer to the organization, Don Álvaro Montero. Don Álvaro was the leader of Río Nuevo, one of the Guaraní communities near Warnes. He had been invited by some of his friends to start attending the meetings in the months previous. His unusual history made him stand out as an obvious leader for his people. He is half Izozeño and half Aba (as Guaranís from the Cordillera region are called) and thus bridged the gap between the different Guaraní groups that inhabit the migrant villages of Zona Cruz.

As a young man, Don Álvaro had worked in the zafra and so knew the hard work of the campesino, but since the mid-1980s, he had done more political work. For many years, he had worked as an organizer for the federation of peasant sindicatos in the colonization zones of Warnes and Montero. Then he had been an official of the agrarian reform, adjudicating land issues between peasants and large landowners. He was a member of the Acción Democrática Nacional (ADN) party, the conservative party of General Hugo Suárez Banzer that had just come into power. He had many connections among the region's politicians. Don Álvaro speaks excellent Spanish and is comfortable in the world of the karai, while still speaking Guaraní with the oratorical skills necessary to appeal to the traditionalists. Most important, he is a consummate politician: he can appear strong and humble at the same time, a key element for traditional Guaraní leadership. (In chapter 3, I discuss Guaraní leadership models and how Don Álvaro fit into them.)

Don Álvaro led the CZC from 1995 to 2002, surviving several challenges to be re-elected in 1998. Although there were many criticisms of his leadership, he was also popular among his people. Many Guaranís have told me how proud they were to have such a strong, well-educated, and "modern" capitán. The fact that he had a car and a cell phone gave him the appearance of a powerful politician, and this was important to people used to being marginalized and dominated (see photo). Moreover, his political connections paid off for the organization, as he managed to use them for grants, donations, and — most important in the highly bureaucratic world of Bolivian politics — to open doors.

One of Don Álvaro's most important contributions to the CZC was his recognition that it had to be more than a cultural organization, through which local leaders exercised moral authority over their people. This was important, of course, but indigenous people no longer lived in an isolated political environment. The capitanía also had to be a regional political organization that mediated its members' relations to the state, and other Indian federations, as well as a sort of grassroots development organization seeking to coordinate economic projects for its communities. In other words, the capitanía needed to function in the world of development projects, NGOs, and high-level national politics.

Don Álvaro was responding to the exciting times in which he was living, a time of multicultural reforms that recognized indigenous claims, where Indian organizing was suddenly becoming financially and politically successful. International money was flowing into the country to support indigenous groups, and Indian leaders were suddenly gaining power and influence. He was feeling the effects of the new regime of multicultural citizenship, in which indigenous identity was a newfound means of inclusion into the nation-state. The Law of Popular Participation (LPP) had been passed, and indigenous organizations were formally recognized as social actors able to intervene in municipal budget decisions. National indigenous leaders were negotiating with the president and political leaders on most important issues, pushing the rights and interests of Indians at the national level. This was the time to organize an indigenous group, and a propitious moment to get funding.

Don Álvaro decided that the capitanía needed to be radically reorganized to meet these new challenges. Because it was initially formed under the auspices of the APG, the capitanía had adopted the internal structure used by the APG, known as PISET. Under this structure (originated by CIPCA, the NGO that helped the APG to organize), each capitanía had a committee made up of officers responsible for production (P), infrastructure (I), health (*salud*) (S), education (E), and *tierra/territorio* (T), or land struggles. Since the beginning of the capitanía, however, it was clear that this system was not working. Don Álvaro explained: "When you look at what [the previous capitán] was able to accomplish, it wasn't much. And when I came in, because I had been educated in another way, I had to get accustomed to all the things I needed to know. When I went to the meetings with the APG or the SAE [the national Subsecretariat of Ethnic Affairs], all I could say was 'yes.' It was all *técnicos* [professional advisers]. The Guaraní way is to give out the jobs at the assemblies to whomever is willing, but that doesn't mean they know anything about the job. 'This person is going to be responsible for education,' and everybody claps! But he doesn't know anything about it, and then he would fail. So, I asked the assembly to allow me to choose my own people to work with, and they agreed."[9]

Don Álvaro picked Samuel Tapera, who had been working as the *secretaria de actas* (recording secretary), and another young Guaraní university student named Enrique Colón. Together they came up with a new idea: the formation of an advisory team of young volunteers who would get training in their areas and act as advisers to the capitán. Samuel believed the old PISET model was not appropriate to the new context: "We tried it under [the previous capitán], but it didn't work here. This was an idea that was imposed from outside, not from within the Guaranís. So we did our own diagnosis, and it was clear from that what we needed to do and focus on."

The new team, called the Equipo Técnico Zonal (ETZ, the technical team of Zona Cruz), was assembled slowly. Young Guaranís willing to work for free for the organization came and joined the team with the idea that when money came into the organization through their combined efforts, they would receive jobs. Meanwhile, they came when they could, went to the many workshops offered by NGOs and government institutions, and began trying to make the organization function. They were a varied group: Samuel was the leader. With a high school degree and computer training, he had been working for the capitanía since its foundation as secretary and continued now as the office manager. His responsibilities varied but mostly he wrote and edited project proposals. The capitán relied on him for almost everything, and his dedication and political commitment were critical to the group.

Enrique Colón, from a community in the Cordillera, was in Santa Cruz to attend the university in accounting. He worked part-time for a local NGO that partnered with Guaraní organizations in the Cordillera to train them to participate in the new LPP. Enrique acted as a coordinator between the capitanía and the NGO. Rosana Moreno, whom I introduced in chapter 1, grew up in La Cañada, the mill town. Her father had a good job at the mill, and so she was able to get her high school degree. Her greatest desire was to make videos about her people. Her responsibility was both women's projects and communication. Arturo López had cut his organizing teeth in his church organization in the small town of Las Palmas and then had joined the APG literacy campaign. Both he and his wife, a strong woman named Estrella Dominguez, had been leaders in their community. Arturo was in charge of economic projects. Ramón Padilla had recently come to the region as part of the APG literacy trainers and had stayed in Barrio Libre. He had a great deal of respect from the rest of the group given his political experience and his ability to teach. He was put in charge of education.

Flor García, also from La Cañada, was a shy young woman who spoke little Guaraní but wanted to be a part of the new organization. She helped Rosana in communication. Lorenzo Valentín was a handsome young man who had recently returned from his military service. He organized soccer teams in the communities, was a romantic poet, and took on the organizing function of the capitanía. Finally, Franco Barragán was the health promoter for Barrio Nuevo. He had been raised outside Guaraní culture but returned as a young adult because he felt drawn to his people and the language. He was tall and quiet, with an easy smile and a gentle assurance about him. Franco became the *responsable* (person in charge) of health projects. The group had a definite team spirit, heightened by the fact that upon joining, every member had to sign a declaration of commitment to the capitanía and to each other.

Proyectos

Right away Don Álvaro and his new team began to go after funding to keep the organization alive. Since its beginning, the organization had depended on outside funding, starting with the CEPAC grants. However much they objected to the way CEPAC had taken advantage of them, it was clear that the initial grant had been important to the capitanía. Through it, they learned about how funding should work and how NGOs should treat their partners: they should share the money. But the most important thing they learned was that outsiders would fund them if they asked in the right ways. The whole point of the first CEPAC project was the *diagnóstico*, without which the Guaranís could not approach outside funders. Once this was done, they would be "the real thing," a group with a plan for its own development, what funders were calling *etnodesarrollo* (ethnic development). I was invited to the public meeting at which the leaders of the capitanía and CEPAC presented the diagnóstico and the plan. It was held at a nice conference center in Santa Cruz, to which representatives of all the major NGOs and funders had been invited. Professional reproductions of the plan, with a shiny cover and beautiful graphics, were handed out to those present. I remember being impressed, thinking, "Well here is a group that is really going somewhere!"

This focus on outside funding was reinforced in several ways. First, the SAE provided a six-month-long training program to indigenous people to learn to propose, write, evaluate, and implement development projects. Two members of the ETZ, Arturo López and Pablo Melgar, attended the training and emerged as *responsables de planificación y gestión indígena* (RPGIs, or people in charge of indigenous planning and management). This government program made it clear that indigenous people were a special category of beneficiaries who should learn how to ask for money from NGOs. The SAE and its successor, the Vice Ministerio de Asuntos Indígenas y Pueblos Originarios (VAIPO, Vice Ministry of Indigenous and Original Peoples Affairs), received substantial funding from international donors, as the Bolivian government did not have the money to fund the reforms it had passed.

Second, the Guaranís operated in a context in which NGO and international funding was a central part of daily institutional life for indigenous organizations. Because CIDOB, the national indigenous federation, had received substantial funding from the Danes during its first ten years, there were always Danish técnicos working in the building, advising the leaders. The APG and its suborganizations, such as Teko-Guaraní, had received much of their funding from CIPCA, a Jesuit NGO. The British aid agency had an important presence at CIDOB during the late 1990s, administering a joint program with CIDOB for indigenous investigation. The director of that program organized the CIDOB library and employed an indigenous staff to foster research. Foreign advisers were often involved in high-level indigenous strategy meetings.

In the regular multidisciplinary meetings held to negotiate the progress of the territorial titling reforms with the government, numerous Bolivian and foreign experts as well as NGO workers acted as mediators and consultants. This meant that there were constantly opportunities for the Guaranís to apply for *proyectos* (projects). One day the capitán grande came running into the office to tell us that the indigenous office at the *prefectura* had just called him, saying they had extra money that they had to give away in the next week. The Guaranís had to get together a proposal right away! Even political parties now require proposals for donations. This irked the capitán grande, who had many political connections and was used to going to visit his cronies and getting enough money for whatever task the organization needed. For instance, when the capitanía moved into its new offices, Don Álvaro took me with him to visit the local ADN party head, whom he had known for years. "Don't worry," Don Álvaro said, "This is exactly the sort of thing the political parties have money for. They will give us a couple of sacks of whitewash." When we got there, however, his friend said things had changed. Now Don Álvaro needed to submit a written proposal. Fortunately, the ETZ got one done and the whitewash was donated.

"Projectism" had important effects on the life of the capitanía. First, the ETZ became a critical part of the leadership in a way that was not traditional. At the meetings approving the *estatuto*, many of the elders disagreed with this change. It is contrary to the Guaraní way, they said, to have such young people making decisions for the group. The only way this was passed was to change the *organigrama* (organizational flow chart) to show the ETZ as a consultant group linked to the capitán grande and not as a substitute for the approval of the larger constituency. In practice, however, the ETZ retained a great deal of influence because they were the ones that negotiated with funders and government authorities — things the elders, who speak less Spanish and live out in the rural areas, did not do well. At one regional assembly, Don Álvaro explained how important the ETZ was: "It used to be that if you needed something, you just wrote a letter. Now you have to submit a grant proposal. It's all *tecnificado* [technical] now. That's why we need the ETZ, to coordinate with authorities."

This ability also gave the capitanía panache with other groups. For instance, in 1998 the capitanía became involved in a land struggle in the Parabanó region south of Santa Cruz. Several Guaraní families were allying with a group of local peasants and landowners to take over some fertile land that had also been claimed by a sindicato of highland Indians. I spent a fair amount of time following this struggle and often talked to the nonindigenous people from Santa

Cruz who were allying with the capitanía. Clearly, the sindicato had more political power and, legally, a better claim to the land. Nevertheless, the cambas chose to work with the capitanía. One reason was ethnic: the cambas felt more at home with lowland indigenous people than with the Indians of the altiplano. But the group's main leader, Roger, told me that they also felt the capitanía was a good partner because they could "*montar proyectos*" — that is, they could apply for and implement development projects. Don Álvaro made this ability clear as he talked to them. "The difference between us and the sindicato," he said, "is that we work with projects."

Multicultural Bolivia seemed to provide a multitude of projects for indigenous groups. Two small organizational strengthening grants from the international funding community helped the capitanía keep the office open and functioning. CEPAC's initial grant had ended in 1996, but they got a "bridge" grant of $19,700 from IBIS-Dinamarka, a Danish foreign-aid agency, to continue the organizational strengthening process. IBIS was a key funder for indigenous organizations throughout Bolivia at that time, providing money for much of the work of national and regional indigenous organizations, including CIDOB, the APG, and CABI, the Izozog Guaraní federation. This money was used for assemblies, office materials, the purchase of a computer, and trips out to the communities. Then the APG funneled some of the funds (about $5,000) they had received from IBIS to Zona Cruz for meetings and office rent. In 1995, UNICEF gave the capitanía a small grant of $2,500 for office furniture. This kept them going until about 1997.

In 1997, the Colectivo de Estudios Aplicados y Desarrollo Social (CEADES, Collective for Applied Studies and Social Development), a local NGO working on LPP training, agreed to work with Zona Cruz. This proved to be extremely important to the creation and training of the ETZ. CEADES had received funding from international donors to foment indigenous participation in the newly passed political reforms that had been intended to democratize municipal government. One of the codirectors of CEADES, Julián Paz, developed with the capitanía a yearlong training program to help them analyze the resources and the problems facing the communities, the staff, and the organization. As I describe in detail in chapter 5, the goal of the year was to help the organization take advantage of the new resources available from the LPP. This meant helping the young team work with the communities to figure out what their needs were and how to get their needs incorporated into the municipal budgets. Besides strategy meetings and trainings about the laws, the CEADES grant also paid for the ETZ to travel regularly out to the communities.

This funding was important in many ways. The ETZ got to know the outlying villages and established a minimal presence for the organization. The meetings they held began a process of organizing at the community level that continues today. Most important, the ETZ began the lengthy process of learning about political organizing and the sorts of rationalities required by the neoliberal regime of citizenship. In practice, the CEADES project became the backbone of the ETZ's activities, as it supported them in their training and their work out in the communities. The grant did not give the ETZ members salaries, but it did provide them with transportation costs and food for the days they were working, so this was an important bit of funding for the working machine of the capitanía.

Several other grants or "projects" were given to particular communities or members of the organization. In 1996, several Guaranís from Warnes created their own small NGO and won a grant from Spain for a health project in Warnes. They were awarded approximately $55,000, three years' funding for a health clinic for the poor. Several young students, mostly members of the ETZ, received scholarships for training projects of various sorts. Rosana Moreno, for instance, got trained in video documentary making through an NGO called Centro de Formación y Realización Cinematográfica (CEFREC, Center for Cinematographic Training and Production) and went on to create a wonderful documentary about Guaraní *zafreros* (sugarcane harvesters). A group of students were trained in journalism and "popular reporting" through another NGO. Franco Barragán received a scholarship to attend nursing school and was sent to do his practice period in a small Guaraní village in the south. Finally, in 1998, Samuel Tapera applied for and received funding from a joint British-CIDOB project to study the uses of medicinal plants in Zona Cruz communities. This provided him and Ramón Padilla with salaries for a year while they carried out the study part time and worked on capitanía projects the rest of the time. The Secretariado Ejecutivo de Pastoral Social (SEAPAS, Executive Secretary of Social Pastoral Work), a local NGO run by the archbishop of the Catholic Church in Santa Cruz, gave two small grants — one to a health post in Los Rios and the other as a loan of $10,000 to the women's organization in La Cañada. The micro-credit project was for twenty women to get small loans of $500 each to start businesses or to augment already existing income-generation schemes. Some of the small businesses the women started, such as small lunchrooms or stores, prospered, but because they did not receive any training about budgeting or accounting, most of these businesses failed.

Meanwhile, the CZC was struggling. For some years, they had no permanent office space and moved several times to spaces loaned to them by other groups or individuals. When I first came back to Santa Cruz in early 1998, they had just moved from temporary space in CABI offices to an office a Guaraní friend of the capitán had loaned them. It was an office front in downtown Santa Cruz, next to a chic boutique. The capitanía did not have enough money to keep the phone line working or to run the air conditioning, so the plate-glass windows were papered with old newspapers to keep the sun out. In the height of the summer, it was sweltering. Fortunately, soon thereafter, CIDOB agreed to give Zona Cruz two rooms in an outbuilding for their office. The rooms had been abandoned for some time and were in bad shape, but the Guaranís were happy to have them. All they needed to do was clean and paint and get locks for the doors. The capitán managed to get one of his political party contacts to donate some whitewash, and in one afternoon, the whole ETZ team (and I) cleaned out the building to prepare the new office. Having their own office was a great boon for the organization, especially offices in the CIDOB buildings, where all the important political action took place. No one had money for the locks, though, so the young men took turns sleeping in the office for a few weeks until finally Samuel Tapera rerouted some of the funds from his medicinal plants study to purchase the locks.

In 1998, the organization got the first bit of stable funding as part of a three-year institutional grant made by the Danes to CPESC, the regional federation to which the capitanía belonged. (CPESC represents Guaraní, Chiquitano, Guarayo, and Ayoreo Indians of the eastern part of Bolivia.) Zona Cruz received $6,000 a year for three years, and although this amount was minimal, it kept the organization afloat once again. This was enough for small salaries of $100 or $200 per month for the capitán, the main officers, and a secretary. It also paid for electricity for the computer, a working phone (at least some of the time), and some money for transportation out to the communities.

Perhaps the most interesting and controversial proyecto during this time came from a young white lawyer I will call Alonso Mendoza, who approached the capitanía in 1997. Mendoza was married to a Danish woman and was getting his master's degree in international development at a university in Denmark. He wanted to write a proposal for a project that would train Guaranís to be better administrators, so they could participate in the ethnodevelopment opportunities available to them.[10] On the surface, this looked very much like the CEADES project in that its goal was to teach the Guaranís to be better administrators. It also resembled the SAE program of training RPGIs to be development officers for their respective groups. Yet there were some big differences, mainly centering on the person of Mendoza.

Mendoza is a camba, a local man from Santa Cruz, from a relatively wealthy family. He acts and speaks like the local elites and tended to order people around. More important, he brought this idea to the capitanía, based on some brief visits he had with some village leaders several years previous. He wrote the project according to what he thought the Guaraní needed to learn and, probably, what he thought he could provide based on his training in international development. There was little input from the capitanía, however, and consequently, there was a strong sense of paternalism about the project. When several ETZ members and Guaraní leaders described the project in precisely these terms, I asked them why the capitanía had agreed to work with him. The answer was invariably, "Well, it's a project, isn't it?" I think this attitude was clearly a legacy from the postrevolutionary years in which subaltern groups tended to rely on strong patrons for resources and access to power. (This model of civil society is described in more depth in chapter 4). In the heady years of multicultural Bolivia, when NGOs and international funders had such financial power and were distributing resources so widely, it was not surprising to see indigenous groups like the Guaraní taking advantage of whatever opportunities they could.

Mendoza was not able to get funding for the project at first, although he applied at all the embassies and big funders, both in Bolivia and Denmark. Nevertheless, he returned to Bolivia in 1998 with what he called the first phase of the project: a huge carton of used furniture and bicycles he had gotten donated by various groups in Denmark. The problem was that the Guaranís did not have any place to store all of this stuff. They did not even have a permanent office. So Mendoza had to pay for the storage of the materials until the capitanía could move into their new office at CIDOB. Then he had to get the capitán grande to call in some favors at a government office to borrow an enormous truck to bring everything first to the office and then out to the communities. The furniture-moving extravaganza was a surreal vision. On top of the huge truck were Mendoza, a short man in expensive cowboy boots, and his tall blonde Danish wife taking photographs — "to prove to those who donated the materials," she said.

The truck got stuck in the muddy bog outside the office, and it took several hours and all the efforts of the ETZ to get it out. They began to unload the most unlikely things from the truck. For the capitanía's offices, Mendoza had brought a gigantic beige velvet sectional sofa. In a cool climate, it must have been lovely, but in the unair-conditioned offices in the tropics of Santa Cruz, this couch was unbearably hot. (It was quickly destroyed by the heat and the water that dripped from the damaged roof during the rainy season.) Next came a strange assortment of used hospital beds, typing tables, an ancient sewing machine, chairs of all shapes, metal bed frames and desks, a couple of battered refrigerators, and forty or fifty used bikes.

After getting some of these items stored in the extra room next to the new office, which was still filthy and filled with rats' nests, the big truck and its captain headed off on the first swing through the communities to deliver the donated goods. I jumped in the back of the truck along with half of the ETZ. We perched precariously atop the odd furniture as the truck sought out the least muddy passages to the villages. We stopped in five villages that afternoon and evening. In each one, the local leader was called and a formal presentation made. None of the leaders (or anyone in their respective communities) knew anything about this delivery, so everyone was surprised and places first had to be made for the goods. In one community, the school-teacher's room was taken over for a dented hospital bed. I couldn't imagine what they were going to do with such a thing. There was no health post, no doctor, not even a health promoter in that village. After receiving the goods, the capitán was asked to sign a document Mendoza handed him, affix his seal, and pose for a picture. And then off we all went to the next village.

This way of "doing development" seemed to me to put these Guaranís in the category of victims of some disaster or refugees who had lost everything in a war. It also established Mendoza and his gringa wife as benefactors, the understanding Peron-like couple who cared about the little people. Interestingly, however, when I spoke to Guaranís during the year and visited many of those villages again, most of them seemed genuinely grateful for the things they received. One local capitán told me that it was wonderful to have a type-writer out in his village. This meant that he didn't have to come to town every time he needed an official document. Few of the hospital beds ended up being used, as I had guessed, but the bicycles were a great success, given the long distances between villages and the lack of regular public transportation. I got a ride on one of them myself one night when I accompanied Samuel Tapera from town out to Bella Flor, before the taxi service began running regularly. But the comment that best explained the Guaraní's reaction was from the capitán of Bella Flor. He said that although it was a surprise to get those items, and a bit strange, since they weren't the things the community could most have used, still, it was something tangible. Most projects consist of words, work-shops, or seminars, he said. This, at least, was something they could use.

This "first phase" was all that happened for some time, as no funds were forthcoming. Then, at the end of 1998, Mendoza was back. He had gotten some funds for the second phase, but not all that he had hoped for. He had convinced ten or fifteen young Guaranís to come to classes at CIDOB, where he began teaching them Guaraní history. The hoped-for funding was to have provided full transportation and *viáticos* (food allowance). Instead, the lim-ited phase two gave no transportation, but it did provide a cooked meal for all the students. Because of this, the participants were few in number, and grew fewer still over the weeks. Eventually, the classes ceased, until more funding could be found. Again, although the project might have seemed a failure to an outsider, when I asked the capitán grande about Mendoza's classes, he shrugged, saying, "Well, it was something. We have to keep trying."

The Estatuto Orgánico

At the same time the CZC was struggling to get on its feet as an insti-tution, its communities were having problems of their own, mostly about land issues. At each assembly, leaders would air their communities' problems and ask for help from the capitanía. One community was having problems because the *kollas* (highlanders) in their sindicato were not cooperating. Other communities had no land at all and were desperately trying to find some. Some people were fighting with their neighbors over limits to the land or with the rich landlords who previously owned the lands. Others were in trouble with debts they had accrued for agricultural credits. Nowhere was the situation worse than in Bella Flor, however, where Guaranís began to sell what most residents believed was collective land. From the beginning of the assemblies, the arguments over land in Bella Flor spilled over into the life of the capitanía. In assembly after assembly, aggrieved parties would address their concerns to the capitán, begging for him to help. If he were a traditional *mburuvicha guasu* (leader of the federation), he should intervene and solve the problems, many Guaranís felt.

These issues brought up serious questions about the purpose of the capitanía. It was fine to have a Guaraní organization that represented the people before the state, especially a state that seemed to be instituting new rights for Indians, but what was the purpose of the capitanía if not to resolve internal problems? What was the basis of the organization's authority and what were the rules by which it was to be carried out? In essence, what did it mean to be an indigenous organization in these new times? These questions had not been clearly formulated or answered at the founding of the capitanía and, as a result, those Guaranís who wanted specific problems solved often felt frustrated.

Some of these ideas were formally expressed in 1998, when the capitanía was forced to draft and approve an *estatuto orgánico* (organizing statute). One of the first steps in gaining representative status under the Law of Popular Participation is to be formally recognized as an indigenous organization by the *prefecto* (a prefect, roughly the equivalent of the governor). The capitanía had not gotten this formality accomplished, despite its years of existence, so CEADES and the ETZ team set about writing the organization's estatuto orgánico. The ETZ worked on the statue for almost a month and then presented the draft proposal to the communities. In June 1998, the capitanía held a workshop assembly at which representatives of all the communities worked through the draft and made amendments and changes. They then returned to the communities to distribute it among the people. Finally, in August 1998, the new act was approved by the full assembly. I attended every step of this long process of institutional self-definition. According to the statute, the CZC is constituted under both the Constitution of the Republic and the customary laws (*normas consuetudinarias*) of indigenous people. It defines itself as "a non-profit indigenous organization with autonomy of management, dedicated to the defense of the rights and social, economic, political, and cultural claims of Guaraní people and communities."[11]

The ETZ debated long about the organization's objectives, and then the assembly made several changes to them. It is worth detailing the statute in this regard. According to Article 11 of the statute, the objectives of the Capitanía Zona Cruz are:

A. Its democratic and participatory incorporation in the state.
B. Its traditional, cultural, social, political, and economic development and the improvement of its conditions of life.
C. The participation as an organization, a zone, provinces, and communities, in the work of all kinds of projects.
D. The defense of the fundamental rights of the persons and the Indigenous People (*Pueblos indígenas*).
E. To search for unity with the other *Pueblos* and peasants.
F. To preserve natural resources and the environment.
G. To consolidate the access to, property rights to, and preservation of *Tierra Territorio* (land and territory) of the Guaraní indigenous people of the integrated area of Santa Cruz de la Sierra for social and economic development.
H. To consolidate Intercultural Bilingual Education, for the development of culture and the relationship with the rest of society.
I. To promote the elaboration and participatory management (*gestión*) of development plans at the level of the zone, the provinces, and the communities.[12]

The majority of these stated objectives are part of the organization's daily practices, as I observed them. Particularly interesting are items A and D, which reflect the discourse of inclusion of indigenous citizens. These echo the language of the International Labor Organization's Convention No. 169, outlined in 1989, which recognized indigenous people's human rights and their rights to participatory democracy. A second group of objectives (B, C, G, and I) focus on the importance of development for the capitanía. Thus the CZC is to act to promote development at multiple levels and to preserve the Guaraní's rights to their lands.

It is interesting to note, however, the inclusion of several items that did not prove to be on the practical agenda of the capitanía during my study period. The two most obvious examples are item F (preserving natural resources and the environment) and H (consolidating bilingual education). The Zona Cruz communities are not in forested areas, nor are the people dependent on the forest for hunting, gathering, or collecting, as are many indigenous groups in Bolivia. This makes their concerns for the environment less critical and, perhaps, more abstract than these concerns might be for other groups. Preserving the environment is, though, an important part of the national discourse about indigenous rights. Similarly, as a rule, bilingual education was not highly valued in the Zona Cruz communities. The inclusion of these articles, which are incidental to the lived realities in the CZC, demonstrates how much influence the international discourses of difference, cultural recognition, and the link to environmentalism have had on indigenous groups like the Guaraní. A final note of interest is the inclusion of objective E, which advocates unity with other indigenous people and with peasants. During the period I worked with these Guaranís, although there was substantial solidarity with other lowland groups, there was little expressed interest in campesino or highland groups. In fact, like many other groups in the lowlands, the Guaranís for the most part perceived these groups, especially kolla migrants to Santa Cruz, to be in competition for their lands. They did not work with them or, frankly, especially like them. Ethnicity was the unifying trope of their activism, not class solidarity.

Who Are We?

The elaboration of the estatuto was an important process for the capitanía, as many critical questions were answered. It was particularly good about establishing clearer rules of institutional functioning.[13] The statute did not, however, resolve fundamental questions about what it means to be an indigenous organization. I suggest that the frustrations aired about these issues were not merely the result of an incomplete formulation of purpose by a young organization. Instead, they result from the fact that the capitanía is a site through which profound questions about the nature of indigenous relations to the nation were being continually formulated and reformulated.

In the era of multiculturalism, indigenousness began to take on a new valence: according to the discourse at play at the time, Indians were being included in the nation as citizens. The post-1952 regime of race and nation that defined Indians as peasants tied to the nation through sindicatos was fading, giving way to new forms of representation. But those new forms were not yet solidified. On the one hand, indigenous organizations were supposed to arise from traditional cultural forms, what were referred to as *usos y costumbres* (uses and customs). On the other hand, as I describe in detail in chapter 4, the new reforms strictly prescribed the sorts of participation Indians could engage in at the municipal level. And such organizations were only legitimate in the eyes of the state once they were approved by the prefecto and given *personería jurídica* (legal status). Most important, as the struggles in Bella Flor explored in chapter 3 show, the overarching problem the Guaraní faced was poverty. This left federations like the CZC in an ambiguous state and its founders with numerous questions. Would indigenous organizations like the CZC bring state support? Would they lead to NGO funding? What new kinds of leadership were necessary to ensure this, and what would be sacrificed in exchange for it? What should the role of tradition be?

From the beginning, one of the founders' main desires was to put into practice "traditional" forms of organization instead of the old sindicato model imposed by the Movimiento Nacional Revolucionario (MNR, National Revolutionary Movement). This desire was part of, and encouraged by, the growing movement of indigenous people to protect and reclaim cultural forms of sociopolitical organization, language, and land use. The activism of the APG, CABI, and CIDOB (which were in turn influenced by international indigenous organizing) influenced the Guaraní of Zona Cruz to express their rights to be and act "indigenous" and to use their new organization as a vehicle for this cultural expression. Implicit in this push is the defense of indigenous rights and of indigenous people in general. The pan-indigenous movement values unity among indigenous groups. This cultural reclaiming was extremely important for migrant Guaranís of Zona Cruz, many of whom felt their link to their Guaraní identity and culture was slipping away as the city life overcame them and their communities. In fact, it may have been more important to them than to indigenous groups that lived in more isolated conditions where there was less insecurity about the loss of language and group solidarity.

These Guaranís looked to the capitanía for this *reinvindicación* (claim or vindication) because it acted as a node of relationships for its members and communities. It mediated for Guaranís in their relations with other political and social forces, such as other indigenous organizations, the government, NGOs, and international funders. It was thus a response to multiple people's various concerns, so this meant that there was always tension between the purposes of the institution and the expectations of its constituents. The overarching question that united these relationships was that of indigenous identity. The questions the Teko-Guaraní representative asked the assembly ("Where do we come from, and where are going?") are underscored by a deeper question: "Who are we?"[14] This is the question the young members of the ETZ were asking, as they watched the city take over. It is also the question the Bella Flor elders were asking as they saw their lands being sold.

One afternoon, I sat with a group of the young leaders in the CZC offices, talking about the role of the capitanía. Samuel Tapera from Bella Flor, Rosana Moreno from La Cañada, and Arturo Lopez from La Palmas were there. Samuel said he thought there were three important aspects of Guaraní identity. The first was a feeling of belonging, something unexplainable and unmeasurable. The second was the language, the ability to communicate to each other in their own common language. But maybe the most important, he said, was the Guaraní organization, the *mboati guasu* (the big tent) that united them. This was different from the sindicatos, because it was a Guaraní way to come together, based on collective life, territory, and work. Rosana agreed, saying that the most important thing was a sense of solidarity, of being united. And that was precisely the thing they were losing by living in the city, where each family has to pay rent and feed itself. The capitanía was the best hope to fight this loss, by providing a space to be Guaraní. Arturo chimed in, saying that the capitanía was important because all his life people had discriminated against him, saying the Guaraní people were *flojos* (lazy). "So maybe this generation can be the example." "Yes," Samuel answered, "this is a long process, for the next generation. We are like *recién nacidos* [newborns]."

Of course, there is no single answer to the abstract, socially constructed question of identity. As is clear from the historical account of the construction of race in Bolivia, the meaning of "indigenousness" has changed over time in relation to discourses of race and nation. The Guaraní's efforts to construct their own meaning through their organization and institutional relations with the state were firmly embedded in a new regime of citizenship and nation: that of neoliberal multiculturalism. The following chapters demonstrate the inherent tensions these Guaranís encountered as they attempted to enact their newfound citizenship rights and to find new resources for their communities.

3 A Crisis of Leadership in Bella Flor

> The social, economic, and cultural rights of indigenous
> peoples that live in the national territory are recognized,
> respected, and protected within the framework of the law,
> especially those rights regarding their lands of communal
> origin, guaranteeing the use and sustainable development
> of the natural resources, their identity, values, languages,
> customs, and institutions.
> — Article 171 of the Bolivian Constitution

A Village Meeting

October 1998: Several hundred Guaraní Indians sit in the large metal-roofed warehouse that doubles as a meeting hall in Bella Flor, on the outskirts of Santa Cruz. Sweat is streaming as the tropical sun heats the hall to oven-like proportions; people glare at each other, muttering in Guaraní and Spanish. In the front of the room, government officials from the Instituto Nacional de Reforma Agraria (IRNA) land reform office try to bring order so they can conduct their business: an inspection of the lands that form the basis of the intra-indigenous land conflict that is tearing Bella Flor apart. One group of residents claims they have individual titles, which they rightfully sold. The other group insists that Guaraní lands have always been held communally and that no one can sell the land. This divisive battle has been going on for several years, during which the titleholders have made substantial profits selling land parcels. Bitter recriminations have led to lawsuits, and now the state is attempting to resolve the case.

One by one, the parties try to speak, getting out only small bits of argument before the crowd interrupts, shouting conflicting versions. One man, the leader of one faction, stands and says, "We hold clear titles to the land and have legally sold them. You have copies of the titles in the files —" "You have no right!" shouts a voice from the crowd. "That land is not yours to sell! It belongs to the community!" His lawyer takes over the argument. Because there is an order "immobilizing" or freezing all further sales, he says, the government has to intervene. A strong, powerfully built man interrupts the lawyers, his booming voice taking over the room. This is Don Rafael Vaca, leader of the neighboring village of El Futuro. "Those people have sold

the land without the agreement of the people," Don Rafael says, "I am selling the land but we are doing it our way, the Guaraní way, collectively."
There is a smattering of applause. Next, a woman stands and addresses the
first man in loud, emotional Guaraní: "You are taking our lands! We have
worked this land with our own sweat! We have raised our families here! We
won't let you take what is ours! That is not the Guaraní way. What kind of
leaders are you? You have betrayed us to the *karai* [white people]!" She sits,
shaking with anger. Cheers and hisses erupt from the audience. An argument
breaks out, and the INRA officials end the meeting, which is quickly getting
away from them.

After the meeting, the people break up into two factions to discuss the
event. Both sides claim they have prevailed. Each group holds a victory dinner, talks through what happened. At one party, the capitán grande, Don
Álvaro Montero, sits with a lawyer, discussing the next steps. At his side sits
Don Fernando Santos, the leader of the Confederación Indígena del Oriente
de Bolivia (CIDOB, the national indigenous organization), who has come to
observe. When it is his turn to speak to the assembled people, Don Fernando
says, "What I have seen here is that economics has taken over politics and
allowed personal interests to intervene. This is causing us to lose our native
indigenous culture. We must act as a community! We must be unified as
always!"

Land and Leadership in Bella Flor

In the late 1990s, as the city lapped up against the borders of Bella
Flor, the Guaraní residents fell into a vicious dispute over landownership.
While most Indians in Bolivia, and across the continent, were struggling to
hold onto their territories, many Guaranís in Bella Flor were selling their
lands to the highest bidders, trying to cash in on the boomtown economy that
made their lands suddenly valuable. Other Guaranís, like those in the meeting just described, resisted the sales, asserting indigenous tradition, identity,
and solidarity. The result was a community split into bitterly opposed
camps: those who held onto "traditional" values of land as an inalienable
group resource, and those who adopted the capitalist vision of land as a commodity. Far from being "united as always" by their indigenous culture, the
Guaranís of Bella Flor were divided about what parts of their culture they
could or should hold onto in boomtown Santa Cruz.

This story is not just about one village fighting to meet its own needs.
Rather, it describes struggles over material and symbolic resources in a
moment of rapid social, economic, and cultural change. Personal motivations
played a part but, as this chapter explains, this conflict was also profoundly

embedded in ongoing contests over the meanings of indigenousness in contemporary urban Bolivia. Indeed, the most frequent expressions of what it means to "be Guaraní" were in the context of the land struggles, like that of the woman at the meeting: "That is not the Guaraní way!" Her cry shows that property relations *are* social relations. Property is not just a "thing," but a right to have control over and to gain income from that thing (Macpherson 1978).[1] Property is a relationship embedded in a cultural and moral framework that produces a particular vision of community. This is critical because, as anthropologist Tania Murray Li has pointed out, "representations [of community] produced in the context of struggles over resources form part of the 'practical political economy' through which different parties defend interests and advance claims" (Li 1996: 502; see also Moore 1998).[2]

As chapter 1 has made clear, representations of "indigenousness" do not occur in isolation but are mediated by discourses of race and nation. In every Bolivian regime of citizenship, Indians' ownership and use of land has been a central part of the boundary work by which Indians have been included or excluded from society. In colonial periods, Indian rights to communal property were tied to a definition of Indians as a separate category of colonial subject. In the republican period, Indians were "liberated" from their communal ties to the land to convert them into individual and modern subjects. In the postrevolutionary period, Indians were redefined as "acceptable" citizens through their participation in the agrarian reform, which gave them individual titles and membership in territorially based unions. In each of these epochs, Indian leaders acted as mediators in the delicate negotiations between local society and the larger forces of state, market, and nation. In the colonial period, local leaders protected communal lands by honoring and policing the tributary pact. Eighteenth-century Indian leaders protected the lands by mounting resistance to the republican appropriations, often by creative uses of the legal system. After the 1952 revolution, peasant leaders secured land under the agrarian reform and garnered resources from the state through participation in state-sponsored unions.

These mediations took place at what historian and anthropologist Thomas Abercrombie has called the frontier between distinct but interdependent cultural realms (Abercrombie 1998: 10). In this chapter, I carry out a close examination of Guaraní leadership models and practices to shed light on the political and discursive processes by which such frontiers are created and maintained. I also illustrate how actors on each side of that ever-changing frontier are engaged in an ongoing intercultural translation, taking elements from each other's repertoires and reworking them in a "delicate communicative negotiation" between local societies and global and state forces (ibid.). Here I make clear that simple dualisms often invoked in discussions about Indian activism, such as tradition versus modernity, are insufficient to understand the complex ways that Indians, like all of us, negotiate between multiple registers. There is no single way to be Indian, or even one unified set of Indian values about land.

In Santa Cruz in the late 1990s, when the Guaraní leadership was formed, it was charged with the protection of urban and suburban Guaraní communities. The Capitanía Zona Cruz (CZC) had multiple roles, from representing the communities before the state to securing development moneys from NGOs. These roles reflected the tension between the need to assert cultural difference in the multicultural 1990s (under a politics of recognition) and the need to facilitate the economic welfare of the people (under a politics of redistribution). At the local level, two goals were especially important: consolidating Guaraní land rights and preserving traditional forms of leadership. Both of these goals were severely challenged by the land struggle in Bella Flor, where residents questioned the viability of "traditional" forms of land tenure and models of leadership in the urban context.

This chapter traces the ways in which the Guaraní adopted different leadership models during different epochs, sometimes incorporating particular traditional Guaraní notions of land and leadership, sometimes adopting corporatist models from Bolivian politics and, recently, balancing state land reform laws. Although the leaders' actions demonstrate innovative reworkings of a number of cultural narratives, the results for the majority of Bella Flor's citizens have not been beneficial: the village has been taken over by suburban housing developments, and few Guaranís have received much compensation. The Bella Flor case shows the newest phase in the long process by which Indian lands have been assimilated to fit the needs of Bolivian society and points to the critical role of Indian leaders in that process. The discussion begins with an analysis of historical patterns of Guaraní land use and leadership styles. This is followed by a history of the founding and development of Bella Flor, drawn mostly from interviews with community residents. Finally I describe the land dispute of the late 1990s and the leadership models enacted by local leaders and the capitán grande of the capitanía.

Guaraní Repertoires: Historical Tensions and Contingencies

When the Spaniards arrived in the late 1500s in the Cordillera region between Paraguay and the Andes, they found a thriving society of Guaraní-speaking people they called the Chiriguano Indians, living scattered across the region. The history of the Guaraní response to the Spanish incursion is a centuries-long story of missionaries, massacres, domination, resistance to military campaigns, and the extension of the cattle frontier (see Meliá 1988;

Pifarré 1989). The patterns and discourse of both land use and leadership styles have evolved through these changing social and political contexts.

A cautionary note about the use of historical material is in order. The history of the Guaraní people is inextricably tied to the histories of the Spanish who invaded Guaraní lands, the missionaries who subjugated them, and the Bolivian nation-state. Much of the Guaraní's history is based on accounts by military conquerors or missionaries and then synthesized and rewritten by historians with particular indigenist sympathies. As a result, I do not propose that the historical trends I describe here are essential cultural patterns from some deep or "true" Guaraní history. Rather, the trends are contingencies of the political and cultural contexts at play at the time of their enactments. Nevertheless, a study of the variety of options and patterns in the Guaraní cultural tool kit is instructive, especially as those tools continue to be employed in current conditions.

Historian Bartomeu Meliá has explained that in Guaraní origin stories, the First Father, in his wisdom and generosity, created the land and gave it to the Guaraní to unfold and use for the good of the people. Land was to be used for the sustenance of the people, and the reciprocity required was the *fiesta*, feasts in which the plenty of the land was shared among the people. For the Guaraní, Meliá says, land and agriculture were "impregnated with religious categories" (Meliá 1995: 301).[3] Land was held in common by the community, and parcels were given to individual families to cultivate for their personal use. "It falls entirely outside the mental scheme of the Guaraní that land could be negotiated and converted into an object of merchandise, any more than could air or water" (Meliá 1988: 40).

An equally important aspect of this historical view of land is migration. The historical search for the Tierra Sin Mal, or land without evil, has led Guaranís to migrate from Brazil to the Cordillera and Chaco as well as to their present homes in Santa Cruz. This may stem from the tension between the instability of the land and its abundance. The Guaraní vision of land included leaving lands for a variety of reasons. People might have depleted the land's natural resources through their slash-and-burn cultivation methods; the weather may have changed (this is represented by the myths of the great floods or the great fires); or the lands may have been invaded and devastated by outsiders (this is represented in myths about grasshoppers) (Meliá 1995: 301–2).[4] The invasion by the Spaniards was the most extreme version of this, which left no alternative but to flee to farther lands. Thus, Meliá says, "Migration is always a dialectic of scarcity and plenty" ("La migración es siempre dialéctica de carencia y plentitud") (ibid.: 306).

Guaraní land use patterns underwent tremendous changes through the centuries, as the Spaniards settled the region. Franciscan missionaries entrusted with "taming" the wild Chiriguano people formed reductions, or mission communities, where the indigenous were put to work in agricultural projects. This process produced numerous insurrections, however, as the Chiriguano were not easily tamed. Ironically, it appears that cattle accomplished what missionaries could not. The large haciendas became the rule, and the Chiriguano were forced by population losses, massacres, and land invasions to leave their lands (see Meliá 1988; Pifarré 1989). Soon the rubber booms of Santa Cruz and the Beni attracted indigenous labor, and after that came the sugarcane boom in Argentina. Thus colonialism and international commodity markets disrupted and altered Guaraní land use early on.

That is not to say that the Guaraní people were totally swept away from historical land use patterns. Many continued to live in communities in the Cordillera, Izozog, and Chuquisaca on communally held land (Albó 1990: 84–87). But migration and changing patterns of use may be seen as an equally traditional trend for the ever-mobile Guaranís. Even in recent generations, land use patterns continued to vary widely. In many communities in the Cordillera, the *peón-patrón* model has been the predominant one for many generations (Healy 1984). In other communities, however, Guaranís had individual titles. In the Izozog, title to community lands was sometimes given to the leaders (Albó 1990).

Yet even in communities that held land collectively, the meaning of "collective" may not be what is commonly imagined. My friends in Bella Flor told me differing stories about how "real Guaranís" held land, reflecting how dichotomies of autonomy and collectivity are intertwined. Sitting with me in his shady yard, drinking mate after he returned from Plan Tres Mil, Don Jesús Tapera told me many stories of his home pueblo in the Cordillera. There, he explained, although land belonged to the community, each Guaraní household head had the individual right to the use of his *chaco* (cultivation plot) and to his home. This was inviolable, because "every Guaraní is a king" ("cada Guaraní es un rey"). This refrain was repeated many times. In some villages, there were collective work systems, where people joined together to clear and cultivate the land, especially the lands of the community leaders or of elderly widows. But in many other communities, there was no such system, and Guaranís were solely responsible for themselves and their families. Thus there is a wide variety of so-called traditional ways of holding land and organizing communities, although people often use the term as if there were only one.

Anarchist Warriors

The same thing is true for Guaraní leadership models. The leader of a Guaraní community is called a *mburuvicha*. The meaning of the word *mbu-*

ruvicha in Guaraní is not clear, but most current translations define it as a person with authority or a leader (Albó 1990).[5] The Spanish called these leaders *capitanes* (captains), which is still used in Bolivian Spanish. The mburuvicha of a community is called a *capitán* or a *capitán comunal*. A regional leader is called a *mburuvicha guasu* ("big leader," or *capitán grande* in Spanish).

The modern-day Guaranís of the CZC claim that their mburuvichas should be given great respect. Many Guaranís told me that mburuvicha guasus are often descended from families of leaders, somewhat like royalty, and are therefore trained to be thoughtful and humble servants of their people. They are generally elder men, considered to have gained much experience and wisdom. They do not run for office, but rather are called into service by the people who respect them and want to follow them. Furthermore, the leadership model most often invoked by the Guaranís in the CZC was that of the military, a vestige of the reputation the Chiriguano people had as fierce warriors. In the military model, the mburuvicha guasu is the head of the warriors, and he must be obeyed for the good of the group.

The capitán grande of Zona Cruz, Don Álvaro Montero, often referred to himself as the general of the group. "I am their leader, and the youths that work here with me are my *queremba reta*," which he explained were the troops of the bravest soldiers that surrounded the military leader, giving their lives if necessary to protect him. Don Álvaro used this military metaphor in several ways. He often told the story of how in the past, if a queremba failed his leader, he would tell the mburuvicha he was tired and sit down next to a tree. There the leader would cut his throat. This interpellating story seemed to work on the young Guaranís who worked with Don Álvaro, who in private moments spoke to me of the importance of their loyalty to their leader. Don Álvaro also used the image of himself as a fierce military leader ironically. "Yes, I am the brave leader," he told me as we got into his shiny car, "and this is my white stallion with hooves of rubber!" This slightly self-deprecating presentation, which he repeated numerous times for varying audiences, nevertheless reminded the listener of his authority as a reworked modern general.

This model was based in some historical fact. Certainly Guaranís are widely known for their reputation as warriors. One of the main traffic circles in Santa Cruz has a giant statue of El Chiriguano, a muscular Chiriguano Indian armed with bow and arrow and an inscrutable and determined expression (see photo). Driving by the statue one day with Don Álvaro and several of the young team members, he said, "See? A queremba, ready to die for his leader." The CZC office has a small version of El Chiriguano, and he also appears on the logo of the capitanía's office stationery. Warrior imagery abounds. Yet there was also evidence of other attitudes, like the one Don Jesús had expressed, that each Guaraní is independent.

Although the Guaranís of Zona Cruz most often represent the traditional past through this military model, this ignores one fact. Throughout the known history of the Guaraní, there has existed a tension within Guaraní communities between a strongly felt sense of personal and family autonomy, on the one hand, and a respect and need for strong leaders in time of war, on the other hand. Historian Thierry Saignes has noted that "one fundamental principle governs the world of the Chiriguano: the independence of each one in whatever kind of grouping. The testimonies are abundant on this point and do not permit argument: 'each Chiriguano Indian is a king because none recognizes the superiority of the other,' 'each one is lord of himself and respects no one,' 'they do not have king or recognized leader: each group has their *cacique* who is little recognized outside of war'" (Saignes 1982: 79).[6]

Meliá has said that this "free spirit" and the right to make decisions autonomously was integral to the notion of being a Chiriguano. He explains: "If there was a leader, it was for very occasional or particular instances, for concrete cases and things. The authority was retained by the group and its decisions were made known by formal mechanisms, by assemblies, and by informal ones, by the formation of opinion. This structure, anarchist in principle, gives to the Guaraní a great pride and independence before those who try to dominate him" (Meliá 1989: 65).[7] Since it was the group that retained the power, a family or group of families easily abandoned a leader they thought was no longer working in their interests (ibid.: 66). It was the family, or the extended family, that prevailed over the interests of the larger community, but these family heads expressed themselves through the *asamblea*, the real voice of the community. The mburuvicha was simply one member of the assembly, charged by it to carry out certain functions in service to the community (ibid.: 67). Other roles of equal importance were also assigned, such as the *ipaje* (shaman).

Meliá argues that this model began to change as a result of the interference of the Spanish colonial authorities, who for their political needs pushed the "role of *cacique* as a unique and privileged interlocutor, who spoke and made decisions in the name of the people and over it, all of this in the manner of a Spanish captain" (ibid.: 66). The long-term result of this, he says, was an increase in the authoritarianism of the leader and an intimidation of the people, who refused to participate. "The famous *capitanes* of the Cordillera have had more outward influence than inward" (ibid.). As the Bolivian state has expanded its presence in the lives of the indigenous people, the outward role of the mburuvicha has become ever more important as a mediator between the communities and public institutions.

Certainly in the case of the CZC, the need to interact with the greater society is critical in choosing a leader. The leader who held the role of capitán grande during my research, Don Álvaro, had several important attributes in this regard. He spoke Spanish, was a government official in the land reform administration, and knew how the karai political and legal systems work. He had contacts with powerful politicians and was fluent in the idioms of power: he had a cellular phone and knew how to make appointments with officials and whom to take drinking. Although people acknowledged that this "modern" attitude was a main reason for Don Álvaro's election, it nevertheless proved a source of criticism, as I show below.

"Good" and "Bad" Mburuvichas

The most thorough source of information about modern forms of Guaraní leadership in the Cordillera and Izozog areas comes from Bolivian anthropologist Xavier Albó (1990). In the late 1980s, Albó compiled opinions of Guaranís about what makes an ideal mburuvicha.[8] First, according to his informants, leaders should be *hatangatu*, which Albó glosses as "truly strong, valiant, audacious, and without fear of anyone or anything. He [most mburuvichas have been male, although this is beginning to change] should have sufficient bravery to defend his people against their enemies and to encourage his people to go forward" (ibid.: 96).[9] Critical to this is an ability "to know how to look directly or eye to eye at the white people" (*"saber mirar de frente a los karai"*). This implies having the knowledge and courage to deal with the authorities in whatever way is necessary (ibid.: 96–97). Next, the leader should "know how to defend his people," meaning that he "should watch out for his people, be with his community, with his people; that he does not sell himself, nor his people." This implies that he does not take advantage of his position to benefit himself, but rather serves the community (ibid.: 97–98). Finally, he should "give and receive advice," meaning that he should give advice with respect using persuasive oratory skills, and he should listen to elders and others to be able to represent the desires of the community (ibid.: 98–99).

This list describes a certain idealized leadership style, the sort of person that Albó's informants hoped for in a leader. It is important to look beyond the ideal type, however, recognizing that what people say they want in a leader and the behavior they actually accept are often extremely different. In addition, the type of leader one wants may depend on social, economic, or symbolic positions one holds in the village. Contestations over power and meaning exist within any group, and they may affect the choices people make in their leaders. My analysis below of leadership styles in Bella Flor shows precisely this point. Most important, the ideal Albó describes appears as a static and fixed cultural concept, while the evidence shows a continuing tension between strong leaders and autonomy in Guaraní history and important changes in leadership models across time. Unfortunately, Albo's model does not shed light on how and why this seemingly unitary discourse of leadership developed. What about the other critical Guaraní discourse of autonomy and assembly?

Despite this lapse, the history and ethnography in Albó's work goes a long way to answer these questions. For instance, he describes the lives of several modern Guaraní leaders. One was a rebel leader who organized commando raids on karai merchant caravans. Another leader was completely assimilated into karai society and lived like a rich Bolivian *hacendado*. Most interesting is Albó's description of one of the most important regional leaders, Aurelio Aireju, who held the position of mburuvicha of the community of Gran Kaipependi in the Cordillera region from the mid-1950s to 1986. Aireju established what Albó calls a "cacique-patronage scheme," which operated "more for his own benefit than for that of his people" (ibid.: 130). He ordered community members to work for free in farm plots for him and his relatives, charged informal taxes on local production, and entered into corrupt agreements with local ranchers and politicians. Aireju charged community members exorbitant prices for fetching supplies from town or for his intervention with authorities on their behalf. He even used colonial punishment methods, sometimes putting people in stocks or burying them alive. Aireju also exploited his followers in his role as a *capitán-enganchador*, the community leader who recruits people to work in the *zafra* (sugarcane harvest), earning bonuses for each worker recruited and transported to the *zafra*. The people finally stopped accepting this behavior when Aireju was quite old, and he fell from power. Even then, though, he was not dethroned, but allowed to live out his days as capitán grande (ibid.: 130–32).

If Aireju is the ideal "bad" mburuvicha for Albó, Bonifacio Barrientos (known among his followers as Padre) from the Izozog region is the ideal "good" mburuvicha. (He is the father of the current Izozeño leader of the same name.) After escaping the travails of the Chaco war, Barrientos returned to the Izozog, reestablished the region's communities, and restructured the capitanía, allying the upper and lower regions of the Izozog. Most important, Barrientos was seen as a hero for his defense of community lands against the karai, as he prevented the entrance of further colonizers into the area. Although Barrientos was also an enganchador for the zafra, and also made money this way, Albó argues that he was not abusive in the way Aireju was. Instead, these payments to Barrientos were seen in the Izozog as just payment for the long work he did for the community. If the leaders described in this historical view differ so much, what makes a good or bad mburuvicha? The case of Bella Flor shows that such characterizations depend on the political and economic contexts as well as the dominant models of state-Indian relations.

Gathering History in Bella Flor

I constructed this history of Bella Flor by stringing together the narratives of many actors, trying to make sense of the multiple points of view and interests, and especially the meanings the actors gave to events. There was one written account of the community's early history, the 1987 dissertation of British anthropologist C. P. P. Davison, which was based on research carried out in 1985. I relied on this source, particularly about the founding of the first community, Barrio Lindo, but I did my own interviews with most of the people Davison had interviewed. (Only one important actor had died in the meantime.) I also carried out a house-to-house survey in Bella Flor and its neighboring spin-off, El Futuro. Part of this survey was recording individual histories to determine how and why people had come to the communities and what they had done since arriving. Once I had a general idea, I interviewed the most important actors, the leaders and critics. Mostly I asked my neighbors endless questions, comparing peoples' memories. The history I present in this chapter is my synthesis of those narratives, my "narrative of narratives" (Donham 1999: 12), in which I make connections between the many contingencies, positions, and discourses I observed. This story is partial and selective, based on my position in this terribly conflicted community.

My initial contacts with the Guaraní people were through the capitanía, and I was accepted as an observer and student of capitanía life. I spent a great deal of time with capitán grande Don Álvaro, interviewing him at length about his views of the problems in Bella Flor. I often accompanied him in his dealings with various parties and legal institutions. I heard his "side" of the story in Bella Flor, as well as that of the parties he supported in the land use conflict, those with titles. When I began living in Bella Flor, I was introduced as someone working with the capitanía. This was problematic but necessary, because even though there were struggles between the capitanía and the community, it was still critical for me to have entered the village through the "appropriate channels," having respected the indigenous political organizations and their hierarchies.

I sought to find a position within the community that would allow people from both sides of the debate to trust me, so that I could come to a fair understanding of the situation. My entrance into Bella Flor was gradual, through visits to Samuel Tapera and eventually by living with his family in Bella Flor. The critical point about the Tapera family is that they are without title, which means they were part of the group that severely criticized the capitán. Don Jesús Tapera, the head of the family, is the former pastor of the community and is well respected. Thus, although I entered the community seemingly allied with one faction, the trust and affection the Taperas showed me altered my position.

As part of my household survey, I interviewed every family in the community and told all of them that I was talking to parties representing both sides of the conflict. In fact, I believe I was the first person to do so, which seemed interesting to many residents. I mapped the village, crossing lines that the Guaranís themselves no longer crossed. I was invited to village meetings in which the landless complained about the capitán; I was also invited to meetings of the titleholders and their lawyers. I told all parties what I was doing and did not hide my participation on both sides. I was most concerned about not being perceived as a spy for one side or the other. I tried to avoid this by disclosure, which required quite a bit of discretion and tact. Sometimes that did not work. For the most part, however, I believe I was successful. Nevertheless, my position determines my narrative of the following history.

Let me address one other issue relevant to my ability to gather information — my gender. I think that being a woman was often an advantage. Much of my community survey was done during the day, when men were gone and women were at home working. Some women were reticent to talk to me because I was a stranger. But because I was a woman, they often brought me into their domestic spaces, sat me down with a child on my lap, or a *porro* of mate, and talked to me about their families' histories. A male interviewer would not have had such freedom and might have only been able to talk to the men. I, however, was received by both men and women. In fact, I seemed to hold some hybrid role that was functionally both (or maybe neither) male and female. I was allowed into women's spaces and gossip, once I got to know people, but I was also treated like a man in many situations. For instance, on the many occasions of public dinners, like weddings or celebrations, the custom was to have men sit at the table and be served by the women. No matter how much I insisted on helping the women, I was never allowed to do that. Instead, I, *la invitada* (the invited one or guest), was placed at the table with the men.

This special role, no doubt based on my being American or *gringa*, also allowed me to attend endless meetings between male political leaders and have lengthy talks with male capitanes on subjects Guaraní women rarely discussed in public. In fact, because the subjects I was investigating were mostly in the male realm, I spent most of my fieldwork with men. There is no doubt that this access was strategic on the part of some of these men, in that it gave them power to be seen as an associate of an American woman. It is also clear that being a woman placed certain limitations on my research. I sometimes declined invitations to accompany men to male-only situations I found too dangerous or that I thought might cause gossip. Of course I cannot know the situations to which I was not even invited because of my gender. In those cases, a male interviewer would have had access that I did not. Again, these considerations color the following narrative.

Formation of the Guaraní Communities

In the mid-1960s, Guaranís who had come to Santa Cruz in the cane harvest began to form their own communities, taking advantage of the agrarian reform laws in the post-1952 revolution years. Barrio Lindo was one of the first communities founded, just southeast of Santa Cruz. Four individuals applied to the agrarian reform for land and received ten hectares each to found an evangelical Guaraní community.[10] It grew rapidly, as Guaranís from all over the Santa Cruz area and as far as Argentina flocked to the village. Soon it was clear that the forty hectares of Barrio Lindo would not be enough for all the families that had arrived, as that certainly did not provide enough agricultural land to take advantage of the newly opening markets in Santa Cruz.

In 1964, these Guaranís decided to apply for a large plot of land (approximately five hundred hectares) a few kilometers east of Barrio Lindo, in which to form a new and larger community, Bella Flor. Helped by the local Movimiento Nacional Revolucionario (MNR) political organizer, they formed a *sindicato* (a peasants union) and made an application. The sindicato model, in which peasants are organized collectively but receive title individually, had been used widely in highland regions to organize Quechua and Aymara groups. This Western model does not correspond with highland people's historical social organization, however, and many critics now argue that this model was imposed on these groups as a form of social and political control, to incorporate sindicatos and labor federations into political parties (Ströbele-Gregor 1996). Nor was it the historical model for the Guaraní.

From the founding of Bella Flor, there were conflicts about a fundamental issue: how was the land to be held? The answer to this question varied depending on the participants' histories and expectations. There were three camps, each of which expressed a distinct vision of how land should be held. Those who had lived in the Santa Cruz area and had experience with sindicatos expected to get individual titles. This was consistent with the revolutionary image of peasants and poor people owning their own land and becoming part of a national market. Land in this "modern" view is a commodity, which contributes to the landowners' ability to make money.[11] Rural Guaranís from the Cordillera and Izozog areas, however, had lived in villages where land use was an automatic right of community membership (Davison 1987: 162). In this "collective" or "traditional" view, land was not seen as something individuals own, but rather as a part of nature to be used by all the people. A somewhat hybrid approach was held by those who had lived through the Barrio Lindo founding. They expected the Bella Flor process to be similar and to produce a flexible arrangement in which individuals would get title but other Guaranís would be allowed to come to the village and live in a communal or collective way.

The history, and ultimate fate, of Bella Flor revolves around the struggle over which of these visions would prevail. Corresponding to each view of land is a particular discourse, a form of leadership, and, most important, a set of actors likely to benefit from it. It is critical to note that although there were several points of view based on history and experience, certain of these came to be seen as "traditional" as a result of the village's struggles over power and resources.

Don Amalio Vega: The "Traditional" Leader

Despite the fact that various ideas about land tenure coexisted, Barrio Lindo leaders and the agrarian reform officials encouraged the sindicato that was by then operating informally. In 1964, Guaranís broke ground in what would become Bella Flor. In 1965, Don Amalio Vega, a dynamic Guaraní from the Izozog, arrived and in a short time became the community leader, taking charge of the land application process. He was apparently a man of great charisma and personal power.[12] He arrived at an opportune moment and immediately engaged the landowner in a battle for the land, using a leadership style that combined physical fights with the rich landowner, heroic rhetoric, and savvy political alliances, including one with the mburuvicha guasu of the Izozog, Bonifacio Barrientos (hijo). Don Amalio argued for the "collective" view of land, saying that Bella Flor should be a "new Izozog," where all Guaranís could live together in the "traditional" way. His reputation as a brave warrior leader gave him the moral authority to impose his views of tradition on the newly forming migrant community.

Through his political connections, Don Amalio approached the agrarian reform to try to change the application from a sindicato to a corporate indigenous community. The process had apparently gone too far to make such a change, but a compromise was reached that was to have far-reaching implications. The fifty-three members of the sindicato would still receive titles, but instead of receiving individual plots, each would receive a title that named him and all the others. The legal term for this is *proindiviso*, meaning that each owns a share but not a particular share. The idea was to ensure that none of these titleholders could exercise any more control over the land than a community member without title, since they could not point to a particular plot of land they owned. Don Amalio also got the authorities to agree to call him the capitán of the community, the traditional leader, rather than the president, thus in essence changing Bella Flor from a sindicato to an indigenous community. (This was before the 1994 Ley de Servicio Nacional de Reforma Agraria Ley INRA, which formally recognized indigenous territories.) Clearly, he knew the importance of names in the garnering of power.

This compromise resolved many problems, but at the same time it sowed the seeds of great dissension. For the many families who came to Bella Flor after its initial founding, it was fine. They came to the community with the permission of the capitán, built houses, and began farming without having to make any arrangements with landowners. The majority of the people who live in Bella Flor are these latecomers, who naturally were supportive of Don Amalio. The people listed on the title, who are referred to as *titularios*, or titleholders,[13] were less enthusiastic, but most of them went along with Don Amalio because he was able to marshal civil and political authority and begin the improvements necessary for establishing a community, such as a school, a health post, and so on. Just below the surface, however, the old debates lived on, waiting for the appropriate time to be reopened.

Don Amalio enacted his vision of landownership through a combination of personal charisma and the strategic deployment of a discourse about being "traditional." For the migrants in the Santa Cruz area, who made up the large majority of Bella Flor's first residents, he was the embodiment of the traditional capitán. He claimed to know what was traditional and to want to enforce it on these wayward migrants who had been tainted by their contact with the karai, the patrones, and the city. Don Amalio is still held up today as the iconic leader. My friends in Bella Flor described him as a great man, an elder they respected. One friend reverently told me he wished the current leaders had the same great vision as Don Amalio had.

But this so-called traditional vision also had substantial benefits for Don Amalio and his supporters. It established a patronage system in which Amalio had great power, a status that a community of individual landowners would not have provided. It took me some time to discover this part of Don Amalio's leadership style. One of the ways I gathered history was to go back many times to the people who had given me information, to read them what I had written based on what they and others had told me. This never failed to elicit critical information that had not emerged the first time. In my fourth interview with one of the early capitanes, Don Jaime Diego, he finally told me stories about how Don Amalio had exercised his power. I later elicited much the same from other people. It turns out that Amalio's leadership style was very much like that of the "bad" mburuvicha Albó described.

Don Amalio had often enforced his power with physical violence, and he used his position to make money. Don Jaime told me that during the period in which the titles were in La Paz, for example, Amalio had hired a lawyer to work on the case and forced the community members to provide three months of labor as payment for his legal fees. Those who disagreed with this became his enemies, and he tried to get their names taken off the title. When the titles came to the agrarian reform office in Santa Cruz, Amalio tried to get control over them so he could charge the titleholders a fee, but the officials prevented this. For several periods, the people of Bella Flor kicked him out of his role of capitán, putting other community members in his place. Somehow he managed to get back into power until 1980, when the people of the community could no longer tolerate his authoritarian and violent approach. Nevertheless, Don Amalio's "traditional" leadership kept him in power for many years. People with opposing interests were forced to go along with him because he had political connections and the support of one section of the community.

Major cracks appeared in the early 1970s, when several of the titleholders split off from Bella Flor and formed a separate community called El Mangal. By that time, so many families had entered the village that the titleholders felt their rights would soon be impossible to assert. They decided to move their village to the eastern part of the land and to demarcate their land rights.[14] The new community was based more on the old Barrio Lindo model, where titleholders "owned" the land and allowed others to farm on it. Today there continues to be a grudging but widely shared understanding that the El Mangal land is separate from the rest of the parcel. For instance, when I began to live and work in Bella Flor, I asked the Tapera family to help me draw a map of the area so I could orient myself. They did not feel comfortable doing the drawing but told me how it should look. I drew according to their instructions. Together we mapped the city of Santa Cruz, the road out from town, the whole parcel of Guaraní land, and we located the villages of Bella Flor, El Futuro, and El Mangal. Then one of the mapmakers marked a line with his finger, cutting off El Mangal from the rest. "Their land comes to here," he said.

The Encroaching City, Development, and Land Sales

From 1973 until the early 1990s, the two villages remained mostly as they were. Their populations began to grow, and the number of houses increased slowly. Schools and health posts were built in each community, electricity was brought in, and finally potable water reached them. The biggest changes came from outside the villages. Throughout the 1970s and 1980s, the city grew rapidly in the direction of the Guaraní villages, especially after 1983, when the massive city flood resettlement program developed a giant new barrio — Plan Tres Mil (Plan Three Thousand) — on the road out to the villages. As I described in chapter 2, the Plan is a sprawling city within the city, which continues to expand at an amazing rate. Its barrios have reached out to within six kilometers of Bella Flor, and the area between the Plan and Bella Flor is also filling in with settlers.

The rapid growth of Santa Cruz and its markets had big effects on the Guaraní villages nearby. As those markets developed in the mid-1970s, Guaranís in Bella Flor began to try to take advantage of these resources by entering into the commercial agriculture market. In 1975, they formed a farming cooperative and mortgaged community land for a loan. When their projects failed over the following years, they defaulted on their payments, and with interest the debt grew.[15] In 1982, the cooperative made a fateful decision: they sold thirty-three hectares to pay off the debt. It was tragic timing. In the next two days, just as they were receiving the money, the government put into effect emergency measures to curb the by then astronomical inflation, the peso plummeted, and the money they got for the sale could not pay off the debt.

With these sales and loans, however, the debate began again about who owned the land, who had the right to sell it, and what would become of the people living on the land without titles. More important, people saw that the land could in fact be sold, which began the disintegration of whatever sense of unity had existed in the community. From then on, small pieces of land began to be sold off in various ways, and the situation became increasingly complicated. The original title had never been changed, and none of the sales were registered with agrarian reform, so they are probably illegal. This must, though, be seen in the general context of land sales and land titles in Bolivia. The history of land tenure and the resulting jurisprudence is beyond the scope of this book, but without getting into the details, it is fair to say that there is little security or monitoring of titles. When buying land in Bolivia, it is common for several people to appear with "valid" titles and claim ownership. Record keeping is flawed, corruption widespread, and forgery endemic. The way landownership cases are most often resolved is through expensive litigation, where one party is jailed for *estelionato* (fraud) and eventually settles. Money, lawyers, and political connections count as much as legal right. In this context, as Guaranís learned their land was valuable, they found lawyers and buyers who helped them overcome the "obstacles" in the titles. What is "legal" is now hard to understand, and each party has its own perspective, but it is clear that lawyers have played important parts as interlocutors between Guaranís and the state. This continues to be the case, as I describe next.

The Great Divide in Bella Flor

In Bella Flor, this loan-debt-sale process came to a head in the early 1990s. The now defunct cooperative was being pressured again to pay off the loan. A group of titleholders, including the capitán comunal, got together and sold fifty-four hectares, paid off the debt, and cleared about $10,000 each.[16] Other titleholders sold their own land for even more money. Although the majority of the community violently disagreed with these sales, the power had switched to the titleholders, who had money, political connections, and allies in the capitanía.

The sudden infusion of this kind of money into Bella Flor was extremely divisive, creating two entirely separate classes of people in the village of sixty-three houses: those with title and those without. A division was made even more salient when those with titles began to sell land and build new houses next door to their neighbors (see photo). A strictly legalistic ethic might be able to justify the division: either your name is on the title or it is not. In practice, however, the division caused moral indignation to those without title, many of whom had been living in Bella Flor since the time of its founding, or within a few years of it. These Guaranís had migrated to the community partly because they believed they would be able to build a secure future for themselves and their families. Many of the younger generation were born there, as were their children. Those with titles and those without had grown up together and built the community together. A description of two families shows how the land sales affected the two classes differently.

The first family, headed by Oscar Cruz and Angelina Nuñez, had come to Bella Flor within a year of its founding, too late to get their names on the title. In his early fifties during my research period, Oscar had worked on the land all his life, and the sun and effort showed in his leathery face and strong wiry body. He showed me his *chaco* (farm plot) with pride, pointing out the yuca, papaya, beans, and corn he cultivated. Angelina, a cousin of Don Jesús Tapera, in her late forties, was a busy matriarch, supervising the house, her daughters-in-law, and grandchildren when she was not suffering from the frequent fevers that plagued her. Their house, right up the alley from the Tapera family, was a one-room *pahuichi*, a traditional mud and thatch Guaraní house. The endless task of washing, mending, and remending the clothes was always under way, as were the jobs of cooking, gathering firewood, and feeding the animals. Their large family lived mostly on the foods Oscar grew in his chaco, as well as from what he earned selling that food in the market in town. This money was supplemented by his occasional day labor on the nearby farms. When they needed money for the electric bill or for medicines for a sick family member, Angelina went into town to find work washing clothes. Their oldest son, Feliciano, was trained to be a health promoter, but because there was no government money for salary, he farmed as well. A small father-son brick-making business had fallen on hard times, since the firewood necessary for the ovens became scarce as the city grew around them. Finally Feliciano found work in the city as a night watchman for a store.

Although this brought in additional income, Feliciano did not like having to live in the city during the week and to only be able to come home for his day off on Sunday.

The second family, the Diegos, had come to Bella Flor a few years earlier and were named on the title. Jaime Diego, the patriarch, was the capitán comunal for many years after Don Amalio stepped down, and he loved to talk about the community's history. He was a cane grower and a small farmer, like Oscar, but since his family had sold some of the land they owned, Jaime had been able to stop working. During my research period, he spent most of his time under the large mango tree, surrounded by his prosperous family. His five sons, about the same age as Feliciano, built new houses near their father, made of bricks with metal or molded fiberglass roofs. The family bought several cars as well as a large truck for transporting cane. The sons had a fancy four-wheel-drive sports utility vehicle, a silver sports car, and a more modest vehicle they used for a taxi. One son was working as the driver of the truck, bringing in substantial sums. Another son drove the taxi. The Diegos wore expensive clothes such as jeans and athletic shoes, went to parties in the Plan, and traveled around to soccer games on the weekends. The brothers' wives did not work outside their homes and had propane stoves that did not require firewood.

Those families without titles, like Oscar and Angelina, feared that sooner or later, the titleholders would sell all of the land, and they would have no recourse to force the issue politically since they had no titles and no money. This was the source of a great deal of anguish, as the people had nowhere else to go and no resources to fall back on to buy new lands. I attended many village meetings in which person after person decried the situation as unjust and unfair. At one meeting, Oscar cried, "We have lived here all our lives, and now our *hermanos* [literally "brothers" but in this case referring to a fellow believer] are throwing us out! How can they call themselves Christians?" Others echoed his complaints. After this meeting, Oscar took me back to his house to show me the receipts of nearly thirty years of electric bills. He held them in his gnarled hands, icons to prove the truth of his claim before any just judge. "This is our home, too!"

In a short period, many Bella Flor families began to stop farming, saying they believed it was too risky to invest more time and money into their chacos if at any moment the land could be sold out from under them. This fear and the continued land sales completely altered the village. In 1998, 81 percent of families relied on farming for their own consumption, and 63 percent sold products on the market. By 2000, not one family in Bella Flor was continuing to farm.[17] Although there are some wealthy families with trucking and taxi businesses like the Diegos, the majority has been absorbed into the urban economy like Oscar's son, as taxi drivers, domestic workers, construction workers, and manual laborers. Their main resource — the land — had been appropriated by a small portion of the community.

Enter Rafael Vaca, the Guaraní Entrepreneur

The sale of the community's land did not go uncontested, however. The main champion for the dispossessed of Bella Flor was the vociferous Rafael Vaca, an evangelical pastor who advocated "traditional" landownership and railed against the leaders and titleholders of Bella Flor. At *asambleas*, in public meetings like the one described at the beginning of this chapter, and in interviews with me, Don Rafael argued that the leaders of Bella Flor had lost their way and were betraying the Guaraní people. In 1995, as a form of protest, Don Rafael and his followers moved out of Bella Flor and formed a third community, El Futuro, about a kilometer away from Bella Flor. Vaca became El Futuro's capitán and pastor.

Like Don Amalio Vega, Don Rafael has a positive and commanding presence. He is a big man, half Guaraní and half karai, with a big smile with a gold tooth right in front. His wife is a dour, reserved woman from the Izozog, strong in her faith and her belief in discipline. They have grand visions, starting with their large family of handsome sons and daughters. Seeing that the land around them was getting sold off, they decided to get in on it and start a Guaraní enterprise run by the Vaca family. Don Rafael convinced his followers in El Futuro that he had their best interests at heart and that they should leave it all up to him. He ran the village in a top-down manner, calling himself the capitán grande of El Futuro. (According to most other Guaranís, this term should be reserved for the leader of a federation of villages.)

The people of El Futuro seemed to respect and fear Don Rafael, and they were careful not to cross him or his plans. Therefore, during the time I was there doing the surveys, El Futuro had a character that was quite different from Bella Flor. The people were banded together as dissidents, having cast their fates in with Don Rafael and his family. Some resented his authoritarian dealings, but having come onto his team, there was no easy way out. Moreover, Don Rafael brought several new families into the village to bolster his position. These were Guaranís from the Izozog or elsewhere, who had some long-lost interest in one of the titles but had never lived in Bella Flor until then. He also invited a non-Guaraní family who served as his *caseros* (caretakers) on other lands he owned. This mongrel mix had strange and ironic results: although Don Rafael claimed to be maintaining the "traditional" Guaraní ways, he also introduced a number of people into the community who do not speak Guaraní and did not intend to learn it.

Similarly, despite all his previous rhetoric about the selling of land being unethical and against the traditional Guaraní way, Don Rafael and his sons formed a land sales company. The other titleholders had sold big plots to one buyer. Don Rafael saw this as foolish and shortsighted. Why sell the land to a rich person who would then turn it around and sell it in urban lots for a huge profit? Instead, Don Rafael and his company made a plan for the sale of the whole five hundred hectares, a new urban housing development neighborhood, and began selling urban lots for $1,200 each. It was to be called the Ciudadela Guaraní, the Guaraní Citadel. His grand plan included saving the Guaraní villages, upgrading the housing there, and incorporating the rest of the land into the growing city of Santa Cruz.[18] I visited his land sales office in the Plan one afternoon. There were colorful maps on the walls and handsome brochures advertising the future of the region.

Don Rafael was savvy and he knew that he would have to have support from a lot of people in the community to pull this off. So he made an alliance with the disenfranchised Guaranís of Bella Flor as well as his own people in El Futuro. He called a meeting and offered those without titles in Bella Flor a piece of the action. They, too, could sell their *patrimonio* (patrimony), by which he meant their right of possession under the agrarian reform law, in exchange for interest in the company. This was a good deal for the people because patrimonio is a potential that would only have cash value once the government made a settlement that validated and valued residency. Given the way the INRA process was going, this looked extremely unlikely. In exchange for their patrimonio and their compliance, Don Rafael promised they would get money and materials to upgrade their houses. The large group agreed and signed a document giving Don Rafael their permission to carry out the urbanization plan.

On the surface, this industrious scheme had many merits. It was all to be done without any funding from outside organizations, and it offered a great deal of hope to the young Guaranís who didn't just want to become part of the urban poor. It took the land that was their "right" and converted it into businesses and more land. And it was an all-Guaraní-run enterprise, something of which the people were extremely proud. Even from the beginning, though, the scheme also had huge downsides. First, the land they sold or traded was not clearly theirs to sell. Just as the other titleholders could not be sure which land was theirs to sell, neither could Don Rafael. Nevertheless, with lawyers arguing for him, he began to sell lots anyway. Second, this scheme was totally controlled by Don Rafael and his sons. There was no transparency in the business deals, and people were too scared of him to demand it. Although Don Rafael had a reputation in the village for dubious dealings, the people without title saw him as their only hope. So they followed him and worked for him regardless of their lack of trust. This proved to be disastrous. Everyone watched as Don Rafael amassed more and more money, building himself a big new house in the Plan, giving his sons new trucks and well-paying jobs in the business, and generally living big. Resentment and accusations began flying, but for several years the people of El Futuro stayed with him.

Why? Don Rafael Vaca compellingly combined a number of leadership models to convince his followers of his authenticity and power. First, he used both sides of the "traditional" leader tension. On the one hand, he asserted his ideas and his authority as the capitán/patrón, and even more than Don Amalio had, Don Rafael took full advantage of his position to make money at the expense of his followers. On the other hand, he claimed autonomy and independence from other leaders, rebelling and forming his own village. He also loudly criticized the capitanía for its relations to NGOs, saying the present leaders had lost the traditional independence of the Guaraní, which only Don Rafael and his followers understood. (In chapter 5, I discuss more fully the debate over NGO-funded dependence.) He was an expert at managing a discourse of communal harmony and tying that back to so-called traditional notions of reciprocity and unity.

Second, Don Rafael Vaca enacted the role of the evangelical pastor, a crucial road to power in evangelical communities, where most of the community members are believers who owe special respect and deference to their religious leaders. Don Rafael assumed this position, using his substantial oratory skills to claim his enemies were immoral, greedy, or sinners. He controlled the community partly through the regulation of church services and the *culto* (bible services) that are held Tuesday and Thursday nights. Don Rafael was thus the community's religious father, with all the beneficence and paternalism that such a position implies. I attended a wedding in El Futuro in which he and his wife were the *padrinos* (sponsors) of the wedding. They walked the bride and groom down the aisle, provided food for the whole community, and then Don Rafael presided over the service. Even the music was under his control: he managed a Guaraní evangelical mariachi band called La Buenas Nuevas (The Good News) that played at the wedding. In this interesting twist, "tradition" is a blend of Guaraní custom and Christian authority.

Most important, Don Rafael emulated Bolivian politicians of the post-1952 revolutionary clientelist system. Many Guaranís told me their leaders needed to be connected with politicians to obtain indigenous access to those resources and services they need. Don Rafael managed this role well, bringing officials to the village, showing his proximity to power. Although community members had grave doubts about Don Rafael because of the many power grabs he had carried out over the years, he offered to be their savior, to protect them and their land. This is what the good mburuvicha is "supposed" to do, so the people, who very much needed protection, accepted his leadership for a time.

Don Rafael Vaca's discourse played on yet another cultural narrative, although he certainly did not allude to it openly, as far as I know. Throughout the history of Guaraní resistance to the Spanish, at times of great despair, a person or prophet would rise up and issue a call to the people to leave the lands and go in search of the Tierra Sin Mal (see Meliá 1988: 23). These prophets claimed to be *hombres-tumpa* (god-men), and they would give oracular messages from God showing the way to return to the Guaraní's traditional and virtuous path. The last great such prophet was Hapiaoeki Tumpa, who had led his people to the terrible massacre of Kuruyuki in 1892 (Pifarré 1989: 373ff). Although Don Rafael did not ever openly make such claims, I suggest that his leadership may have appealed to the people, in part, because it echoed the prophets' call. As part of the Guaraní enterprise, for instance, Don Rafael bought some land several hundred kilometers from the city. He talked a group of young people, whose prospects seemed dim, into going out to the land to work it for several seasons without pay. When their harvest was sold, he promised, the proceeds would go to establishing a new prosperous community for them. Naturally, the proceeds were small and went into Don Rafael Vaca's pockets.

Questioning the Legitimacy of the Capitán Grande

Because Bella Flor was one of the founding villages in the capitanía, it had a great deal of influence over the rest of the villages in the regionwide assemblies. One important impact of the Bella Flor situation was to call the legitimacy of the leadership of the capitán grande into question.

In 1995, when Don Álvaro Montero was elected capitán grande of the CZC, the local authorities asked him to step in to try to resolve the Bella Flor land problem. He already knew about the struggle, as it was discussed in detail at the asamblea of the capitanía at which he was elected. Several members of Bella Flor had warned him about this conflict, telling him it would be one of the most difficult issues facing the capitanía. Don Álvaro was especially suited for just this sort of decision making, however, as he had worked with the agrarian reform department for many years. Shortly after his election, he called for a meeting of all the parties and named a commission of community members, made up of both titleholders and nontitleholders and including some of the village's most esteemed members, such as the local capitán and the pastor. Some people argued that Don Álvaro's previous experience made him predisposed to favor those with titles and to work toward a solution in which those who held valid titles would get their land, but he had also worked for years with La Federación del Norte, a federation of peasant farmers who had taken over land under the agrarian reform laws. Don Álvaro's job had been to help those peasants obtain titles to the land.

The Bella Flor meeting broke down in a mass of accusations. Some of the people claiming to hold titles did not have them. Others had obviously false documents. Still others had given their titles to other Guaranís to hold and administer for them, creating confusion. Don Rafael Vaca led the fight against the titleholders (even though he controlled the title of his wife's father and several others). He argued that selling the land was wrong and against everything that Bella Flor stood for. He and others claimed the whole meeting was a sham, and that the capitán grande had been bought off by the titleholders to decide the case on their behalf. The accusations were bitter and ugly, and no resolution seemed possible. Don Álvaro told me that although he tried to find a solution, he refused to intervene in a Guaraní-Guaraní fight. He says he told the people it was up to the law now to decide who had title. If the people were not willing to compromise their differences, he recalled, the only solution was to turn the case over to the agrarian reform offices and let them decide.

The titleholders hired lawyers and the case went before the INRA. (The meeting with which I opened this chapter was one step in the INRA decision process.) Over the years I followed the case, the two sides became increasingly bitter and Don Álvaro refused to act as a mediator. Instead, he often met with the titleholders and their lawyers. Accusations that he had been bribed by them circulated across the federation, yet he always denied this. He said only the law could resolve the case, so it was understandable that he followed the legal process. Nevertheless, he was widely perceived as having taken the titleholders' side, the side of those who were benefiting from urbanization and the growing market in Santa Cruz.[19]

The fact that Don Álvaro chose this solution reopened the larger question of what was a good mburuvicha in contemporary times. His leadership was a reflection of the transition the Guaraní faced as they incorporated into the politics of multicultural indigenous Bolivia. That is, the context in which Don Álvaro was forced to exercise his leadership style required him to tack back and forth between models: the warrior leader, the local politician, and the corporate administrator. On the one hand, he held himself out to be the "general" of the capitanía. This was accomplished both through his management of the discourse of "tradition" — using the military metaphors and Guaraní titles — and through such practices as his hierarchical relationships with the younger members of the technical team, his habit of "holding court" in the office, and his role at assemblies. This overtly "indigenous" leadership style was important to the capitanía's efforts to revitalize its cultural identity in multicultural Bolivian politics.

On the other hand, however, Don Álvaro was chosen for his ability to operate within the "modern" world of the karai, to maximize the ability of the capitanía's members to obtain and preserve resources. Under the influence of NGOs and outside funding, he and his technical team attempted to run the capitanía as a corporate entity, following the logic and practices of the karai world. As I discuss in chapter 5, under this model the indigenous leader is essentially an administrator, acting as a facilitator between institutions of the state, NGOs, the community, and constituent indígena citizens. Thus it was enormously beneficial to the capitanía as a whole to have a leader function in this new sphere, but the fights in Bella Flor showed the tensions this created for some Guaranís. Here we see the articulations between the politics of recognition and the politics of redistribution. Because he had to be in good standing with such institutions to be able to channel potential resources through NGOs and state agencies, the capitán had little choice but to pay attention to karai laws and institutions. In fact, I often heard Don Álvaro speak about this in meetings in the communities, to encourage his people to understand the changes: "We can no longer deal with problems as we did in our fathers' times. Then the mburuvicha would simply order those in error to be tied to a tree." Usually the people laughed nostalgically at that point, as did the capitán. "Now, we must submit to the karai laws." Nevertheless, it was just this abdication that got him in trouble with his constituents in Bella Flor.

Interestingly, this tension echoes that found in early Guaraní leadership models between the desire for autonomous community members with a strong voice in the assembly, on the one hand, and the need for a strong leader to work for community interests in time of war or threat, on the other. When Don Álvaro abdicated to the karai systems of conflict resolution, in essence refusing to be the strong warrior leader fighting to protect his people, he became suspect to those who needed his intervention and advocacy. To those whose interests were being met, however, such as the "autonomous" titleholders and leaders of Bella For who were making money from the land sales, Don Álvaro's failure to intervene in their business appeared appropriate and "traditional." Once again, we see how "tradition" is strategically deployed regardless of historical accuracy.

The crisis in Bella Flor would have benefited from a leader who could have bridged the gap between the severely divided factions, but Don Álvaro was not able to balance the multiple roles required of him to do so. Many times, the people of Bella Flor asked him to take on that role, to protect them, to protect the land. But although he used the rhetoric of the warrior, his actions were that of the administrator who followed the karai laws and the politician who made money when his clients' interests were met. In this case, Don Álvaro used the discourse of the traditional mburuvicha to maintain the respect and obedience of the communities and the technical staff, but he was unable or unwilling to rework it sufficiently to produce the kind of cultural or political power necessary to confront the crisis. Collective land was part of the rhetoric surrounding his warrior leader image, but ultimately under his leadership Bella Flor's land came to be a commodity to be administered within the context of the market. In essence, although he enacted a so-called traditional Guaraní leadership role for the benefit of the outside, such as the NGOs and the state, he was not traditional enough for Bella Flor's poor. As a result, no one was ever totally satisfied with him.[20]

Nevertheless, Don Álvaro kept his leadership for the same reason all the other leaders I have described did — not because he was the guardian of tradition, but because he served enough interests to maintain power. Despite his opposition from Bella Flor, Don Álvaro and his technical team had managed to gather enough grants from NGOs to keep the capitanía afloat. There were small development projects in some communities. But mostly, he managed to maintain an image of political power that convinced enough people that he would help them get what they needed to survive. Don Álvaro was a member of Acción Democrática Nacional (ADN, National Democratic Action), the political party in power. General Hugo Banzer Suárez, then president of Bolivia, was the head of ADN, and Don Álvaro often showed a picture of himself at Banzer's side from his early days in politics. At the 1998 assembly in Warnes, a midsize city to the north of Santa Cruz, Don Álvaro got several of his political allies to make an appearance at the meeting. The mayor of Warnes came with his armed bodyguards. The regional *subprefecto*, a sort of lieutenant-governor, a well-known wealthy rancher (picture a Bolivian Lorne Greene), came to the meeting, threw his arms around Don Álvaro, and said he was delighted to be here with his good friend. He then pledged to be of whatever help he could to the capitanía. "My door is always open to you!" This was proof of a critical ally at the governmental level. (This was pure theater, of course. As the next chapter shows, today's Guaranís remain excluded from most political participation.)

A New Leader

Throughout 1998 and 1999, the land sales continued and the city began to push its way into the communities. Barbed-wire fences and wide roads cut into the farmland between the villages, connecting the highway and an adjacent housing development that had grown to several thousand units. The new owners of lots within the community, mostly *kollas* (highlanders), began to build brick and wood houses on their lots. Large signs posted in fields advertised new subdivision sales. Slowly, people gave up fighting about whether the urbanization should happen or not. It seemed beyond their control, so they tried to join in gathering the benefits. Many of those who had been vehemently opposed to such things joined the fray.

Oscar Cruz and Angelina Nuñez, the family without title described earlier in this chapter, are a good example. They had supported Don Rafael Vaca and the local capitán who followed him. Their son-in-law was especially anti-capitanía and had given several impassioned speeches about his betrayal. When I visited them in 1999, I was amazed to see what was going on. Their mud house had been converted into a store, and behind it a new brick house was being built. Angelina looked beautiful; it took me a minute to notice that she had new prosthetic teeth covering the gap that I had learned to consider normal. Her daughter had new teeth too. They had a new propane stove in the cooking house, and when they offered me some mate they brought out a thermos with water that had been heated on propane instead of the blackened kettle heated from embers. I congratulated them on their good fortune and walked around looking at everything with them.

What had happened? Oscar had found one of the original titleholders who no longer lived in the area and made some sort of a deal with him to take over his title and share some of the benefits. They had sold several hectares of land, and with it had bought the materials for the house, the new teeth, and a car for their son-in-law to drive to bring in additional money for the family. The store in the old house brought in even more money. And to top it off, they were selling part of their house lot too, to a man from the city. Not only were the outsiders coming into the community, in this case they would be a matter of meters away, building a house right next door. It was telling that the leaders of the resistance had so completely, and without irony, joined the land sales rush.

In August 1999, the people of El Futuro finally tired of Don Rafael Vaca and threw him out of the community. One night, Jorge López, a young man who had been one of Don Rafael's employees, picked up the capitán grande to take him to El Futuro in his new Landcruiser, and I hitched a ride. Jorge was to be elected the new capitán. The *ceremonia de posesión*, the formal ceremony giving the new capitán possession of his new role, was held in the large yard of Doña Elba, the head of a large family, and witnessed by the capitanes from nearby communities, lawyers for all the parties, and all the neighbors. Doña Elba gave an emotional speech about how Don Rafael Vaca had taken all of their sweat and work and put it in his pockets. Apparently, the problems resulting from Don Rafael's schemes had finally become too great and the "corruption" too obvious or too extreme.[21]

Don Jesús Tapera of Bella Flor explained how he had found out that Don Rafael had managed to put all the land in his own name and was using the community's permission to urbanize for his own purposes. When this got around, people got mad, organized, and hired a lawyer, Jaime Fernández, who had promised to represent them for free. Don Jesús motioned to Fernández, a handsome white man in expensive cowboy boots, who smiled proudly. Then, Don Jesús continued, the community retook the land, setting up roadblocks into the land. Resentful that Don Rafael had benefited so much from the sales, the community members began negotiating with the buyers who were still paying for their lots to start making their payments to the community instead of to Don Rafael.[22]

With that, a quick election was held to validate the decision already made in favor of Jorge López. The capitán grande gave a speech welcoming the community back into the capitanía (it had withdrawn during Don Rafael's leadership), formally addressing the new *mesa directiva* (governing council) that had been elected with the new capitán. The elected made the sign of the cross with their thumbs and first fingers and vowed their loyalty to the community. Then Victor Román, the current president of the Confederación Indígena del Oriente de Bolivia (CIDOB), the national indigenous federation, a grim-faced Guaraní from Camiri, addressed the crowd. "Congratulations," he said to the happy group. "But," he warned harshly, "you must beware, because in other communities, the lawyers who have promised to help have ended up owning everything." When the party began and the barbequed pork (pig courtesy of lawyer Fernández) was served, Fernández approached Don Victor, saying, "No, I am not like that. I am here to serve the people." Don Victor eyed him dourly: "Time will tell" ("El tiempo verá"), he said.

Don Victor had reason to worry. Although López became the official capitán, in many aspects the karai lawyer Fernández took over as the real leader of the community. Fernández made his fortune importing and reselling used vehicles (like Don Álvaro's transformer) and from land sales in boomtown Santa Cruz. He had purchased titles in El Futuro (eleven hectares) and Bella Flor (thirty hectares), which he began to subdivide and sell for a large profit over the next few years. He also received some land in exchange for legal services. In a short time, Fernández assumed the role formerly held by Don Rafael: he became the community's new patrón. At the public meetings, he had said he would represent the people without payment, because of the injustice Vaca had perpetrated on them. Then he fronted the money necessary for the legal case, making him the new hero of the communities, the leader who would confront the legal authorities on the people's behalf. Moreover, Fernández began using the same economic tactics that had made Don Rafael so popular. First, he loaned his four-wheel-drive vehicle to the community and paid for gas. Then he began giving vehicles to the important people in the "revolution" against Don Rafael, such as Jorge López and Don Jesús Tapera. This would be an "advance" against the money they would make when they won the case, he said. So just as when Don Rafael was in power, those close to the patrón got vehicles and ways out of poverty.

When I asked Don Jesús about these parallels, he agreed this was the same way Don Rafael had exploited the community, but once again people were willing to go along with this because they had realized that the land was slipping out of their hands. They would never get what was their due even if they won the case because there were already people living on the land and Don Rafael already had the money. "The only thing we can do," he said, "is get our land's value in these small ways, through vehicles we can put to work, and perhaps through the money the lot buyers will pay us. What choices do we have?"

During a trip to the communities in January 2000, I interviewed the lawyer Fernández about his role in the communities. I had seen him the Sunday before in the community, driving with his wife in their brand-new four-wheel-drive vehicle, stopping to talk to the villagers who had flagged him down. Fernández told me about his life and why he was involved with the Guaraní. He was raised in a poor family in Santa Cruz and was a street vendor, he said, so he understood the misery of being poor. Now, he said, he "could not continue to live in a world with so much pain." "The people here don't have the head for these things [*no tienen cabeza*], I have to help them, to guide them [*orientarles*]. They are put off [*postergados*] and forgotten, and I want to raise them up." Unlike Don Rafael, Fernández said he was working for the interest of society, to "help them fight for what is theirs." Granted, others have said the same thing, but "they have come broke, but I come with money, capital in service to the community." He also has long-term aspirations: one day he hopes to be the *diputado Guaraní* (roughly, "the Guaraní's senator"), representing all the Guaranís of the Chaco region.

In this way, Fernández, the white lawyer-cum-Guaraní leader, played the role of the reconfigured "enlightened patrón" who saves the poor indigenous people from poverty, inability, and abandonment. The paternalism hardly needs historical reference but is, unfortunately, all too reminiscent of the missionaries of previous centuries (see Pifarré 1989). Fernández also used the rhetoric of poverty alleviation and development NGOs, naming the indigenous groups as underdeveloped and needy (see Ferguson 1994; Escobar 1995). Like the other leaders, he tied his leadership to the land, but in his case he promised to save the people through purchasing the land and giving them some limited benefits. Why were the people attracted by this new pseudo-leader? The answer may be as simple as the fact that Fernández had money and some power and appeared willing to share these assets in a time when the Guaranís really needed them. The fact that he is a lawyer is critical. Throughout Bella Flor's history, lawyers have played key roles as mediators with the Bolivian institutions, especially when it comes to land. If the good mburuvicha protected the community's land, the good modern-day mburuvicha should be a lawyer who can manipulate the land-tenure process. Don Álvaro had been forced to tack back and forth between a rhetoric privileging collective land and practices that worked exactly to the contrary. In the context of rapid urbanization, Fernández did not have to make such compromises.

In December 1999, Don Rafael Vaca managed to get the new capitán and Fernández jailed, charged with interfering with his land and with assault. The Guaranís and Fernández all claimed that Don Rafael had bribed the prosecutors to bring this about. Three hundred Guaranís from the six suburban Guaraní communities marched with placards to the police station, and after several days of political pressure, the two men were released. Mutual claims of bribery and death threats flew. Meanwhile, the outsiders who bought the lands continued to move in at a rapid rate.

The City Takes Over

Over the next few years, the legal case continued but the conflict in the community finally settled down, as the inevitable urbanization continued. A settlement was finally reached among some of the Guaranís. The people who threw in their lot with lawyer Jaime Fernández received some parcels in the new urbanized areas that they could hold onto or sell to the new neighbors, almost all of whom are from the highlands. Don Rafael Vaca continued his fight but did not come onto the lands, where he was not welcome. Fernández continued to develop the area and made an enormous amount of money. Although some of his followers named a Guaraní cultural center after him, most Guaranís do not consider him a trustworthy ally, but rather a rich camba who took advantage of their troubles. "Yes, he gave us lots," said Don Jesús Tapera, "but he never gave us the titles. So that makes it very hard to sell the lots."

In 2004, the communities looked entirely different. The once separate Guaraní communities had become part of a huge suburban housing development. Several bus lines travel from Plan Tres Mil to the communities, which by then had more than five thousand inhabitants. There were markets and two new schools as well as several restaurants. Women sold fried chicken and empanadas at the bus stops. There were bars and *chicherías* (the locales where highland women sell their corn-based liquor) and several video game arcades. A few beauty shops advertised from the patios of the houses. The original Guaraní neighborhoods were still somewhat identifiable by the remaining *pahuichis*, but many dwellings had been replaced by brick houses.

When I visited in the summer of 2004, the Taperas told me they hoped that their small landholdings would help their family to get ahead. Don Jesús, who had supported Fernández against Don Rafael, received twenty-four lots in the settlement. His three oldest sons — Samuel, Miguel, and Tuto — each received three lots.[23] They have sold a few, but they assured me it was not enough to get rich. First is the problem that they don't have the legal titles, and this may never be resolved. Also, the new buyers put down a small amount of cash and pay the rest in monthly payments. As most of the buyers are poor, the payments are not very secure, and often months pass without any income. But, said Don Jesús, "we understand each other, and we know we will eventually get *algito* [some little something]." The Taperas' mud and thatch house had not been replaced, but a large stack of red bricks awaited. "When we get some cash . . . ," they said. The oldest son, Miguel, and his wife had a new brick house in El Futuro, and they had bought a used radio transmitter along with all the equipment necessary for running a small radio station. Their Radio Guaraní transmitted twenty-four hours a day on a short bandwidth, playing popular dance music, Mexican music, and, two hours a day, an all-Guaraní program hosted by Don Jesús Tapera. Miguel's ten-year-old son acted as the radio operator on the day I stopped in.

Things were not all rosy, however. Many Guaranís had already spent all their money. Miguel Tapera looked to be in danger of doing just that. The radio station was not making money yet, as advertisers were few for a station with such a small broadcast area. He spent a lot of money on drink, as his wife and family told me uncomfortably. His swollen dissolute face verified their accounts. This was, sadly, not unexpected. When the first land sales started in 1997 in El Mangal, the same thing happened. Guaranís with little experience with cash quickly spent their money on booze, parties, and cars. Soon they found they didn't have the money to repair the cars. My friends from Bella Flor would shake their heads as we passed by the sad sight of a car stalled, getting dirtier as the dust storms passed over. "We don't have the custom" ("No tenemos costumbre"), Don Jesús would lament, meaning that the people are not accustomed to handle this kind of money. "They are going to lose everything" ("Van a perder todo").

In Bella Flor, the changes were a little less sudden, so perhaps the risk of economic ruin is less. The changes in village life, though, were difficult for the Guaranís to handle. Doña Susana, Jesús's wife, complained about the teenagers. "Pot smokers" ("Son pitilleros"), she said, "They do drugs and play video games all night. The parents tried to shut down the video game store, because so many kids were going there, missing school." Their son Tuto was beaten up by a gang of kolla kids who stole his money, probably to buy alcohol. "There is a lot of fighting," Doña Susana said, "the gangs

rob people and their houses." Neighbors told me Tuto is also involved in such
activities and has started sniffing glue. This sort of atmosphere has changed
the behavior of Guaraní teenagers. Few now go to culto, the religious meetings that were so highly attended only a few years ago. Now the Guaraní kids
hesitate to speak Guaraní and get teased for being Indians. When asked, they
often say their parents are Guaraní but they aren't.

The changes reflect a simple fact: these are no longer "Guaraní communities." Their customs and organization are peripheral to the life of this busy
and growing suburban neighborhood. Accordingly, Guaraní leadership, the
capitanía, has been replaced. Guaranís are no longer the majority in the
neighborhood, and their capitanía is no longer eligible to be the official
territorial-based organization (OTB) that mediates between the residents and
the city under the Law of Popular Participation (LPP). (Chapter 4 describes
how this new law works.) Now the neighborhood is represented by a *junta
vecinal* (JV), a neighborhood association run by the kolla and camba neighbors. Guaranís may participate in the JV, but their interests as Guaranís are
not an overarching issue. The capitanía and the JV occasionally collaborate
in making requests to the municipality, but this is mostly symbolic. The JV
has the political power in the community now. This is not all bad: as a result
of the JV's efforts, electric lines from the city come all the way to the community, and the water collective in the Plan has extended its services. Now
all lots in the entire parcel have water and electricity.

While I was there in the summer of 2004, Don Jesús Tapera took me to
visit the new president of the JV. As we walked through the neighborhood,
Don Jesús greeted his neighbors. "This lady's son is paying me for a *lotecito*
[a little lot]," he said, "and that man over there is paying Samuel for his lot.
Así estamos viviendo [That is how we are living]." The president, Juan Otero,
is a tall, kind-faced man from Cochabamba, who runs a big cantina a few
blocks away from the Tapera household. He told me the neighbors get along
well with the Guaranís, who are just another part of this urban barrio. "The
Guaranís have no choice," he said, "they have to integrate themselves with
us." He told me the barrio had been organizing. They had already staged several mobilizations to get their needs met, one to get the transportation union
to put in another bus line and another for increased security for the residents.
"We have to mount these *bloqueos* [road blockades]," he said. "If we just
file papers, we are forgotten."

Walking home, Don Jesús summed up the situation in Bella Flor. "It's just
as I predicted — our Guaraní community has disappeared. The Guaraní are
full of envy and are divided amongst themselves." This, he says, is the fault
of the leaders, who failed their people. The result is that the capitanía has
lost all force and has fallen into corruption, while the leaders try to pocket
money on whatever projects they can.

Narratives of Leadership in Changing Contexts

The case of Bella Flor points out that notions of indigenous representation and participation have always been complex and contested constructions influenced by state institutions and conflicting discourses. As in many previous eras, Indian leadership models were determined by and articulated with a political economy of the land. The history of Bella Flor's land-tenure process has shown how Indian leaders have adapted and reworked their roles in various eras. After the revolution, the Bella Flor Guaranís acted as campesinos to receive the land for the community and set up a cooperative farming project. During the 1990s, Bella Flor became an indigenous community, under the leadership of the capitanía. In the context of rapid economic and social change in boomtown Santa Cruz, the leaders of Bella Flor made strategic use of a variety of culturally acceptable narratives about land and leadership, merging traditional Guaraní notions of the good mburuvicha with the karai patrón/politician. None of these models is inherently good or bad. Under each system of leadership, some people benefited and some people did not. Ultimately, the newest model privileges powerful strongmen, who sold what was thought of by most Guaranís as collective lands on the market. The result is that today suburban Guaranís are torn about what makes a successful leader, which leaves them open to corruption and clientelism and ultimately to negotiation of land as a commodity. Again, some benefited and others did not.

This, too, has historical echoes. In the colonial period, bad *kurakas* (leaders) profited from their intermediary role with the Crown, taking advantage of their power to amass lands and businesses. In the *sindicato* period after the revolution, peasants union leaders were co-opted by the strong patron state. It is not surprising that Indian leaders and their followers play into the interests of those more powerful than they are. An important way in which this is accomplished is by the diffusion and strategic use of particular narratives of leadership that are tied to particular schemes of state-Indian relations. Although these are always negotiated and contested, the case of Bella Flor shows that this sort of innovation does not always result in empowerment or inclusion. In the cases of Don Amalio Vega and Don Rafael Vaca, we saw a melding of the "traditional" warrior model with the patrón model from Bolivian corporatist politics. For the most part, these merely reproduced the inequalities that continue to structure Bolivia. Don Álvaro Montero attempted an additional change, blending the multicultural indigenous model with the neoliberal corporate officer model. Although this creative form of leadership was successful to some degree at the federation level, at the local level the tensions inherent in this mixture essentially paralyzed the capitán. For the people of Bella Flor, faced with a runaway boomtown economy, a leader whose representation was marked by a politics of recognition and a cooperation with the market economy was insufficient to save their lands.

This chapter has described one community struggling with the meaning of indigenous identity and leadership as they faced rapid urbanization. Leadership became a critical issue for all Indian communities during the political reforms of the 1990s, when Indians were invited to participate in politics at the municipal level through a new scheme of citizenship and political participation. Chapter 4 looks at this issue, as I examine the effects of the Law of Popular Participation in multicultural Bolivia.

Part **2**

CITIZENSHIP IN NEOLIBERAL BOLIVIA

4 Multiculturalism and the Law of Popular Participation

> Bolivia, free, independent, sovereign, multiethnic, and pluri-
> cultural, constituted as a united republic, adopts representa-
> tive and participatory democracy as its form of government,
> founded in the union and solidarity of all Bolivians.
> — Article 1 of the Bolivian Constitution

Hailed by the Man in the Hat

In April 1998, the Vice Ministro de Asuntos Indígenas y Pueblos Originarios (VAIPO, Bolivia's Vice Ministry of Indigenous and Original Peoples
Affairs) sent a team of its officials to the Santa Cruz headquarters of the
Confederación Indígena del Oriente de Bolivia (CIDOB), the national federation of indigenous people. The VAIPO team was carrying out a diagnostic
of the women of various lowland indigenous groups to see what kinds of
training would be most helpful for them. On this day, they met with female
representatives from Guaraní communities around the city. Also invited were
the capitanía's male leaders and the young members of the Equipo Técnico
Zonal (ETZ), the technical team that helps the capitán grande. Celia, the
head of the VAIPO team, agreed I could sit in.

The day began with a short workshop led by Arturo López, one of the
ETZ members. He spoke about the International Labor Organization's
Convention No. 169, which Bolivia had adopted in June 1997. As I
described in chapter 1, this international treaty lays out a series of human
rights that indigenous peoples should be given by nation-states and becomes
domestic law when adopted by particular countries.[1] After Arturo explained
the treaty, he encouraged his audience to fight for their rights as indigenous
people, keeping in mind that Bolivia had signed the convention. Celia clarified his talk with a few points. She told the Guaranís that as a result of the
ratification of this international law, two basic concepts of state-indigenous
relations have appeared. The first is respect. Bolivia must respect indigenous
people, their culture organizations, and especially their identity. Who will be
considered indigenous? The fundamental criteria, she said, will be "consciousness of your indigenous identity," as evidenced by indigenous organi-

zation. The second concept is participation. "The government has to assume the responsibility of development, with the participation of the interested peoples, to provide a coordinated program to protect and guarantee the integrity of indigenous peoples."

All of this, she concluded, had an important result: "You have been converted into subjects of rights and responsibilities. You are citizens." Then she drew a diagram, a network of Bolivian laws and reforms (such as those guaranteeing political participation, indigenous territory, bilingual education, and so on) intersecting with ILO Convention 169. At the top of the diagram stood a big man wearing a hat, representing the Bolivian state. All the supposed benefits of the laws flowed from him to the indigenous people.

Celia's words reflected the multicultural regime of citizenship offered to Bolivia's indigenous people in the mid-1990s as part of the economic and political reforms passed by the neoliberal government of President Gonzalo Sánchez de Lozada. This chapter examines the most important of these political reforms, the Law of Popular Participation (LPP), a form of decentralization that established new forms of local political participation and specifically named Indians as participants. As in previous regimes of Indian citizenship, this new one created categories of membership and established practices and institutions to define the boundary between those included and those excluded. This chapter shows how the political technologies underlying the LPP acted to include some new citizens and to exclude many others. Although its advocates touted the LPP as a remedy for many discriminatory forces of Bolivian history, the experiences of its supposed beneficiaries demonstrate that in many cases the neoliberal prescriptions reproduced the illness they claimed to cure.

Neoliberal Multicultural Reforms

In the mid-1990s, under the first administration of Sánchez de Lozada (1993–97), Bolivia's congress amended the constitution to declare Bolivia to be "multiethnic" and "pluricultural." Over the following few years, it instituted a series of political reforms intended to transform the traditional relationship between the state and indigenous peoples. Lauded across the continent, these state-led reforms were intended to construct a new form of indigenous citizenship, based on indigenous participation in local politics, collective ownership of territories, and intercultural education. This was seen as a long-needed step toward social justice, as the indigenous people who make up approximately 60 percent of Bolivia's population have traditionally been excluded from political participation.

The reforms, which I call "state-led multiculturalism," were the result of strategic articulations between the ruling Movimiento Nacional Revolucionario (MNR) party and indigenous groups. By the mid-1990s, Indians from both the highlands and the lowlands had been able to bring the so-called Indian Question into the national agenda. This "push from below" — supported by the church, NGOs, and the international indigenous movement — gained strength as lowland people carried out widely publicized marches, the most famous of which was the 1990 March for Territory and Dignity. When Sánchez de Lozada ran for office, he was under great pressure to address the issue of indigenous rights and to expand democratic participation. Making a strategic choice of Aymara Indian leader Víctor Hugo Cárdenas as vice president, he promised to address these goals.

At the same time, however, Sánchez de Lozada was under pressure to extend the economic restructuring that had begun in the mid-1980s. The neoliberal project in Bolivia was initially begun by a group of technocrats supporting former dictator General Hugo Banzer Suárez for president in the postmilitary elections of 1982. Banzer's economic team included leading figures from the mining and finance sectors as well as members of the Confederación de Empresarios Privados de Bolivia (CEPB), the businessowners association, many of whom had been educated in the United States. When Paz Estenssoro was elected, he assembled his own emergency economic team that included several members of the ADN group. Heading his team was CEPB leader Gonzalo Sánchez de Lozada, a wealthy mining entrepreneur. The team developed an orthodox neoliberal emergency plan called the New Economic Policy (NEP), which was instituted in 1985 (Conaghan, Malloy, and Abugattas 1990: 13–14). Harvard economist Jeffrey Sachs joined the team to advocate on behalf of the government to the Washington, D.C.– based International Monetary Fund (IMF).

The Paz Estenssoro team concluded that the disintegration of state authority was the major problem underlying Bolivia's ills.[2] Sánchez de Lozada justified the severity of the plan, saying "the state is practically destroyed. . . . [It] lacks the capacity to execute and implement any economic policy. . . . Therefore, the first political goal consists of reestablishing the authority of the state over the society" (ibid.: 18). Thus, although neoliberalism's advocates often argue that the main goal of neoliberalism is to pare down the state, the Bolivian version has always been tied to an ambitious state-building project. The plan this team developed was a shock treatment approach with a tight sequencing of measures. It included (1) a devaluation and float of the exchange rate, along with a commitment to a full currency convertibility; (2) an immediate reduction in fiscal deficit through a sharp increase in public sector prices (especially oil and gas); (3) a tax overhaul to raise revenues; and (4) the signing of an IMF standby arrangement to be followed by rescheduling government debt owed to foreign official creditors. The implicit fifth element was the continued moratorium on repayments of principal and inter-est to the commercial bank creditors, despite the IMF's urgings to do so (Sachs 1987: 281). The plan was almost immediately effective in halting the hyperinflation, which had reached the 60,000 percent mark.

The plan's success came at an enormous social cost, however. In addition to the fiscal measures just described, Paz called for the national budget to be balanced, making across-the-board cuts in government spending in health education and other services. Public sector employment was reduced by 10 percent. Co-authors Jennifer L. Bailey and Torbjorn L. Knutson have called this restructuring process "surgery without anaesthesia" (Bailey and Knutson 1987). Probably the most severe part of the plan was the decen-tralization of the chief state enterprises: Corporación Minera de Bolivia (COMIBOL, mines), Yacimientos Petroliferos Fiscales de Bolivia (YPFB, oil and gas), and Corporación Bolivian de Fomento (CBF, development). The mining sector was drastically restructured, as mines were closed and tens of thousands of miners were laid off in what was euphemistically called *re-localización*, or relocation (ibid.: 49).[3] One striking result of the massive lay-offs was the migration of the *relocalizados* to urban zones in El Alto, Cochabamba, and Santa Cruz, as well as to the coca-growing Chapare region, where coca cultivation tripled in the late 1980s (Sanabria 1993; Acción Andina 2001).

The neoliberal model imposed by the Paz government was similar to the structural adjustment plans instituted across the developing world at the time. It may seem ironic that the leader of the MNR revolution was at the helm of such a radical turnaround. But the same kinds of strategies were being put in place in many Latin American countries during this time. Many researchers have noted that given the international context, few alternatives remained for the political elites. International funders required that debtor countries abandon the import substitution model and adopt the other prescriptions of the neoliberal model to avoid financial crisis and to facilitate insertion into the new order (Kruse 1994: 23).[4]

The basic tenets of the NEP were continued through the 1980s by the gov-ernment led by Jaime Paz Zamora, despite the high social costs and frequent popular protests.[5] These were somewhat mitigated by the adoption of the Fondo Social de Emergencia (FSE, Social Emergency Fund), a palliative pro-gram intended to absorb some of the shock of the NEP. The main goal of the FSE was to stabilize the adjustment program through massive short-term employment creation. Similar emergency funds were created in other coun-tries to meet the popular crises of rises in food prices, unemployment, and social service cuts. In Bolivia, the FSE brought in $239 million from outside funding. More than one million people (in a country of 6.3 million) directly benefited from the program (Kruse 1994: 137–38). Much of this funding was administered by NGOs, which began to find a place working with the government. Given the widespread disruption caused by the adjustment process, this emergency program had an important impact in securing popular acquiescence for the NEP (Graham 1992).[6]

When Sánchez de Lozada was elected in 1993, he wholeheartedly adopted the neoliberal vision of capitalist development and instituted a campaign to deepen the restructuring of Bolivia's economy. The wide-ranging political and economic reforms were intended to streamline the state, make the government more efficient at the local level, open the markets to trade, encourage exports, and make Bolivia more competitive on the world market.[7] Crucial to this was the privatization of five major state enterprises, in an innovative program called capitalization.[8] Following the IMF's requirements, Sánchez de Lozada also continued Bolivia's structural adjustment programs, slashing social spending, instituting new forms of taxation, and attracting foreign capital investment to try to resolve the deficit and repay foreign debt (Aguirre Badani 2000; CEDLA 2003).

One of the central political reforms accompanying these economic restructurings was the LPP, Bolivia's version of decentralization.[9] "Decentralization" is the term used for programs to divest the national government of its overarching financial and political control over the hinterlands, often calling for more power to be given to municipal or regional governments (see McCullough and Johnson 1989; Morris and Lowder 1992; Kohl 1998).[10] As regional planner Ben Kohl and journalist Linda Farthing have noted, decentralization has been pushed by modernizers in high- and low-income countries for several decades (Kohl and Farthing 2006). Scholars who have studied the effects of decentralization, especially in francophone Africa, where it was implemented in the 1960s, have debated its effectiveness. Many critics have noted that rather than empowering local actors, decentralization reinforces the power of the central government by fortifying both the informational nexus and the infrastructure, allowing for greater government surveillance (Slater 1989; Ferguson 1994; Wunsch 2001). Others point to the potential for democratic participation, in which local actors can mount challenges to national and local elites (Slater 1989; Samoff 1990; Kohl and Farthing 2006).[11] This position was taken up by the multilateral funders, who pushed decentralization as a central part of neoliberal restructuring packages, linking it to the production of increased social capital and to locally implemented poverty alleviation (World Bank 2004; see also Davis 2002).

The LPP was thus created in the context of international pressures to decentralize, during a time in which many other Latin American countries were also doing so. Nevertheless, one cannot see the LPP as simply the imposition from without of a neoliberal prescription assumed to be universally valid. Rather, it was the product of a long history of seminars, dialogues, and theorizing carried out by Bolivian intellectuals and politicians concerned with the specific problems of Bolivian society. Especially important were the tensions between the center and the outlying regions like Santa Cruz, where regional elites have traditionally chafed at control by La Paz and advocated regional or departmental decentralization.[12] In the 1980s, Santa Cruz lawyer Carlos Hugo Molina began advocating for municipal decentralization as the only viable route for Bolivia (Van Cott 2000: 138). Furthermore, the need for autonomy at the local level had long been the position of campesinos and indigenous groups, as elaborated in various proposals, such as the 1984 Fundamental Agrarian Law, proposed by the Confederación Sindical Única de Trabajadores Campesinos de Bolivia (CSUTCB), and the 1990 Indigenous Peoples Law, proposed by CIDOB.[13] Elements of this sort of structural reform were also found in the 1991 Law of Communities, proposed by the political party Movimiento Bolivia Libre (MBL), as well as the 1991 book *Por Una Bolivia Diferente* (*For a Different Bolivia*), written by the Jesuit NGO known as the Centro de Investigación y Promoción del Campesinado (CIPCA) (see Van Cott 2000: 134–38; Urioste Fernández de Córdova 2002: 158). Sánchez de Lozada's campaign platform, the Plan de Todos (Plan for Everyone), contained many of these tensions and interests, which had matured over the previous decade in multiple seminars and dialogues. Thus when it was enacted, the LPP was a particularly Bolivian version of international neoliberal practices.

The LPP was intended to correct several major problems that were the legacies of earlier government policies. The first was the continuing imbalance between the rural and urban areas. In the colonial era, there was a pronounced absence of the royal administration in the lands administered by *hacendados* or in *comunidades indígenas* (indigenous communities). This continued through the republican period, as political power was centered in the towns and essentially inaccessible to the peasant and Indian sectors (CEADES 2003: 227). The LPP was intended to correct this lack of equilibrium by reconstructing the state in such a way as to give indigenous citizens access to local power. The 1952 revolution had made some strides toward this goal with its focus on rural peasants. However, the LPP had a new goal: bringing the rural population into the nation by extending the arms of the state to all parts of the country (Blanes 2000: 5). This was accomplished by a radical reconfiguration of the political entities with a new focus on municipalities. Before this reform, only 10 percent of national funding was spent on municipalities. Of that, 93 percent went to the three largest cities, leaving the large rural population with little attention or financing. Another 10 percent of national monies went to regional development corporations. The LPP divided the country into 311 municipalities and shifted the regional development money to the municipalities for a total of 20 percent of national budget money. This was divided across all the municipalities according to population. The money was to be used for local development, especially in the areas of education infrastructure, health and sports, local roads, and micro-irrigation (Pérez Luna 2004).

It also established a new system for citizen participation in decisions about how these *co-participación* (revenue-sharing) funds should be spent. Under the law, mayors and councils were to make yearly development plans based on the petitions of constituent population groups called *organizaciónes territoriales de base* (OTBs, territorial grassroots organizations).[14] The OTBs were to canvas their members' needs and make proposals for the city's yearly budget, then act as watchdogs through the *comités de vigilancia* (oversight committees) to make sure the budget was correctly implemented. As President Sánchez de Lozada himself suggested, this was to be "the most important redistribution of political and economic power since the 1952 Revolution," which would correct the centralist, statist bias and channel state attention and monies to the whole country (Sánchez de Lozada 1996: 19).

The second major problem that the LPP would correct, the LPP's architects contended, was the colonial legacy of exclusion of Indians from full citizenship by expanding democratic participation. The LPP would accomplish this by recognizing indigenous organizations as OTBs and traditional indigenous leaders as representatives of the OTBs, chosen according to their uses and customs.[15] For the first time, Bolivian law gave some measure of political recognition to indigenous social organizations and their customary leaders and acknowledged their collective identities. This was an important step toward including indigenous groups in the social fabric of a democratic, multicultural Bolivia and, as such, was a victory of the indigenous organizations that had been so active in advocating for indigenous inclusion into the national agenda. It also reflects the influence of anthropologists in the Sánchez de Lozada ministries, who pushed to have the indigenous cultural constructions recognized in the state's new structure.[16] Vice President Cárdenas pointed out the importance of the reform in frank ethnic terms. Bolivia, he said, is "a society defined by an internal colonial structure of exclusion," whose state is "colonialist and exclusionary." The great hope of the LPP was to move from a "democracy reduced to the vote, to the electoral, to the political, towards a broader democracy, a social, ethnic, cultural, and economic democracy" (Cárdenas 1996: 21).

It is critical to note, however, that although the LPP was certainly a response to political pressures from indigenous groups and popular sectors since the 1982 democratic opening,[17] this was not a new system of participation designed by indigenous people in a bottom-up process to gain political power or control over the state. That is, it was very different from the agrarian reform following the 1952 revolution, which did respond directly to the demands of the popular sectors (Ayo Saucedo 1999; Blanes 2000; Pérez Luna 2004). Rather, the LPP was formulated by lawmakers with an urgent project of state building. As a result, as Bolivian political scientist Diego Ayo Saucedo has noted, the promulgation of the LPP was a paradox from the beginning: "The national government promoted the participación of civil society in the state through a regulatory framework elaborated and put forth 'from above,' without the participation of the affected and supposedly benefited population" (Ayo Saucedo 1999: 30). Ayo Saucedo suggests that the law has a "technocratic halo" that is the legacy of its technical birth, which represents the "complete absence of discussion of its forms and contents with the different representative social organizations" (ibid.).

The goals of the reform were documented at its inauguration. In a volume distributed by the government, lawmakers acknowledged that the state, as constituted, was bloated, corrupt, and overly centralized. As a result, there existed a rift between politicians, who were seen as a corrupt elite class, and civil society, which was isolated, marginalized, and excluded from the state's activities (Molina Saucedo 1996: 33). The result was a dangerous opposition between a state unable to govern efficiently or serve its people and often forced to rely on violence and coercion, on the one hand, and a population that did not trust its government, on the other hand. Lawyer Carlos Hugo Molina Saucedo, one of the principal architects of the law, described the problem this way: "Civil society, organized in all its expressions, as a reaction to its subjugation (*avasallamiento*), has developed a capacity of confrontation (*enfrentamiento*) which has prevented it from producing a relation of integration, of articulation between the exercise of power and the full development of its citizens' capacity for liberty. A State that lacks a level of relationship between political society and civil society is a State which will have difficulties consolidating its democracy" (Molina Saucedo 1996: 33).

To prevent this gap from fragmenting further, the MNR needed to reform the state and forge a new relation with its citizens, including the indigenous groups clamoring for inclusion. The solution was to decentralize, passing some of the management responsibilities from the "inefficient" national government to a supposedly more "efficient" local level. President Sánchez de Lozada explained that the reform was intended to "transfer political power so that the rural communities and neighborhoods have both the authority and the responsibility to define their priorities and keep watch to ensure the correct use of the assigned resources" (Sánchez de Lozada 1996: 19). This new responsibility would not only involve the citizens in the public arena, it would also make the government enterprise run more smoothly, since grassroots organizations would (supposedly) be less corrupt and better managers of resources intended for their benefit (Cárdenas 1996: 25).[18]

At the time, some questioned the compatibility of Sánchez de Lozada's economic and political strategies. One the one hand, he was implementing classic neoliberal policies that cut social spending and privileged market forces. On the other hand, he was funding social and political reforms that responded to the demands of marginalized sectors. Ramiro Molina, the prior director of the Subsecretario de Asuntos Étnicos (SAE, Subsecretariat of Ethnic Affairs) worked closely with the president. He explained that Sánchez de Lozada came into power with a vision to change the model of the state to the model of the market. Nevertheless, "he knew the market was no panacea, and had to be combined with the social side, with a state that provided health, education, and the rule of law, that is democracy."[19] This duality was expressed in his pairing entrepreneurs on the economic side of the cabinet and progressives on the social side, including the indigenous affairs office. Clearly, Sánchez de Lozada had learned a lesson from the success of the FSE in garnering public acceptance of harsh economic reforms.[20] We can also see this hedging of bets as a sort of pragmatic version of economist Karl Polanyi's theory of the double movement: liberal strategies to create a market economy have always generated corresponding and opposing measures to make the transitions feel more humane, if only temporarily until all parties adjust to the new situation (Polanyi 1944).[21]

Sánchez de Lozada was not the only one to combine neoliberal economic logic with a focus on social relations at the local level, however. It is worth noting here how strongly the language promoting the LPP echoes the broader discourse put forth by development practitioners at the World Bank as well as by neoliberal advocates at large. They promote market liberalism and political decentralization as the most efficient mechanism for delivering the economic and social development desperately needed by the poor, especially the indigenous, who remain among the poorest.[22] They argue for "community-driven development" (CDD), which results when local community groups with strong "social capital" pressure the state and the private sector to deliver goods and services (Putnam 1993, 1995; see Mohan and Stokke 2000 as well as Davis 2002). The World Bank Group on CDD applies a market logic to the question of development: in CDD, community groups work with "demand-responsive" support organizations like local and central governments, the private sector, and NGOs "to provide social and infrastructure services, to organize economic activity and resource management, to empower poor people, improve governance, and enhance the security of the poorest" (World Bank 2004). Transferring responsibility to the local/community level would force local governments to "respond dynamically to communities" and ensure that local governments were "held accountable to their constituencies" (ibid.). Under this logic, decentralization and community-driven development are entirely consistent with neoliberal philosophies.

Similarly, I would argue that the LPP was not an anomaly, but a central part of the overall neoliberal strategy of the Bolivian elite facing the challenges of globalization. The complex of reforms was designed to secure the greater efficiency of the state and the governance of the population. I agree with Ayo Saucedo, who points to three components intended to "harmonize" the process: "capitalization, intended to attract foreign investments by making strategic enterprises competitive; educational reform, intended to form human resources oriented to the market; and the LPP, which was to counteract this economic impetus with a socially palliative design, searching for equity as the other face of the efficiency proposed by the other reforms" (Ayo Saucedo 2003: 84).

A Radical Challenge to Corporatism

One of the most important ways in which the LPP acted to support the logic of neoliberalism is by proposing a radical change in the site of the articulation and processing of community demands. Before the reforms, most civil society demands arose from collective organizations like *sindicatos* (unions), which represented particular social sectors. These were often hierarchical organizations based on traditional values, arising from territorially based social structures, with culturally defined forms of leadership. These sorts of state–civil society relations were perceived by modernizers as anachronistic, costly, and, worst of all, inefficient. The LPP was designed in part to redirect political activity to a new public space — the municipality — and to establish new forms of sociopolitical relations in which OTBs, rather than sindicatos, would act as the link to the state.

Why did the architects of the reforms think such a change was required? Bolivian civil society has been organized along corporatist lines for many years, especially since the 1952 revolution. The union movement briefly cogoverned the country in the first few years after the revolution and continued to be an important political force for the next thirty years. Although political parties operated and elections were held, the majority of Bolivians participated in politics not through voting for political parties but through supporting their union representatives in the sindicato movement. (This was especially true, of course, during the military dictatorship years.) Sindicatos obtained concessions from the government for its constituents through mobilizations, strikes, and the threat of popular violence. Thus politicians and sindicatos shared power in an uneasy truce, an equilibrium regularly broken by violence and conflict. This *poder dual* (dual power) first described by Bolivian political scientist René Zavaleta (1987) was an essential part of Bolivian politics. This was characterized by a fairly regular cycle of "forced negotiation": social sectors organized in corporate organizations — be they peasants, miners, or *gremialistas* (merchants or street vendors) — mounted

The Tapera family.

(above) The Tapera home
in Bella Flor.
(right) Samuel Tapera.

(above) New and old homes
in Bella Flor.
(left) Capitán Grande
Álvaro Montero.

El Chiriguano statue in Santa Cruz.

protests, the government negotiated with them directly, and then the parties reached an agreement that pacified the protest. Equally regularly, the state reneged on its promises, and the protests began again (Laserna 2002: 8; see also Lazar 2004).

This cycle continued until the mid-1980s, when the union movement's power to convoke popular support and veto government policies began to be eroded (Ayo Saucedo 1999: 42). This was accomplished in part by the return of democratic processes of elections and legislative functioning, which appeared to bring long-hoped-for stability. More important was the strict implementation of the structural adjustment policies of the NEP imposed in response to the deep economic crisis in the immediate postdictatorship years. Although there were loud and violent protests by unions mortally wounded in the process of economic restructuring, the need to defend the fragile democracy was equally forceful and ultimately overwhelmed union resistance. The closure of the mines and the relocation of the miners silenced the strongest part of the trade union movement. This was the first blow to the sindicatos, and it allowed the political parties to begin to take power, especially assuming the role of representing the people before the state, a role formerly held by the unions (ibid.: 43–44).

If the miners lost power in the 1980s, so did the peasants unions. Anthropologist John McNeish has pointed out that in the rural areas of Oruro, for instance, by the late 1980s peasants had lost faith in the representative power of ineffectual peasants unions and left-wing politics in general (McNeish 2001). One important result in the rural areas was a resurgence of interest in indigenous politics of difference and a rethinking of the importance in traditional ayllu leadership. In some areas, campaigns began to reinsert the local ancestral leadership positions within the local government structure (ibid.: 255). This was taking place, of course, in the context of the evolving indigenous rights movement that I described in chapter 1.

Nevertheless, despite these blows to organized labor, sindicatos have continued to be a fundamental form of organization for many Bolivians. Peasants unions, such as the CSUTCB, have remained the strongest segment of the labor movement, especially with the added force of the militant *cocaleros* from the Chapare (Albó 2000). In the urban areas, small trade or producers associations are extremely important in the lives of the majority of people working in the informal economy, such as street venders; bus, taxi, and *trufi* (shared taxis) drivers; and merchants. Anthropologist Sian Lazar has described the work of the organizations and federations for this sector in El Alto as holding a critical dual role: mediating between the workers and the state, on the one hand, and carrying out the work of the state, particularly regulating commerce and mediating conflict, on the other (Lazar 2004: 9). She also points out that membership in these organizations is not necessarily linked to politics, but might be considered more like belonging to a guild or professional organization. This reveals that these corporate organizations continue to have substantial appeal for their members, as they provide not only economic benefits, but also an important sense of collective belonging (ibid.: 10). Moreover, in times of crisis, the unions still command strong loyalties and have demonstrated the power to convoke massive demonstrations. (Chapter 6 describes the role these corporate organizations continue to play in the current Indian and popular struggle.) Thus, although disciplined by the harsh realities of the market (Rivera Cusicanqui 1993: 103), the sindicato movement was by no means defeated.[23]

The 1994 reforms, particularly the LPP, were intended to further disrupt the power of unions, as modernizing elites sought to dismantle this corporatist system of politics. Economist and planner Roberto Laserna has argued that the reforms were part of a move toward a normative institutional system, which proposed that social conflicts be negotiated through democratic institutions and regulations rather than by political deals seeking to avert another political emergency (Laserna 2002: 27). Particularly during the economic crises of the 1990s, the state could no longer continue to take direct actions to meet demands of popular sectors. By breaking the power of the clientelist system, the hope was to make political and economic decisions more rational and effective, rather than to continue the costly and often corrupt expenditures needed to silence vocal political actors (ibid.).

The LPP was a key piece in this challenge to traditional corporate political systems. As the following analysis shows, however, there was insufficient political will to really institute the sort of normative institutional system that Laserna has described (ibid.). Furthermore, the political technologies that were at play in the implementation of the law reinforced the underlying racist exclusions that had kept indigenous people from participating in the state. Although the power of traditional collective organizations was certainly substantially diminished, elite-run political parties replaced them as the current form of corporatist clientelism. To illustrate this, let us see how the LPP was implemented on the ground and how it was experienced by the supposed beneficiaries.

Initial Responses: Indian Subjects, NGOs,
and the Symbolic Power of Citizenship

When the LPP was enacted in 1994, there was a substantial amount of fanfare about the revolutionary changes it represented. As the government began to enact the law, there was a recurrent buzz about the "pluri-multi" nature of the country and the extension of participatory citizenship to

Indians. Iván Arias, then an official of the Popular Participation project, explained that in this stage of state-indigenous relations, which he called the "*canto a diversidad*" ("song to diversity") stage, participation would forever change the relation of indigenous people to the state. Instead of seeing the state as the source of resources and making *reclamos* (demands) against it, now indigenous people would see themselves as citizens, with rights and obligations: "We want fewer inhabitants and more citizens" ("Queremos menos habitantes, y más ciudadanos").[24]

The process of molding new citizens is complex, however, and involves many actors. First were the legislative changes to the constitution and the actual laws naming indigenous people as actors. These were followed by administrative regulations that detailed the manner in which participation was to be carried out. But indigenous people outside political channels — that is, those not in the national leadership circles — understood little about how the new laws would function, and less about how to gain access to the supposed benefits. Government agencies, with limited funding from international aid agencies, made some efforts to teach indigenous people their rights and obligations as citizens. The SAE, its successor VAIPO, as well as the Secretary of Popular Participation and the Ministry of Education organized workshops to disseminate and educate about all the reforms that had been passed.[25] The meeting described at the beginning of this chapter, where Celia explained citizenship as a function of rights and responsibilities, is an example of how those workshops functioned.

One problem that bears mentioning about these workshops, however, is the difficulty in presenting complex legal and political information to rural, often illiterate participants who speak little or no Spanish. The majority of the Zona Cruz women that attended the meeting spoke some Spanish, but few of them had attended elementary school for more than a handful of years, if that. At the end of the meeting, several women stood up to thank the organizers. Doña Estela from Bella Flor told Celia how grateful she was to have received the *capacitación* (training). "This has really opened my eyes," she said. In my discussions with people later, however, it was clear that they had gotten little out of the meeting. That afternoon, Don Álvaro Montero said he thought that Celia had no clue about the realities facing his people, and the discussions did not seem to address their particular issues. The next week, I spent the afternoon with Doña Estela in her home. She told me she had no idea about how Guaranís could use the laws Celia had discussed to bring about changes in their communities. "This was just one more workshop about some law that doesn't really help us." It was like all the other useless workshops she had attended, where the presenter didn't learn anything about them and they didn't learn anything helpful. What they needed was information about how to run a little business, or something they themselves could do. What she had gotten from the workshop, though, was that Guaranís were *citizens*, in some sort of relation to the man in the hat, the state. Maybe that would eventually lead to something good.

Extremely important in all of this were the NGOs, which got funded to help train indigenous people to exercise their new rights as citizens. Because of the "revolutionary" nature of the reforms, many international agencies funded projects to support the state's limited ability to put the reforms into effect. I was able to observe one such NGO program in detail throughout 1998. In chapter 1, I described how the Guaranís of Zona Cruz entered an agreement with a Bolivian NGO called the Colectivo de Estudios Aplicados y Desarrollo Social (CEADES, Collective for Applied Studies and Social Development) to work with its young leadership team, the ETZ. For two years, CEADES trained the team to diagnose the situation of the communities that make up the capitanía, to analyze the problems and potential solutions, and to find resources available through the new reforms. This project is described in more detail in chapter 5. The training was especially tailored to teach the communities to learn to participate in the new municipally administered Popular Participation program, the LPP. CEADES worker Julián Paz, a geographer from Chile, worked closely with the Zona Cruz team. One afternoon, after a long meeting preparing the Guaraní team to go out to the communities, Julián and I talked about CEADES's role. He told me the big risk in Bolivia was that the people were being given the job of citizens without the training to do it. So, he said, NGOs like CEADES were taking on the role. This points out, of course, the rigid ways in which citizenship was being defined at the time. Of course, the many forms of participation in trade unions or indigenous organizations could be characterized as citizenship, but under the strictly defined categories of the LPP, they were discounted, even by someone like Julián who had worked with this sort of protagonism for years.[26]

The discourse surrounding the reforms exercised a strong symbolic force. While some indigenous people were concerned about the effects the law might have on their traditional organizations, many others felt the law gave them new rights, which entitled them to participate in a national public dialogue.[27] For instance, Pablo, the same Guaraní friend who described his identity card as a birth certificate (recounted in the introduction to this book), told me that now that they were citizens, their bosses at the local ranches could not treat them as badly. "We have rights now," he said. "They can't steal from us like before." In this, he and his neighbors considered themselves to have moved from a position outside the dominant "legitimate" political agenda — what feminist scholar Janine Brodie might call "pre-political subjects" — to a position of shared membership in the Bolivian society (Brodie 1994: 53). To be sure, the Guaranís in this community did not have equal power in that sphere, but through the LPP and the discourse accompanying it, they began to feel entitled to exercise the political rights that the reforms offered.

Other symbols of the nation were also important in this interpellation. For instance, during the VAIPO workshop Celia led for Guaraní women, the leader had the participants break up in groups and describe what would be an ideal community. Each group drew their vision on brown butcher paper, with schools, health posts, agricultural areas, parks and playgrounds, and so on. In each drawing, the red, yellow, and green stripes of the Bolivian flag flew over the schoolhouse. Similarly, when I attended a national assembly of CIDOB, at which new national leaders for the group were to be elected, the indigenous organizers had affixed a Bolivian flag over the podium, and the opening ceremonies began with the singing of the Bolivian national anthem.[28]

One particularly interesting example of symbolizing the new multicultural pluri-ethnic nation had to do with the vice president, Víctor Hugo Cárdenas. The Guaranís of Santa Cruz often invoked his name as a sort of code for all the ideological values of democracy and participation. His symbolic value was enormous, as merely saying his name invoked notions of inclusion and equality. If an indigenous man was vice president of the country, well, then, what was not possible for them? The records of the Zona Cruz asambleas show a fascinating evolution of this usage. In the first asamblea, a representative from the national Guaraní association, the APG, warmly greeted the newly formed capitanía as part of the APG and brought greetings to them from Víctor Hugo. Some time later, at another meeting, during a heated discussion about the land struggle in Bella Flor, Guaranís who felt the situation was becoming unfair claimed that one of their leaders had been in communication with Víctor Hugo about the situation. Although that was unlikely to be the case, it showed how his name was beginning to signify justice. Finally, at an asamblea in which the land struggle was discussed again, one of the most combative of the parties to the struggle arrived, saying he had only come because he had heard that Víctor Hugo was going to be at the asamblea. There was no basis to the rumor, but invoking his name in this way acted to remind the rest of the participants that there were greater powers watching — the Guaranís were no longer acting alone; now they were part of a larger system of laws and justice.[29]

Changing the Rules of the Game

Although the Guaranís of Zona Cruz received symbolic benefits from the new reforms, the LPP promised much more concrete benefits. Under these regulations, territorially based organizations (called OTBs), including indigenous groups, can take part in the city's development decisions. The OTBs make claims to the city, asking for the city to invest revenue-sharing funds on their proposed projects. The city council and the mayor are supposed to take these demands into account in the preparation of the *plan anual operativa* (POA, the annual operating plan).[30] The oversight committee, made up of representatives of the OTBs, is supposed to oversee the POA's design and implementation. This new system meant that mayors and city councils, which had formerly not been important sites of economic activity, suddenly became much more important.

Because they had the power to disperse large sums of money — revenue-sharing funds were roughly 20 percent of the national budget — municipal elections had real meaning. Bolivian political scientist George Gray-Molina has noted that the structure of national public investment shifted radically from a central to local or departmental expenditure of 75 percent to 25 percent before the reforms to the exact opposite, when the figures flipped to 25 percent central spending and 75 percent local or departmental spending (Gray-Molina 2001: 70). Moreover, he documents that in the first three years alone, aggregate social spending (education, sanitation, and health) tripled from US$75 million in 1994 to US$178 million in 1996 (ibid.). This meant that suddenly municipal elections were fiercely contested by political parties, which until that time had focused their money and energy on national elections. Now political parties that had little presence in the rural areas have become a daily reality at the local level (Calla Ortega 2000: 87).[31] Some analysts, like Gray-Molina, argue that the reforms produced not only a significant urban-to-rural redistribution of fiscal resources, but also increased indigenous and peasant political representation and participation in public decision making (Gray-Molina 2001: 64). My research shows a different outcome: while the law did provide indigenous groups with the possibility of participating in municipal elections, the biggest effect of the law was to increase the power of traditional political parties and the elites who controlled them.

Gray-Molina and other analysts have reason to suggest increased participation. In the first elections after the LPP was instituted in 1995, Indians and campesinos ran for municipal office across the country to take advantage of this new political space. Their success varied widely. For some communities with strong local leaders and large numbers of indigenous people, the traditional elites saw their positions challenged by indigenous and campesino newcomers. El Alto, the satellite city above La Paz, is the most significant case. There the large Aymara population has been quite active in city politics since the influence during the 1990s of the Conciencia de la Patria (CONDEPA, Conscience of the Fatherland), a La Paz–based political party.[32]

Since the reforms, representatives of the extremely well-organized *junta vecinales* (JVs, neighborhood associations) regularly attend city planning meetings and negotiate with their city officials and *subalcaldes* (submayors) for public works. The federation of juntas, FEJUVE, has become a powerful and effective political force (Lazar 2004, and pers. comm.). Another area where Indian leaders were able to take advantage of this opening was the Chapare region in the Cochabamba tropics. The *cocaleros*, the mainly Quechua and Aymara coca growers union, won a number of municipal elections. They translated this power in the municipalities to increase pressure against national coca eradication policies (Albro 2005). A third example is the Guaranís of Alto y Bajo Izozog, where the capitanía formed what is called a *distrito municipal indígena* (DMI, indigenous municipal district) and won the subalcalde position. The capitanía was able to manage a substantial amount of funds for the benefit of the Guaraní people.[33] (There are several such DMIs and they have had varying success. See Balslev 1997 and Lema 2001.) Gray-Molina has also documented a success story in Capinota, Cochabamba, where grassroots organizations took active part in the oversight committee and were able to lobby the municipal council to invest in important irrigation, water, and sanitation projects (Gray-Molina 2001: 76).[34]

Nationwide, the elections brought a substantial showing for indigenous candidates. Of the 1,624 *consejales* (city council members) elected in 1995, 464 were indigenous or campesinos (Ayo Saucedo 1996: 338).[35] This electoral success was largely in the highlands, in the rural areas where Indian populations are largest and most concentrated. The officials at the Secretary of Popular Participation (SNPP) trumpeted this figure, arguing it showed how the LPP was working to democratize the decision making.[36] Although 29 percent indigenous representation was still insufficient given the fact that Indian population makes up between 65 percent and 70 percent of the country, it was a substantial change in the makeup of local authorities.[37]

The numbers don't tell the whole story, though. Until a recent law change in 2004, all candidates were required to be affiliated with a political party to run for office. So the indigenous leaders who ran for city council were required to find a political party that would sponsor them (Gray-Molina 2001: 68). The case of Faustino Auca is illustrative.[38] He told me the story of his political career when I met him in La Paz in 2004. Don Faustino had served his rural community in the department of Potosí through a number of posts. As a young man, he was a leader in the campesino union. Then, under the rotating cargo system, he held a number of other local leadership positions. In 1995, his community put him forward to run for *consejal* (city council member) in the first round of elections after the LPP was enacted. He described the difficulties he had working with his chosen political party. "We were conditioned," he told me, "by our need to *prestar consignas* [borrow party insignias]. We had to vote for the interests of the party." So despite his election as an indigenous leader, Don Faustino did not feel able to act on behalf of the people he represented. He served as a councilor and for a time as mayor, and although he was able to push forward some projects for the rural communities, he complained that the operating plans of the municipal budgets were overwhelmingly beneficial to the town. He said his frustration was shared by his people, as well as by many other leaders, who felt the continuing power of the political parties eviscerated their participation as public officials. "We were trapped," he said. "We needed our own party so we didn't have to do the bidding of the politicians." This eventually lead many of them to join the Movimiento al Socialismo (MAS, Movement Towards Socialism) party, headed by cocalero leader Evo Morales in the 2003 elections. Don Faustino followed this path, and in 2000, he was elected to the national congress as a *diputado* (congressional representative). (I provide more on these elections in chapter 6.) Not everyone had such success, however. Other leaders gave up their efforts to use the political parties to the benefit their constituencies and accepted the money and material benefits that party loyalists receive (Albó 2002: 83).

Faustino Auca's experience with political parties is not unique.[39] Bolivian historian Ana María Lema has studied the election of indigenous council members in the lowland communities of Urubichá, Gutiérrez, and Villa Monte in Santa Cruz and Chuquisaca. She has argued that even though these leaders were elected in a triple process of selection — put forward by their indigenous organizations, sponsored by the political parties that loaned them their party affiliation, and then voted in by their indigenous electors — once in office, they found that the authoritarian and paternalistic forms of doing politics in the small towns left them a limited margin of action. Moreover, the political parties often laughed at the agreements they had made with the indigenous leaders before elections. In some communities, the local politicians expressed hostility toward indigenous politicians, either simply because of their ethnicity or because of their reputation for conflict. In others, where the indigenous councilors were in the minority, the mayor and other council members just ignored them or gave their demands low priority. Overall, the indigenous leaders were either badly manipulated or badly marginalized (Lema 2001: 203).[40]

Why was this so? Of course, the reasons for success or failure in each community depend on the particularities of each case. The experiences of Guaranís in Santa Cruz suggest four main reasons why the LPP as enacted did not result in inclusive political participation: First, the colonial legacy of racism continued to operate. Second, the law instituted new technologies of knowledge management, which were hard for indigenous leaders to access. Third, it operated to fragment indigenous organizations. Finally, the LPP was limited in scope and funding. Let us look at each factor in turn.

Colonial Relationships

During the spring of 1998, I accompanied the capitanes of three Guaraní communities in the Warnes jurisdiction to meetings of the oversight committee. Warnes is north of Santa Cruz, in an area of large agribusiness, cattle ranches, and sugar refineries. There are about seven Guaraní communities in the area, mostly Guaranís who came to work the sugarcane and stayed on to farm. The Guaranís here had not managed to run any candidates for public office. Instead, they were trying to access resources by sending representatives to the oversight committee, so as to get their requests placed in the city budget. This was their first time these local leaders had attempted to participate under the new law.

Don Víctor Ortiz was a man of about sixty, wearing thick black glasses and speaking heavily accented Spanish. He had the quiet proud bearing of many of the elder Guaraní leaders. His village, Villa María, was a farming community about forty kilometers out of Warnes. Don Gregorio Ambrosino was a younger man, near forty. He spoke good Spanish and had worked many years on nearby haciendas. He was the newly elected leader of his village, Nuevas Palmas, and seemed more confident about being involved in the meetings. The third leader was a man I had met years before, Don Marco Solórzano, head of the small community of Guaranís that lived right in Warnes. In 1996, I had visited this group during my first summer's work with the capitanía. Several extended families of Guaranís had come to Warnes to find work and were living in abandoned train cars. Since then, they had built *pahuichis* along the outskirts of Warnes, and the small suburban community had organized itself. Don Marco was shy but accustomed to interacting with townspeople.

We met in Warnes, in the large open meeting room of the Warnes Chamber of Commerce. It was another rainy morning, and many of the OTB representatives had not been able to get into the city on the muddy roads, so the meeting got off to a slow start. At the front of the room, at the dais, was a group of white politicians (including the subprefecto, a sort of lieutenant governor, and several important lawyers from Santa Cruz) sitting and talking loudly among themselves. Several more of them continued to arrive, talking on their cell phones, holding small meetings with various clients in the back of the room. By comparison, the representatives of the territorially based organizations sat in chairs at their feet, waiting quietly. The president of the oversight committee, a cheerful camba merchant who represented an urban neighborhood organization, asked the assembled people what they wanted to do, given that the majority of the representatives had not arrived. The OTB members agreed they wanted to postpone the meeting, because they knew those missing would want to hear the lawyers' talks explaining the process. The politicians agreed and then went right on and held the meeting anyway.

For approximately two hours, the lawyers on the dais — including Carlos Hugo Molina Saucedo, the Santa Cruz lawyer who drafted the LPP — talked to each other about politics and complex legal questions. For the first few minutes, they addressed the OTBs. Molina urged the OTBs to take advantage of the potential Warnes had for development. They should make decisions that supported its agriculture and industry, such as building hotels and an exposition fairground to show off its products. "It is up to you to take advantage of the money available," he said. Soon, though, the politicians began interrupting each other and arguing. The OTB representatives were silent, watching. At the lunch break, I sat with the Guaraní leaders and asked them what they thought. I admitted I had been appalled at the behavior of the blustery camba politicians. They laughed patiently, agreeing that the patrones had essentially done what they always do: control the meeting. The Indians were used to that, they said. They considered it more important that they had an opportunity to get some money from the city. They liked being at the meeting and were going to come back to make a proposal for their community.

Some weeks later, I met Don Víctor and Don Gregorio again at a meeting of the oversight committee. This time, only the OTB representatives were there, presenting their proposals to the committee president. He listened patiently to the representatives' statements about what their community wanted. He then commented on the statements, helping the group make its proposal more likely to be accepted by the mayor and the council at budget approval time. First, they each needed to remember that the coparticipation funds were approximately 11 Bolivianos per person (about US$2) so the project proposed must be within that amount. The committee president had a list of population figures of each community (although many of the Guaraní villages either did not appear or were seriously undercounted). Several communities presented their requests for money under the next year's budget. At one point, the committee president looked down from the podium to the assembled community leaders and said it was good they had come to participate, because, roughly translated, "He who doesn't cry, doesn't get breastfed" ("El que no llora, no mama"). This often heard refrain in Bolivian politics represents the legacy of the clientelistic system of politics described earlier. An English-speaking reader might make a comparison with the saying "the squeaky wheel gets the grease," which implies that insistence is often rewarded by attention. The Bolivian version, however, contains an inherent paternalism (or perhaps maternalism) in that it assumes the crier is both subordinate and dependent and must rely on crying to get his or her needs met.

When Don Gregorio spoke, he said that the people of Nuevas Palmas had decided they wanted to fix up the school. It needed a new roof, two rooms for the teachers to stay in, and two bathrooms. No, the committee president said, that is way beyond the budget. Why not ask for two latrines, instead? That is much cheaper, since it doesn't require a water tank. That way there will still be money for the teacher houses. Don Víctor's village needed a retaining wall built against the curve of the river that had been eating away at their land. No, too expensive, the committee president said. Why not a well? The Japanese embassy had recently been offering to provide the drilling equipment for wells, so now the oversight committee was pushing wells. One woman said her community needed two things: some land for a playground and a new schoolroom. "Well," said the president, in a slightly condescending voice, "you have to decide on the one thing you really want."[41]

Perhaps one reason for the president's response was his impatience with rural people who did not completely understand the process. He was trying to corral these demands into a form the council might actually act upon. But another, larger part of this response, I believe, was a continuing gendering and infantilizing that reflect colonial power structures still very much a part of societal relations in Bolivia.[42] This was evident in the diagram of the VAIPO worker, with which this chapter began, which depicted the Indians waiting below the great father from whom benefits were to flow. Here, although the oversight committee president believed he was enacting the liberal democratic practices of participation, his culturally based notions of Indians as children without the capacity to reason well led him to override their political demands. Because of the region's long-term patron-client relationships, this local elite man has social and cultural capital that allows him to take part in the city government. The Guaraní leaders do not have such capital, so it seemed "natural" to all parties that the committee president should act on their behalf. Once again, liberal elites believe they "know best" and act as parents for the untutored Indian citizens.

In these everyday practices of the LPP, we see unwitting exclusions that result from the underlying hierarchy of power, which the existence of the LPP does not alter. These practices remind us of the continuing force of what Mexican anthropologist Adolfo Gilly has called "racial subalternity," naturalized forms of domination based on perceived inequalities that continue even when they are outlawed (Gilly 2003: 20). They also remind us again that liberal inclusions are tied to culturally based conceptions of Otherness, which inevitably lead to exclusion (Mehta 1997). Although the LPP was supposed to overcome these cultural biases, the practices of the law do not prevent their influence. In fact, the law continues to privilege political parties, the bastions of elite thought and interests. The internal structures of parties are not regulated and reflect the race, class, and gender hierarchies common across the country. Thus whatever seemingly democratizing policies the LPP may contain are often undermined by the exclusionary biases that continue to operate in the political parties.

The description of this oversight committee meeting should not be taken as an argument that no Indian groups were able to exercise their agency or make their collective voices heard. It is, however, characteristic of the challenges indigenous people have had to meet to put their demands forth. During the first few years of the LPP, those Guaraní villages that did participate at this level did, in fact, receive some improvements. They were not necessarily the things they asked for initially, but they were helpful and needed. The majority of the improvements were schoolrooms and living spaces for teachers, who usually come to the villages on Monday mornings and leave for their homes in the city on Friday afternoons. Several other communities received potable water systems. Often these projects came in stages, since the whole project typically exceeded the yearly budgets. These small projects were extremely important to the people of the outlying Guaraní villages. Not only did these improvements make their lives easier — the difference between hauling water every day and having it delivered to your village square is enormous — but they made the Guaranís feel that the government was paying some attention to them after many years of being ignored.

Presenting a project does not automatically mean getting it approved by the municipal council, however. This involves political power that indigenous groups may not have. The success of getting these *obras* (public works) depended greatly on the municipality in which the community was located, the particular *gestión* (administration) that was in power, and the relation the Guaranís were able to forge with that leader. For instance, the Guaranís were not able to make much headway in Warnes, where there were multiple conflicting groups seeking funding. Since 2002, the city has been in complete chaos, as infighting between council members has closed down municipal functioning completely. For one period, there were two mayors and two councils, each claiming legitimacy. These conflicts had to be taken up at the national level, which takes a long time and during which no obras are implemented. When I was in Bolivia during the summer of 2004, I went to Warnes to verify with the city how many projects had eventually been carried out in the Guaraní communities in its jurisdiction. The city hall was closed down and the local leaders, including the Guaraní regional capitán, were all in La Paz, trying to get the Supreme Court to lift the freeze on municipal funds.[43] The capitanía told me none of the communities had received any obras as far as they knew.

In Santa Cruz city district, where Bella Flor and its neighbors are located, the communities have also had a tough time. For example, the leaders of Las Palmas community started asking for funds to build a schoolroom in 1997.

The first year, their petitions were denied, as the committee said other communities' demands were more pressing. Each year, the leaders went back with their demands, and finally in 1999, the request was granted, or so the municipal authorities said. Nothing happened, however. In 2002, the leaders went to the mayor's office and complained. They were shown a list of the thousand works the mayor of Santa Cruz, Jhonny Fernandez, had accomplished during his tenure, and there they saw their schoolroom listed! But it was never built, they argued. The work is in progress, they were told.

By summer 2004, however, there was still no sign of work. In Bella Flor and El Futuro, a few schoolrooms have been built, along with a bank of bathrooms next door to the school. Revenue-sharing funds provided part of the materials, and the community had to provide the "counterpart," in the form of concrete and construction labor. In other cases, such as in El Mangal, the community received a third of the material for a new schoolroom from the city and the rest from NGOs. The Guaranís in the region complained to me that the reason they didn't get any obras was because the decisions were made in Paurito, the *subalcaldía* to which they belong, and the subalcalde there had used all the funds for building a big soccer stadium and a hospital. "But we're thirty kilometers away from there!" Samuel Tapera, my friend from Bella Flor, complained. "How are we ever going to use that hospital?"

The attitude of the Santa Cruz city officials toward the Guaraní communities was even more telling. First, just finding someone in the administration who would talk to me was nearly impossible. I finally had to do it the Bolivian way: I got a friend to call a friend who worked in city hall to arrange a meeting. Then, when I went to interview the official, he couldn't even find the Guaraní communities on his map. "They must not be part of this municipio. Try the prefectura," he told me incorrectly. I finally tracked down the proper city engineers in charge of the obras, and while they looked up the figures, they asked me why I was bothering with these people. One engineer said, "Oh yes, the Guaraní, they are so hard to manage, they really don't adapt well. Look at those in the plaza." (He was referring to Ayoreo Indians, who often beg in the main square or offer their woven handicrafts for sale to the tourists. The Guaraní people typically do none of those things, but many middle-class cambas consider all Indians the same: lazy and dirty.) "I think it is the fault of the NGOs," he continued, "they have given them bad habits by giving them handouts. Now they don't want to work."

When I went back a few days later to get the printed-out results, the engineer told me the reason why these Guaranís had gotten so few obras was that they didn't have good leaders. "There are two ways to get the city to give you attention," he told me, "either by requests or *por bloqueo* [by blockade]." That is, communities get more city investment if their leaders "move more" and when they "belong to normal society." The Guaranís, though, "they just raise their hands, they don't really want advancement. . . . They are just *testarudo* [stubborn], *cabezadura* [hardheaded]." Is it any wonder the Guaranís in Santa Cruz received few projects when the people in charge maintain such overtly racist attitudes? Here we see how everyday racism acts in conjunction with liberal multiculturalism.

By comparison, in Minero, the municipality just to the north of Warnes, the Guaraní communities had done fairly well. One village had received a "poly-functional" building, which served as a schoolroom and had a kitchen for community functions, another separate schoolroom, a new potable water well (which cost US$7,200), and an *item* (salary line) for a bilingual primary teacher. The 2005 budget promised an electric pump for the well. Another community had received a small public lighting system, an electric meter, and several latrines. What made the difference? In Minero, there was a populist mayor who appeared to care about the outlying communities. When I went to verify the obras in Minero in 2004, the civil engineer heading the popular participation office was entirely forthcoming, called in all the *responsables* (those in charge of) the communities I asked about, and gave me all the figures I needed. He said the previous mayor had been run out of town for corruption, and this new one was determined to work for all the people. The Guaranís came to the public meetings and were able to communicate their needs to the administration. This engineer anticipated bringing more works to their growing communities in the coming budgets. The fact that this municipio was able to respond to the needs and demands of the Guaranís shows how important political will is in the functioning of the process. Where there is a "good" liberal mayor, the LPP has benefited the subalterns, but where public officials are motivated by corruption and personal interests or where colonial power structures continue to hold sway, Indians continue to be excluded.

Technologies of Knowledge Management: Obras *and Training*

The experiences of these Guaranís show that, despite the rhetoric about cultural recognition, they view the LPP primarily as a vehicle for the distribution of resources. Communities have traditionally gauged both their value as a community and the success of their leaders on the quantity of obras (public works) the state carries out for them (McEwen 1975). Residents of local communities have often been ignored by the distant or ineffective state and have sought ways to obtain benefits and resources from it. In the past, the mechanism for redistribution was via corporate organizations and patronage relations. The LPP has changed this in several ways.

First, the LPP has brought the production of obras to the local polity, instituting new institutional pathways for the fulfillment of constituent demands for resource redistribution. Second, as a result of the LPP, there was suddenly a great deal more money at stake, and a great deal of propaganda about the works that would flow from the municipalities. This heightened community expectations. And third, whereas before, public works were seen as lucky benefits flowing from a *caudillo* (political patron) in exchange for loyalty or votes, or the result of hardworking leaders pushing for resources from those patrons, now obras are seen as the right of citizens under the law. This is because the law redefined citizenship as the right to participate in local development. The municipal section, the organizing unit of the LPP, is the new unit of reference in the daily life of Bolivians, the new source of patronage (Lema 2001: xxii). The result is that communities expect their city council to provide them their due. The overarching question for communities is "When is it our turn? (¿Cuándo nos tocará a nosotros?)" (Blanes 2000: 36). Or, more bluntly translated, When do we get ours?[44]

This means that communities in the same jurisdiction are in competition for obras, as the coparticipation funds are limited and must be divvied up by the city council for the year's budget. The Guaranís in Warnes described earlier were not very successful, precisely because they were not able to compete well against other communities who were favored by the municipal leaders. Sociologist José Blanes, who carried out a study of the LPP in three Aymara municipios in the La Paz department, notes that this competition has radically changed social life in the countryside, where "solidarity was an important piece of the survival of poverty." Although there were always intercommunal conflicts, this new form of competition has deepened them and made them much more complex (ibid.: 53). Moreover, this focus on obras puts intense pressure on local leaders. If they fail to bring home the obras, their communities express great discontent and may reject and replace them. This is complicated by the fact that in the highlands, leaders often rotate leadership roles every year, under the traditional cargo system. Blanes found that as a result, the Aymara leaders in the communities he studied pushed for short-term works that had immediate payoffs rather than long-term projects that might benefit future leaders (ibid.: 54). Thus it was more important to have a flashy ritual celebration opening a small water pump, with all the community acknowledging the leader's success in obtaining it, for instance, than to have pushed through a three-year irrigation plan that would benefit more people but come to fruition when other leaders would be standing at the head of the celebration.

Across the country, in the first years of the LPP, observers noted the many short-term but highly visible urban development projects like public plazas, public health clinics, and jeeps for the mayor (MDH/SNPP 1997; Kohl 1999;

Blanes 2000: 37). Lema has said this "cement conspiracy" was not true over-all, however, and that such massive works occurred mostly in the department capitals.[45] Nevertheless, it is clear that the works carried out by municipal-ities tended to be more social than productive and to favor urban residents more than rural ones (Calla Ortega 2000: 86; Lema 2001: 150). Ayo Saucedo has argued that even though the LPP is supposed to focus on local development, the push for obras actually accomplishes the opposite, as it interferes with rational municipal planning. Instead of being able to come up with coherent plans for regional or intercommunity productive devel-opment projects, the cities are forced to respond to the OTBs demanding small obras for their communities. This demonstrates once again that the LPP was intended as a socially palliative project in tandem with the other neoliberal restructuring. So, instead of really contributing to development, it acts to redistribute limited but visible resources to a population demand-ing attention (Ayo Saucedo 2003: 94).

The demand for obras acts as a technology of power that changes accept-able forms of leadership. In the world of obras, indigenous leaders have to perform according to new requirements. Where success is measured by pub-lic works carried out in the community, leaders no longer gain status in their communities through moral standing, or from access to powerful political patrons. What counts now is the ability to work well in the bureaucratic world of city administration and municipal elections. This has greatly dis-advantaged indigenous leaders, few of whom have the technical abilities or education to fulfill these roles. A look at the Guaranís of Zona Cruz shows how formidable an obstacle such bureaucratic requirements can be.

To get the mayor and council to place their communities' needs on the annual operating plan, each Guaraní community needed to form as an OTB, the grassroots organizations entitled to participate in the oversight com-mittee. This proved to be much harder than expected. First, to be recognized by the municipality, the community had to have a *personería jurídica*, a for-mal registration of the community as an indigenous organization, signed and sealed by the office of the prefecto. For the Guaranís, this required a com-munity meeting; the drafting of a formal document by the capitanía's office staff; the seal and approval of the capitanía; and then the processing and approval of the prefecto's office. These steps might not seem difficult to urban readers, but for the leaders of rural communities without offices, typewrit-ers, computers, or sometimes even electricity, each of these steps takes an enormous effort and many costly trips to the city.

I worked in the capitanía's office several days a week and observed the dif-ficulties the local leaders encountered. Samuel Tapera, in Bella Flor, was the capitanía's secretary of acts, the person responsible for drafting the documents and getting the proper signatures and seals. A local leader would make the difficult trip into the city and ask Samuel to type the required resolution for his community. Then the leader would return to his home village to get the signatures of the local village leaders and affix the seal of the community. (That meant each community had to go out and get a rubber seal made ahead of time.) Then the signed document, usually carefully wrapped in a plastic bag, was returned to Samuel, who had to get the signatures of the directorate of the capitanía. This might take a few weeks or a few months, because this group only assembled irregularly. Invariably, someone was missing, stuck in an outlying community by mudslides or a death in the village. Perhaps the electricity of the office was out because the organization couldn't pay its bills. Such details are not just administrative snafus, but the very difficult coming together of two ways of life — one a bureaucratic city life determined by forms and seals, and the other marked by poverty, transportation obstacles, and the uncertainties of those living on the margin of disaster. Each member of the ETZ, the technical team that helps the capitán grande, was assigned various villages to help their leaders accomplish these steps, but the process lasted for several years. Many of the Zona Cruz communities still have not accomplished this first step.

Once a community had a personería jurídica, its leaders must learn how the LPP process worked. This meant going to a workshop or getting someone else who had been to one to explain the process. I attended such a workshop in Santa Cruz, put on by one of the many NGOs that received funding to give popular participation training. It was in a fancy seminar room in the Spanish cultural center downtown, and community and urban neighborhood representatives from many nearby towns were present. The workshop lasted two days and taught the participants the basics of drafting and reading budgets, as one of the important roles of the OTBs is to monitor the mayor and city council's execution of annual budgets. Although these topics were taught in as accessible a manner as possible, the lessons were nevertheless quite technical. Indigenous and community leaders were scribbling into their lined school notebooks, silently taking notes. For Guaraní capitanes and representatives, many of whom have attended only a few years of primary school, these technical terms were almost unintelligible. Yet these workshops were part of the process by which citizens were trained to speak a common language of administration, financing proposals, development, budgets, monitoring — the idioms of modern bureaucratic democracy.

Critics have argued that the laws, regulations, and training that leaders must master are not unlike the pre-1952 requirements for citizenship, in which a voter must have been able to read and write and have a "respectable economic patrimony," meaning to be a landowner or to control wealth. Being able to formulate a an operating budget or elaborate a proposal is much the same: it demarcates new hierarchies of citizenship, in which the illiterate have fewer opportunities (Ayo Saucedo 2003: 56). The practices of the LPP thus tend to privilege those people who can easily manage these technologies and to segregate ethnic authorities without the requisite social capital.

This has another serious effect: communities tend to promote to leadership those people who have the most education and who will be best able to manage these requirements. Studies of the levels of education of local officials — mayors, council members, and community representatives to the oversight committee — show that more and more of them have higher education. Three-fourths of council members elected in 1999 had university training, and a third of oversight committee members had high school degrees (SNPP-UIA, cited in Ayo Saucedo 1999: 103). This proportion is above the norm for Bolivians in general, and far above the norm for Indian people. This is not surprising in and of itself, as young men with some formal education have been assuming positions of liaison with the Spanish-speaking world for many years.[46]

Yet some critics have argued that the need for elevated technical knowledge under the institutions of the LPP is at odds with the *usos y costumbres* (customary usages) of the sociocultural groups that populate Bolivia. It can interfere with traditional forms of authority, where moral authority and respect accrues to older men and women who have fulfilled their responsibilities under the Andean ritual fiesta and cargo system (Abercrombie 1998). While it is certainly possible to be Indian and to be educated, it is unfortunately not a common situation in Bolivia, where Indians continue to have some of the country's lowest educational levels.[47] The result is that for many indigenous communities, the social values that used to underlie choice of leadership have been replaced by skills valued in neoliberal notions of the modern state: efficiency, administrative abilities, and the mastery of bureaucratic language. (Chapter 5 describes the efforts of an NGO to teach these skills to young Guaraní leaders.) Thus the practices of the LPP act as a space where new forms of relations between Indians and the state are constructed, recontextualizing Indian leadership and privileging seemingly neutral political skills over "anachronistic" or culturally determined social relations.

It is critical to understand, however, that these technologies are not neutral. Instead, they act to politicize local governments so that traditionally favored groups, mostly the white elite, are able to control the municipal budgets. Despite the seemingly inclusive participatory planning process and the rhetoric of inclusion, what happens in practice is that the mayor and the political parties in control of the municipality make the decisions about the obras. This means that the "ability of the local leaders to push, personal influences, the ties of friendships, and even political affinities come into play at the moment of the prioritization of projects and the elaboration of the POA" (Blanes 2000: 47). Interestingly, even in some communities that were converted into indigenous municipal districts (DMIs) (where a submunicipality or subalcaldía was created that contains only indigenous communities), the power of the local elites can continue. For example, Lema's study of the Guaraní DMI in Gutiérrez showed that the indigenous leaders found it difficult to act as the subalcalde, because of the dual responsibility to the community and its interests on the one hand and to the municipal government on the other. In this DMI, as well as in the Weenhayek DMI in Villa Monte, Lema found that ultimately the indigenous subalcaldía remained dependent on the decisions of the mayor of the larger municipio to which it pertained (Lema 2001: 180ff).[48]

The technical and educational requirements I have described had another result: they fostered indigenous dependence on NGOs. CEADES's LPP training project with Zona Cruz was not unusual. All over the country, NGOs took advantage of the money flowing in to fund neoliberal decentralization and political reforms. In some places, there was an invasion of scholars and NGO workers seeking to find work in this new field. (To be honest, I must count myself among them. Although I was not part of an NGO, I was carrying out participant observation in their midst.) Some NGO workers installed themselves in city halls, while others limited themselves to sending representatives to develop particular activities. Many of them turned themselves into the spokespersons for indigenous demands and claims (Lema 2001: 228). Thus, where local organizational capacity is relatively weak, there may be a "tendency for even the best-intentioned NGOs to take over and control the process" (Kohl 2003: 161).

In other places, NGOs acted in more favorable ways. For example, planner Ben Kohl carried out a study of popular participation in several municipalities across the country. He concluded that where local organizations are strong and backed by NGOs able to provide technical expertise while supporting grassroots leadership, the LPP has been able to strengthen rural development. Moreover, municipalities that have active NGOs working for them have generally fared much better under the LPP than those without them. He describes the city of Uncia, where an NGO that worked in the region for more than fifteen years won the contract to write the municipal plan. "The thorough planning undertaken by the NGO served to educate communities about their rights and empowered them to confront corrupt local officials" (Kohl 2003a: 161). But this may come at a high cost. Anthropologist Carmen Medeiros has studied the workings of the LPP in the highland town of Arque, where a development NGO had been working for some years before the law's implementation. She argues that the involvement of local peasant communities in municipal meetings was only possible because of the pressure and active involvement of the development institutions working in the province. They provided technical training for the city officials as well as the peasants union, gave additional funds for the agreed-on projects, and, most important, had the technical knowledge necessary for the projects. "The concrete outcomes of the meetings had to be specific project ideas, and only the experts had the skills to evaluate their feasibility and to formulate them following the jargon and requirements of funding agents" (Medeiros 2001: 416).

Fragmentation of Traditional Organizations

A crucial factor in the ability of indigenous leaders to exert the necessary pressure to get obras is the makeup of their communities. The Guaraní leaders described so far came from ethnically homogenous Guaraní communities with a single representative organization, the capitanía. Many Guaraní communities in Zona Cruz are ethnically mixed, however, and this posed a serious problem in organizing participation under the LPP. In Bella Flor, Guaraní residents ended up folded into the neighborhood association after the land sales had changed community demographics. The situation of Barrio San José is similar.

About twenty Guaraní families live in urban San José, a rapidly growing neighborhood in the city of Santa Cruz. In San José, the junta vecinal is controlled by kollas, migrants from the Andean regions, most of whom speak Quechua. The Guaraní residents had formed their own organization, a community capitanía, in the early 1990s as part of the Capitanía Zona Cruz (CZC). The local capitanía was an important part of the San José Guaranís' lives. It offered a source of ethnic pride, a way for urban Guaranís to spend time with others who spoke their language, and it was a vehicle for organizing efforts to get city resources. Relations between the Guaraní and kolla groups were civil, but efforts to work together on several economic projects (like a small store) were not successful. Don Lorenzo Rivera, the capitán and the patriarch of the extended family that made up the Guaraní community there, explained that the kollas hated them. The kollas, he said, wanted to run the organization "their way," and they had such a forceful, abrupt manner that the Guaranís did not feel comfortable. Moreover, the kollas had different ideas about money. They were "*mesquinos*" (stingy), and the Guaranís couldn't convince them to spend any of the money for things they felt were important. Don Lorenzo's use of the negative stereotypes about Andean people (conservative, stingy, overbearing) points out the difficulties of intraethnic organizing.

Before the LPP, each group found it best to work on its own to garner resources. But the LPP allows only one OTB from each region or community, because the organizations must have a "territorial base." So after the

LPP began, the Guaranís (who are outnumbered by far) had little choice but to try to work with their neighbors. They sent a representative to the junta meetings, because they knew the only way to get economic benefits for the Guaranís was to have a Guaraní on the junta board. But soon the problems began. Don Lorenzo's wife, Amalia, told me the Guaranís were treated badly by their neighbors, "like Indios." Although there were interests in common with their neighbors — everyone was concerned with street lighting, teacher salaries, and so on — what the Guaranís wanted was money to make a Guaraní meeting center. Naturally, this did not go over well with the rest of the community. A division among the Guaranís developed over how to (and who should) work with the junta. Most Guaranís withdrew, but one family remained, trying to overcome the differences. This caused further division in the capitanía, which more and more seemed to lose its reason for existence.

Don Lorenzo expressed his frustrations: "We have to try to get what we can from the LPP, but it is difficult. The danger is that we are going to be absorbed into the kolla organization. They will just run everything anyway." His solution was to return to tried-and-true traditional Bolivian clientelism: he joined a political party to try to form a relation with the powerful party boss in his section. "This is the way to get money and resources for my people," he told me some months later. He was considering running for local office, because he knew that if he did, the party would give him food and clothes to give out as part of the campaign. "The politicians never come through after the elections," he said, "but you can get some good things that way. Maybe I can get latrines for the community."

A similar problem arose in Las Palmas, an ethnically mixed community near one of the sugar refineries in the Warnes region. The small Guaraní community was a member of Zona Cruz, and its leader, Doña Rosa Montes, was trying to use the capitanía as a tool for bringing development to her community. The Guaranís decided that the community's main priority was getting a potable water system, so they called their non-Guaraní neighbors together and began to work together. Just then, the LPP began to function. A non-Guaraní woman who was a *militante* (literally "militant," meaning an active member) of one of the political parties organized her own OTB, got recognized using her political connections, and started a campaign for potable water. When I talked with the capitana in 1998, she lamented how the Guaranís had been marginalized from the political process, and she assured me that a major reason was racism. The head of the new OTB despised Guaranís and had been quite open about taking the project out of Guaraní hands. Doña Rosa said that although she was glad that it appeared the city would fund the water project through the LPP, she feared the racism of the people in charge might negatively affect service to the Guaranís. Would their part of the neighborhood get left out? The whole thing had been a terrible blow to the capitanía. Not only had the Guaranís lost their connection to the city since they were not welcome in the OTB, but the capitanía had also lost force. Now Doña Rosa could never get anyone to come to meetings. Slowly, the Guaranís of the community stopped participating in any capitanía activities, as their daily lives were regulated more through the junta vecinal.

These examples support political scientist Iris Marion Young's argument that in societies characterized by marked inequalities between groups, "universalist" citizenship practices often end up reinforcing the values and power of the dominant group. This is because such practices, which give equal representation to all citizens, make the erroneous assumption that all citizens have equal power and abilities to articulate their interests. Since this is not true in practice, Young advocates for what she calls "differentiated citizenship," which would institute special representation rights for disadvantaged groups. Without such protections for the minority groups, democracy tends to reproduce existing power relations (Young 1996). This helps to explain why the LPP, which was supposed to recognize and institutionalize ethnic and cultural difference, in fact often results in the fragmentation of indigenous organizations. The examples cited earlier took place in multiethnic communities, but this fragmentation has been documented across the country.

One problem is that the law imposes a generic requirement for representation in municipal meetings that is based on Western cultural models. This "New England town meeting" model, as one USAID official described it to me, with its clearly defined roles of president, vice president, and so on, does not match indigenous forms of authority or representation. For instance, many lowland indigenous groups make decisions like the Guaranís, in large assemblies in which decisions are made by consensus. Leaders are then given the responsibility to carry out the will of the group. In Andean communities, communities are often organized into *ayllus*. These sociopolitical entities have a dual and complementary structure as well as a couple-based (man and woman) system of authority (Calla Ortega 2000: 83). Despite the discourse of honoring the customs of indigenous peoples, it is clear that neither of these traditional forms of organization is compatible with the requirements of the LPP.

In addition, the new system of representation, compatible or not, acts as an alternative and parallel institution to the traditional forms of sociopolitical organization. Busy people, especially poor subsistence farmers, have little time for political functions. The ETZ técnicos spent an enormous amount of time trying to encourage the leaders of local Guaraní communities to get involved, to go to the municipal meetings. They had little success in this, though, as most of the people in the communities simply did not have any time to leave their day labor or agricultural jobs. Who would provide money for their families in the meantime? The cargo system in Andean communities recognizes this, rotating the burden of service every year (Abercrombie 1998). Where communities have traditional organizations, like the capitanía or an ayllu, it is an additional burden to have to serve on both this and the OTB. This is aggravated by the fact that OTBs are the new point of access to the state and to its resources. It is not surprising that traditional organizations are losing meaning and force at the local level, replaced by OTBs and the oversight committees. The result is that instead of institutionalizing the *usos y costumbres* of native culture, participation in the OTBs acts as a form of acculturation that weakens the indigenous organizations.

Bolivian anthropologist Ricardo Calla Ortega has pointed to another factor that threatens indigenous organizations, particularly in the highlands. There the traditional sociopolitical organization, the ayllu, often covers large discontinuous areas of land and vertical territorial management of distinct ecological niches, which do not map onto municipal boundaries. This has caused major disruptions within the ayllus, as one part of its members may live in one municipality and others in another. To seek the benefits as an OTB means to abandon the traditional social relationships of authority and responsibilities under the traditional cargo system, as organized across the territory, generations, and genders, and instead to adopt the generic system imposed by the LPP. Calla Ortega suggests that the resulting deconstruction of the ayllu system is causing some to lose control over their territories (Calla Ortega 2000: 83).[49]

The same issues have confronted lowland groups, particularly those with extensive territories (Balslev 1997; Orellana Halkyer 2000). The INRA reform, which gave indigenous groups the rights to receive title to their territories, can be seen as a form of "parallel decentralization" (Ayo Saucedo 2003: 142). The law establishes *territorios comunitarios de origen* (TCOs, communal territories of origin), which are controlled and administered by communities or federations of communities of Indians. The problem is that the boundaries of the TCOs, like ayllus, do not map onto municipalities. One third of TCOs are in two municipalities, and another third are in three or more municipalities. This makes it nearly impossible to manage the territories outside the framework of municipal systems described earlier.

Fighting for Small Change

Finally, although the LPP shifted the focus of citizenship to the local level, promising popular participation in local development decisions, in fact the issues at stake in the municipal realm were limited to such local administrative matters as infrastructure, water, roads, and health provision. The LPP shifted 20 percent of federal budget money to the cities, but in practice there is limited money available to the communities and the municipalities control the kinds of projects that are implemented. Remember the admonitions of the oversight committee president to the Guaranís in Warnes? He told them there was only about $2 per person for projects per year. The result is that inclusion in municipal politics has effectively limited the range of demands indigenous people could make there. Instead, these new citizens struggle to gain access to limited revenue-sharing funds for small obras. As I described earlier, in the process in Warnes, this often means deciding between small projects like potable water and schoolrooms in villages. This is not problematic in itself, because the villages do in fact want potable water and more schoolrooms. It is only to note that this set of practices is homogenizing, as cultural and political demands have no place within the local pragmatics.[50] The annual operating budgets are written to reflect the kinds of projects that the municipalities and their governments and NGO partners know how to accomplish. They do not reflect indigenous desires for their communities or regions. Lema has noted that even in Urubichá, where indigenous leaders were elected to the council, the budget did not reflect indigenous values or customs. The things that were important to the local people — the forest, local flora and fauna, ritual relations with the lands — were invisible. Social and cultural-based demands had no place in the process, so few indigenous people were interested in participating in the planning (Lema 2001: 196).

Although participation in local activism can be empowering, even transforming in certain situations, my work with the Guaranís in Santa Cruz has shown that in practice inclusion at the local level has fragmented and refocused indigenous demands to the immediate decisions of local governing, precluding more critical responses to existing inequalities. This left little room for challenging the bases of political power. Rather, the poor, and in this case the indigenous poor, were brought into the system in an orderly way at the local level.[51] The Guaraní communities around Santa Cruz do need water, but they need other things much more. They need land, education, and jobs. Across the country, Indians are the poorest Bolivians, facing centuries-old structured inequalities. The most important issue for indigenous groups has been the struggle to obtain titles to their territories. Yet the inequitable distribution of land and conflicts between rich patrones and the poor employees are not subject to discussion in the sphere of municipal politics. The result is a sad competition among the poorest communities for the crumbs from the tables of the rich. These small projects do not alter the underlying economic or social facts in the municipio, nor do they redistribute resources in any substantial way.[52] The LPP may provide a means by which peasants and

Indians claim respect for their civil rights and recognition of their ethnic identities, but these may not matter if they cannot overcome unequal land distribution, unfair labor exploitation, and overarching poverty.

Good Democracy?

The Law of Popular Participation promised to redefine the relation between citizens and the state, allowing all citizens, including Indians, to participate in local development. By establishing a modern and regulated form of mediation between communities and the state, its architects further hoped to abolish the inefficient and anachronistic corporatist models of politics that had characterized Bolivia since the 1952 revolution. Through these measures, the neoliberal government intended to pass some of the responsibility for governing onto the citizens themselves, make the population more governable, and soften the costs of the painful economic policies it was imposing. The experiences of the Guaranís in Zona Cruz and the other Indians described in this chapter demonstrate that few, if any, of those goals were accomplished. Instead, the political technologies embodied in the practices of the law reinforced the exclusion of Indians from political power and strengthened the power of political parties controlled by the dominant elite. In many areas, the law weakened existing corporate models and eroded their leaders' political and cultural authority.

By radically altering the process by which indigenous communities make demands, these technologies have profoundly affected indigenous leadership practices, replacing social relations arising from the groups with the need to relate to the municipio. This forces community members to consider themselves more as members of the municipio and less as members of the ayllu or capitanía. As people consider themselves in relation to the municipality — and by extension, in relation to the state — their identity as members of indigenous communities is subsumed in part to their identity as individual citizens (see Blanes 2000: 95). This is not a coincidence, but the result of the institutional design of the law and practices that favor homogeneity over social differentiation.

I am not lamenting the loss of tradition here, or expressing nostalgia for the loss of a particular model of leadership. As we have seen in the preceding chapters, relations between Indians and the state have always been mediated by local leaders, and indigenous leadership models and forms of authority have always mutated in the process. Instead, what I am calling attention to is the damaging effects such changes can have for these leaders' followers. In chapter 3, I described how the Guaranís in Zona Cruz chose Don Álvaro Montero as *mburuvicha guasu* in part because of his abilities to manage the modern political challenges the capitanía faced. His leadership, questioned by many, ultimately supported a notion of land as a commodity, and this led to the disintegration of the community. In this chapter, I have described a weakening of the authority of indigenous community leaders as a result of the institutions of the LPP.

In most indigenous groups, leaders are tied to the community through carefully regulated rituals of social control. In the Andes, leaders are required to *rendir cuentas*, to give an accounting of what was done, how money and time were spent, and what the results were. They are held to the basic requirements of the community: do not cheat, do not lie, do not be lazy. The constant need to give information to the base and respond to the community's questions and requirements is an essential part of Andean culture and custom (Patzi 2002; Blanes 2000; Lazar 2005). In the lowlands, the asamblea performs the same function. Guaraní capitanes are required to submit to the desires of the whole community. The LPP has replaced these systems of authority and social control with a discourse of "good democracy," in which municipal administrations guarantee the well-being of citizens and politicians demonstrate their worthiness through the provision of public works (Blanes 2000: 76). More important, it substitutes traditional forms of social organization with foreign models, homogenizing all models into a single acceptable one. Under the LPP, there is only one way to participate and only one way to present demands: through the OTBs to the municipality.[53] The experiences documented in this chapter demonstrate that this "good democracy" model does not function in many parts of Bolivia. Municipalities are not efficient and do not act to benefit all citizens. Rather, municipal administrations are often based on personal clientelist relations between the mayor and communities. This is representation without real social control, and it is not surprising that it often leads to corruption and a lack of real democracy, and eventually to social protest (CEADES 2003: 234).

Because these institutions are controlled by the dominant classes, the racially structured inequalities that have marked Bolivian society have been recontextualized but not substantially altered. Thus the inclusion promised by the LPP has turned out to be profoundly exclusionary. Moreover, the hope of dismantling the clientelistic state model was stymied by an ineffective elite class that continued its prebendal practices, paralyzing the viable functioning of the democratic institutions.

The response of Indians to this experiment in popular participation has been multiple and various. In the Capitanía Zona Cruz, as the next chapter shows, young Indian leaders endeavored to master the logic underlying the reform, so they could be responsible citizens and bring obras to their communities. In other places, Indians soldiered on, trying to overcome the racism and institutional blockages described in this chapter. Perhaps the most important effect of the LPP is one its architects would never have anticipated. If, as this chapter has shown, the old ethnic or corporatist allegiances have been somewhat diminished as a result of the LPP, what has taken its place? Certainly, the political parties have continued their grabs for power. But at the same time, a new form of citizen activism has emerged, precisely as a result of working through the institutions and practices of the LPP, such as OTBs, oversight committees, and municipal political offices. As the following chapters make clear, Indians have taken many lessons from their experiences with the LPP, perhaps the most important of which is their roles as citizens deserving of equal treatment by the state. As Don Faustino Auca, the diputado from Potosí explained, Indians decided they could no longer expect the mestizo elite of Bolivia to share power with them. Instead, they would have to take power and make their own democracy by entering the electoral field at the national level. These experiences are the foundation for postmulticultural citizenship.

5 Forming Neoliberal Subjects: NGOs and "Responsible" Self-Government

> Making [the collective conscience] genuinely collective is
> always an accomplishment, a struggle, against other ways
> of seeing, other moralities . . .
> — Philip Corrigan and Derek Sayer

"We Have to Organize"

Late one hot afternoon in May 1998, two young Guaranís working for the Capitanía Zona Cruz (CZC), Arturo López and Flor García, and I got off the bus in the community of La Primavera, about thirty kilometers east of Warnes. The small village is one of the communities that make up the capitanía, and Arturo and Flor were there to "organize" the community. When it cooled down a bit, the local capitán rang the school bell and slowly a few of the community's residents made their way to the schoolhouse. A few farmers, still dirty from their day's work in the fields, sat in front. Thin women with babies at the breast and toddlers at their feet sat in the back. Arturo and Flor unrolled a colorful chart and taped it to the blackboard. Arturo told the group that he was sorry he had not been able to come visit them since the year before. Now, though, he said, they had funding from an NGO called the Colectivo de Estudios Aplicados y Desarrollo Social (CEADES, Collective for Applied Studies and Social Development), so he had the means to visit. He explained how important it was for the Guaranís to begin to participate in local municipal decisions, a right made possible under the new Law of Popular Participation (LPP). "We have to organize, so that we can get resources for each community." To begin this process, the capitanía needed to be consolidated, and to do so, it needed an organizing statute, the *estatuto orgánico*. Arturo and Flor were there to share a draft of this statute that the technical team, the ETZ, had drafted.

In a few weeks, all the communities were to come together to discuss it. Arturo made his pitch: "Once we have the statute, we can negotiate with the prefectura's office. It is like our first and last name [*nombre y appellido*]. Then we can be recognized under the Popular Participation Law. So you must all get involved. This statute needs to be the responsibility of all the people of the organization, not just the capitanía workers." Flor passed out a few copies of the draft, one to the capitán, and the other to the young camba school-teacher, to whom the community members looked with respect. While the school teacher asked a few questions about the statute, I talked to the man next to me, a quiet Guaraní of about fifty, with the rough hands and feet of someone who had spent his life in the cane fields. "Do you know what a statute is?" I asked him. "No," he said, looking down, but he wouldn't ask Arturo to explain. He just listened quietly and later put his mark on the list of those who had participated at the meeting.

After the meeting, Arturo and Flor were pleased with the results. They had introduced the idea of a statute, left copies for the leaders to review, and gotten a promise from the capitán to attend the upcoming meeting to vote on the statute. Even if the people didn't completely understand the details, Arturo said, it was a start. Most important, they had argued for the need for the Guaranís to start contributing their energy to the capitanía. This, they said, was the first step to "real development." Neither Arturo nor Flor stopped to ponder the many meanings that term might hold, nor did they consider the possibility that the community members might have different ideas about development than the capitanía. Those issues could get worked out in the future. For the moment, what was important was getting the ball rolling, starting the conversation.

What did Arturo and Flor mean when they encouraged the rural Guaraní to "participate" in local government decisions? Why should the illiterate community members of La Primavera feel "responsible" for the terms of an institutional statute? According to historical accounts of Guaraní leadership (described in chapter 3), the *asamblea* (assembly of the community) made decisions orally and by consensus. No formal rules bound them, although they were guided by a roughly held and changeable sense of the ethics of good leadership. In recent times, the *capitanes* have taken on more administrative power with extensive authority to negotiate with the state and local elites. Therefore, the notion of individual participation in local government is quite foreign to these Guaranís, as is the idea of being responsible for drafting a set of formal legalistic rules to order their institutional behavior. Where do these ideas come from, and why were Arturo and Flor so enthusiastic about the participation of the villagers of La Primavera?

The previous chapters have argued that as part of a neoliberal regime of indigenous citizenship, the Bolivian state interpellated indigenous people as citizens. This had been accomplished on one level through the practices and institutions of state-sponsored multiculturalism, which named indigenous people as actors in the administration of local government, intercultural education, territorial titling schemes, and so on. As chapter 4 made clear, one important effect of these reforms is that to take advantage of these rights, indigenous citizens and their leaders are supposed to participate in local government meetings. This is because under modern forms of government advocated by neoliberal philosophies, citizenship should be an active exercise of responsibilities, including economic self-reliance and political participation (Schild 1998: 94). This is consistent with Arturo and Flor's message to the villagers of La Primavera: "We must participate." This is not the only way citizenship could be defined. Under previous corporatist models, for instance, Indians exercised their roles as citizens through membership in organizations or through relations with political patrons. Here, however, we see that differing regimes of citizenship bring with them different forms of identity and behavior, what can be termed a new subjectivity. How do we understand this change?

Governing Citizen Conduct

Previous chapters focused on the practices and discourses of the state (at both the national and local levels) to show how the multicultural regime of citizenship impacted indigenous people and their leaders. As those analyses demonstrated, state institutions are powerful mechanisms for integration, which create pivotal categories of collective and individual identities (Corrigan and Sayer 1985; Schild 1998). In this chapter, I examine the practices of another set of actors, who also act as an interpellating force: NGOs that fund certain forms of indigenous development projects called *etnodesarrollo* (ethnic development). I expand the argument begun in chapter 4 to show that when neoliberal states privatize many of their functions, NGOs can play a predominant part in enacting the discourses and goals of the state and state formation. This chapter shows how NGOs act as a mechanism of governance, doing the state's "work," although this happens without an apparent or obvious link to the state.

This argument is based on the recognition that power is not only exercised by the state, but also is generated from multiple sites in many ways. French social theorist Michel Foucault described differing modalities of power at play in modern societies, contrasting sovereignty with a form of power he termed "governmentality" (Foucault 1991). Sovereignty is about control over territory and people; governmentality is "the conduct of conduct." For Foucault, governmentality refers to two separate but related forms of conduct: on the one hand, "all the endeavors to shape, guide, direct the conduct of others" and, on the other hand, "the ways in which one might be urged and educated to bridle one's own passions, to control one's own instincts, to govern oneself" (Rose 1999: 3). Such governing may be formally rationalized through programs, laws, or policy, but it may also be less formally articulated in terms of a variety of practical rationalities within particular types of practice.[1]

As Foucault scholar Nikolas Rose has suggested, there are "multiple encounters where conduct is subject to government," and many of those are outside the rigid boundaries of state action (ibid.: 5). In this perspective, "the state now appears simply as one element — whose function is historically specific and contextually variable — in multiple circuits of power, connecting a diversity of authorities and forces, within a whole variety of complex assemblages" (ibid.: 5). Using this approach, scholars have noted how neoliberalism regulates and rationalizes conduct through what is defined as "public" or state mechanisms *as well as* through what are defined as "private" arenas, such as corporations, NGOs, and individual actions (Rose 1996; Merry 2001). Thus many of the duties of the state — health, education, policing — are passed to private actors, by selling state enterprises, by reorganizing service providers along economic enterprise models, or by outsourcing to NGOs or private actors (Burchell 1996; Schild 2000).

The state–civil society divide is blurred even further by the increasing role of such international agencies as the World Bank and the International Monetary Fund (IMF) that set political and economic policies like structural adjustment programs as conditions for loans, on the one hand, and international NGOs that sponsor programs and interventions, on the other. This amounts to a kind of transnational governance that acts to transfer sovereignty away from the state (Ferguson and Gupta 2002). Neoliberal notions of development also privilege such local initiative. In what World Bank practitioners call "community-driven development," local community groups and individuals become "assets and partners" in the development process, taking responsibility for decisions and demanding accountability of governments and NGO partners (World Bank 2004).

This chapter explores this form of neoliberal government by showing the work of an NGO with young Guaraní activists in the capitanía. Bolivia's LPP emerged in part from a neoliberal administration eager to pass along responsibility for governing to citizens exercising their rights and obligations at the local level. Although the LPP opened up spaces for indigenous people to make these demands on the state, in practice it made participation in those new spaces dependent on a certain kind of rational behavior: "responsible" participation. Indigenous groups had to organize their own villages to make diagnoses of their needs, to attend meetings where budgets were discussed, to make arguments backed by rational arguments, and to speak a particular kind of bureaucratic jargon defined by the new law. Because these skills were not held by the majority of the supposed beneficiaries of the law, the state and municipalities relied heavily on NGOs, often funded by international organizations, to carry out the widespread training necessary to "educate" citizens about how to access their new rights. In this chapter I show that NGOs funded, taught, and reinforced certain behaviors among their indigenous partners, traits that conformed to the definition of "good" indigenous citizenship pursuant to neoliberal multiculturalism.

The NGO Sector: International Trends

First, why look at NGOs? International funding for indigenous development — "ethnic development" — is part of an international system of aid and policy making that has been enormously important in Bolivia, as it has in the rest of the so-called developing world (Keck and Sikkink 1998). This system has a number of actors and kinds of institutions. Aid may come directly from foreign governments and be sent directly from one government to another as bilateral aid. A substantial amount of foreign aid, however, is administered by international agencies like private nonprofit organizations or transnational advocacy networks with a particular cause or multilateral agencies like the United Nations or the World Health Organization. Any of these donors can give the money or services to particular national or local governments, or they can choose to give the funding directly to local nonprofit organizations. They may give the aid to local grassroots organizations (GROs), membership organizations that represent their members' collective economic, political, or cultural interests, like cooperatives, unions, or indigenous groups (Arellano-López and Petras 1994). Donors may also give money to local NGOs, institutions formed to carry out some particular mission like economic development or social justice. Thus there is a wide spectrum of organizations called NGOs, from small groups doing volunteer work to large institutions administering million-dollar budgets.

Giving aid directly to NGOs or GROs is a particularly important mechanism in situations where the national government is not a reliable channel for the aid, where warfare or internal corruption is present, for example, or where the government is causing the problem the aid is intended to alleviate. During the 1970s, the years of military dictatorships in Latin America, NGOs were important spaces for those opposed to the economic and political policies of the authoritarian states. These NGOs worked closely with GROs, providing political support and organizational training. As democratization occurred across the continent in the 1980s and neoliberal economic policies began to take precedence, however, NGOs began to change their focus from grassroots support to implementing development projects on behalf of government and international development agencies.

Since the early 1980s, there has been a major change in the nongovernmental sector, as the number of development NGOs has skyrocketed. Bolivia is no exception to this general rule: since 1980, the number has gone from between fifty and a hundred NGOs to more than five hundred in 1996 (DCONG 1996; Richards 2000). Especially since the end of the Cold War, bilateral and multilateral donor agencies pursued a "new policy agenda" that gave prominence to the roles of NGOs and GROs in poverty alleviation, social welfare, and the development of "civil society" (Edwards and Hulme 1996: 961). Development scholars Michael Edwards and David Hulme have suggested two main reasons for this trend. Both reasons are based in the neoliberal philosophies in vogue in international lending circles for the past few decades. First, NGOs were "viewed by official agencies and members of the public as more efficient and cost-effective service providers than governments, giving better value-for-money, especially in reaching poor people" (ibid.). NGOs were often seen as less corrupt, more locally based, and more capable of reaching areas with limited resources and infrastructure. Because they are less likely to be paralyzed by bureaucracy, they can be more innovative and flexible in solving problems. In practice, it may not be simply a matter of efficiency but rather a matter of possibility: NGOs took up many of the roles that governments used to fill, as financial crises and structural adjustments of the 1980s and 1990s forced governments to reduce broad areas of social spending (Arellano-López and Petras 1994; Schild 1998).

Second is the notion that good democratic governance is essential for a healthy economy. NGOs were seen as "an integral component of a thriving civil society and an essential counterweight to state power, opening up channels of communication and participation, providing training grounds for activists, and promoting pluralism" (Edwards and Hulme 1996: 962). NGOs were seen to be connected to the people they attempt to serve, to understand their needs more, and to be more cognizant of sociocultural differences than government or international agencies. As such, they were supposedly able to promote the kind of local participation that is not only the basis of liberal notions of democracy, but also is seen as likely to promote project sustainability (Richards 2000).

Whether or not these claims are borne out by the evidence has been the subject of substantial debate in the development literature (see Bebbington and Farrington 1993; Arellano-López and Petras 1994; Edwards and Hulme 1996; Atack 1999; White 1999). Furthermore, scholars have argued that NGOs' claims to legitimacy as agents of "civil society" (however that term might be defined) ignores the complex political, economic, and class interests enacted through NGOs (Arellano-López and Petras 1994; Ferguson 1994; Dougherty 2003). Nevertheless, there has been a striking proliferation of NGOs in development work throughout the world. Some NGOs have acquired substantial political power and act as strong lobbyists with both national states and international organizations, often pressuring governments to obey the laws that protect the most fragile segments of national societies (Ramos 1998: 268). Not only has the number of NGOs risen dramatically, but the proportion of total bilateral aid channeled though them has also increased substantially. This has had important effects: NGOs are growing in size and are becoming more and more involved in implementing state- or international agency–designed projects, rather than the grassroots or "bottom-up" projects that gave them the reputation for being closely connected with their constituencies (Edwards and Hulme 1996).

NGOs in Bolivia

NGOs have been active in Bolivia since the 1960s, when the Alliance for Progress funded nonstate development groups (hoping to stave off Cuban-style resistance to poverty). Similarly, the Catholic Church's "preferential option for the poor" formulated in the 1960s brought funding to grassroots social action groups (Sandoval 1992). These developmentalist NGOs were eclipsed in the 1970s, when a second group of NGOs arose in response to the military dictatorship. These NGOs were part of the resistance movement against state capitalism and the dictatorship (Duran 1990) and "tended toward a political interpretation of development and poverty" (Richards 1998: 22). They formed alliances with campesino and trade union groups, radical miners, and progressive religious sectors of the church. Many were part of leftist political parties, especially the Movimiento de la Izquierda Revolucionario (MIR, Revolutionary Movement of the Left), actively fighting the government. Thus NGOs in Bolivia tend to be made up mostly of urban, white-collar professionals, while GROs tend to have social class origins corresponding to the particular group — peasant, indigenous, and so on (Arellano-López and Petras 1994). In those years, NGOs' goals were to protect popular organizations through human rights and support work as well as through intellectual and training services (Kruse 1994: 134).

When the country returned to democracy in 1982, the NGO sector faced a major shift in identity. Suddenly they were able to work without fear of repression, and there was an enormous amount of aid from large overseas funding organizations (ibid.; Duran 1990; Van Niekerk 1992). Many NGOs foundered during this time, as they found their resistance role eliminated and their experience in administrative roles limited. NGOs' need for a coherent mission was met, in part, by the enormous changes that swept over Bolivia after democratization. In 1985, the government implemented the first neoliberal restructurings of the economy. The economic transformations were accompanied by enormous social costs. In response, the new government instituted the Fondo Social de Emergencia (FSE, the Social Emergency Fund), a palliative program intended to absorb some of the shock of the New Economic Policy (NEP).[2]

The FSE gave NGOs a new role. International agencies responded to Bolivia's financial crises and massive poverty with record assistance, giving $392 million in 1988 and up to $738.2 million in 1990 (Van Niekerk 1992: 133). International donors, especially European governments, preferred to provide the Bolivian government resources it could administer through the FSE, for poverty alleviation efforts implemented by NGOs (Arellano-López and Petras 1994: 562). Throughout the 1980s, the number of NGOs grew rapidly to accommodate the available money. In addition, the Paz Estenssoro administration realized it would need NGOs to help administer the programs, because existing government ministries were lacking or inefficient. As a result, approximately one-third of all the FSE funds were channeled through NGOs. The NGOs were crucial in increasing the breadth and reach of the FSE programs, since they worked with local and grassroots groups and were able to get projects out into places government ministries never could have (Kruse 1994: 138–39). Clearly, the boundaries between governmental and "nongovernmental" agencies began to blur here. On the one hand, the state was able to attract international monies because they would be administered by NGOs, and on the other hand, the NGOs grew because of this arrangement with the state.

The FSE-NGO relationship during the late 1980s fundamentally changed the way NGOs operate in Bolivia. First, it amounted to a thaw in relations with the state. After the initial suspicions were satisfied and it became clear that the FSE was not driven by the power of partisan politics, many NGOs found the state was an acceptable partner. Planner and economic analyst Thomas A. Kruse has argued that NGOs weren't compromised in strictly partisan terms, but because the FSE promoted popular support for the government, working with the FSE meant a de facto acquiescence to the logic and viability of an antipopular program (ibid.: 140). That is, the NGOs were "in some capacity rendered functional to the logic of neoliberalism . . . at the same time that they (potentially) took advantage of the available resources to other ends" (ibid.:142).

Second, the other big change was the increasing professionalization of the NGO sector. As NGOs began to administer larger and larger projects, they had to develop accountability and the ability to engage with government and funding organizations. The relationship between NGOs and external funding again posed the difficult question of co-optation. One of the most critical arguments on this point was made by sociologist James Petras, who argued that Latin American intellectuals generally have been transformed by their incorporation as research functionaries in institutes dependent on external funding. He says the hegemonic political projects of the funders are masked by the appearance of local autonomy and by the use of seemingly neutral social science jargon, depoliticizing their claims (Petras and Morley 1990: 150). Petras (with coauthor Sonia Arellano-López) suggests that Bolivian NGOs became so dependent on outside funds that they were obliged to join the chase for funds. As a result, they say, "the diversity of views that these institutions represented has largely been lost as they have competed with one another to become the favoured clients of international donors" (Arellano-López and Petras 1994: 567).

These pressures created new winners and losers among NGOs, depending on their ability to adjust to these new conditions (Schild 2000). For instance, under neoliberalism, bilateral and multilateral funding has flowed away from development and toward decentralization and governance projects. As a result, funders are increasingly directing resources through municipalities, and this has meant the loss of direct funding for NGOs as well as increased competition for limited funds (Kohl 2003a: 160). This has caused NGOs to sell their services as consultants to municipalities (Bebbington 1997).[3] In many Bolivian municipalities, NGOs were hired as consultants to help implement the new LPP, drafting budgets and plans, organizing community members, and advising community leaders (Kohl 2003b). These structural changes have led NGOs not only to compete for funding to implement government programs, sometimes usurping the political space that once belonged to grassroots organizations, but also to change their missions to accommodate to the logic implicit within those programs. The case of CEADES is illustrative of this point.

The Evolution of an NGO: CEADES

CEADES is a small Bolivian NGO based in Santa Cruz. Its four principal workers are educated intellectuals with long histories of social activism. Three are Bolivian (a sociologist, an economist, and an agronomist), and one is Chilean (Julián Paz, the geographer).[4] CEADES began working with the capitanía in 1996 on various projects, the most important of which was training of the young workers of the organization, the Equipo Técnico Zonal (ETZ). This "institutional strengthening" work was designed to form a new kind of indigenous leader, capable of exercising his or her rights as citizens of the new democratic Bolivia. A brief history of the organization shows the multiple influences on its work with the Guaranís: the Catholic Church, leftist populist ideologies, international NGO funding agendas, and personal trajectories.

The group's three Bolivian members had attended a progressive Jesuit high school in Cochabamba founded by a Belgian priest, and they wanted to find professional work that would repay their "debt to society." Two of them began working with the Centro de Investigación y Promoción del Campesinado (CIPCA, Center for the Investigation and Promotion of the Peasantry), the Jesuit-led NGO in Camiri that supported local indigenous groups, particularly Guaranís. Others in the group began working in a medium-size Bolivian NGO called PROCESO, which focused on two separate projects. The first was indigenous literacy, which was a joint program with the Asociación del Pueblo Guaraní (APG), the national Guaraní federation. CIPCA funded and encouraged the work of the APG to use literacy to politicize and organize Guaranís throughout the country, valorizing indigenous languages and identities. The program caught on and began to get international aid money. Soon the program covered three departments and twenty-three regions, and PROCESO joined the team to design the program's methodology, in consultation with the APG, which then trained the literacy teams.

Out of this process came the second component of PROCESO: environmental education. The idea was to use the literacy program to begin a discussion about the environment and the need for indigenous people to participate in the decisions that affected their environment. Julián Paz joined PROCESO at that time, hoping to put his expertise to work in the interface between environmental, political, and social issues. This environmental project was funded by a German activist with the Green Party and the German Parliament, which wanted to encourage environmental conservation. They provided enough money for the PROCESO team to travel all over Bolivia, holding workshops with indigenous groups. Through this they developed long-term ties with Guaranís in southern Bolivia.

Julián told me that it was an important time for NGOs, because they had the chance to enact the progressive theories they held about adult education, mostly based on the writings of education scholar Paolo Freire.[5] Julián was part of the group the Consejo de Educación de Adultos de América Latina (CEAAL, Council for Adult Education in Latin America), a movement of educators trying to form and educate popular leaders during the 1960s. He explained that the movement's primary tenet was the belief that the people themselves are the carriers of theory, that they are capable of producing transformation as a result of their own social, political, and economic experience. They can recuperate their traditions and their experience through a process of critical analysis of their reality. The question for the Bolivian NGOs was how to apply this to the world of the campesino and the *indígena*. The work of the APG and PROCESO was an attempt to figure this out in practice.

Unfortunately, Julián told me, they never got the chance to come to any conclusions, because the political circumstances changed and neoliberal strategies took the fore. Many of the NGO workers engaged in this struggle joined the government or the political parties. Some saw a possibility to effect more political change from within the government. Others, tired of the difficult life of the marginalized NGO worker, opted for the (relative) security of government jobs. For those who stayed in the NGO world, he said, there was a period of radical and pragmatic redefinition. For Julián and for PROCESO, the decision was to step back from the role of political actor and to work instead to facilitate the assumption of that role by the people they had hoped to educate, the *capacitados* (the trained or educated). Julián explained:

> JP: So what are we preaching now? Organize yourself, train yourself, fulfill your obligations, and exercise your rights! The social control of the state and the democratic process must be carefully watched, and the controllers controlled. What are the means for this? Organization, training, projects. They are not the ends in themselves, but means to this end.
>
> NGP: Then you believe in democracy?
>
> JP: Yes, of course. [Claro que sí]. Not as a formal system, but as a future. As an individual you can be recognized, that is a sphere of liberty that is possible. Right now, the democracy of Bolivia is limited to the sphere of elections. This is the only level of participation, the rest is still held prisoner to certain groups. But what we want to promote is participation at all levels, beyond the vote. Human rights should be broad: liberty and access to resources that all should have. Institutionally, we are calling for this to happen at many levels: environment, health, work, for children and the aged.

One of the ways Julián and his colleagues decided to put their ideas of democracy to work was to engage with their old friends the Guaranís who, under the new Popular Participation laws, might be able to gain political control of the municipalities. The Goni years were exciting for people who had experience and interest in working with indigenous groups. In a short time, the government passed the reforms that I have described earlier, and there was quite a lot of international attention paid to them. The LPP was of particular interest, as it combined neoliberal notions of decentralization with traditional liberal notions of local democracies. Suddenly, all over the country, people in government and in NGOs were talking about participation, citizenship, and democracy — as ideas but also as practices that had to be learned. In this way, we see how the particular definition of citizenship began to be enacted: through projects.

So it was not surprising that PROCESO, like the many other NGOs around Bolivia that were jumping on the Popular Participation bandwagon, began to turn its programmatic work in that direction. It was in a good position to use its continued desire to empower popular leaders in the new political context, and it was fundable. PROCESO applied for and got a grant from a Swedish NGO named Diakonia to help indigenous people take advantage of their rights as citizens under the new reforms. The grant paid for the salaries of the PROCESO workers, for overhead for the Santa Cruz office, for various travel costs, and for the costs of workshops in indigenous communities.[6]

PROCESO began by working in one Guaraní community in the south, near Camiri, where Guaranís are in the majority. A mixed group of Guaraní and *karai* (white) educators went to the community and led participatory workshops along with the local leaders. The result was that one of the indigenous leaders was elected mayor, one of the first indigenous mayors in the country. The surprising success of the process led to a huge influx of international money into PROCESO with the goal of reproducing its success in other Guaraní communities. This resulted in a leadership crisis in the NGO. According to Julián, one of the main conflicts was about who was going to be the leader of this new larger program. This was important, because whoever directed such an influential program could be catapulted into a government position as a minister or the head of a government agency like the Subsecretario de Asuntos Étnicos (SAE, the Subsecretariat of Ethnic Affairs).

Of course, this would have been one way of co-opting NGO success, Julián said, but some of the NGO workers, weary of years working in the countryside and having to be away from their families, saw the possibilities as a way out. CEADES was formed after the rupture, when Julián and his current colleagues left PROCESO. The rift also affected the funders, recalled Julián, because much of the funding was the result of personal confidences. While that can be good, he said, it also can be unfortunate, as "we are often subject to the whims [*ánimos*] of some gringo who is making choices about his own career." Some of the funders stayed with the PROCESO project, but Julián and the CEADES group managed to convince the Swedes to fund them to carry on with the Guaraní project.

Unfortunately, during the crisis, PROCESO had withdrawn from the Camiri Guaraní project and left the capitanía without advisers and in chaos. The results were disastrous: ultimately, the Guaraní mayor was convicted of corruption charges, and the mayorship returned to the hands of the local white elite. These sorts of problems were endemic across the country. After a hiatus of several years, the newly formed CEADES reentered the arena to find another community in which to start a pilot program. They had the money; they just needed another Guaraní community in which to administer it. Through their contacts with the APG, they made connections with the Capitanía Zona Cruz (CZC) and explained what they wanted to try. The Zona Cruz leaders were excited about it, they told me, because it was quite a large amount of money to be invested in the training of the youth (although no one at Zona Cruz could remember the amount of the grant, and it is not in the written agreement). So in 1996, CEADES and the capitanía signed an agreement in which CEADES was to help train the ETZ and to strengthen the CZC's ability to exercise its civil rights under the new law. (This was part of a larger agreement between CEADES and the APG, in which CEADES agreed to work both with Zona Cruz and another capitanía in the region of Charagua in the south.)

This brief history shows several things that lead us back to James Petras's concerns about NGOs. First, it is clear that international funding has been given with the intent to influence behavior and policy. Belgian, German, and Swedish money has provided the possibilities for the work of many NGOs. Second, the evolution from activist-progressive education to a strategy of withdrawing from direct political action follows the trends Petras and others have shown to be the result of the neoliberal moment. Yet CEADES has hardly left political work. To the contrary, its practices are intended to regulate the conduct of political actors. More important, Julián Paz's story also shows how these international discourses are enacted and lived through individual people, whose feelings are structured by the times in which they act. Julián's notion of multicultural citizenship as a potential political opening is the result of having lived through Bolivia's return to democracy. This opened spaces for political action that had been impossible before. It is also the result of the neoliberal context, which constrains his actions in many ways and makes only limited institutionalized forms of citizenship possible. Finally, it is the result of the maturation of his own personal philosophies. That is, the hopes of a radical twenty-year-old longing for democracy are quite different from those of a mature activist with a now tempered vision of what is possible.

What runs through the historical trajectory of the NGOs is an overriding faith in democracy and participation. I suggest that Julián and his fellow NGO workers were interpellated by the discourses and practices of democracy in the same way that the indigenous citizens were interpellated by the multicultural reforms. That is, they were citizens of a country that had come through years of military dictatorship into a functioning, if far from perfect, democracy, in part due to the civil and political actions of people and NGOs like Julián and CEADES. It is partially through the practices of NGOs working toward democracy that the ideology of citizenship is built. Thus, like all citizens, NGO workers are both the agents and the subjects of the current regime of citizenship — they are constituted by the lived experiences of being citizens, and then they have a role in constituting what citizenship means. These practices have been supported by international money, but this is not an overdetermining factor. Although there can be no doubt that NGOs offer an important source of employment for middle-class educated people like the CEADES workers, my analysis convinces me that NGO agendas are a complex articulation of multiple factors. These include international funding pressures, roles in the formulation and reproduction of discourses, personal experiences, and current political constraints.

What is of particular interest here is how NGO workers — themselves constructed as subjects of the nation-state through their experiences and faith in liberal democratic ideals — act as agents of the government. They also act as mechanisms of neoliberal governance by reproducing the discourse and practices of neoliberal multiculturalism with the intended "beneficiaries" of their work. CEADES's work with the ETZ was an exercise in making Guaranís into citizens, reproducing discourses of citizenship and democracy the workers themselves had internalized. How did they do this?

The Zona Cruz Project

The CEADES project was officially entitled the Proyecto de Fortalecimiento Organizativo de Zona Cruz para el Desarrollo Local (Zona Cruz Organizational Strengthening Project for Local Development). The main idea was to help Zona Cruz communities to take advantage of the new reforms, particularly the Law of Popular Participation. By learning how to participate in development decisions at the municipal level, Guaranís would not only begin to have access to some part of the resources the state was giving other communities, but they would also begin to learn how to be responsible citizens exercising *gestión* (management skills).[7] In practice, the main work of the CEADES project was to train the ETZ, because CEADES couldn't go out to all the twenty-six communities and train all the local leaders. Instead, CEADES was to train the trainers, who would then go out to each community, diagnose the particular needs, and encourage the communities themselves to push the municipalities to include those needs into each municipality's annual operating plan.

CEADES began training the ETZ in 1997, holding workshops in its offices in town. They paid for the travel expenses and *viáticos* (daily expenses) for the team of young Guaranís. (These payments are crucial to the participants, who truly do not have enough money for the twenty-five-cent bus fares into town.) In chapter 1, I described the group in more detail. They were, for the most part, in their twenties and among the most educated Guaranís of their generation. Most had graduated from high school, a real accomplishment among the poor in Bolivia. They lived in the closely surrounding communities (that is, none of them came from the most rural of the communities), but they often had to take buses for several hours to attend the workshops. They were eight men and four women, and each had a particular responsibility to the capitanía — Arturo López was in charge of development projects, Rosana Moreno was in charge of women's issues, and so on. Besides their area of programmatic responsibility, each ETZ member was also made responsible for a certain number of the communities, to carry out various tasks.

The workshops varied in length and content, but usually they were day-long meetings attended by the whole ETZ team and facilitated by a CEADES staff person. The group would gather in the conference room and spend the entire day in discussions, recording their ideas and decisions on brown butcher paper taped to the blackboard. The overall goal was to get the participants to come up with a plan for the organization's future and to begin to enact it. This entailed information-gathering and analysis of the issues confronting the Guaraní communities that made up the capitanía. So, first, the team had to think through the issues, then design a diagnosis instrument to be applied, and then go out and do some research. These steps took several months. Follow-up meetings took up the reports and the problems they identified, as well as reasons why the research trips failed. The lengthy workshop meetings were spaced around these goals and took place every three weeks or so. In some periods, they were held more frequently. While the team was formulating the organization's organic statute, for instance, they met almost every day for several weeks. As the team and its plans for the organization gathered more coherence, they also met outside the formal meetings at CEADES, particularly at the capitanía offices. After the meetings, the team and I would often continue our discussions at a restaurant or bar near the downtown bus station, after which we would disperse to our homes for the night.

The CEADES staff member responsible (most often it was Julián) worked to mold these young people into political organizers. The training was both practical and theoretical. The main task was to teach the ETZ members how to identify goals in a rational, consensus-driven manner and then to decide how those goals could best be reached. Julián told me he was trying to teach a process rather than the answers. By teaching them to be good political organizers, he was also imbuing the Guaranís with the characteristics of good citizens, according to the current definition thereof, which includes participation, efficiency, and responsibility.

Techniques of the Self: Participation as Responsibility

Teaching young Indians about citizenship began not with a civics class or a lesson about the new law but with workshops designed to teach new personal skills to the ETZ team. The workshop was aimed at fomenting a sense of individual responsibility in the young adults and women of all ages —

segments of the Guaraní community that are typically ascribed secondary roles in the Guaraní communities. These young leaders wanted to learn these skills because they considered them essential to success in the *karai* (white) world, but they found doing so both stimulating and unsettling. Such personal skills are tied to particular political and cultural contexts, and their adoption brought to light a number of contradictions for Guaranís.

For instance, the most important skill Julián taught was the ability to speak and participate in public discussions. The younger Guaranís in the group told me they found this difficult because they had been taught by their parents to guard their tongues in public, especially in front of wiser and more experienced elders. Women are at an even greater disadvantage, as they are expected to defer to their husbands and fathers. Once, for example, I was at the home of Oscar Cruz and Angelina Nuñez, friends in Bella Flor. One night, when Angelina was speaking to me, Oscar interrupted her as if scolding a small child. "How can you be talking like this when your husband is right here? Be quiet like a good woman." Women and young people do express opinions about what is at stake in the community, but most of this discussion takes place in private conversations. This reflects a system of hierarchies within Guaraní cultural formations, but I suggest it is also the result of a Guaraní sense of self in which individual interests are always balanced with — in fact formulated through — one's sense of belonging to a collective unit.

These customs, and the related sense of self, are changing as the younger generation and women gain education, employment, and experience in the urban environment. The NGO training was a further step in this direction because the entire team was expected to develop a sense of individual responsibility cut loose from culturally structured social formations. Each "citizen" of this small democratic republic was supposedly equal and was expected to have a voice and an individual position. Some of the ETZ members had little problem with this, especially those who had been to school outside their communities like Samuel Tapera and Arturo López. Others needed training to accomplish it, however. Some of the methods Julián used were right out of pedagogy trainings, but they were immensely successful. For instance, when no one would talk, Julián took out colored index cards and had people write their ideas on the cards. Then he would read the cards and attach them to the butcher paper hanging at the front of the class. Or he would break the group into smaller groups, each with the responsibility to present their answers to the larger group. These all taught a different sense of responsibility. Over the course of the training, I noticed a remarkable change in the ability of the ETZ members to speak out and argue their points. Of course, it is difficult to know how much this translated into the ability to speak up outside these gatherings. Some of the leaders — like Samuel, Arturo, and

Rosana — continued on in their leadership roles with the organization over the following years and made good use of the training. For others — like Flor, who drifted away from the group — this "self-help" training may not have had lasting effects.

Drafting the Estatuto Orgánico

During the year that I accompanied the project, the group realized it needed to take all the steps necessary to obtain the *personería jurídica* (legal recognition) for the parent organization, the Capitanía Zona Cruz, as well as for the local capitanías. This meant drafting an *estatuto orgánico* (literally, an organic statute), a sort of articles of incorporation and constitution. The ETZ and CEADES took on this task, and over several intense months of discussions about what they wanted the capitanía to be, they produced a draft statute. (This is the statute Arturo and Flor were talking to the community about in the opening anecdote of this chapter.) In chapter 1, I describe the contents of the statute and the meaning it had for the organization. In this chapter, I discuss the effects of the process of drafting the statute. One effect was that the Guaranís were forced to codify their "traditional" rules and to submit those rules to government approval. As the ETZ team labored over the new articles and rules for the draft statute, Julián encouraged them. This statute is "an act of constitution," he said, "a coming together of sovereignty and citizenship. The state is making an offer, and you are accepting it." More important, however, the process of drafting of the statute demonstrated to the ETZ that neoliberal citizenship begins with orderly participation. Two important sets of practices demonstrated this connection.

The first set of practices Julián taught was the rational and participatory way of running meetings. Guaraní assemblies in Zona Cruz had tended to be mostly a matter of the leaders reporting what they did during the previous term, introducing powerful political allies, and answering the complaints of their constituents.[8] For the consideration of the statute, the ETZ implemented a new model of assembly procedure, faithfully reproduced from the NGO workshops. They began taking copies of the draft to the communities to encourage attendance. Then they held a two-day-long conference for the leaders and delegates of all the communities. The ETZ team presided, and after a full oral reading of the draft (because so many Guaranís are illiterate), they broke the assembled group into small sections, each with the responsibility to review a certain section of the statute. Many Guaranís had grave doubts about the process and about particular elements of the statute. For instance, the conservative elders felt the ETZ was getting too much power. They participated in the groups, however, and there was a lively debate about the contentious issues. These conversations went on long into the night, even among archenemies. This process facilitated certain discussions, but it also precluded other equally important debates. For example, one family felt the capitán Don Álvaro was corrupt and should be kicked out. Their objections were silenced by the format the ETZ pushed through. In the end, the groups got back together, raised the concerns and suggestions about the statute, and the entire group voted on changes. At the end of two long days, the statute was passed with minimal amendments. Even those who opposed the capitán grande and the ETZ ended up giving their consent to this new process and with the results it produced.

This shows how some of the practices of citizenship taught by the NGO were adopted and reproduced by the ETZ. It also shows how these practices were productive in the Foucaultian sense. For instance, throughout the year, the most salient value presented to the ETZ by the NGO leaders was to *want* to participate, and to urge other group members to be responsible for their own villages' welfare. The trip with Arturo and Flor recounted at the beginning of the chapter demonstrates how the neoliberal discourse of "responsibilization" was reproduced: the young leaders felt responsible for their conduct and urged their charges to feel and act in the same way. Whether it caused the community members to want to participate is hard to tell. Many Guaranís had already planned to come to the meeting because they saw it as in their community's long-term interest. It was a well-attended and participatory community decision-making event, which resulted in a statute that the federation has since used as its magna carta, turning to it in times of internal conflict. Like the rest of the tasks, the drafting of the statute was orderly, rational, and based on group consensus, with occasional input from the capitán grande, who sporadically attended such meetings. In this case, the ETZ members learned not only that rules were important to good government, but also that they could design the rules and get the Guaraní assembly to agree to and abide by such rules.

Corporatizing the Organization

The second means Julián used was a strategy of "selling" the statute, by adopting an economic model of the capitanía. Julián suggested that to have meaning for the people, the capitanía had to offer a packet of services to the people so that they would support it. This packet needed to be visible in the statute and in the public meetings to approve it. This is reflective of the changing roles for leaders, as I discussed in chapter 3. Thus, he said, the capitanía had to look beyond the "traditional" models of government —

in which leaders were seen as humble servants of the community, or, after the Spanish conquest, as strong personalistic leaders — to adopt a corporate service model, with clear designations of who is responsible for what organizational tasks. Crucial to this service model was the notion of efficiency.[9]

The focus on efficiency was evident in the NGO workshops, where ETZ members were taught to account carefully for all the money they spent on their community-outreach trips. Julián wrote in large letters on the board the word *eficiencia* (efficiency). He continued: "What is efficiency? One of the most important parts of a modern team is efficiency — cost to benefit, we spend less than we make. . . . The farmer who invests more into his *chaco* [farm plot] than he can sell his products for loses. So if you spend all your salary in the first weekend on parties and drinking, then what do you do?. . . . The other half is *eficacia* [effectiveness] — fulfilling the goals. . . . Efficiency is related to honesty and correct administration, and effectiveness to responsibility, commitment, and realistic and reachable objectives." Preparing a chart of all the places they had gone, how many community members had shown up, and how much the ETZ had spent in each place, it turned out that meetings were only held in thirteen of the communities. "That is only a 59 percent return," Julián said. He concluded that if the community doesn't get organized and show interest in working with the ETZ team, the ETZ should stop spending time and money on them. "The capitanía needs results! It's better to work with one community with results than twenty without."

Another key element of efficiency Julián taught was good money management. There are some obvious reasons why NGOs feel they must teach their indigenous partners these skills. First, most Guaranís have lived in rural communities, where cash is less important than in urban environments. Although the Guaranís in the ETZ were not subsistence farmers outside the cash economy, neither had they lived in circumstances where they controlled much money. Second, the Guaranís distrusted banks, which they considered racialized spaces of power. After hearing several stories about how other Guaranís had been ignored or treated poorly at banks, I accompanied Rosana Moreno, one of the ETZ members, to open an account for money that had been donated to her for a college scholarship. Like most banks, it was enormously bureaucratic, with long lines, bored and uncommunicative tellers, and complicated forms to fill out. Even worse, the teller at the new accounts desk was disregarding the line, serving the loudest clients first. Anyone would have felt intimidated — I certainly did. The teller looked right through Rosana, who has recognizably indigenous facial features. Even after we got the teller's attention, she displayed disdain and doubt that Rosana could manage the details of her savings account. When we left, Rosana explained that this kind of humiliation — "They make us feel ashamed" ("Nos hace sentir vergüenza") — kept many of her friends out of banks altogether.[10]

Finally, NGOs have to deal with money issues because there is so much concern about corruption among NGO beneficiaries. This is tricky for NGO workers. As I have discussed elsewhere (Postero 2000), the subject of indigenous corruption is avoided in public yet often acknowledged in private.[11] Because funders have a great deal of pressure to make sure that the monies they disburse for development projects are actually used by the intended beneficiaries and not squandered, there are often quite rigid reporting and accounting requirements, which can be frustrating and difficult for all involved. In one meeting of the capitanía, for instance, the treasurer, Enrique Colón, a young Guaraní who was enrolled in accounting classes at the local university, tried to remind the capitán grande that the accounting for their biggest grant (a grant from the Danes for general institutional support) was due soon and that the leader should be getting his report ready. "Oh, you know how hard it is for me to do this!" the capitán exclaimed. Soon, all the young ETZ members were bending around the capitán, going through his agenda, trying to count the hours he had worked for this project. (Even my field notebook was enlisted in the accounting project.)

An even harder problem was how to account for money the capitán had personally been granted. He had been given a certain amount for transportation money, to get him out to the rural communities to maintain the ties. When he had to report how he had used the funds, the capitán said he had run out of money to get to the communities because he had had to take several people out to lunch, including the office secretary. The assembled group debated this issue a long time, because they understood that the capitán has obligations to be a generous father figure and that political connections necessary to smooth the workings of the capitanía require such social stroking. Yet the younger generation also felt constrained by the funder's bureaucratic requirements. "If we don't follow the rules of the funders, we won't get the next installment of the money, and then what?" argued Enrique Colon, the treasurer. This generational difference shows how well the CEADES trainings (and all the previous NGO contacts) worked — perhaps too well. Yet it was not merely the younger Guaranís who could master the discourse (if not the practices) of good money management. On several occasions, I heard the capitán grande talking about the need for an honest treasurer. So, when he needed to look trustworthy, the capitán knew that "transparency" was attractive.

Spaces of Neoliberal Citizenship

The practices on which the NGO focused — orderly and transparent meetings, the reliance on rules, a participatory meeting process, and good money management — are part of modern life. It is not surprising to see indigenous people get drawn into the requirements of modern office life, or the "efficient bureaucratization" required of NGOs by neoliberal-minded funders (Mohan and Stokke 2000; Schild 2000). Indians are not frozen in time, nor is this the first time they have adopted new practices into their livelihoods. They, like all peoples, are in a constant process of engaging with new discourses and institutions throughout their lives, choosing and adapting their ways according to what seems to work for them (Shepherd 2005). What is striking, however, is how the NGO tied these particular forms of conduct to citizenship. For the NGO, successful neoliberal citizenship is marked by efficient organization, rational participation, and self-government.

What, then, were the effects of this subject making? Did the Guaraní leaders internalize the logic the NGO workers tried to teach them? That is, did the training go beyond the reproduction of the practices and language of responsible participation to change the way capitanía members govern themselves? Was this a matter of style the Guaranís learned in order to gain the confidence of NGOs, or, to use Foucault's terms, did this form of government produce subjects responsible for their conduct? Or was it a combination of both effects?[12] This is a difficult question to answer, partly because subjectivity is hard to measure. The data gathered in my research demonstrate the discourse and behaviors of the trainers and the trained during a limited period. What the supposed subjects may internalize over the long term is difficult to predict. Moreover, it is important to recognize that subject making is never so simple or unidimensional. The Guaranís were responding to a number of discourses and desires structuring their actions and ideas, not just to the neoliberal rationalities CEADES was teaching them.

Julián told me he did not feel the time and energy CEADES had put into the project had paid off. He compared it with other work the organization was doing with another indigenous group, the Chiquitano people, in the far eastern part of the department. There the community was much more cohesive, and the leaders were able to enter the municipal government more successfully. They were struggling against more identifiable enemies, such as petroleum companies and loggers. Although Julián did not blame the ETZ members personally, he was disappointed in the results of the training and had decided not to work with the capitanía again.

The ETZ team's perception was more mixed. On the one hand, they felt the training project had been productive for the team. The project had provided financial support for a year and a half, which meant that for all that time, these young people had gotten money for *viáticos* as well as for travel into the city and out into the rural communities. They had had a place to meet and to discuss the issues facing the organization. They had had an adviser to help them strategize. There was a phone, a fax, and a bank account to support them. Their connection to this institution and the educated karai workers was a resource that they might need in the future.

On the other hand, the ETZ team realized that they had not been able to internalize all the skills Julián had tried to teach them. Obviously, the young Guaraní trainees were not instantly converted into corporate businesspeople or even professional Indians. Instead, they practiced the new skills to see how the skills could best be used in combination with what they felt were the values and traditions of their people. For instance, despite his strong desire to participate in the capitalist economy, Samuel Tapera spoke often about the difficulty he and his fellow Guaranís faced as they tried to enact the values CEADES had taught them. Their lives had not prepared them for this, he said. "We aren't trained, we don't have that kind of discipline." Nevertheless, Samuel understood that the new rationalities and forms of conduct could open a wide range of possibilities for the Guaranís as tools for political and economic advantage. Samuel and his father, Don Jesús, often talked to me about the difficulties the Guaranís had with "*la lógica de la ciudad*," as they called it, "the logic of the city."

Don Jesús lamented: "We aren't good capitalists. We want to be a part of the world of goods and cars and comfort, and stop being discriminated against because of our poverty. So our people are becoming more individualist, forgetting the old collective ways. But, really, they aren't good at it." Moreover, the Guaranís in Zona Cruz wanted to learn these skills so they could avoid the terrible *vergüenza* (shame) of looking like unsophisticated peasants. I have had many conversations with Guaraní friends in which they recounted their humiliation in situations where they did not know what to do or how to act with white people. Their typical response was to fade away, to retire and not try again out of shame. "Our biggest fear," Doña Estela told me one time, "is being laughed at or made fun of [*burlado*]." So these skills have much more importance than merely imposing other people's models of modernity on them. They are tied to a sense of dignity, particularly a pride in their own indigenousness.

Relatively new to these "techniques of the self," Samuel Tapera recognized that gaining them entailed a long process. He told me that the crucial challenge for his federation was to bring together the youth like himself, who were beginning to learn these new logics, with the elders, who held onto the old ways. Reconciling the two Guaraní cohorts in a new and creative way was, for him, the future of indigenous identity. The CEADES training instilled a certain *kind* of indigenousness: a bureaucratic, professional indigenousness, which, in Bolivia, was being produced in articulation with neoliberal notions of citizenship. By that, I mean that the Guaranís were encouraged to act on the basis of certain permissible cultural differences and to support their Indian communities, but to do so in "authorized" ways that reflect the logic of neoliberalism — transparency, efficiency, and rational participation. This supports anthropologist Charles R. Hale's contention that the core of neoliberalism's cultural project is "the creation of subjects who govern themselves in accordance with the logic of globalized capitalism" (Hale 2004: 17).

Nevertheless, the experience of the ETZ showed that even adopting this role and trying to act within the rules and rationalities of the dominant class did not guarantee the promised benefits. A year after the end of its training, CEADES held an evaluation meeting to see what progress the ETZ had made. After a rundown of the disappointments — few communities had been able to gain their legal recognition from the prefecture, only a small number had been able to present proposals as territorial grassroots organizations to the municipalities, and fewer still had received funding for their projects — the young Guaranís paused to consider the obstacles. Many of the young people blamed themselves or their people for not being able to follow through with the plans they had made in the training. Others expressed their frustration at the limits they found in the reform. One woman remembered what a local capitán had told them. She had been kept waiting for hours to speak with the mayor of her small town. When she finally complained, the secretary told her the mayor was busy meeting with *gente grande* (big people).

Despite their organizing, the Guaranís continued to confront the barrier of the political elite's power and racism. Samuel Tapera said the efforts to overcome this through participation as territorial grassroots organizations had provoked a "*choque de visiones*," or a clash of visions within the capitanía "about how to live in this economic system that blocks its doors to people like the Guaraní." The team agreed that rational planning and responsible participation in civil society were helpful strategies for urban Guaraní leaders, but they were not sufficient. They did not provide answers to the painful process of urbanization and social disintegration occurring in Samuel's community of Bella Flor, for instance. They did not resolve the colonial legacy of racism and the massive corruption these new citizens found in the municipal governments they were trying to access. Nor did they provide any relief from the economic crisis that makes life in the margins of a large city a terrible struggle. All the responsible participation in the world couldn't give these Indians the education or the social capital it takes to exercise the knowledge management skills necessary under the LPP.

The arts of neoliberal government may have powerful effects and may act to influence behaviors and practices through the diffusion of neoliberal rationalities. Nevertheless, the effects must always be understood in the context of particular social formations and relations of power. Even where, as in this case, Indians wanted to adopt parts of the neoliberal project, the continuing structural inequalities facing them made that difficult. The obstacles the ETZ faced rendered visible what neoliberal notions of privatizing social issues often obscure: the fundamentally political dimension of such social issues as poverty, development, and inequality (Dagnino 2003: 7–8).

The profound obstacles facing the Guaranís also show the limitations of Foucault's notion of governmentality. Governmentality is useful here to identify the nonstate actors that act to regulate conduct and enact the discourse of citizenship articulated with neoliberal government. It also explains the particular rationalities at work and shows how they are embedded in the particular scheme of private and public spheres favored by neoliberal governments. I believe that governmentality theory is particularly helpful to explain subalterns' seeming consent to ideas put forth by dominant sectors. When I began my investigation of Bolivian politics in the early 1990s as a reporter, indigenous people were mounting defiant marches, making claims against the state. During my field research in the late 1990s, however, indigenous leaders were working *with* the state and NGOs to try to take advantage of the articulations made possible by state-sponsored multiculturalism, to see what resources this new form of government might provide them. In that context, I found governmentality helpful to explain the subtle ways in which neoliberalism (as both a philosophy and a set of practices) organized consent by establishing appropriate forms of conduct.

But focusing on the acquiescence and the internalization of the logic of responsibilization can obscure the other equally strong forces and discourses at work. The discourse and rationalities of neoliberalism are powerful, but so are the ongoing discourses of racism and class as well as long-term patterns of state-civil society opposition. While one discourse may create Bolivian neoliberal subjects responsible for their own governing, the other reminds those subjects that they are lazy Indians. One creates a citizen expecting to benefit fairly from the state's resources, and the other empowers the traditional *patrones* (masters) to continue their control. This focus on acquiescence also tends to erase the subjects' agency. They become subjects of the discourse and attention is turned to the strength of the discourse and the resulting passivity of the subjects. The Guaranís consented in some ways to the new rationalities, or tried to. In the long run, however, they did not *only* consent. They also evaluated, tried, and weighed the possibilities of the neoliberal political reforms. Where they worked, Guaranís took advantage of them. Where they didn't, Guaranís rejected, modified, or ultimately, resisted the reforms.

Foucault made it clear that governmentality is just one modality of power that works in tandem with other modalities. He also reminded us that where there is power, there is resistance. Yet I think we tend to forget that when using his theories. Perhaps it is because his writings always seem to describe moments in which only one modality is predominant, so we are not used to seeing them in contact or tension with other modalities or forces. The Bolivian case points out the complex interactions between power, discourse, and cultural formations that must be examined separately in each conjuncture. If this chapter has described the ways in which indigenous people consented, at least in some ways, to neoliberal rationalities, the following chapter describes the many ways in which they resisted neoliberal economic restructuring, enacting new forms of political protagonism assembled through engagements with neoliberal political reforms.

6 *Popular Protagonism since 2000*

In simple terms, democracy for us answered — and still
answers — the questions who decides what? A tiny minority
of politicians and businesspeople, or we ourselves, the
ordinary working people?
— Oscar Olivera, speaker for the popular alliance in
Cochabamba's 2000 so-called water war

In the midst of winter, you can feel the inventions of spring.
— Lawrence Durrell

The Costs of Neoliberal Reforms

The previous chapters have described the ways neoliberal reforms and
policies have affected indigenous peoples and their leaders in Bolivia. Chapter 4 detailed the political reforms of the 1990s, which were intended to modernize and decentralize political participation, while dismantling corporate
models of state-civil society relations. Chapter 5 described the effects of
neoliberal government on the subjectivities of indigenous leaders, arguing
that neoliberal notions of citizenship are tied to such rationalities as efficiency,
economic models of leadership, and responsible participation. In this chapter, I turn to another aspect of neoliberalism — the economic restructuring
process and its effects on Bolivia's poor and indigenous populations. I argue
that the economic restructurings begun in the mid-1980s and deepened with
the 1990 economic reforms had immense and debilitating effects on popular sectors. The consequence in Bolivia has been a social crisis marked by
demonstrations, national strikes, and mass uprisings, as popular and indigenous sectors have contested the hegemony of the traditional political parties,
the legitimacy of the neoliberal state, and the increasingly privatized decision
making inherent to it.

This chapter describes the crisis and analyzes the ways indigenous people have responded to it. Indians have taken much from the reforms of the
1990s and their interpellation as citizens, developing new expectations
about both their roles and their rights. The combination of a widely accepted
discourse of indigenous citizenship and the continuing lack of effective Indian
participation has resulted in profound frustrations. This sense of violated

rights not only contributed to the mobilization that led to the resignation of the president in 2003, but also fostered important new forms of Indian leadership and representation. The successes of Evo Morales and the Movimiento al Socialismo (MAS, Movement Toward Socialism) party in the December 2005 elections are the outward reflections of an ongoing process in which the changing meaning and roles of "indigenousness" are contributing to what I call a postmulticultural Bolivia. I argue that this new conjuncture can be traced directly to the workings of the 1990 reforms, which provided new subjectivities and resources for resisting marginalization while at the same time reinforcing the colonial ordering of class and race.

The Economic Reforms

The political reforms I call neoliberal multiculturalism, described in previous chapters, did not take place in isolation. Rather, they were paired with a radical restructuring of the economy. Since the mid-1980s, Bolivia's governments have religiously implemented the fiscal and monetary reforms associated with neoliberal policies. The structural adjustments imposed across Latin America by the World Bank and the International Monetary Fund (IMF) were intended to replace the developmentalist state projects of the 1950s and 1960s, which put into effect national circuits of accumulation and expanded productive capacity in the post–World War II years. Under the state capitalism model, surpluses were appropriated by national elites and transnational corporations, but they were also redistributed through populist programs, including social wages like subsidized consumption, expanding employment opportunities, and rising real wages (Robinson 2004: 136–37).

By the late 1970s, however, in light of the global economic downturn and the debt crisis, this model proved unable to bring about sustained development and was increasingly replaced by the neoliberal model of the so-called laissez-faire state. The new model pushed countries to abandon their inward-looking models based on domestic market expansion, import substitution, industrialization, and domestic protectionism. Instead, they were urged to integrate into the global economy with an export-led development model, opening their borders to transnational capital (ibid.). Although neoliberal policies have brought some benefits of global capitalism to the region, they have also led to social instability, pauperization, and the escalation of inequalities (Robinson 1996, 2004; Alvarez, Dagnino, and Escobar 1998; Oxhorn 1998, 2003; Portes and Hoffman 2003). The turn to more left-leaning leaders across Latin America (Luiz Início Lula da Silva in Brazil, Hugo Chávez in Venezuela, Néstor Kirchner in Argentina, Tabaré Vásquez in Uruguay, and Ricardo Lagos in Chile) along with popular uprisings

(Argentina's *caserolazo* of 2001 was the most extreme of these) shows Bolivians are not alone in rethinking the promises of neoliberalism.[1]

In Bolivia, the reforms of the 1980s began to change the state's role in the economy. Since the ambitious populist programs following the 1952 revolution — land reform, universal suffrage, nationalization of the mines, and universal education — the Bolivian state had played a central role not only in capital formation but also employment (Arze and Kruse 2004: 24). Called "el Estado de '52" (the State of '52), the nationalist-developmentalist state directed the economy, provided services and jobs, and was a focus of social demands (Rivera Cusicanqui 2004: 20). By 1985, however, that model was in crisis. Bolivia faced huge debt, hyperinflation, and plummeting tin prices, and the New Economic Policy was instituted to reverse the downward spiral. Neoliberal governments since then, especially that of President Gonzalo Sánchez de Lozada in the 1990s, continued the policies, deepening the transformations. Economic analysts Carlos Arze and Thomas A. Kruse have argued that the years of unraveling the State of '52 have been traumatic for Bolivians. They paint an agonizing picture of the consequences.

First, they say, the reforms removed the state from all economic activity and caused it to abandon its role as the country's principal employer. This had severe consequences for labor. During the first stage of adjustments, thousands of miners were retired and mid-level bureaucrats were laid off. In the 1990s, capitalization (privatization) of most publicly owned enterprises further cut public sector employment. Whereas the government once provided jobs for a quarter of the employed population, now it does so for only 12 percent (ibid.: 27). This restructuring of the labor market was accompanied by a new regime of flexible accumulation that employs labor on a contractual and contingent basis as well as an increase in capital-intensive, technology-driven businesses that employ a relatively small labor force. The result is a huge pool of unemployed workers who turn to the informal market for fragile and uncertain subsistence.

Second, while privatization was supposed to stop the hemorrhaging of spending and bring in profits from foreign investors, in fact the state lost money in the process. Promised dividends from capitalization partners did not appear, and the shares retained by the state went to pension plans also controlled by the capitalist partners. This meant that control over most of the country's economic surplus passed into the hands of foreign investors without producing new income for the state (ibid.: 25). The result was a state of permanent insolvency that was met by a tax reform based on consumption, which weighs proportionally more heavily on the poor. This was particularly difficult in combination with the other common element of adjustment packages: a drastic cutback of social spending on health and education services.

Third, market liberalization reforms severely affected Bolivian industry, which had been supported by protective barriers. Instead of becoming more competitive by modernizing their productive processes, however, most Bolivian enterprises responded simply by squeezing labor and reducing wages. This has "deepened the exploitation of their employees and, by lowering workers' salaries, limited the development of the internal market on which the sector's growth depends" (ibid.).

Finally, Bolivia's farm economy, which is the principal provider of products for domestic consumption, has been devastated by the commercial liberalization. Large numbers of rural farmers and herders have been bankrupted because they were unable to compete with cheaper supplies from abroad. This has led to a massive increase in agricultural imports that substitute for national production (ibid.: 26; Pérez Luna et al. 2001; Pérez Luna 2004). This gradual and sustained liquidation of peasant production has led to an emptying of the countryside, especially in the altiplano, and a massive migration to urban areas (El Alto is the most spectacular case) and to neighboring Argentina (ibid.). A corollary to this pressure on the campesino sector is the U.S.-driven policy of coca eradication. The program has caused the loss of substantial resources (a government office estimates $610 million between 1997 and 2000) and the destruction of thousands of jobs directly or indirectly linked to this agricultural production (ibid.).

The resulting generalized sense of crisis, what anthropologist Lesley Gill has termed "teetering on the rim," has been palpable in the country for some years (Gill 2000). This gloomy situation is made all the more painful by an increase in incomes for the dominant classes, especially those in the "transnational capitalist class" and local economic and political elites tied to transnational capital (Robinson 2004: 142). Sociologists Alejandro Portes and Kelly Hoffman have demonstrated that in most Latin American countries, including Bolivia, while the average income for the subordinate classes, including urban workers and urban petty bourgeoisie, declined during the years of neoliberal adjustments, the incomes of these dominant classes (which they describe as capitalists, business executives, and elite workers and academics) increased, exacerbating what was already a gulf in the economic condition and life chances of the wealthy and the poor (Portes and Hoffman 2003: 65). The crisis has caused a huge migration of Bolivians to other countries. There are already a million Bolivians in Argentina, and now there is a growing wave of migrants to Europe, especially Spain.

I began an investigation of this phenomenon during the summer of 2005 in Madrid, where Bolivians are working in the labor sectors Spanish workers no longer can or wish to fill: in restaurants and hotels, in construction, and in private homes caring for elders and children. Some are poor rural people and work mostly in agriculture or domestic work. Many more are middle-class Bolivians, with education and enough family resources to fund the expensive trip. One young couple from Santa Cruz was typical. Both were in their twenties and had dropped out of college to come work in restaurants in Madrid. They saw their older brothers and sisters unable to make a living in Bolivia, even with college degrees, and decided to try Spain. Living in a tiny studio apartment, they both work long hours but manage to send several hundred Euros home each month as a nest egg for their eventual return.

A final effect has been the increasing sense among most Bolivians that the elite, in conjunction with the transnational capitalist classes, have commandeered control of what was formerly considered national patrimony, the economy of the country. Neoliberal policies have reinforced the bargaining power of a handful of privileged collective actors, whose demands gain direct access to the upper echelons of the government and the central bureaucracy (Boron 1995: 211). This was especially clear at the end of the Sánchez de Lozada government, when it was revealed that the president had secretly signed contracts with transnational gas companies in which the royalty percentages were far below that demanded by law.

As a result of all these effects, the years since early 2000 have been marked by social convulsion as those bearing the costs of the economic crisis have raised their voices in protest. Although these costs have been borne by all the country's poor, indigenous groups have been particularly active, especially recently. Aymara development analyst Mamerto Pérez Luna has speculated that perhaps the limited practices of participatory democracy granted under the LPP distracted indigenous organizations from these long-term structural problems for a time (Pérez Luna 2004). By 2000, however, the optimism of the 1990s began to wane, replaced by a renewed Indian activism that has moved the focus of contestation beyond the local level of territorial grassroots organizations to a national critique of neoliberal economic policies.[2] The following section briefly reviews this period to show how indigenous actors have begun to combine their interests and struggles with other sectors to build a new postmulticultural civil society based on citizenship rights and inclusion in the state.

Taking the Struggle to the Streets: The Water War

The year 2000 began with what was called *la guerra del agua* (the water war). In October 1999, bowing to pressure from the World Bank and the Inter-American Development Bank, Bolivia passed a new law allowing privatization of water supplies (Laurie, Andolina, and Radcliffe 2002).[3] Shortly after, the city of Cochabamba granted a contract to the Aguas de Tunari consortium for a badly needed water development project in the

Cochabamba valley. The city's population had grown enormously as dislocated rural farmers migrated into the urban zone. The municipal government had not been able to keep up with demand from the growing households of domestic users or from peasant farmers reliant on customary use of irrigation water. These farmers were mostly Quechua-speaking Indians who perceived their water rights as inherited through customary law. Many also referred to these rights as sacred according to Andean *cosmovision* (worldview) (ibid.: 265; Albro 2005: 435). Many communities had dug their own wells and established local water cooperatives, furthering the chaotic situation and, some say, lowering the water table (Laserna 2002). The new law and the contract allowed the consortium (the majority interest holder of which was a subsidiary of Bechtel Corporation) to raise local water users' rates and to make illegal any private water collection schemes, in essence seizing the water rights of these associations.

By April 2000, discontent over this privatization of the city's water supply erupted into massive popular demonstrations. A successful alliance between urban workers, rural peasant irrigators, members of local water collectives, students, and ordinary Cochabambinos was formed, calling itself the Coordinadora en Defensa de Agua y Vida (Coalition in Defense of Water and Life). The Coordinadora staged marches and such acts of resistance as burning water bills en masse in the public plaza. The conflict escalated as protesters took to the streets. Thousands fought the police across the barricades, dozens were wounded, and one killed. Finally, the government backed down and cancelled the contract with the consortium.[4]

The water war was widely heralded as a victory by "the people" against corporate globalization in Latin America, a sort of David and Goliath–like victory for the opposition (Assies 2003; Finnegan 2002). Oscar Olivera, union activist and spokesperson for the Coordinadora, argues that the Cochabamba struggle was much more than a local conflict over water. Rather, it was the direct result of neoliberal restructuring in Bolivia. In his *testimonio*-style book, Olivera contends that Bolivia suffered a loss of sovereignty by turning itself into "a servant of big capital" (Olivera 2004). Pointing to crushing debt service, slashed social spending, high unemployment, a disastrous pension reform scheme, and the fragmentation and destabilization of social movements and labor unions, he argues that "one and only one goal defined the purpose of neoliberalism in Bolivia: to intensify the exploitation of our natural resources in order to increase corporate profits" (ibid.: 14). The water war was the response of people who felt the government had stripped them of their material inheritance and natural resources, and commercialized the conditions for basic social reproduction (ibid.: 71). Even the very name of the Coordinadora reflects that, says Olivera. During the organizing assembly, one peasant *compañero* said:

"Let's not just have 'water' in our name, but 'life' as well, because they are taking everything away from us. All that's left to us is the water and the air" (ibid.: 27).

Olivera's account of the water war provides an illuminating window onto the sentiments of the allied popular sectors that came together in Cochabamba in 2000. Central to this was the sense that "they," the political class tied to transnational capital, were controlling public decision making. The quotation from Olivera at the beginning of this chapter captures the essence of the concern: Who decides what? Would politicians and elite businesspeople make decisions over something as basic a human right as water? He concludes that members of the coalition wanted to make their own decisions: "That was what democracy would mean in practice, and that was what the Coordinadora set out to accomplish" (ibid.: 29).

Another central component of the Cochabamba struggle was the defense of cultural heritage and collective "indigenous" rights to water (Laurie, Andolina, and Radcliffe 2002). Although this was not a struggle led by indigenous organizations, as the campaign developed, the language centered more and more around the protection of *usos y costumbres* (traditional custom and usages, or customary law) and the inherent paradox between Andean spirituality and neoliberal notions. Olivera (who does not hold himself out to be indigenous) proclaimed water to be sacred and tied to "beliefs of rural people since the time of the Incas" (cited in Albro 2005: 435). Even those members of the Coordinadora who were battling to protect their water cooperatives on the city's outskirts used language invoking collective rights based on Andean imagery and history. One poster, for instance, matched the motto "Water Is Ours" with a phrase invoking Andean deities: "Pachamama, Woracocha and Tata Dios gave it to us to live, not to do business with" (cited in Laurie, Andolina, and Radcliffe 2002: 267).

This was not just a strategic use of the discourse of indigenous rights in the context of the identity politics of multiculturalism. Rather, as this chapter demonstrates, it is a new form of coalitional politics that is emerging as the most important form of social movement protagonism in Bolivia today. In the Cochabamba campaign, most of the poor were Indians or urban migrants with some Indian heritage. Yet the protesters did not unite around their identity as Indians but around a "common idea of how cultural practices were threatened by market forces" (ibid.: 265). Instead of organizing around class or ethnicity, the Cochabamba protesters came together around a shared notion of exploitation based on both culture and poverty. The language of indigenous rights, argues anthropologist Robert Albro, provides persuasive cultural analogies that frame deprivations of indigenous and urban nonindigenous popular sectors that have suffered together in Bolivia's free-market democracy (Albro 2005).

The results of the water war were significant: the contract with the transnational corporations was abrogated, the water service was returned to the city and "democratized" with the addition of popular representatives to the governing board, and the national water law 2029 was amended to include the recognition of such customary laws as indigenous collective water rights Yet these "victories" did not lead to sustained political organizing in Cochabamba or even to a substantial improvement in the water supply for poor barrios.[5] Another cloud remained on the horizon, as Bechtel filed a claim against Bolivia in the World Bank's Center for Investment Disputes for US$25 million, which is still pending. Nevertheless, the Cochabamba struggles set an important precedent in Bolivian — and international — circles, showing that indigenous and poor people can successfully protest neoliberal privatization policies in particular conjunctures.[6] The Cochabamba example continues to have resonance. In 2004, for instance, residents of El Alto protested a similar contract to the Aguas de Illimani project led by the French water company Suez. President Carlos Mesa Gilbert conceded to this protest, admitting that the company had not fulfilled its obligation to the community, and in January 2005, he cancelled the contract.

Peasants and Cocaleros at War

Beginning in 2000, strikes spread across the country as several years of economic crisis took their toll. By September 2000, angry peasants and workers, disgruntled teachers and transport workers, and *cocaleros* (coca growers) mounted protests and blockaded the highways. There were two main focuses of the protests. The first was in the highlands near Achacachi, close to Lake Titicaca, where the farmers union CSUTCB, led by Aymara nationalist and former Katarista guerrilla Felipe Quispe (El Mallku), mounted aggressive demonstrations. Community members covered kilometers of roadways with tree trunks and large stones, making it nearly impossible for the military to break the blockades. The strikes began in solidarity with demands by cocaleros in the Chapare but later continued on their own, focused on the neoliberal water law and the trade liberalization policies that affected altiplano Indians so severely. In the process, Quispe employed an aggressive discourse of ethnic *reinvindicación* (claims or demands), advocating a separate Aymara nation. He described the struggle of poor Aymara peasants against the colonial powers that continue to control the country and threatened to repeat the terrifying siege of La Paz that Túpac Katari had carried out in the eighteenth century (Laserna 2002; Patzi 2003).

These protests (dubbed Black September by the media) became quite violent; several farmers were killed and many were wounded in struggles with the police. Quispe's position included demands that all the lands and resources in the zone should be the property of original peoples and not the neoliberal state; that Decree 21060, the 1985 law that had privatized the mines and decimated the power of labor, should be overturned; and that the state should recognize self-determination for all of Bolivia's "nations, communities, and original people" (Patzi 2002: 63). After some months of stand-offs, the protests ended when the state agreed to modify various laws, including the INRA, forest, and mining laws; to assign more lands to a colonization program; and to place more money in rural development (ibid.: 58).

A second mobilization occurred the next year, in 2001, with similar demands. It was eventually resolved as Quispe negotiated a seventy-two-point agreement with the central government in which, among other things, a thousand tractors would be distributed through the CSUTCB, $47 million would be designated to development plans, and $11 million would be earmarked for micro-credit programs and other projects (ibid.: 64–65). These protests showed the strength of the militant Aymara campesino organizations and made clear Quispe's power to use the media as well as to convoke mobilizations (Albó 2000: 103). However, these demonstrations also demonstrated the continuing strength of the traditional corporatist style of union politics, in which social movements mobilize their constituents in opposition to the state in order to gain resources and concessions. While the neoliberal state reforms were intended to end inefficient state interventions and distributions by substituting more "rational" forms of popular participation, the 2000 and 2001 protests made clear not only that these new forms of politics had not succeeded in satisfying the Indian populace of the altiplano, but also that the traditional peasant organizations still had strength to protest the rest of the neoliberal agenda (Laserna 2002).

The second focus of protest was in the Chapare, in the tropical region of Cochabamba, where the struggles of the cocaleros became particularly important in the eyes of the popular sectors. A large number of the coca growers are Quechua and Aymara miners who lost their jobs in the late 1980s, when the government closed and privatized the national tin mines as part of the first structural adjustment programs (Sanabria 2000; Gill 2000). Coca has long occupied an important role in Andean social and cultural institutions; it has been grown since the time of the Incas. During the 1960s, as migrants moved into the Chapare, government extension agents promoted the cultivation of coca as a cash crop. Coca is legal to grow and sell, as it is used regularly by Andean people as a mild stimulant and hunger suppressant. By the mid-1970s, coca was the region's main cash crop.[7]

Increased coca cultivation does not benefit the state directly, and it threatens foreign aid. In 1986, for example, the United States withheld $7 million in aid as a result of the Bolivian government's failure to meet eradication goals (Bailey and Knutson 1987: 49). Nevertheless, a large sector of peasants continues to be engaged in the production of coca, seeing it as one of the few options available to fend off starvation given the continuing financial crisis Bolivia has suffered (Kohl and Farthing 2001; Farthing and Ledebur 2004; Potter 2004). A number of interesting analyses of coca production have argued for legalizing traditional production (Mirtenbaum 1995; Rivera Cusicanqui 2003; Spedding 2003), yet coca and cocaine production continues to be a key focus of the United States–Bolivia relationship. The United States continues to push for coca eradication while also encouraging what is euphemistically called "alternative development," that is, trying to find alternative crops that coca producers could grow instead of coca (Bailey and Knutson 1987: 49; Kohl and Farthing 2001).

As a result, the coca growers have been fighting a low-intensity war with the antinarcotics forces led by U.S. Drug Enforcement agents and the U.S. embassy (Kohl and Farthing 2001; Farthing and Ledebur 2004). This decades-long struggle has been marked by violence, as narcotics agents brutally put down demonstrations and highway blockades staged by the cocaleros.[8] In 1988, Bolivia passed the draconian Law 1008, which justified the war on drugs and allowed arbitrary arrests and incarcerations. Through the ironically named Plan Dignidad (Dignity Plan), in 1998, the United States promised $700 million in debt reduction, alternative development projects, and counter-narcotics assistance in exchange for Bolivia's promise to reduce coca production (Potter 2004). President Hugo Banzer Suárez's implementation of the plan further militarized the Chapare, raising the death rate of coca growers and security personnel (Farthing and Ledebur 2004: 36). In 2001, the Bush administration passed the Plan Colombia, a $1.3 billion package for the Andean region (ibid.; Albro 2005).

Without a doubt, this military presence fortified the incipient coca growers union. Led since 1988 by Evo Morales, the cocaleros union acted at first as the region's central institution of local governance. It joined the greater peasant union movement and eventually came to dominate the national federation, the CSUTCB (Albó 2002). The cocaleros have been successful at promoting both peasant agriculturalist agendas as well as identifying themselves as indigenous people within the terms of international indigenous rights discourse. While human rights workers characterize them in terms of poverty, the cocaleros themselves, especially in international circles, spotlight themselves as representatives of Bolivia's indigenous movement (Albro 2005). For instance, Morales and the cocaleros were active in the 1992 commemorations of the "Five Hundred Years of Indigenous Resistance." More important, they characterize their rights to grow coca not just as a matter of economic survival, but as a matter of ethnic heritage, since the "sacred coca leaf" was bequeathed to the Andean people by the gods (Albó 2002: 76).

Under Morales's leadership, the coca growers union assumed a dynamic role in oppositional politics in Bolivia, arguing against both U.S. imperialism and human rights violations by the Bolivian government (Petras 2004). They were also one of the first groups to take advantage of the political spaces opened by the 1994 Law of Popular Participation (LPP). They created a new political party, the Asamblea Soberana del Pueblo (ASP, Assembly for the Sovereignty of the People), and ran candidates in both the 1995 municipal elections and the 1997 national elections. They were successful in gaining seats in municipalities in the Cochabamba area, particularly in the Chapare, and sent six members to congress in 1997, including Morales. Shortly after, however, Morales broke from the CSUTCB and created the MAS party, which did well in the 1999 municipal elections (Albó 2002; Albro 2005). (Chapter 4 describes the ways in which local indigenous leaders were able to use the MAS political affiliation to avoid the pressures of traditional political parties.) In the mobilizations of 2000, the cocaleros built on this increased institutional support to call for an end to the militarization in the Chapare and Banzer's policy of total eradication of coca, what was called *coca cero* (zero coca) (Albó 2002: 79). The government made some concessions, agreeing to stop the eradication in the Yungas, the region of "traditional" coca production, but did not relent on its policies in the Chapare. This isolated the coca growers from other protesters and eventually, despite a march to La Paz, the mobilization fizzled (Kohl and Farthing 2001: 36).

The Alternative Path: The 2002 Elections

The mobilizations of 2000 in the highlands and the Chapare made clear that Indian and popular sectors did not feel included in "multiethnic, pluricultural" Bolivia. Months of social strife and blockaded roads were only partially resolved through negotiated settlements, none of which resolved the underlying tensions. In 2002, after having been impeached from his congressional post because of his support of the Chapare blockades, Morales began to campaign for president, clarifying the position of the MAS party to build its power as a national party that would be able to exercise power at the national level. This strategy was not entirely new. The CSUTCB had long considered the necessity of forming a political instrument to advance its interests (Albro 2005), and the Kataristas had also formed political parties for years (Albó 1987 and 1994). Nevertheless, Morales appeared to have the right idea at the right time. The MAS emerged at the conjuncture of growing expectations of indigenous citizens and the problems and frustrations indigenous leaders had encountered in attempting to access the institutions of the LPP.

MAS brought together the old Left, an influential leftist lawyers' group, current leaders of campesino and workers unions, members of the new Movimiento Sin Tierra (Movement of the Landless), and some lowland indigenous leaders, presenting a varied popular front. While still strongly weighted toward the highland people, MAS declared itself to be a party for all the popular and indigenous groups of Bolivia who had suffered indignities and oppression by the white elite. In another example of the merging of class and ethnicity, Morales declared: "The MAS is born and draws its strength from the struggles of the indigenous peoples, for the defense of out identity, which is the coca leaf, for the defense of our land, who is our mother, for the defense of our natural resources, which are our hope and our patrimony" (cited in Albro 2005: 447). This ethnic message was blended with strong anti-imperialist and anti-neoliberal ideology, decrying the growing power of transnationals and the continued domination of the United States. It was also mixed with a simple populist message: There are rich people and then there are the rest of us — poor, hard working, and excluded. Now it's our turn.

This combined message convinced many voters in the June 2002 presidential elections, in which Morales won second place, thanks to an outpouring of indigenous and popular support. His party won 20 percent of the votes, just 1 percent behind Sánchez de Lozada's Movimiento Nacional Revolucionario (MNR, National Revolutionary Movmement) party. When I visited Santa Cruz in 2003, I found that many Guaranís supported him, even though he was a *kolla* from the highlands. One of the most surprising MAS supporters was the capitanía's former leader, Don Álvaro Montero. Throughout the 1990s, Don Álvaro had trumpeted his indigenousness as central to his and the capitanía's activism. He had been a member of Banzer's right-wing Acción Democrática Nacional (ADN, Nacional Democratic Action) party, and had pursued connections through that party during Banzer's presidency. Now the director of a campesino union in the colonization zone north of Warnes, Don Álvaro had become a militant MAS supporter, espousing a newly learned socialist discourse about the tensions between rich and poor. When I asked him about the big change, he said he had not forgotten his heritage. "I am just working for justice from another angle," he said. "The reforms did not give rise to much political power; perhaps a broader based political movement will."

MAS was not the only electoral option for Bolivian Indians in 2002. Although he asserted a strident antigovernment policy, Aymara leader Quispe also ran for congress in 2002 and was elected on the Movimiento Indígena Pachakuti (MIP) ticket. MIP managed to win almost 6 percent of the national vote. Sánchez de Lozada built a tentative coalition allowing Goni to assume the presidency, but in August 2002, Bolivians watched in awe as thirty-five MAS and six MIP congresspeople — highland Indians, lowland indigenous people, and campesinos — took their places in the national congress, vowing to change the way the Bolivian state governed its people (Van Cott 2003). Initially they held marginalized positions as opposition parties, but as time has passed, and because MAS continues to win in municipal elections, the party's influence in national politics has grown, culminating of course in the 2005 election of Morales to the presidency.

Lowland Struggles

In the lowlands, indigenous groups also organized in opposition to neoliberal policies. Although the overall crisis also affected them, there was a particular aspect to the neoliberal economic reforms that involved them: the resource extraction projects that became the focus of the Sánchez de Lozada administration. A central part of the economic restructuring policy was to open the way to international capital investment in Bolivia (Postero 2005). By ending its own productive activities, the state could encourage the private sector to develop. Nowhere was this clearer than in the hydrocarbons sector, where the reforms pushed by the World Bank set the stage for the entrance of multinational oil corporations.[9]

First, the state oil company, Yacimientos Petrolíferos Fiscales de Bolivia (YPFB), was capitalized: the state sold 50 percent of its equity to multinational corporations, including Enron, Shell, and BP. Second, the Sánchez de Lozada government passed the 1996 Hydrocarbons Law, which granted concessions to foreign companies with extremely low royalties and taxes, especially on newly discovered oil and gas reserves. Such changes produced dramatic foreign investments in exploration, production, and distribution, to five times as much as YPFB had invested before capitalization (Hindery 2004: 4). These investments, however, have been the subject of enormous criticism. They have allowed foreign companies access to and control over resources many Bolivians consider to be national patrimony. Although it is clear that these companies are able to invest capital that the Bolivian state could not afford, it is also rankling to most Bolivians to have foreign companies profit off of Bolivian natural resources. This was precisely the reason the tin mines were nationalized after the 1952 revolution, and such sentiments run deep in Bolivia.

Under Sánchez de Lozada, transnational companies had enormous freedom to carry out their exploration and production with little oversight from the administration, which did everything possible to encourage their investments. Geographer Derrick Hindery has argued that even the environmental monitoring agency set up within the government was funded and controlled by the multinational oil corporations, resulting in a serious conflict of interest (ibid.). Most important, however, was the tremendous environmental and social impact this new push to extract oil and gas produced, especially on indigenous peoples, whose lands were the site of the oil development. Despite government commitments to indigenous claims to territory (codified in the INRA law), the privileging of foreign investors resulted in the devastation of indigenous lands with little or no democratic participation by the affected communities (ibid.: 12). This was another example of the privatization of resources and the very decision making about them.

So in September 2000, at the same time the campesinos and cocaleros were striking, the Chiquitano Indians in eastern Santa Cruz began a sixteen-day protest that shut down work on an Enron pipeline project. The Chiquitanos were fighting against a pipeline that Enron and Shell were constructing from Cuiabá, Brazil, through the fragile ecosystem called the Chiquitano Dry Forest, "one of the world's richest, rarest, and most biologically outstanding habitats on Earth," according to the World Wildlife Fund (cited in Langman 2002). The Chiquitanos filed lawsuits, formed alliances with conservation NGOs, and mounted blockades to demand the pipeline route be changed (Cortés and Tito 2004). They did not stop the pipeline, but under pressure from international conservation NGOs, Enron eventually agreed to fund a multimillion-dollar fund designed to mitigate the social and environmental damage caused by the pipeline.

This fund and the top-down way it was established, however, were widely debated among indigenous people and their advocates (see Langman 2002). As a result, the World Wildlife Fund pulled out of the fund at the last minute, citing potential conflict of interest, the lack of indigenous participation, increased social and environmental conflicts, and a risk to the sustainability of the forest and indigenous populations (ibid.: 3). Eventually, Enron, Shell, and the Bolivian company Transredes established a separate conservation fund, run by four environmental NGOs. Critics claim the pipeline has proven a disaster for the Chiquitanos. Geographer Jorge Cortés and economist Henry Tito, who work for an NGO that has advised the Indian organization, contend that it has become "a[n] impoverishing project which threatens the rights of affected communities and condemns generations present and future to live in a degraded environment and conditions without dignity" (Cortés and Tito 2004: 354).

Hindery points out another detrimental side effect of the project: the need to attract foreign investment through deregulation kept state institutions from addressing environmental impacts. Since the construction of the main Bolivia-Brazil pipeline began, he says, Enron, Shell, and their local consortia have been responsible for four major oil spills, a gas leak, and various ramifications on local environments and livelihoods (Hindery 2004: 295). Although the Chiquitanos were ultimately unsuccessful in blocking the pipeline, their public protest became well known both in Bolivia and internationally (see Amazon Watch 2003), highlighting popular dissatisfaction with energy privatization and the increasing power of transnational energy companies, a sentiment that would prove to be critical in the 2003 uprising.

The Chiquitano protests were not the only mobilizations in the lowlands during this period. Frustrated with their continued vulnerability to transnational interests, the agonizingly slow progress on titling of indigenous territories under the land reform law, and the limited success provided by the LPP, in 2002, lowland indigenous organizations, including many young Guaraní leaders from the Capitanía Zona Cruz, held a national march for a constituent assembly. They called for the rewriting of the constitution through a democratic process that included the voices, interests, and values of indigenous and popular sectors. This demand was based on a widely held feeling that the 1994 constitutional reforms under Sánchez de Lozada's administration were instituted by the political elite and responded to the influences of the multilateral funders and the ideology of the free market. They were not, in other words, the product of a dialogue with broader sectors of society, and did not include the changes that these sectors felt necessary to ensure real democratic participation or an efficient and just political system (Almaraz 2003). The most urgent demands were an abolition of the monopoly of the political parties and the establishment of institutional systems of transparency to stop the rampant corruption by government officials. To these general concerns, indigenous groups added their own: they demanded better and more extensive rights to territory and the control of natural resources found there, autonomous territories administered by indigenous groups, and special indigenous municipalities (ibid.).

The march was to highlight these demands. A significant problem arose, however, when long-held divisions within the national indigenous movement broke open during the run-up to the 2002 elections. Many leaders of the Confederación Indígena del Oriente de Bolivia (CIDOB, Indigenous Federation of Eastern Bolivia) allied themselves with the MIR party, several of them running for congress on this ticket. Others allied with Morales's MAS party and his politics of class unity between highland and lowland Indians. Lowland indigenous groups have been wary of such alliances, because of their continued fears that landless and poor highland people will invade the lands the lowlands people have struggled so hard to protect.

This tension became more salient when indigenous leaders disagreed over strategies in organizing the national march.[10] The march to La Paz began in a fragmented way, as one sector began from Santa Cruz, while another hung back, debating. Eventually both groups marched, but they remained separate during most of the march, making a divided and confusing public representation. Nevertheless, the march received a great deal of public and media attention, especially the symbolic coordination with the highland groups of Aymara and Quechua peasants. The march was not successful in forcing the government to hold the assembly, but it was important in reasserting the lowland indigenous people as political actors in 2002. Moreover, the issues brought up by the march — the need to reform the constitution to allow indigenous groups and peasants to have a voice in government — expressed what many at the bottom of Bolivian society had been feeling and expressing throughout the conflictive previous years: that the rich white politicians and the constitutions and reforms they had instituted in the past just did not represent them or their interests.

Such marches require enormous sacrifices by the participants. They march, sometimes for months, from the tropical lowlands up the mountains to the severe cold of the Andes. The marchers do not carry tents but are housed wherever they can find shelter — in schools or churches in welcoming communities, or just by the side of the road. They suffer exhaustion, cold, and the uncertainty that their efforts will amount to anything. Yet the experiences are also profoundly moving, as people from different groups across the country meet, exchange stories, and share hardships for a common cause. A few months after the march, I was in a Yuquí village in the Chapare and interviewed several young Yuquí leaders who had been on the march.[11] They described how their entire federation had supported them by voting a part of the community forestry project's budget to buy them tennis shoes, blankets, and food for the trip. Although they hated the cold, they said they had learned a great deal about national politics in the process and were proud to have represented their small village in the march.

The march was also pivotal for several young Guaraní leaders from Zona Cruz. Rosana Moreno from La Cañada came back to the work of the capitanía reinspired. Echoing the "responsibilization" she had learned in the NGO training from CEADES, she explained to me that the only way to overcome the injustices they faced was to push the politicians to reform the constitution to allow the country's poor and indigenous to participate in all the decisions that affected them. I asked, But hadn't the constitution already been reformed in 1994 to include indigenous people? "Yes, but we are still marginalized," she said. Therefore, Rosana asserted, it was important to register loud and clear opposition to a political system that appeared to value corporations more than its indigenous citizens.

Rosana's activism showed the paradoxical effects of the 1990s reforms. On the one hand, she argued they had not worked. On the other, she was out on the streets, acting as a "responsible" citizen asserting her rights. The march had also brought her deeper into the national political scene, where she said indigenous and poor people were starting to act together to remake Bolivian society. Rosana found the reception of the indigenous march moving as it went through the Chapare, the home of the cocaleros. She and the other ETZ leaders said they were inspired by Evo Morales but were being cautious. The rest of the capitanía felt the same way. After the march, I met with the capitanía's current board of directors. Sitting around their big table, part of the remnants of the Danish furniture from the "Mendoza project" years before, they debated whether they should align themselves with Morales's MAS party. Doña Estrella reminded us that joining in any political party is risky: if the party gets burned, we do, too. The new capitán grande, José Morales, said, yes, those political party types are *vivísimo* (super clever). Even Evo. "What we need is our own party," he said, "with our own T shirts." But, Evo was powerful, so they would think carefully about it. After the meeting, however, some of the younger Guaranís proudly confided that their former leader, Don Álvaro, had met Evo and was part of his political machine in his new job.

The Gathering Storm: The Impuestazo

The feeling that the politicians were untrustworthy was not only the verdict of indigenous people. In 2003, Vice President Carlos Mesa Gisbert issued a report after his first year in office in which he decried the corruption that marked the government and acknowledged the frustration of the public: "After twenty years of representative democracy, the political system continues to reproduce the long history of discretional management reflected in a clientelist, patrimonial, and basically prebendal logic of the public. In the perception of the citizens, the democracy of political pacts has ended up being nothing more than an instrument for the division of power and an open distribution [of resources] through public administration" (cited in Quiroga 2004: 35; translated by the author).

President Sánchez de Lozada had inherited from the Banzer/Quiroga administration a country with an enormous fiscal deficit and shocking levels of corruption. Having won only 20 percent of the vote, his government was an unwieldy alliance of parties that had been unable to accomplish much to improve the crisis. To gain standby loans from the IMF, Sánchez de Lozada promised to reduce the fiscal deficit from 8.5 percent down to 5 percent by creating a new direct income tax. Under the plan, a 12.5 percent tax would be levied on all employees who made more than four times the minimum wage. This would mean that for many, salary deductions would have increased to more than 30 percent, in a country where the per capita GNP is US$900 (Andean Information Network 2004).

The president imposed the tax (the *impuestazo*, roughly, "the big tax") with little debate by the congress in a moment of mounting violence in the

Chapare. Only a few weeks earlier, four people had been killed in a clash with security forces there (Amnesty International 2003). The announcement of this newest neoliberal measure was met by immediate protests in La Paz. On February 12, 2003, the national police expressed their discontent by mobilizing at their headquarters close to the presidential palace. Shortly after, large groups of workers and students began to stone government buildings. When the protesters burned several ministry buildings and began to loot, the military intervened to disperse them. The day ended in horror, as shocked Bolivians glued to their televisions watched military sharpshooters fire on police and civilians in Plaza Murillo, the crowded square in front of congress (Quintana 2004). The next day further clashes ensued, including military shootings of civilians during a march organized by the Central Obrero Boliviano (COB), the labor federation. In two days, at least 31 people (16 civilians, 10 police, and 5 military) were killed and 189 wounded (Orduna 2004; Amnesty International 2003).[12] Most of those killed, including the police and military, were Aymaras. Sánchez de Lozada quickly withdrew the tax, but by then his presidency was profoundly shaken.[13]

The Uprising of October 2003

In October 2003, the tensions brewing for several years culminated in six weeks of dramatic public protests. The uprising was centered in El Alto, the satellite city north of La Paz, where the majority of the population are Aymara Indian migrants.[14] Although the uprising focused ultimately on the president's plan to allow transnational corporations to export Bolivia's natural gas reserves via a pipeline through Chile to the United States and Mexico, it was the result of the convergence of many separate demands from differing sectors of the Bolivian population. Campesino groups, neighborhood associations, labor unions, street traders, and university students all came together to protest, and their massive mobilizations forced the president's resignation. Like all popular uprisings, it is important to see the October insurrection as an articulation of long-simmering injustices, particularly against Indians, with current local and sectoral tensions.

Beginning in late September, the CSUTCB, led by Felipe Quispe, began a highway blockade in the rural areas of the altiplano, with several demands. First, the confederation wanted the government to fulfill the agreement it had made to end the 2000 peasant protests. Second, it demanded the release of jailed peasant leader Edwin Huampo (Lazar 2004). Finally, the mobilizations objected to the president's economic policy and specifically the proposed pipeline through Chile. The blockades continued while Quispe and several hundred followers held a hunger strike in El Alto. Then the COB, the national trade union confederation, called for an indefinite general strike to contest the government's economic policies. They demanded the government renationalize the hydrocarbons sector that had been privatized in the first Goni administration and use the natural gas resources to fuel development of Bolivia's own industries (Cherian 2003).

Meanwhile, in El Alto, Indian residents from neighborhood councils organized to protest a painful new local property tax (known as the Maya and Paya *formularios*). Organized by the Federación de Juntas Vecinales (FEJUVE, the federation of neighborhood associations), the poor city dwellers objected to the new tax, which was based on the value of their homes. Given the terrible and widespread poverty in El Alto, it seemed unreasonable to penalize those who had managed to improve their homes. This protest was successful, and the mayor rescinded the tax on September 16. Nevertheless, many urban protesters continued their strikes in support of the peasant struggles, even though the blockades affected their livelihoods as street vendors or merchants.[15] This link between the city and rural protests was central to the outcome of the uprising. Many Alteños have migrated from the rural areas precisely because of the harsh economic measures the campesinos were protesting, and they understood the crises their *hermanos campesinos* (peasant brothers) were facing (Pérez Luna 2003). Moreover, there is a fluid boundary between the city and the countryside, as most migrants retain strong economic and kinship ties to their *pueblos* (home communities). Anthropologist Sian Lazar has argued that peasant leaders like Quispe recognized the strategic nature of El Alto as an "indigenous city" and intentionally sought to strengthen the rural-city links to gain a foothold there (Lazar 2004).

Alteños' support for the peasants only increased after September 20, when the government sent the military out to the altiplano to remove roadblocks on the road from Sorata to La Paz, to rescue a large group of foreign tourists "held hostage" by peasant blockades. In the process, a gun battle erupted in the village of Warisata, leaving five civilians and one soldier dead and twenty people injured (Amnesty International 2003). This inflamed Alteño passions further. Several members of the neighborhood councils told me later that this was further proof that the Sánchez de Lozada government was more concerned with the fates of rich white people than its own citizens. The protests escalated. FEJUVE called an indefinite general strike on October 8, and the peasant unions began to demand the president's resignation (Lazar 2004). Large crowds marched down into La Paz, filling the plazas carrying signs declaring "The gas is ours" ("El gas es nuestro") and "No to export, yes to industrialization" ("No a la exportación, sí a la industrialización"). Spokespeople demanded that Bolivian people rather than private companies be the beneficiaries of the exploitation and sale of the gas. Blockades continued, bringing the nation's commerce to a halt. The death toll mounted, as the military killed thirty-eight people trying to stop the gas tankers down from El Alto into La Paz.

By mid-October, the neighborhood associations had organized massive public protests, controlling the streets and manning twenty-four-hour blockades across the city. They closed police stations and invited the police to join in the uprising or be subject to popular justice (Hylton 2003). Hundreds of miners, carrying dynamite and weapons from the 1930s Chaco war, marched into La Paz from Oruro, protesting the gas pipeline and the Free Trade of the Americas Accord. Market vendors and transport syndicates joined the fray, paralyzing the city and closing the markets. University students demanding autonomy for the University of El Alto held massive marches (Hylton 2003; Lazar 2004). Several popular radio stations in El Alto were critical to the mobilizations, sending reporters to the scenes of massacres and reporting instantly to the public.[16] The churches were the repositories of bodies and the wounded, who were unable to break through the blockades to seek attention. Finally, middle-class residents from all over La Paz joined the protest to register their dismay at the violent repression. Hunger strikes were established even in the chic neighborhoods in the southern part of La Paz. There were matching demonstrations in other cities, notably in Cochabamba, where the trade unions and the Coordinadora en Defensa de Agua y Vida, which had led the water war, led marches echoing the demands of the Alteños.

On October 16, two hundred thousand people gathered in the Plaza de San Francisco in La Paz, calling for the president's resignation. Former Ombudsperson Ana María de Camperos, members of the Permanent Assembly, intellectuals and members of the church began a high-profile hunger strike, decrying the violence and loss of life. Then Vice President Carlos Mesa and most of the president's cabinet resigned. By October 17, with nearly eighty people dead and several hundred wounded, the president was forced to resign. He flew to Miami that night, as the country erupted in celebrations.

The former vice president, Carlos Mesa Gisbert, a historian and well-known television journalist, was sworn in as president. In his inaugural speech, he promised two immediate responses to the protesters' demands: to hold a public referendum about the uses of natural gas, and to convene a constituent assembly to rewrite the constitution and reform the state. He ended his speech calling for a Bolivia in which there is "unity in diversity." We will design a nation, he said, with "more equity, more justice, and with the security that comes from making that which we have not made in centuries" (La Razón 2003a). In this, he evoked a multicultural democracy in which there would be equitable participation, which none of the constitutional reforms or state-led multicultural reforms of the 1990s had accomplished. The following day, Mesa appeared before throngs of Aymara Indians in El Alto, where the majority of deaths had occurred. Asking for patience from the nation's Indians, he promised "neither forgetting nor vengeance, justice" (*"ni olvido, ni venganza, justicia"*) (La Razón 2003b). He said he would do his job thinking of them, "the country's most excluded" (Arrington 2003).

Objections to the Natural Gas Plan

What exactly brought together the "angry workers, peasants, Indians, street vendors, and the unemployed" who made up this unprecedented mass uprising (Petras 2004)? First, there was a shared sense among a wide spectrum of Bolivians that the gas plan was squandering Bolivia's patrimony. They were not eager to see repeated the traditional pattern of sale of raw materials to more developed countries, which traditionally profited from Bolivians' resources and labor. Having experienced earlier versions of elite-controlled global commerce — the exploitation of silver, rubber, guano, and finally tin — many Bolivians saw little reason to trust the twenty-first-century version. In essence, this was a popular iteration of a sort of dependency theory critique, arguing that the core was to benefit once again from the periphery's raw materials (see CIPCA 2004).

Second, the plan hit a strong nationalist nerve with its proposal to pipe the gas to Chile. Bolivia had lost its coastal territory and seaports to Chile in the War of the Pacific (1879–83), and Bolivians continue to lament this loss, which left the country landlocked and dependent on foreign ports to transport goods. As president, General Hugo Banzer Suárez had framed the issue as one of sovereignty, keeping alive the possibility of recovery of what he saw as Bolivia's natural right to the ocean. Although some saw this as posturing, the idea gained purchase with many others because of Bolivians' strongly held feelings that the sea had been "stolen" from them. In fact, one of the most important results of the protest is an ongoing negotiation with Chile about access to the sea, with the United Nations as an interlocutor (La Razón 2004).

Third, the fact that the gas was to go to the United States, via Sempra Energy of California, made the plan all the more unpalatable to many Bolivians. As with other countries in the region, the United States has a long history of political and economic influence over Bolivia (Malloy and Gamarra 1988; Klein 1992; Petras 2004). In more recent years, the United States has asserted this influence in two main ways. The first is its insistence on neoliberal restructuring as a condition of foreign aid. The "Washington consensus" is well known in Latin America, and many Bolivians complain that IMF structural adjustment programs are straightjackets that violate Bolivian sovereignty.[17] Yet Bolivia's poverty makes it dependent on U.S. and international funding and debt-relief programs.

More salient for the popular sectors that made up the bulk of the protesters, however, was the United States' role in drug eradication in Bolivia. As described earlier, the violent repression of the cocaleros in the Chapare is widely acknowledged as the result of a U.S. agenda rather than a Bolivian one. Evo Morales's description of Bolivia as "a country occupied militarily by the United States" subject to "permanent intervention by organs of U.S. intelligence agencies" was widely accepted among poor and middle-class sectors (Morales 2003). This perception may also have been partially increased during the 2002 elections, when U.S. ambassador Manuel Rocha threatened a trade and aid cutoff if Morales were elected president. Sociologist James Petras has echoed the feeling of many observers, suggesting that this "precipitated a big shift to the left among the majority of anti-imperialist Bolivians" (Petras 2004: 2). The anti–United States sentiment was furthered during the October protests, when the new ambassador David Greenlee made it clear that the United States would not support anyone else for president but then-president Sánchez de Lozada. Many Bolivians perceived this as a strong-arm tactic that denied the legitimacy of civil society's right to challenge their government and bypassed Bolivian constitutional procedures that would allow for a smooth and democratic transition.

There can be little doubt that public reaction to the government's use of violence formed a fourth element bringing together this unlikely coalition. The protest began initially with the "likely suspects," members of the unions and organizations that traditionally filled the oppositional role in Bolivian society. As the demonstrations grew, however, and the president ordered the use of more violent methods of crowd suppression, the horror of the deaths brought formerly undecided people into the protests. Bolivia has had a relatively low level of state violence compared with other Latin American countries, even during the period of its military dictatorships. The growing violence during the second Sánchez de Lozada administration had begun to take its toll. The February 2003 gun battle in La Paz over the impuestazo was said to be the most lethal day in Bolivia's history since the 1952 revolution. The violence in the Chapare also mounted, as coca growers, their families, and security personnel were killed and wounded in frequent confrontations (Amnesty International 2003; Washington Office on Latin America 2003). Altogether, human rights advocates estimate that in the fourteen months of Goni's administration, the government was responsible for more deaths than in any one year of the military dictatorships of the 1980s. The Commission of Human Rights estimates the toll as 140 dead and more than 500 wounded (Los Tiempos 2003).

While neoliberal rhetoric describes neoliberalism as minimizing the state to privilege the market, the Bolivian case shows a somewhat different reality: some segments of the state, such as social spending, are minimized but the repressive apparatus of the state is ever more present. Anthropologist Lesley Gill has argued that the repressive apparatus of the state in neoliberal Bolivia has been supported and paid for, not to defend the human or civil rights of the Bolivian people but to defend the property rights of those who control the market (Gill 2000). The violent government responses in February and October 2003 appear to justify her assertion. Ironically, this strategy boomeranged: it brought together the traditional victims of state violence — the poor, coca growers, miners, peasants, Indians, and the unemployed.

Interestingly, the protests were largely centered in the highlands, especially in the La Paz/El Alto area, where the population is heavily Aymara. There were few protests in Santa Cruz, where there is a much smaller percentage of indigenous residents. When I spoke to my Guaraní friends later about the October gas war, they said they watched the process on television along with everyone else in Bolivia. Samuel Tapera told me that he and his Guaraní friends longed to join the protests, but they were a small minority in Santa Cruz, where there was little echo with the popular mobilizations of the highlands. The people of Santa Cruz expressed substantially larger support for the president and for the economic potentials of the gas pipeline. The traditional social movements — like the sindicatos, miners, and cocaleros — are all part of the highlands tradition and have focused their attention on the dominant powers in La Paz, the capital. Santa Cruz, which has a different ethnic makeup, with fewer Indians and more European immigrants, has always felt separate from the rest of Bolivia (Stearman 1985). It has created its own development path, tied more to international markets, and has its own camba elite, who more than anything long for autonomy and control over the resources of the Oriente.

This long-held sentiment has blossomed since early 2000 in what is known as the autonomy movement, the strongest manifestation of which was a massive march and demonstration in Santa Cruz in January 2004. This regional division has faced the country for many years but in recent times has caused many to question whether Bolivia is a viable country. Without doubt, this will be a fundamental challenge for Bolivia's future. In the October 2003 uprising, the regional division revealed itself mostly through the limited participation of Cruceños in the popular protests. Nevertheless, the resignation of the president and the promises of Mesa to hold a referendum on natural gas were widely welcomed by the region's majority.

The lowlands indigenous movement was not entirely silent, however. CIDOB, the national indigenous organization based in Santa Cruz, sent out a public press release supporting the protesters in El Alto and threatening to raise a regionwide demonstration of lowland indigenous groups if Sánchez de Lozada did not resign. Then CIDOB and the APG, the national Guaraní organization based in the southern city of Camiri, mounted a joint demonstration in the community of Taparenda. Some regional groups also held demonstrations, like the Chiquitano Indians of San Javier. This response was probably all they could do on such short notice, given the difficulty of organizing small indigenous groups dispersed across the huge area of the Oriente. But even this represented a fairly important shift, publicly linking the agendas of lowlands and highlands indigenous groups. Other social movements in the lowlands also joined the protests, most notably the campesino sindicatos and the Movimiento Sin Tierra (MST, the Movement of People Without Land), who blockaded the highway in Yapacaní, north of Santa Cruz.

Public Participation in Decision Making

Although Bolivia's October 2003 revolution was sparked by the Sánchez de Lozada gas proposal, it was clearly about much more than populist concerns about gas. I suggest it was centered on the sense that Sánchez de Lozada's government had systemically excluded Bolivia's poor and Indian populations from participating in political decision making at the most important levels. Transactions giving foreign companies the right to profit from natural gas exploitation seemed to exemplify the president's neoliberal focus on the market as opposed to the welfare of the people. Like most Latin American countries, Bolivia owns rights to all subsoil resources. The capitalization of the YFPB changed this in part because it gave YFPB's foreign partners rights to 50 percent of the company's profits. In 1997, at the end of his first term, Sánchez de Lozada took this privatization process one step further, passing a decree that allowed multinational corporations (MNCs) to explore and exploit natural gas fields under concession from the government, apart from YFPB projects. In the seventy-eight contracts the government signed secretly with MNCs, the companies were granted ownership of natural gas *de la boca del pozo* (literally, "from the well-head"), meaning that although the gas belonged to the Bolivian state while it was underground, the gas became the property of the MNCs when it was pumped and sold (Petras 2004: 3).[18]

Private contracts with these companies also fixed the Bolivian share of the profits at 18 percent in the case of new wells, as opposed to the 50 percent share publicized under the capitalization scheme. Under the proposed plan exporting the gas to Chile, the price would be fixed at the Chilean port rather than as a proportion of the price received from U.S. buyers (Petras 2004). To make this scheme competitive, the corporations would have had to sell the gas at low commodity prices to the companies that liquefied it and transported it north. Bolivian consumers, however, would pay much higher prices for domestic use.[19] Given the tremendous sacrifices Bolivians have made since the mid-1990s, during this period of financial crisis and structural adjustment, it is not surprising that this arrangement sparked growing anger among the Bolivian population. While such a deal may have made sense from the point of view of capitalists trying to sell a commodity on an unstable international market, for poor Bolivians it seemed an all-too-familiar formula for the rich to get richer.

Chaos and Elections

The October uprising did not result in a peaceful transition to smooth-running democracy. To the contrary, the post-2003 political scene in Bolivia was chaotic. In July 2004, President Mesa held the national referendum on the hydrocarbons law. In the referendum questions he drafted, Mesa proposed a new strategy of gas exploitation to benefit Bolivia, along with the abrogation of the previous hydrocarbons law, refinancing the national petroleum corporations, and a combination of gas exportation and domestic gas use. He argued that the current contracts signed with transnational corporations would have to be respected but that, wherever possible, they would be renegotiated to raise the royalty rates. All future concessions would pay at least 50 percent royalties.

Mesa's proposal was not convincing to all. Many of the Aymara protesters of El Alto, along with the trade unionists of the COB, saw the referendum as a sellout. They believed the referendum ignored the clear message of the October uprising: that the people wanted immediate nationalization of the gas wells and a reformulation of the hydrocarbon policy to promote national industrialization without export, especially through Chile. Economists argued that such a strategy would amount to a foolhardy return to inward-focused development, which proved untenable during the import substitution industrialization years. Even if Bolivia did decide to turn to a domestic industrialization program, where would the capital for this investment come from? And what would be the market for its products?

While Mesa's proposal ultimately prevailed in the referendum voting, the MAS party and other sectors continued to exert pressure during the parliament's rewriting of the hydrocarbons law. He advocated that 50 percent of all oil and gas profits go as royalties to the Bolivian treasury, while the president proposed 18 percent royalties and 32 percent as taxes. In March 2005, faced with a crippling round of massive strikes and blockades by MAS, the COB, Central Obrera Regional (COR, Regional Workers Federation), and other organized groups, Mesa resigned, criticizing Morales and other Left leaders (La Razón 2005a).[20] His resignation was rejected by the parliament, but the strikes continued, plunging the country into further chaos.

That was not the only problem Mesa had to face. At the other end of the spectrum, the civic committees of the so-called Media Luna departments (Santa Cruz, the Beni, and Tarija, where the gas resources are located) called instead for a strategy of export with increased royalties to be paid at the regional level. In January 2005, these leaders mounted enormous marches, calling for regional autonomy and the direct election of department governors. (At that time, departmental prefects were appointed by the president.) Mesa agreed to elections and urged that it happen in the context of the constituent assembly tentatively scheduled for 2005 and 2006.

Finally, in June 2005, as Mesa and the congress failed to agree on the dates and process for holding the constituent assembly, national strikes began again. After weeks of political uncertainty and blockades paralyzing the country's economy, Mesa resigned again. As part of a compromise among all the political parties, including MAS, Eduardo Rodriguez (the head of the Supreme Court) was named interim president. In collaboration with the main political parties, the entire congress resigned, and Rodriguez scheduled elections for December 2005 for president, vice president, and all congressional seats. In a concession to the autonomy movement, elections were also scheduled for the first time for prefectos, the governors of the nine departments.

This was the context for the momentous elections of 2005. Morales and his vice presidential running mate, social scientist Álvaro García Linera, faced a strong opposition from Jorge "Tuto" Quiroga, who had been Banzer's vice president and after Banzer's death from cancer, president. His Podemos party campaigned for a continuation of neoliberal reforms and was the clear favorite of the U.S. embassy. A third strong candidate, at least early on in the campaign, was Samuel Doria Medina, who had left active politics in the early 1990s to win a fortune in the cement business. He campaigned as a populist who could provide jobs and make the economy grow. Until the last weekend, it appeared from poll results that Morales was in first place, but with less than the 50 percent necessary to take the presidency. The election results were stunning: Evo won 51 percent of the vote, more than any other president since the country's return to democracy. Morales won the support of a wide spectrum of Bolivians, but most of his support came in the highlands. He won all the departments in the western part of the country, but Podemos won the eastern departments of Santa Cruz, Pando, Beni, and Tarija. Even in those eastern regions, however, Morales garnered the support of labor and peasants unions, the poor and landless (like the MST), and indigenous organizations (like CIDOB, the CPESC, and the APG).

When there is no outright winner, Bolivian law dictates that the congress chooses a president. This has happened in every other election since the country's return to democracy. In 2002, even though Sánchez de Lozada only received 21 percent of the vote, he and his party negotiated a pact with other parties to allow him to take the presidency. In 2005, however, for the first time the president was chosen directly by the Bolivian people, demonstrating the growing power of postmulticultural citizenship.

Conclusion: Toward a Postmulticultural Bolivia

> What they don't understand is that the mentality of the people
> has changed. Once we were imaginary citizens. Now we are
> real. And we are not going back.
> — Andrés Manuel López Obrador, mayor of Mexico City,
> describing popular support for his campaign to challenge
> the elite's control over Mexican politics

This book has examined the emergence of a new social formation in Bolivia that has crystallized since 2000 in response to the promises and exclusions of neoliberal multiculturalism. Chapter 6 described the convergences of a number of complaints and demands differing social sectors brought against the government since 2000, culminating in the election of Evo Morales as president. In this final chapter, I draw on the analysis provided earlier in the book to propose four important shifts that have shaped this activism. I also explain the implications this activism has for democracy and neoliberalism.

The Death of the State of '52

First, the reforms of the 1990s brought an end to the "State of '52," the social pact between the national developmentalist state and the social sectors. As I wrote in chapter 4, the assault on what has come to be seen as the "traditional" model of state-civil society relations began with the first neoliberal adjustments in 1985, when the mines were nationalized and the miners union silenced. Nevertheless, collective associations continued to be the fundamental form of citizen activity as well as the means by which citizens were represented in the political system. Although their clientelist nature often distorted their democratic potential, collective organizations such as trade unions, indigenous social groupings, and neighborhood associations are essential to everyday life in Bolivia's popular sectors. Since the mid-1980s, however, these collectivities have been less able to produce results for their constituents. In the 1990s, as privatization and the privileging of global capital altered the economic relations between the state and labor, labor was pushed from its strong negotiating position. As Bolivian sociologist Silvia Rivera Cusicanqui has pointed out, since the 1980s the marches, strikes, and mass mobilizations of indigenous and popular sectors have become "increasingly confrontational, testifying to the exclusionary nature of formal democracy. Bolivian democracy, as it currently exists, is incapable of processing indigenous and popular demands unless forced to do so by insurgent action" (Rivera Cusicanqui 2004: 20).

This is true in part because although neoliberal reformers tried to transform the model of state-civil society relations, they were unable to replace it with a viable democratic alternative. The 1990s multicultural reforms, especially the Law of Popular Participation (LPP), were the mechanism by which both the government and civil society were to be modernized. Yet, as chapter 4 demonstrated, the forms of inclusion codified by the LPP proved to be quite limited. Rather than promoting a functioning system where Indians and popular sectors found an arena in which to present their demands, the municipalities became the site of expanded patronage, clientelism, and corruption. Patrons, in the form of political parties and increasingly NGOs, continue to wield enormous power over indigenous and poor citizens. Frustrated, these people turned back to the tried-and-true model of conflictive mobilizations. They also undertook a new strategy of forming their own political parties.

If the so-called State of '52 is dead, the collective form of organization and political action is decidedly not, however, as the October 2003 uprising made all too clear. The protagonists of the insurgency were trade unions, *juntas veci-nales* (neighborhood associations), peasant federations, student organizations, street vendor syndicates — corporate groupings with well-established patterns of political behavior based on decades of direct negotiations with the state (Lazar 2004). Anthropologist Sian Lazar has suggested that the reason why the October uprising reached such dramatic heights was that the state refused to attend to the social sectors in the traditional way (Lazar 2006). Rather than engage the normal cycle of protest-negotiation-agreement (with the government reneging on promises and the people renewing their protests), President Gonzalo Sánchez de Lozada resorted to denigrating popular demands and then, tragically, to using massive state violence. For Bolivians, this was an unacceptable violation of a social pact, which, if moribund, still held moral sway.[1]

Legacies of Neoliberal Multiculturalism

The second important shift that informed the convergence of the events in October 2003 was one experienced at the level of what literary critic

Raymond Williams has called the "structure of feeling" (Williams 1977). Here I refer to the important ways the multicultural reforms of the 1990s contributed to the production of indigenous subjects. In chapters 2 and 3, I described how indigenous organizations and leaders, like those of the Capitanía Zona Cruz (CZC), were influenced by the discourse of multiculturalism and the political and funding opportunities it made possible. The Guaranís of Zona Cruz found great pride and solidarity in their indigenous organization and in the knowledge that they were "recognized" by the state. In chapter 5, I described how Indian citizens were imbued with and internalized — to some degree at least — the logic of neoliberalism. By learning "techniques of the self" — such personal skills as rational participation, effective money management, and, most important, "responsibilization" — Indian leaders prepared for the exercise of citizenship in multicultural Bolivia. The case of the Guaraní leaders demonstrates the limitations of these skills, but it also shows how strong the discourse of citizen participation was for Bolivia's Indians. These young Guaraní leaders did not just give up when the municipal government's doors failed to open for them. Rather, they rejoined the mobilizations pushing for more democratic openings, such as the constituent assembly.

How much other indigenous peoples accepted this interpellation is speculation, but it is clear from the events since 2000 that indigenous people are beginning to exercise a new and more powerful protagonism, through both conflictive mobilizations and their entry into electoral politics. The LPP did not create this, of course. As I described in chapter 1, Indian resistance has been ongoing since the conquest, and much of the current drive for participation and inclusion is the result of the sustained advocacy and activism of these indigenous groups. Nevertheless, the LPP opened up new expectations for Indian citizenship and provided some new institutions as well. In many cases the institutions of municipal government proved to be mechanisms for the continued dominance of the political elites, but in other cases these same institutions facilitated the current activism.

For instance, in October 2003, much of the insurgency arose from neighborhood associations in El Alto. El Alto's residents are highly organized and the neighborhood groups exert enormous political pressure on the city's government. Collective organizations, based on rural Aymara communal structures, act as territorial grassroots organizations (OTBs) under the LPP. Through these state-sponsored associations, Aymara residents have been able to organize and make demands for a society based on their own culturally informed vision of democracy. Chapter 4 described the forms of social control common in Andean communities, where decisions are made in assemblies. The October uprising demonstrated how the members of such communitarian organizations were able to use the strength they had gained through participation in the municipal government process to go beyond the limits inherent to the LPP. When the gas pipeline plan was announced, it was these same juntas that organized the protests. Alteños I interviewed in 2004 insisted that the uprising was not led by any national political leaders; rather, they believed, it was the result of a bottom-up response by poor people fed up with marginalization, poverty, and what they saw as the engine of it: neoliberalism.[2]

Organizations already in place in El Alto — the juntas vecinales, the *juntas escolares* (neighborhood school associations), the street vendor associations, and so on — leaped into action during the protests. Doña Beatriz Mamani, who worked selling vegetables in the market, told me she and her neighbors all knew each other and their local base leaders because they had been working together as an OTB to push for more services from the city. They needed paving blocks for the streets and more control by police to protect them from delinquents. So when the uprising began, Doña Beatriz and her neighbors called on this network to get people into the streets. Each block had a leader who knocked on every door to make sure that the families were participating in the blockades. Doña Beatriz said it was quite scary, especially when the military started killing so many people, but there was little choice. Everyone in the association was expected to do their part and to contribute to the fund for supplies and food. None of this would have been possible without the strong and active associations that are part of El Alto's fabric, which have been strengthened by the LPP since the 1990s.

The El Alto case is somewhat special. As I described in chapter 4, in many other communities, the LPP has fragmented and marginalized Indian organizations. But this has also led to new protagonism, most evident in the success of the Movimiento al Socialismo (MAS, Movement Toward Socialism) party. Evo Morales's party decided to work at both the local and national levels, where it has been a vocal opponent of neoliberal economic policies. In the referendum over natural gas held in July 2004, Morales argued against the giveaway of Bolivian patrimony to foreign corporations, supporting the people's "verdict of October" to nationalize the gas resources. The MAS and the Movimiento Indígena Pachakuti (MIP) parties, which came to power precisely in reaction to the LPP, were crucial actors in the debate, as were the local leaders identified by the LPP. In the weeks before the vote, I attended two of the many public hearings about the referendum held across the country. The first was in El Alto at a meeting of Aymara junto vecinales leaders, and the second was in a town hall in rural Oruro, where Quechua campesino leaders came to hear their MAS congressman. In both places, the framework designed for the LPP decisions — OTBs with leaders elected by "responsible" citizens — was being used for public teach-ins about the referendum that were highly critical of the new president's plan.

Here the Bolivian case offers a contrast to most characterizations of the effects of neoliberalism. Indigenous citizens, assuming some of the rationalities of neoliberalism and acting through institutions established during the neoliberal political reforms, posed important challenges to the workings of global capitalism. These are quite unexpected results of the multicultural reforms of the 1990s, which were intended to heal the rift between the state and the populace. Instead, the reforms — through both their inclusions and exclusions — enabled citizens, particularly indigenous citizens, to act against the continuing limitations of state-sponsored multiculturalism and the costs of neoliberal economic policy.

Alliances Across Sectors

The third shift that made the October uprising and Morales's election possible is a change in the form of social movement activism that has been occurring since 2000 or so: that of people organizing across ethnic and class lines. These alliances were evident in the water war in Cochabamba and the formation of the MAS party but became all the more important in the struggle against the neoliberal policies of the Sánchez de Lozada government. Neoliberal adjustment programs affected Indians severely. Indian farmers on the altiplano were heavily affected by trade liberalization and the end of subsidies, and indigenous communities and environments were threatened by resource extraction schemes. But they were not alone in bearing this burden. This was shared by the general public, particularly by workers, peasants, and the urban poor.

This common ground brought together the popular sectors over the past few years in the different mobilizations described in the last chapter. The water war joined residents of urban neighborhoods with rural farmers in battling the costs of a water privatization scheme that would have affected them all. The campesinos' protests in the highlands pointed out the costs to subsistence farmers shut out by imported foods, but they also called attention to the effects these economic transformations have had on the urban poor, whose food prices rose in response. Even the cocaleros' fight against coca eradication, which might seem an issue specific to this particular sector, has implications for the rest of the poor. Morales and the cocaleros have framed their struggle in terms of anti-imperialism, arguing against the overarching power the United States has over Bolivian policy. This question of sovereignty resonates with many Bolivians, particularly those who attribute the economic crisis to the "stranglehold" by so-called Washington consensus institutions.

Similarly, the October 2003 uprising brought together a wide swath of Bolivians united against various dimensions of neoliberal policy. The leaders of the uprising took strategic advantage of these articulations to bring together poor and Indian Bolivians into one heterogeneous group that shared a common experience in the "market democracy" of neoliberal Bolivia. Their shared marginalization and suffering acted as a crucible for the negotiation of a new Bolivian public. This emerging collectivity was a fragmented collection of autonomous but connected groups, like merchant associations, neighborhood associations, or indigenous organizations. It drew strength from the traditional corporate collectivities of the State of '52, such as peasants and trade unions, but it also appeared to go beyond their limitations through these cross-sector alliances. Bolivian sociologist (and now vice president) Álvaro García Linera has described this form of social movement a "multitude-form" (García Linera 2004: 71).[3] In contrast to the "modern" social movement like the union, the multitude-form is the result of participants' free choice, with no mechanism for surveillance or control of membership. It lacks a stable structure of control and relies on the moral authority and persuasive arguments about the justice of its cause to ensure its power of convocation. Yet, like any group with a social identity, it has a collective group narrative that demarcates social boundaries and creates a sense of authenticity and otherness (ibid.: 78).

This new collective identity was revealed most clearly when the protesters asserted "The gas is ours!" ("El gas es nuestro!") during the October uprising. To whom did the "ours" refer? The discursive label most often used was "the Bolivian people" ("*el pueblo boliviano*"). It is clear that even though the faces on the frontlines of the demonstrations were overwhelmingly Indian, especially in El Alto, where most of the violence occurred, "*el pueblo boliviano*" did not signify indigenous — or more specifically, it did not *only* signify indigenous. Rather, the label appeared to mean a coming together of all Bolivians hitherto excluded from the public sphere, most of whom were Indians. Thus poor, urban residents who might identify at times as Aymara and at times as Alteños, and rural people like the Guaraní, who might identify at times as indigenous people and at times as poor peasants, found an articulation in their opposition to neoliberalism and their sense of exclusion from public life.[4]

After the October 2003 events, Morales explained the sentiment this way: "This uprising of the Bolivian people has resulted not only from the issue of natural gas, of hydrocarbons, but from a collection of many issues: from discrimination and from marginalization, but fundamentally from the exhaustion of neoliberalism. The culprit responsible for so many deeds, and also responsible for the uprising of Bolivian people, has a name: it is called neoliberalism. . . . Now, with the recent events in Bolivia, I have realized that what matters is the power of an entire people, of an entire nation. For those of us who are convinced that it is important to defend humanity, the best support we can offer is *to create the power of the people*."[5]

The Turn to Citizenship

But is this alliance truly new? That is, if race and class have always been intermingled in Bolivia, as I have argued throughout this book, what makes this fresh form of activism so different? The answer to this brings us to the fourth important shift: the turn to citizenship and the assertion of citizenship rights. I argue that part of what makes this postmulticultural activism so successful in this moment is that it has turned away from basing its demands on class or race to articulate its demands in terms of citizens' rights. When the protesters of October demanded participation in public decision making about the issues of natural gas, this was not because they were poor or because they were marginalized Indians. Instead, they were arguing that as citizens they had rights to be included in that process. This is a response to the history of political reforms in Bolivia since the return to liberal democracy in the 1980s. It also reflects a continentwide trend, as civil society organizations and multilateral institutions across Latin America have adopted the language of citizenship and citizenship rights.

Citizenship refers to the relation between individuals or groups and the state. That relationship depends on how each society answers the fundamental questions of belonging, such as: What rights and obligations do members of a society have vis-à-vis the state? How does the state determine what kinds of rights to afford? Who qualifies as citizens and what role do they have in determining the ways society is governed? There are many possible answers to these questions, and the tensions between them continue to underlie debates about citizenship today.[6] In his classic 1949 essay, sociologist T. H. Marshall described three sets of rights necessary for full citizenship: civil rights, political rights, and social rights (Marshall 1949: 78). He argued that although civic and political rights were important, they did not eliminate inequalities of social class. It was only in the twentieth century's social welfare states that the struggles for social rights as part of modern citizenship were able to modify the capitalist class system, somewhat altering the patterns of social inequality.

Based on Marshall's model, theorists of democratization and civil society have promulgated an ideal of liberal citizenship in which rights-bearing citizens participate as equals and guide formal political decision making (O'Donnell and Schmitter 1986; Habermas 1989; Avritzer 2002). This model formed the basis of most contemporary Latin American democracies, yet a growing literature points to a substantial gap between the ideal and its implementation. Perhaps most important, critics argue that liberal citizenship is a product of bourgeois society underlain by inherent exclusions of race, class, and gender (Fraser 1993; Calhoun 1997; Eley 1997). Although democratic countries in Latin America like Bolivia claim to have eliminated such exclusions through universal suffrage, in practice, radical disparities continue to mark the exercise of citizenship. Anthropologists Teresa Caldeira and James Holston have argued in the case of Brazil, for instance, that although the poor enjoy full political rights, they do not have sufficient civil rights. Their subjection to systematic crime, police abuse, and government corruption deprives the poor of a sense of individual security. As a result, institutions and practices of law and justice are delegitimized, precluding the democratic rule of law (Caldeira and Holston 1999; Caldeira 2000).[7]

At the same time, however, as military dictatorships gave way to more democratic societies across Latin America, citizens have had more opportunities to exercise their political rights. Civil society actors have increasingly taken advantage of these openings by demanding particular social and economic rights from which they have been excluded, such as housing, clean water, and education (Jelin 1998; Dagnino 2003). By pushing for human rights and inclusion, social movements like those of indigenous groups have broadened the meaning of democracy for all members of society (Van Cott 1994; Dagnino 2003).[8]

The experiences of citizen activists across Latin America make it clear that contemporary citizenship must be theorized in the context of societies marked by structured inequalities. That is, although liberal democratic definitions characterize citizenship as a universal category that can be claimed by any legitimate member of the nation state, it is important to recognize that such categories are enacted in politically structured contexts. Here I suggest thinking about citizenship in another way, as an idea or discourse that orders society. Taking historical anthropologist William Roseberry's notion of "languages of contention," we might say that citizenship is the framework by which social conflicts and power relations are negotiated in modern democracies like Bolivia (Roseberry 1996; Guerrero 2003). I suggest that citizenship is politically and socially constituted in two interrelated dimensions: the politics of belonging and the contest over political culture. Both have been radically challenged and transformed in Bolivia by the new form of social activism.

The Politics of Belonging

The politics of belonging refers to the processes by which members of society are included in the democratic system — in essence, defining who is called to the table. This perspective draws our attention to the technologies, discourses, and practices by which societies organize political participation and exclusion (Lazar 2004). Citizenship in this view is a term of belonging, which is ultimately enforced by the state (Schild 1998; Taylor and Wilson

2004). A central focus of this book has been the contested political processes by which Indians have been included in and excluded from participation in Bolivia's multiethnic society. By characterizing these processes as political, I do not mean to imply that they are strictly or purely political. Rather, the analysis here has amply demonstrated that political technologies are deeply interconnected with cultural formations and economic practices.

Bolivia's LPP established political institutions and practices that promised to make all citizens equal through access to political participation at the local level. Indians and peasants were invited to take an active role in municipal development decisions by participating as OTBs or in municipal oversight committees. The evidence in this book demonstrates, however, that although the reform offered "universal" citizenship rights by expanding political opportunities for Indians and others, the practices of the LPP were underlain by and reinforced a racial hierarchy that, in large part, excluded meaningful Indian participation. Thus although the LPP operated to officially "recognize" indigenous people, it did not amount to "real citizenship." Why not?

In Bolivia, the central distinction that has determined political inclusion is race.[9] In chapter 1, I showed how the concept of race framed colonial and republican regimes. Indians in colonial times were under the jurisdiction of a separate set of laws and courts. This changed in the republican period, when liberal European notions of the nation were adopted. Nevertheless, although Indians were officially subject to the same national laws as others — and so could be considered equal citizens — the constitution still restricted suffrage to those who were literate in Spanish, who held lands or received rents, and who were not domestic servants. This set of distinctions effectively excluded Indians from exercising any political rights. It was not until the 1952 revolution that the country adopted universal suffrage. Thus in modern-day Bolivia, indigenous peoples can vote and (if they have the money and the patience) obtain documents showing their membership in the nation state, like a passport.

The formal granting of citizenship rights did not guarantee inclusion or participation, however. By concentrating on a politics of belonging, I look beyond these legal definitions of citizenship to see how racism continues to operate through the new, supposedly universal, categories of membership defined by the LPP. The reforms did bring about some important changes, as I discussed in chapter 4. The LPP named indigenous organizations and their leaders as political actors who would represent their constituencies in municipal governments, in essence, recognizing indigenous peoples as citizens, acknowledging their culturally based *usos y costumbres* (customary laws). In some areas, the reforms brought Indian organizations to political office and allowed them to participate in budget decisions benefiting their constituencies. This case study also shows, however, that the transformations at the discursive level did not translate into political or material changes for most indigenous peoples. As chapter 4 showed, for the most part, even where Indians were able to use the LPP to gain elected office, the reforms did not substantially alter the racialized power structures favoring the elite. Indigenous peoples were marginalized from political decision making, their traditional sociopolitical organizations were fragmented, and historical leadership roles were diminished. I conclude that the changes institutionalized through the LPP reinforced the ways in which indigenous people's relation to the state is mediated by the dominant elite, traditional political parties, and individualized clientelism. Thus the LPP acted to recontextualize existing hierarchies of exclusion in new "multicultural" forms.

Yet precisely because of these effects, which rendered visible the continuing exclusions, the reforms also had significant positive impact. By engaging with neoliberal state institutions that promised to include them and finding them wanting, citizens began to push to make those institutions more inclusive. That is, in the 1990s citizenship was defined by the state and implemented through the LPP, which carefully limited the institutions and practices of inclusion. In the early 2000s, a newly composed Bolivian public is expanding the spheres of participation beyond local politics, to national protests and electoral campaigns. This explains the strength of the MAS party, which gave poor and Indian leaders a place to express their constituents' demands as well as the hopes for the constituent assembly, which was in fact inaugurated in August of 2006. Today's poor and indigenous Bolivian public demands a democratic government designed by the people themselves, which will go beyond the limited notions of citizenship found in neoliberal multiculturalism.

There are many obstacles to any sort of truly inclusive society. Racism has a strong hold in Bolivia, and this sometimes manifests itself as fear. During the 2004 referendum on the gas, for instance, Aymara leader Felipe Quispe and his followers threatened to boycott the voting, to mount a blockade, and even to burn ballot boxes. Although such activities were seen as heroic during the October uprising, by July of the following year, any groups proposing such tactics were widely labeled "the radical sectors." This was somewhat understandable, since so many Bolivians feared another chaotic breakdown of the country if the referendum failed. But there was no escaping the undertones of racism and classism in these characterizations.

Bolivia's mestizo segment has had little choice but to recognize the fact that Indians are and will continue to be a powerful sector of Bolivian society. The exclusions of the past will no longer pass unnoticed. This is a critical point for indigenous people. After the October uprising, Aymara residents of El Alto described their feeling of empowerment. One woman, a leader in her neighborhood association, told me, "The people feel fearless now, they will rise up just like that." Another young leader told me he was proud of his Aymara brothers and the bravery they all showed in the protests: "Something awoke, I don't know what . . . it is that they value themselves now" ("Se despertó algo, no se que . . . es que ellos mismos se valoran ahora"). This sense of collective self-esteem, which has been growing since the 1990s reforms and the social upheaval since 2000, is most evident in the election of Morales, whom the poor and Indians refer to as "one of our own."

The Contest over Political Culture

The second dimension of citizenship that has been radically altered as a result of the novel form of social activism is citizens' ability to participate fully in the public sphere. If in the first dimension of citizenship I asked who was called to the table, in this second dimension I ask what issues are subject to deliberation and decision once at the table. That is, how do citizens make citizenship rights meaningful in practice? Social movements activists have argued that notions of citizenship must go beyond the idea of legal or political rights to account for struggles over cultural politics, such as the recognition of cultural difference and the feelings that unite collectivities (Jelin 2003: 107). This focus on "citizenship from below" is based on the idea of new social subjects who assert the "right to have rights" (Dagnino 2003). Every society has a "political culture," a historically determined but constantly changing construction of what counts as "political," as opposed to "economic" or "cultural" (Alvarez, Dagnino, and Escobar 1998: 8). Rather than asking simply for inclusion into a previously defined political culture, citizens have the right to rethink what they consider their rights to be.

Central to this is an understanding that the political arena must be redefined to include contestations over cultural meanings embedded in the unequal and hierarchical organization of social relations (Dagnino 2003: 4). This is related to the first dimension, of course, since it is precisely because of their historical marginalization from state power that subaltern groups like indigenous people may have alternative visions for the state and society (Varese 1996). Feminist philosopher Judith Butler has argued that the "abjected," those who do not matter in the dominant discourse, can sometimes create liberatory resignifications of social meanings (Butler 1993). This second dimension of citizenship thus provokes the question, How might indigenous peoples draw from their subaltern position to rethink citizenship?

Many members of Bolivia's indigenous social movements do indeed strive for some sort of culturally informed citizenship by which they can advocate for a government and society based on their histories and worldviews. In fact, it was one of the reasons why so many indigenous people were excited by the reforms of the 1990s, which recognized their traditional practices and customs and allowed their traditional leaders to represent them in municipal proceedings. But, as chapter 4 demonstrated, Bolivia's indigenous and popular sectors found it difficult to exercise this sort of "citizenship agency" through the institutions and practices of the LPP (Taylor and Wilson 2004). The institutionalized forms of participation were often at odds with customary forms of leadership, sociocultural organization, and authority. Much of the contestation since early 2000 has indeed been in response to the sense that political institutions were unresponsive to the Indian majority's deeply held cultural values.

Thus the current wave of activism has pushed to incorporate issues formerly relegated to the realm of culture into the public arena. In the water war in Cochabamba, for example, the protesters were not fighting just for economic rights to water but also to be able to define how water is to be treated and managed, taking into account native Andean cosmology about water and land. They argued that water is a human right rather than a commodity, imposing a cultural framework on a political contest. The long-standing conflicts in the Chapare brought to light similar tensions between foreign-led concerns about the so-called war on drugs and traditional desires to produce and use coca. Finally, in advocating for a constituent assembly, indigenous activists like the Guaraní are hoping to include some sort of social control that emerges from their community values. They hope that traditional methods of leadership accountability might offer another way to fight the ubiquitous corruption in political circles.

Evo Morales used these culturally informed protests to great advantage in his 2005 election campaign. He promised to legalize growing coca, by extending the zones where it can be legally grown (while promising "zero cocaine and zero narco-trafficking") (Forero 2005). Throughout the campaign, Morales emphasized his Aymara roots, describing his childhood of poverty herding llamas and working in the harvests with his father in Argentina. Four of his brothers and sisters died of malnutrition, and his mother nearly died during his birth from a hemorrhage. Because there were no doctors to attend the birth, they relied on an aged *curandera* (traditional healer) to save her (La Razón 2005c). In addition, he promised he would abide by the customary ethics of Andean leaders. Reciting these ethics in Quechua, Morales said they would be vital to his form of government: "*ama sua* (do not be a thief), *ama llulla* (do not lie), *ama kella* (do not be lazy), *ama llunku* (do not be servile)" (ibid.). Through these efforts, he reinforced his image as a poor Indian, proud of his heritage, who would bring the values of the base to the government.

This emerging Bolivian public has not only focused on values we might call "traditional." Rather, they have also challenged neoliberal definitions of public and private spheres, claiming increased rights to participate in public decision making. As the state shifted its enterprises more to private ownership during the 1990s, and as transnational capital emerged as key players in Bolivia's economy, many Bolivians felt that the state had abandoned its duty to act on behalf of the public. The October insurrection was the culmination of these concerns, in which protesters demanded the state protect its resources and distribute the benefits to all the people rather than to a small minority. Echoing the demands of the 1952 revolution, Bolivians fifty years later want a state that includes and protects them. They do not want a return to the paternalist and corrupt State of '52, however, but a new transparent state defined through citizen-driven public dialogue. If citizenship is characterized as participation in a politically constituted public space, then the postmulticultural citizens have fundamentally challenged neoliberal orderings of that space, radically redrawing it through their political pressure.

Most important, though, they hope to construct a government that has the interests of the poor and the working class in mind. When Rosana Moreno and the other Guaranís from the ETZ joined the march for a constituent assembly in 2003, they were seeking a profound change in the goal of the state. José Bailaba, a Chiquitano leader from the Oriente and a MAS congressman, explained in 2003 why his group, CPESC, had organized the march. "Still in this country," he told me, "political leaders continue to defend their own particular interests, which are opposed to the interests of society. Politics is transformed into something totally contrary to the social. We need a government that can generate work and economic resources, that can support the poorest sectors in rural development, health, in land redistribution . . . really, a government that can serve the public."[10] Here we see a clear argument for a politics of distribution to accompany the politics of recognition. Again, Morales responded to these concerns in his campaign. By pushing for nationalizing the gas resources, he indicated that the new Bolivia would take control of its resources and distribute them for the benefit of its people. An advertisement for Morales during the end of the campaign had this message: "Jobs for Bolivians, distribution of land, a law against corruption, nationalization of hydrocarbons. There are proposals, programs, and hope" (La Razón 2005f).

Looking to the Future

The election of Morales has brought to a close a period of great instability and chaos. Since the October 2003 uprising, many Bolivians have questioned whether the continuing social upheavals were undermining the

nation. As blockade after blockade took place, businesses large and small suffered. Commentators in the newspapers debated whether the country was
so divided along ethnic, class, and regional lines that it simply was not viable.
Others pointed out that for the most part, the population had lost all faith
in politicians and the political process. Even Carlos Mesa Gisbert, the popular journalist thrust into the presidency, squandered his popularity and trust
by not being able to accomplish the things he promised. When he resigned
in 2005, the country was at a crossroads. Would the constitution prevail?
Would traditional political parties force one of the elite into the presidency
to protect it from the popular sectors? Several Bolivian friends of mine
expressed concerns that such maneuvering could cause a military coup,
reminding me how recent Bolivia's return to democracy really is. Not that
far below the surface are memories and fears of military control. Fortunately,
the presidency passed according to the Bolivian constitution to the head of
the Supreme Court, who then convened and oversaw fair elections.
Candidates campaigned, pundits opined, and in December the president, vice
president, the entire congress, and for the first time new governors of the nine
departments were legally and peaceably elected.

So has the emergence of postmulticultural citizenship been "good for
democracy"? Of course, this is ultimately a question for historians to answer
in retrospect. Then there is the question of what we mean by "democracy."
Whether an outcome is good or bad depends on one's perspective. For the
white and mestizo elite, the rising power of the poor and Indian social movements may seem a disaster in and of itself. For the indigenous majority, regardless of how "the new Bolivia" actually ends up functioning, the fact of
having an Indian in the presidential palace in the first place might be as good
as it gets. I leave those discussions to future analysts. For now, though, it is
possible to identify certain factors that might affect how the new government
might fare.

First, much depends on how Morales manages the enormous divisions that
face the country. He won with an impressive 51 percent, but there are still
a lot of people who see him as their worst nightmare (this is how Morales
characterized himself in relation to the United States). While saying he represents all Bolivians, he does not count on the support of the traditional elite
or the traditional political parties, or the camba establishment in Santa Cruz.
These deep divisions threaten to make his administration, like the last two,
difficult. How he negotiates with these interests will be critical.

Second, his power base is not stable. He has relied on an assemblage of
social movements to form his base, but these groups have a fragile history
of competition under the corporatist state and have little experience working together. To the contrary, the dominant powers have often used them
against each other, co-opting them with favors and patronage. Moreover,

Morales and his MAS party have been operating as an oppositional force, enacting a politics of contestation and resistance. Now in this new phase, they must elaborate a convincing politics of proposal and government. Whether they can meet this challenge, especially with the profound divisions hanging over them, is the question. Will Morales disappoint his indigenous supporters, who want change and want it quickly? (Vargas Llosa 2005). If he does, will the social formation that brought him to power bring him to task too?

Third, Morales has spoken openly of his admiration and friendship with leaders like Hugo Chávez in Venezuela and Fidel Castro in Cuba, and he has vowed to emulate their social policies and their independence from the United States. Morales has made his objections to neoliberalism, structural adjustment, and the newest elaboration of it (the Latin American Free Trade Pact) a central part of his platform. In the international news, observers have argued this represented a swing to the left in Latin America, making Morales stand in, once again, for the dragonslayer of neoliberalism — a role he clearly enjoys. This image was strengthened on May 1, 2006, when Morales ordered the Bolivian army to seize control of the fifty-two oil and gas installations, fulfilling his campaign promise to nationalize the gas resources. His decree left open the possibility of renegotiating the contracts held by transnational corporations. Although his clearly left position has won him admirers across the world, will it impede his ability to bring investments and development to Bolivia?

This is a crucial issue because of the drastic economic condition that Bolivia suffers. It has enormous resources of natural gas that offer the promise of future development, but those resources are still in the ground, and there are terrible differences of opinion as to how to best develop them. This instability has not been good for foreign investment — only $84 million came into the country in 2005 (ibid.). Morales has a huge challenge ahead to raise the standard of living, stimulate economic growth, and bring jobs to the country. Bolivia has relied heavily on U.S. foreign aid to meet its budget ($95 million from USAID alone in 2005) (Lettieri 2005). Will this critical source of revenue dry up in response to his strongly anti-imperialist, anti-neoliberalism rhetoric and his nationalizing the gas resources? Or will he moderate his tone once in power, as others in his position have done?

Nevertheless, despite these obstacles, the December election and Morales's election have reinvigorated a weary civil society. Although there is still a great deal of cynicism about politicians, including Morales, it is clear that his election will open certain political spaces for social movements that have not been available for some time. As my friend Samuel Tapera told me shortly after the election: "We have to hope that things can change. We have given the political parties their chance. So Evo is the only alternative. He deserves the opportunity to govern! So we are hopeful, hopeful that he will provide work, and bring change."

Perhaps the most important expectation lies in the constitutional assembly, which Morales has promised to oversee. The *constituyente* has long been the site of hope for changing the power structures. Yet after the referendum on gas held by President Mesa, which many saw as manipulated by Mesa, those hopes dimmed. Would the constituyente be another performance like that, where the options were delimited by the state? Now it seems likely that Morales will at least ensure wide participation in the assembly and act to be sure popular sectors are not silenced. His administration has said that the creation of the new Bolivia will be closely linked to the process of constitutional reform that will be the task of the constituyente (La Razón 2006).

Already NGOs are beginning to hold practice assemblies to sound their bases for the ways they want to restructure Bolivia. When I was in La Paz in 2004, I attended a meeting of female activists preparing for the constituyente. It was a little like a high school civics class. The delegates, mostly working-class women from the highlands, many with infants wrapped on their backs, were reading and discussing Bolivia's current constitution. Then, section by section, they began to ask what they would change if they had the chance. One woman complained about the required military service for all men, noting that in practice, it was only the poor who served. Another focused on the role of political parties, reminding her fellows about their corruption. How could they change that? Would the new law allowing social organizations to propose candidates prove a viable alternative? In the section on economic rights, a debate erupted about natural gas resources. Fairly quickly, the women agreed that nationalization was the only option. For several days, they talked through the sections, carefully plotting their suggestions on the butcher block paper in front of the room, just like the Guaraní leaders had learned to do in Santa Cruz. There were arguments, disagreements, and compromises. Then they returned home to talk with the other women in their grassroots organizations, to educate them about the constitution and the issues facing the country.

In Santa Cruz, the Guaranís are also involved in such meetings. But there it will be much harder to come to agreements or compromises. The autonomy movement, led by Cruceño elite politicians, gathers momentum, especially now that its leader, Rubén Costas, was elected governor of Santa Cruz. When I met with the leaders of the capitanía in June 2004, we discussed the constituent assembly. That was the hope, they all agreed. But they worried, would the constituyente turn out to be like the LPP, just a *juego político* (political game)? Samuel Tapera agreed with this concern. Now in law school, thanks to a scholarship, Tapera had just returned from Geneva, where he had served as a delegate to a U.N. meeting about indigenous issues. The

trip had been eye-opening, and it had been wonderful to meet other "indigenous brothers" from around the world who faced such similar problems: oil
exploration, discrimination, and, most of all, struggles to hold onto the land.
But in the end, he said, shaking his head, "All that talk, all these meetings.
So far, there are no real answers."

This will be the challenge for the constituent assembly — to produce more
than talk, to get to some real answers that change the material conditions
for the poor and indigenous peoples of the country. Is this possible? Have
the events of past years revealed irreconcilable divisions in Bolivia? Or can
the alliance of Indians and poor people forge a viable proposal for a new
model of state-civil society acceptable to all Bolivians? What new model of
a multiethnic state might emerge that balances the need for recognition and
equitable distribution? This is the most important challenge ahead, and it
goes to the heart of the issues I have described in this book, because it is a
challenge to neoliberalism. Although there is no doubt that the new social
formation active in Bolivia has engaged with, learned from, and benefited
from some aspects of neoliberalism, the protests since 2000 and especially
the election of Morales are clear indications that the majority of Bolivians
reject the practices, institutions, and effects of neoliberal economic reforms.
Their verdict is that it enriches the already rich and privileged, impoverishes
the already poor and marginalized, and limits the possibilities of democratic
participation. Bolivia's postmulticultural citizens hope they can provide
another option. The rest of Latin America, and perhaps beyond, will be
watching their efforts.

Notes

The epigraphs to this chapter are drawn from the following sources: Anacleto Supayabe (pers. comm. with the author, July 26, 2004, Santa Cruz, Bolivia) and Evo Morales (La Razón 2005e).

1. I use the term "popular" in the Latin American sense, referring to middle or lower classes. It is related to the notion of populism, as something inspired by and appealing to the mass population. Robert Albro and Jeff Himpele (forthcoming) note that this is a different connotation from the North American term "popular culture," which is associated with the idea of mass culture. In Bolivia, *sectores populares* is used to mean those sectors representing the poor, peasants, or labor. It generally has a class connotation rather than an ethnic or cultural one. I use "popular," then, to refer to organizations that do not specifically identify as indigenous. Of course, as I argue in the text, such distinctions are difficult to sustain in Bolivia, where most people are both indigenous and poor. The point of my usage is to illuminate the ways in which ethnicity and class are used as organizing schemas under specific conjunctures.

2. This figure is based on the 2001 census by the Bolivian National Statistics Institute, which gives the following numbers of people who self-identify as indigenous: Quechua 31%, Aymara 25.23%, and Others (including Guaraní, Chiquitano, and Mojeño) 6.10%. Their total is 62.33%. This number is cited in the United Nations Development Program's Human Development Report for Bolivia (UNDP 2004) as well as in a World Bank (2005) report on indigenous poverty.

3. Indian rebellions swept the area in the 1700s, events that left a historical memory among many Bolivians of the possibility of Indian wars. The most important of these were revolts led by Juan Santos Atahualpa in 1742, Túpac Katari in 1780, and Túpac Amaru II in 1781. See Klein 1992 and Stern 1987.

4. In this sense, some similarities can be drawn with the Zapatista movement, which although made up of many indigenous people, advocates about issues that impact all of Mexico, such as free trade and economic justice. See Rus, Hernández Castillo, and Mattiace 2003; Hayden 2002.

5. I use the term "public" following Nancy Fraser's seminal article coining the term "subaltern counter-public" (Fraser 1993). She takes as a starting point Habermas's idea of the public sphere, which she defines as the "theater in modern societies in which political participation is enacted through the medium of talk" (ibid.: 70). She argues that in stratified societies, "arrangements that accommodate contestation among a plurality of competing publics better promote the ideal of participatory parity than" (as Habermas argues) "does a single, comprehensive, overarching public." She proposes the term subaltern counter-publics to refer to the "parallel discursive

arenas where members of subordinated social groups invent and circulate counter discourses, which in turn permit them to formulate oppositional interpretations of their identities, interests, and needs" (ibid.: 81). See also Albro and Himpele forthcoming for an interesting take on the relation between the "popular" and the "public."

6. Recognition of self-identification is an essential part of most definitions of indigenousness. The most widely quoted definition is that formulated by José Martínez Cobo, the special rapporteur for the United Nations Commission on Human Rights: "Indigenous communities, peoples, and nations are those which, having a historical continuity with pre-invasion and pre-colonial societies that developed on their territories, consider themselves distinct from other sectors of the society now prevailing in those territories or parts of them. They form at present nondominant sectors of society and are determined to preserve, develop, and transmit to future generations their ancestral territories, and their ethnic identity, as the basis of their continued existence as peoples in accordance with their own cultural patterns, social institutions, and legal systems" (Martínez Cobo 1987: 29, cited in Assies 2000: 4). Assies 2000 includes a helpful discussion of the different theoretical frameworks by which indigenous identity has been defined. See also Maybury Lewis 2002.

7. Hale 2002 uses similar terms, "state-endorsed multiculturalism" and "dominant bloc–endorsed multiculturalism."

8. Since 1986, constitutional reforms have recognized the multiethnic and pluricultural nature of society in the following countries: Bolivia (1994), Colombia (1991), Ecuador (1998), Mexico (1992), Nicaragua (1986), Paraguay (1992), Peru (1993), and Venezuela (1999) (Seider 2002: 4).

9. In practice, however, neoliberalism does not result in the withering away of the state. Rather, some parts of the state apparatus, such as social services, are minimized or outsourced, or, as I demonstrate in chapter 4, extended into smaller and more remote spheres, such as municipalities. Other parts of the state, like the military or the judiciary, are kept in place or even increased in size and force. See Bierstecker 1990; Gill 2000; and Postero 2004.

10. Information on the radio series is available online at http://www.homelands .org.

CHAPTER 1: REGIMES OF RACE AND CITIZENSHIP

The chapter epigraph comes from Marx 1963 [1869].

1. Throughout this book, I refer to my Guaraní friends by their first names to reflect the informal usage common in Santa Cruz. Even titles of respect, like "Don," can be used with first names only.

2. Like most Guaraní names, there are numerous ways to spell Kuruyuki. Historians Bartomeu Meliá (1988) and Francisco Pifarré (1989) spell it Kurujuky, while ethnomusicologist Walter Sánchez C. (1997) spells it Curuyuqui.

3. This chapter is an assemblage of scholarship carried out by numerous historians from Bolivia, the United States, and Europe. I am extremely lucky to have been able to draw upon these resources. I am particularly grateful for the recent work of historians Brooke Larson (2004), Sinclair Thomson (2002), and Andrés Guerrero

(2003), who analyze questions of citizenship and race in ways that demonstrate star-tling comparisons with the current moment.

4. The exact time of the arrival of the Guaranís in the area is not clear to histo-rians. Pifarré gathers together a fascinating combination of accounts of travelers, Incas, missionaries, and military officers to estimate the arrival at fifty to a hundred years before the arrival of the Spaniards (Pifarré 1989: 27ff).

5. The Bolivian highlands were part of the Spanish *audiencia* of Upper Peru and were ruled from the viceroyalty of Lima.

6. For more on the Andean encomienda, see, for example, Trelles Aréstegui 1982 and Ramírez 1986.

7. There are substantial debates about how destructive the colonial system really was. Galeano's characterization may be the most extreme. Enrique Tandeter sees Potosí labor as essentially coercive, as his 1993 work *Coercion and Market* makes clear. Peter Bakewell, however, challenges the "Black Legend" historiography, suggesting that not only have the conditions facing Potosí mitayos been exaggerated, but the workers actually experienced a degree of autonomy at the mines. See his 1984 book *Miners of the Red Mountain*.

8. For different approaches to race and caste in colonial Latin America, see, for example, Chance 1978, Farmer and Katzew 1996, Poole 1997, and Jackson 1999.

9. See also Sergio Serulnikov's excellent 2003 monograph, *Subverting Colonial Authority*, about Northern Potosí, as well as Ward Stavig's 1999 book, *The World of Túpac Amaru*.

10. Not all historians see the repartimiento as bad as has conventionally been argued. For example, Jeremy Baskes has suggested that indigenous cochineal pro-ducers in Oaxaca, Mexico, actually benefited from the arrangement (Baskes 2000).

11. Spanish-language surveys of the so-called age of Andean insurrection include the thorough studies by Boleslao Lewin (1957), Jorge Cornejo Bouroncle (1963), Carlos Daniel Valcárcel (1970), Alberto Flores Galindo (1976), Jürgen Golte (1980), and Jan Szeminski (1983). In addition to Stern's 1987 anthology, there are several important English-language studies on the rebellion. Lillian Estelle Fisher (1966) and Scarlett O'Phelan Godoy (1985) have examined the rebellion across the Andes. Stavig (1999) and Charles Walker (1999) have analyzed the specific effects of the uprising in Cuzco. And in addition to Thomson's excellent study on La Paz, Oscar Cornblit (1995), Nicolas A. Robins (2002), and Serulnikov (2003) have examined the war in Upper Peru.

12. This is the system whereby community members assume civic responsibili-ties in Andean communities. Usually the roles are taken for a year. Such leadership is often seen as an obligation, which often entails substantial expenditures of money and time. See Abercrombie 1998 and Lazar 2005.

13. As a result, from 1880 to 1951, the number of voting citizens in Bolivia stayed between 2% and 3% of the total population (García Linera 2003: 14, citing Irurozqui Victoriano 1994).

14. This echoes Mamdani's (1996) duality of colonial African indirect rule: cit-izen and subject. Citizens are white settlers or urban Africans, while subjects were the rural "tribal" Africans under the authority of the Native Authorities adminis-

tering "customary law." Mark Thurner (1997) has described a similar duality in Peru, between the tributary subject (those Indians who paid tribute to the Spanish Crown in exchange for their autonomy and their lands) and the citizen taxpayer.

15. Marisol de la Cadena's 2000 work presents a different picture of the acceptability of mestizaje in Cuzco, Peru.

16. This form of corporatism was not unusual in Latin America. Political scientists have long studied the phenomenon and noted its characteristics under different contexts. For an excellent review of the concept and its development since the 1970s, see Collier 1995.

17. See Friedlander 1975, Knight 1990, Bonfil Batalla 1996, and de la Cadena 2001.

18. Gordillo has argued that the perception of the unions as co-opted para-statal organizations fails to recognize the unions' resistance. Although divided and influenced by various wings of the MNR party as well as the Left, the unions continued to act on behalf of their constituencies. The result of their actions was not only the Agrarian Reform Law, but also a radical rethinking of the peasants' role in the nation. Through this period, he says, the "campesinos helped to transform the foundations of society, consolidating a project of the nation that included them as historical actors, but that also permitted them to constitute themselves as the subjects of their acts, thoughts, and discourses" (Gordillo 2000: 239).

19. Sanjinés has argued that Qusipe's radical positioning is a compelling critique of domination and the cultural mestizaje that has been hegemonic in Bolivia since the revolution. While Cárdenas's version of Katarismo "ends up promoting a multiculturalism that does not question neoliberal policies," Quispe has "radicalized Katarista discourse by separating its ideology from the established system of political representation." His goal is to "prevent Katarista ideas from turning into a multicultural formality with little effect in everyday political practice" (Sanjinés 2004: 164).

20. Zulema Lehm Ardaya's excellent 1999 study of the Mojeño organization shows how the 1990 march was an articulation of political demands by young leaders as well as millenarianist projects by the older more traditional leaders. She argues that the march was the result of an accumulation of the experiences of indigenous organizing that began with the earlier Búsqueda de la Loma Santa millenarianist movement. Her close ethnography of the two movements and their interlocking influences is a high point in recent indigenous studies.

21. This was not the first such meeting of indigenous leaders in La Paz, however. Rivera Cusicanqui describes the first national Indigenous Congress sponsored by the MNR party in May 1945, in which hundreds of highland Indian leaders arrived in La Paz and for the first time were allowed to walk freely in Plaza Murillo (where the principal government buildings stand). Before this time, Indians were not admitted in the city. According to Rivera Cusicanqui, the citizens of La Paz were upset and frightened by the sight. She says that "the ideological impact of this Indian conclave, held at the seat of the government and in the presence of its highest authorities was perhaps more important than any of the measures it adopted" (see Rivera Cusicanqui 1987: 50).

22. In our cross-country comparison, Leon Zamosc and I also point out the very

different contexts in which the issue of indigenous rights arises. In some cases, indigenous groups have sufficient political power to raise the issues themselves. The case of Ecuador's Confederación de las Nacionalidades del Ecuador (CONAIE, Confederation of Indigenous Nationalities of Ecuador) is illustrative. It has organized mass demonstrations and roadblocks, which have given the group enough political power to negotiate directly with the state. Indigenous groups may also raise their rights as a result of particular threats to their livelihoods, such as logging or resource exploitation. In other cases, indigenous rights have emerged as relevant issues during negotiations around the resolution of armed conflict. This has been the case in Guatemala, Colombia, and Mexico, although each of these cases presents particular scenarios. Finally, the Indian Question has also been politicized through the framework of the electoral process. Alejandro Toledo made indigenous identity an important element of his presidential campaign in Peru in 2001, and in both Ecuador and Bolivia, indigenous groups have recently formed new and potentially powerful political parties that raise these issues at the local and national levels. For more details, see Postero and Zamosc 2004.

23. But see Chapin 2004, in which the author has argued that although there have been important alliances between indigenous groups and environmentalists, there are also some fundamental differences. Indigenous peoples, he says, invariably begin with the need to protect and legalize their lands for their own use. They emphasize finding ways of making a living on the land without destroying their natural resources. Conservationists, however, often begin with the need to establish protected areas that are off-limits to people and to develop management plans. And, he says, "if they include indigenous peoples in their plans, they tend to see those people more as a possible means to an end rather than as ends in themselves" (Chapin 2004: 21).

24. For an interesting comparison, see anthropologist Diane Nelson's 1999 description of Guatemala's ratification of ILO Convention 169.

25. See the discussion about various forms of power sharing in multiethnic societies in Postero and Zamosc 2004.

26. Ley de la República No. 1585, August 12, 1994.

27. Author's translation.

28. The SAE published a four-point statement of its "ethnic policies": (1) a formal recognition of indigenous peoples by the state and the recognition of their collective rights; (2) the promotion of the participation of indigenous organizations' representatives in the decisions regarding their development; (3) respect for and strengthening of indigenous organizations and cultural systems, based on their own development, and the strengthening of their own capabilities for determining and managing (*gestión*) their own development; and (4) active state support for bettering the conditions of indigenous peoples' lives (see Lema 2001: 7). I thank Luz María Calvo and Ana María Lema for the firsthand accounts of this period in SAE's history.

29. Some examples are laws recognizing indigenous forms of collective land tenure; indigenous people being granted certain collective rights of commercial forestry; certain laws protecting indigenous peoples' customary rights (*derechos consuetudinarios*) to access to water resources; and the new administrative systems allowing the establishment of indigenous municipal districts (see generally Marinissen 1998).

30. La Ley INRA, Ley No. 1715. The reform was accompanied by a complex set of regulations, which established four phases for the titling and use of TCOs: (1) the initial indigenous demands and immobilization of the land; (2) field investigation, in which the lands are mapped through geo-coding and the rights of all parties are established — the result is *saneamiento*, or clearing of the titles; and (3) a so-called spatial study carried out by the Vice Ministerio de Asuntos Indígenas y Pueblos Originarios (VAIPO, Vice Ministry of Indigenous and Original Peoples Affairs) to determine how much land the indigenous people will really "need." Once this is decided, the land is titled. Finally, (4) to make use of any of the natural resources on the land, such as lumber or wildlife, the indigenous groups must develop management plans based on scientific studies that must be approved by the local government (see generally Marinissen 1998).

31. For more about the Ley INRA, see Marinissen 1998 and Martínez 2001. For ethnographic and legal assessments of its implementation, see Roper 2003; the special issues of CEJIS 1999 and 2001; and Opiniones y Analisis 2003.

CHAPTER 2: AN INDIGENOUS FEDERATION IN BOOMTOWN SANTA CRUZ

The chapter epigraph is drawn from Albó 1990: 325.

1. Bolivian literature (not to mention La Paz stereotypes) portrayed Santa Cruz as a lazy tropical backwater, populated by rich *hacendados* on their handsome horses, lovely camba women in revealing dresses, and brutish but good natured mestizo peasants who speak their colorful and humorous camba dialect. Even former President Hugo Banzer Suárez, a native of Santa Cruz, once said that the legacy of the Oriente is the hammock.

2. These clothes are purchased by the ton and resold all over Latin America. Even factoring in the middlemen, the clothing is still inexpensive: shirts for a dollar or two, pants a bit more, dresses two or three dollars. One result of this is that many of the poor of Santa Cruz wear clothes with English slogans on it. This ranges from the innocuous and sometimes even cute ("Pleasant Valley Cheerleading Camp Retreat Weekend") to the comical (a huge muscle-bound man wearing a shirt that said "I'm not fat, I'm pregnant!") to the tragically ironic (a malnourished Indian woman with five starving children hanging onto her with a T-shirt that said "Only in Corpus Christi.")

3. Since the sales of the land have begun and people have had more money to spend on housing, many families have begun building their houses out of bricks and cement. During my stay in Bella Flor, however, there were only twelve brick houses of the sixty-four houses in the village. The new houses were typically small, often retaining the one-room style of the traditional Guaraní house but with cement floors.

4. I use the term "households" to describe a group of people that pool their resources, live as one family, and eat from a common kitchen (*olla comun*) or common cooking pot.

5. In 45% of these extended families, the adult sons brought their partners to their parents' home; in 30% the daughters brought their partners; and in 25% the extended family was made up of both sons and daughters bringing their partners into their own family. There did not seem to be an established gender pattern to these arrangements.

6. I do not know Davison personally. Anthropologist Jürgen Riester of the NGO APCOB in Santa Cruz alerted me to Davison's 1987 dissertation, which I found in the APCOB library. I include his data as he reports it, with no ability to decide how it was gathered or if it is accurate. I counterpose my data to his in the interest of seeing what had changed since the mid-1980s.

7. Pers. comm. with the author, July 17, 1998, Santa Cruz.

8. This quotation comes from the official record book of the Assemblies of the Capitanía Zona Cruz, p. 7, from the September 17, 1994, meeting in the community of Chané Justiniano. The speaker was Jose Domingues of Teko-Guaraní, Camiri.

9. Pers. comm. with the author, July 15, 1998, Santa Cruz.

10. The Mendoza proposal was this: "The project constitutes the alternative of adequately preparing the managers-actors of the indigenous communities in the principal areas of their careers, focusing the support on training and organizational and administrative strengthening of the indigenous movement, with the goal of generating appropriate human resources to participate efficiently in the different activities of social and ethnic development as well as the democracy of the country" (my translation).

11. Article 2, Estatuto Orgánico de la Capitanía Zona Cruz, approved August 1, 1998, by the Asamblea General de Zona Cruz, Warnes.

12. Author's translation.

13. The statute lays out who can be members, how the assemblies should work, who can be the officers and what their duties are, what the sanctions for violations are, and so on.

14. These questions call to mind the famous Paul Gauguin painting portraying social life in Tahiti, which he inscribed with the French title "Where do we come from? What are we? Where are we going?" Deborah Elliston has argued that this was a profound subversion of the common orienting questions Polynesians asked people unknown to them. Gauguin took these "central questions through which sociality was organized by people . . . and appropriated them, . . . changing them to articulate classic existential concerns of French intellectual thought: the questions represented collective searches for meaning" (Elliston 2000: 172).

CHAPTER 3: A CRISIS OF LEADERSHIP IN BELLA FLOR

The epigraph is drawn from Ley de la República No. 1585, adopted December 8, 1994.

1. "What distinguishes property from mere momentary possession is that property is a claim that will be enforced by society or the state, by custom or convention or law" (Macpherson 1978: 3).

2. Donald S. Moore (1998) has noted that environmental struggles may themselves shape the political boundaries of "community." He argues that good ethnographies are needed to analyze the key constituencies in agrarian conflicts, the internal differentiation within groups, as well as the processes through which discursive and material boundaries are shaped.

3. Linguistically, land is identified with the term *tekoha*, which means "the quality of being (*modo de ser*), the condition of being (*modo de estar*), system, law, culture, norm, behavior, habit, condition, custom" (Meliá 1988: 297).

4. Ethnohistorian Bartomeu Meliá has suggested that the depredation by Spanish conquerors became confused in Guaraní memory with the advancing frontier and the destruction of the forest. This destruction of alarming proportions was represented mythically by grasshoppers (Meliá 1995: 304).

5. Anthropologist Bret Gustafson has noted that in modern discourses, the term *mburuvicha* is used interchangeably with *capitán*, so whatever original Guaraní meaning it had has been merged with this colonial construction. It could be construed as "leader" or "authority," depending on the context and the power the mburuvichas hold vis-à-vis their communities and spheres of influence. In old Guaraní, one root of the word is "grande" (*juvicha*). Some etymologies suggest *mburu-juvicha* is the *gran temblador*, the one who possesses the most sacred trance power. Leaders are also called *teta ruvicha* (the *grande* of the community) or *mburuvicha guasu* (*el gran grande*) (pers. comm. with the author, via e-mail, 2000).

6. Author's translation.

7. Author's translation.

8. Albó does not explain his methodology in gathering this information, or whose ideas these represent. All he says is that this ideal is the result of "numerous discussions" he has had in the region (Albó 1990: 96). He has many years of experience in the region, however, and is one of Bolivia's best-known researchers in areas of indigenous culture and politics.

9. Mburuvichas have almost always been men. Albó explains that this has to do with the necessity of his having courage (*hatangatu*), which the Guaraní consider to be a male characteristic. There have historically been a few female leaders, but only in special circumstances, such as when a woman has learned to speak particularly well (Albó 1990: 110). In the CZC, there were two female capitanes comunales (local leaders) during the time of my fieldwork. In both cases, the women explained their leadership to me in that they were acting to fill a void. Both women led Guaraní communities in which the men worked in the sugar processing plant and thus had no time for organizing. These female leaders had begun to organize the women in their communities, and since there was no other leader willing to represent the community at the capitanía level, these women took over the larger role. This characteristic of Guaraní leadership is changing more and more, however, as women are receiving education and as a result of national and international efforts to encourage female leaders. Gradually, women are holding more important roles in both the regional organizations as well as the national-level organizations like the Asociación del Pueblo Guaraní (APG).

10. The large majority of Guaranís in Zona Cruz are evangelicals, as a result of a strong evangelical proselytizing campaign from the 1960s on. Bella Flor was founded as a Christian Guaraní community, and most of its leaders have been educated in evangelical bible colleges. This education has provided many Guaranís with the social and political capital to negotiate karai Bolivian culture as representatives for their people. Although this new religion has been taken up by many Guaranís, it does not seem to affect their notion of themselves as Guaraní. That is, for these Guaranís, there is no inherent contradiction between being Guaraní and being an evangelical Christian. Political scientist José Antonio Lucero has written about the tensions

within Ecuador's evangelical indigenous federation (known as FEINE) and its strategic moves to enter the national political agenda (Lucero 2006). See also Albó's interesting 1995 article (321ff) about Pentecostalism among the Guaraní as well as David Stoll's 1990 and 1993 works for an analysis of the effects of Protestantism across Latin America.

11. Here I use "modern" in the sense that the Guaraní do, to mean a view that conforms with the logic of the Bolivian society that surrounds them in the city. Of course what "modernity" is has been debated endlessly, and I do not try to enter that debate here.

12. I never met Don Amalio Vega, so this is speculation based on reconstruction of his words and reputation from interviews, recollections, and the detailed description of him in Davison 1987.

13. Titleholder would be best translated as *titular* in (official) Spanish, but the residents of Bella Flor use the word *titulario*.

14. This imaginative and very probably illegal bit of lawyering was based on a certain logic: the 595 hectares was divided by the 53 members to give 11.73 hectares to each titleholder. Dividing the land into specific plots is also logical, in that it gives control over the land to those who own it. Nevertheless, the understandable desire to control the land was contrary to the way the title was drafted. The new titles were never presented to the agrarian reform office, but they were proof enough for the foundation of the new community.

15. Worse still, the loan was tied to the U.S. dollar, since the funds came from an international development bank (Davison 1987: 176). So, as the Bolivian peso began to fall in the late 1980s, because of huge inflation in the immediate postdictatorship years, the debt became larger and larger.

16. This group included both people whose names were on the title (that is, the original settlers of the community) and the heirs to these titles in the case of people who had died in the meantime.

17. To put this in context, in 1985, British anthropologist Davison found that families in Bella Flor cultivated an average of 2.55 hectares (including both cane for sale and food for consumption). I surveyed the village in 1998 and found they were down to 1.28 total hectares per family (0.89 hectares for consumption). In 1999, it was down to 0 (Davison 1987; Postero 1998).

18. This was part of a larger holding company that titleholders buy into with their title. The land was subdivided, and the titleholder got shares of the new venture profits. Nontitleholders also were part of the venture, because they were investing what was being called their *patrimonio* (heritage). Essentially, this acknowledged that all the people who have worked the land will be recognized eventually as having some rights to the land by the agrarian reform law. With the money from the lot sales, the company began doing several things. First, they bought cars and trucks to form a fleet of taxis. The titleholders and their young sons were then given possession (but not title) of the vehicles, so they had a way of making a living. Then, the company invested in a big tractor and began mechanized rice planting in the lands between Bella Flor and El Futuro. The profits were to be split between the shareholders. The company also purchased land about two hundred kilometers away, in

the colonization areas. A large number of the people of El Futuro went out in three or four trips in the season, when land is prepared for cultivation, and cleared the land. The idea was that it would be partly collective, growing rice, and then young Guaraní families would have individual plots. A third plan involved the purchase of cattle for yet another area.

19. It is important to note that corruption, defined as taking private advantage of public resources, is not a "Bolivian" or "indigenous" failing, but an all-too-human quality found in every society. I have written elsewhere about how corruption claims in this case stood in for other more important issues, as well as about the difficulty of defining acts as corruption in the first place (Postero 2000 and 2001). For an interesting take on the anthropology of corruption, see Shore and Haller 2005.

20. What, then, could Don Álvaro have done to resolve the crisis? This was, of course, the ever-present question. The most often suggested remedy was a negotiated agreement dividing the land between the titleholders and the nontitleholders, which would have allowed the "legal owners" to sell their land and would have protected the vulnerable who had worked the land for so many years. In fact, Don Álvaro did put forth a weak version of this idea to INRA, but he did not try to convince people at the community level of the plan's wisdom, nor did he exert any effort to make it come to pass. Another idea was to do a collective version of Rafael Vaca's idea of the Guaraní enterprise. If the capitanía or the community formed a fund, it could have sold some of the land and used the proceeds for the collective good of the community members. That would mean buying other farming lands elsewhere, educating the community's youths for city jobs, building better houses, or whatever the assembly decided. Any of these ideas might have been accepted had a strong leader pushed it from above.

21. First, the land colonization plan up north had come unraveled. The plan had been that young and disenfranchised Guaranís of El Futuro would work for free for a season clearing and planting the rice on a collective basis. Then the harvested rice would be divided up for the next season when the people came to live on the land, to clear land to which they would eventually get title. Meanwhile, Don Rafael held the title, since he had purchased it through the Guaraní land sales company. The people did their part for the long first season, but when it came time to divide up the harvest, Don Rafael said there was not enough, and the rest needed to be saved for seed for the next year. This led to a great deal of resentment, as can be imagined. The moral economy of Don Rafael's greed had unraveled.

22. Despite his defeat, Rafael Vaca did not give up. During my visit in January 2000, I met with him as he was holding an extemporaneous meeting with the buyers of the El Futuro lands. The community members had continued their blockade of the land for several months, and the buyers were getting impatient. That morning the buyers had met with the community members, promising them to act peacefully and to cooperate with them. By the afternoon, Don Rafael was there, telling them he had gotten an *amparo*, or writ from the court, prohibiting the blockade and convincing them that they had all the right to go onto the land and start making their homes. Don Rafael was protected by off-duty policemen, who told me they were paid privately by Don Rafael. As a result of this meeting, the buyers told me they were just

going to enter their lands and not bother about any cooperation with the Guaranís. "This is their internal problem," said their leader. "We paid our money in good faith, and all we want is to start settling here. We cannot judge who is right between them."

23. Interestingly, none of the women in the Tapera family received lots. This is not universally true, however. Some women heads of household did receive lots in the settlement.

CHAPTER 4: MULTICULTURALISM AND THE LAW
OF POPULAR PARTICIPATION

The chapter epigraph is drawn from Ley de la República No. 1585, adopted December 18, 1994.

1. See Marinissen 1998 for a description of the treaty and its adoption and significance for Bolivia's indigenous peoples. See Nelson 1999 for an interesting discussion of the debates over ILO Convention 169 in Guatemala.

2. Co-authors Catherine M. Conaghan, James Malloy, and Luis A. Abugattas have described the situation in Bolivia at the time of the NEP's takeover as "a crisis of social domination," the term Argentine political scientist Guillermo O'Donnell coined for a situation in which threat from below menaces the viability of the capitalist system as a whole (Conaghan, Malloy, and Abugattas 1990: 18).

3. This was partly in response to the collapse of the global tin market in the fall of 1985 and partly in response to the falling productivity of Bolivia's tin industry, which during the decapitalization over years of military rule had become more and more antiquated (Crabtree, Duffy, and Pearce 1987).

4. Thomas A. Kruse has noted that previously "the market was subordinated to the interests of a national community . . . now the order was inverted, as the nation was 'structurally adjusted' and subordinated to the logic of the market, now of global proportions" (Kruse 1994: 23).

5. Popular opposition was strong but immediately repressed. The Central Obreros de Bolivia (COB, the Workers Federation of Bolivia) declared its opposition to the plan, and Paz declared a state of siege, with congressional approval, and sent hundreds of COB leaders into internal exile. In August 1986, a massive protest called La Marcha por la Vida (the March for Life) was lead by unemployed miners into La Paz (see Nash 1992 and Sanabria 2000). The protest, which included hunger strikes and hundreds of miners "crucified" on crosses lining the roads into La Paz, was put down by the army (Crabtree, Duffy, and Pearce 1987: 87–88). The trade unions' failure to move the government shows how successful the NEP was in restructuring the balance of power in the country. The closing of the mines and the severance pay given to the *relocalizados* to soften their opposition to it eroded the power of this traditionally radical oppositional force, which had a pivotal role in the revolution and brought an end to the dictatorship.

6. After four years, the program was renamed the Fondo Social de Inversión (FIS, Social Investment Fund) and made into a semipermanent fixture in Bolivia (Graham 1992).

7. For a general discussion of neoliberal policies and practices, see Bierstecker 1990 as well as Mosley, Harrigan, and Toye 1991.

8. The five state enterprises were oil and gas, telecommunications, airlines, power generation, and the railroads. Ley de Capitalización, Ley No. 1544, March 21, 19944.

9. Ley de la República No. 1551, April 20, 1994.

10. Both Laserna (1994) and Martínez Montaño (1996) describe the history of decentralization in Bolivia, pointing out that there has been a back and forth debate in Bolivia since the 1930s between regional capitols and the centralized state. During the dictatorships, for example, the regional civic committees served as a space for the expression and strengthening of civil society. They also point to the importance of international support (especially from the German aid agency GTZ) in the strengthening of regional sectors.

11. As Kohl and Farthing have noted in their 2006 book, decentralization's role in challenging established power structures has been particularly apparent in Brazil, where participatory budgeting in hundreds of cities has allowed the left to challenge regional elite.

12. Much of the impetus for this debate about decentralization came from intellectuals and politicians from Santa Cruz, nonindigenous elites who sought more local control over the departments (Molina Monasterios 1996; Van Cott 2000:137ff). The concerns about autonomy have continued to be central for Cruceños, as I describe in chapter 6.

13. In 1985, there was also a reform to the Law of Municipalities, which expanded the roles of municipal officials. Some people see this as a step toward decentralization. Indigenous groups, however, pushed to amend the law to establish indigenous and peasant municipalities, which do not yet exist (Marinissen 1998: 233ff).

14. OTBs are defined as "the basic unit with a communal or neighborhood character that occupies a determined territorial space, comprises a population without differentiating level of education, occupation, age, sex, or religion; and maintains a principal relation with the public organs of the State through the Municipal Government of the jurisdiction where it is located" (author's translation). Regulation D.S. No. 23858, September 9, 1994, and additions in D.S. No. 24447, December 20, 1996.

15. Article 3 of the LPP. See also Cárdenas 1996: 25.

16. Anthropologist Javier Medina was especially influential in the crafting of the law. See his accounts of it in Medina 1996 and 1997.

17. This point has been emphasized by both Diego Ayo Saucedo (1999: 27) and Silvia Rivera Cusicanqui (1987).

18. This, unfortunately, did not prove to be the case. In the many analyses of the LPP during its ten-year anniversary in 2004, the most salient criticism has been the rampant corruption at the local level (Iván Arias, pers. comm. with the author, July 2004, La Paz; Ayo Saucedo 2003). This has been reflected in the numerous *votos de censura* (censure votes) by which mayors were removed from office. A USAID/Bolivia study estimated an average of 129 mayors (40%) were replaced every year from 1995 to 1999, most through censure votes. See Kohl and Farthing 2006.

19. Ramiro Molina, pers. comm. with the author, November 10, 1997, La Paz. Many observers credit the contradictions between the two sides of Goni's government for the eventual disintegration of the political alliances on which it was based.

20. See Benería and Mendoza 1995 for a discussion of the role of social emergency funds in other countries. Co-authors Sonia Alvarez, Evelina Dagnino, and Arturo Escobar have referred to these funds and the discourses they engender as "apparatuses and practices of social adjustment." They suggest that these funds operate by creating new individualizing and atomizing discourses such as "self-help" and "active citizenship," which ultimately might depoliticize the basis for mobilization against structural adjustment (Alvarez, Dagnino, and Escobar 1998: 22). This is certainly the conclusion of public sector scholar Carol Graham's in-depth study of the Bolivian FSE. She says that although it is difficult to establish a direct causal relationship between the FSE and the sustainability of the NEP, it is certainly plausible to assume that it played a role in strengthening support for the Paz Estensorro government, if not directly for economic adjustment. Moreover, she says, one can only speculate about the outcome of the structural adjustment process without the FSE. "While the implementation of economic reform may have been possible, Bolivia's fragile democratic institutions could have been substantially weakened" (Graham 1992: 1244–45.)

21. Political scientist Wendy Brown has said, "As the social body is stressed and torn by the secularizing and atomizing effects of capitalism and its attendant political culture of individuating rights and liberties, economic, administrative, and legislative forms of repair are required" (Brown 1995: 17).

22. In his 2002 work, anthropologist Shelton Davis describes the World Bank's projects to address indigenous poverty in Latin America, drawing on what are called "participatory approaches to indigenous development."

23. Here, I make reference to Silvia Rivera Cusicanqui's famous 1987 book about Indian and campesino movements, *Oppressed but Not Defeated.*

24. Iván Arias, pers. comm. with the author, October 23, 1997, La Paz.

25. The SAE, with funding from the United Nations Development Program (UNDP, or PNUD in Spanish), also established a six-month-long training program for indigenous leaders to become *responsables de planificación y gestión indígena* (RPGIs, indigenous planners and managers), in which they were taught not only about the new laws, but how to write proposals, engage with the local and national government, and make development plans for their communities

26. I thank Sian Lazar for this insight, among many others.

27. Bolivian historian Ana María Lema has collected the positions of several indigenous leaders from that time. See Lema 2001: 31–34.

28. Sarah Radcliffe and Sallie Westwood have noted the importance throughout Latin America of the three common symbols of the *patria* (fatherland): the flag, the shield, and the national anthem. "The nation is symbolized by a number of material artifacts which identify themselves as being unique to the nation, or which through their visibility and wide diffusion through the country, come to stand in for it" (Radcliffe and Westwood 1996: 58). They also discuss how nations mark the territory as national through the use of maps, museums, and educational geography texts.

29. It is worth pointing out how much Indian estimation of Cárdenas has dropped after the initial hopes. Aymara intellectual Félix Patzi has argued that Cárdenas was nothing more than a 1970s *indigenista* who was easily used by the national integrationist project of capitalist multiculturalism (Patzi 2002: 42–43).

Most of my Guaraní informants now just think of Cárdenas sadly, as someone who was used and discarded by powerful politicians.

30. These were later called *planes de desarrollo municipal* (PDMs, municipal development plans).

31. Bolivian anthropologist Xavier Albó summed up the thoughts of many when he suggested the LPP should perhaps better have been called the Law of Municipalization, since that more accurately reflects both its content and its subsequent implementation (Albó 2002: 80).

32. Sian Lazar argues that to understand the political activism of the Alteños since the mid-1990s, one cannot underestimate the importance of the CONDEPA party in the 1980s and 1990s (Lazar, pers. comm. with the author, February 6, 2006, via e-mail). That party, led by a radio journalist named "Compadre" Carlos Palenque, focused on urban Indians in La Paz and El Alto, forging a new identity for Aymara migrants to the city. Palenque used his role as a journalist, and later in his popular TV show *La Tribuna Libre del Pueblo* (*The People's Free Tribune*), to make the lives of urban Indians (*cholos*) visible to the rest of Bolivians. He shared his platform with an Aymara woman, Doña Remedios, a *cholita* dressed in the traditional clothing of velvet skirt and bowler hat. See Archondo 1991 for an account of the Compadre's rise to power; and Soruco, Pabón, and Sanjinés 2000 for an update on the strategic use of the media for popular struggles.

33. See the 1998 work by regional planner Jordi Benería-Surkin on the political and economic strategies of CABI. With institutional allies such as USAID and the Wildlife Conservation Society (WCS), the Izozeños have managed to carry out a triple strategy: (1) they control a large territory as an indigenous organization, (2) they control an indigenous municipal district as an indigenous OTB, and (3) they co-manage (with the WCS) the largest national park in South America.

34. Of the three case studies he presents, however, two (Sacaca, Potosí, and Asunción de Guarayos, Santa Cruz) demonstrate the complex problems facing the LPP (Gray-Molina 2001).

35. There are reasons to question these figures, however. Most of the sources of this statistic, from academics to official Popular Participation documents, characterize these newly elected consejales as "indigenous," without defining the term or detailing their origins. As this term has had and continues to have such widely varying meanings, this makes it difficult to judge exactly who was elected and what their relation to "indigenous" causes might be.

36. The LPP training manual, widely distributed to popular organizations to teach people about their rights and obligations under the new law, included the election results in a section entitled "successes of Popular Participation." According to the manual, the election of 460 indigenous consejales is a "historical fact that demonstrates the profoundly democratic nature of the popular participation process" (MDH 1996: 49).

37. The municipal elections in 1999 also saw substantial indigenous and campesino candidates, but figures are not available for ethnic makeup for this election (Albó 2002). Gray-Molina has also noted that the elections were disastrous for female representatives, as their proportion fell from 27 percent to 8 percent (Gray-Molina 2001: 68).

38. I interviewed Faustino Auca and several other indigenous congressional leaders in July 2004, at the congressional offices in La Paz.

39. Albó's study of Indian council members showed that although many of the elected leaders had been party members before their nominations, a large number (36%) were nominated by their own grassroots organization (Albó 2002: 82). These first-time candidates were forced to negotiate with various political parties to see who could offer them the best terms.

40. This was made more disastrous by the disappointing actions of some of the indigenous leaders themselves. In the town of Urubichá, for instance, where Guarayo leaders elected to the council had the majority, they took turns being mayor, making the most of the position to rake profits. Lema contends that once in office, "the personal interests of the Guarayos prevailed over their indigenous identity and their ethnic conscience. They limited themselves to enjoying the position and forgot those who brought them there. They dedicated themselves to the 'good life,' traveling to the city . . . far from their communities, escaping slowly from the social control of their people" (Lema 2001: 205).

41. This part of the meeting of the Warnes oversight committee reminded me of the movie *Bienvenido, Mr. Marshall*. In that movie, made in Spain in the 1950s, there is a scene in which the city fathers of a small town in Andalucía believe that the Americans are coming to give out money for development under the Marshall Plan. They have every person in town line up and tell the town secretary the one thing they most want to receive. A piano? A set of weights? From a hilarious comedy about the foibles of international politics and development, the movie turns into a lovely allegory about how to find your own dreams.

42. Indian political psychologist and sociologist Ashish Nandy has shown how cultural traits of femininity, childhood, and primitivism were rejected by European colonizers and projected onto colonized populations. Indian subjects of the Raj were represented either as innocent and ignorant children who were still willing to learn (which called for civilizing, modernizing, or Christianizing by colonizers), or unwilling, oversexed, ungrateful savage children (which called for harsh repression by colonizers). These views were tied to liberal notions of progress in which colonizers had the duty to help the children mature so as to be good partners in the liberal utopia (Nandy 1983: 16).

43. Kohl reported that in May 2003, 25 municipalities had their accounts frozen by the National Treasury, and another 185 had failed to file one or more financial reports. In some cases, outgoing mayors refused to give the receipts and accounts needed to file annual reports. Commentators suggest this practice is preferable to facing corruption charges (Kohl 2003a: 160).

44. Author's translation.

45. Lema cites Iván Arias, who points out that these public beautification works are not all vanity projects. Rather, they provide spaces of conviviality for the public as well as symbolic spaces of power. Moreover, they demonstrate the prestige, modernity, and status of the officials who built them and may even help to forge a municipal identity (Lema 2001: 151).

46. For instance, anthropologist Jan Rus's work in Chiapas has shown how younger, educated "scribes" act as mediators between indigenous communities and

the state (Rus 1994). Anthropologist Terence Turner has also documented how young leaders of the Kayapo of central Brazil educated in Brazilian schools were able to translate their expertise into social control, as they negotiated concessions for extractive activities on community lands. Turner's analysis of how this monopoly was challenged is a fascinating study of the dynamic relations between generations (Turner 1995).

47. A World Bank–funded study in 1994 found that Bolivia's indigenous people have on the average three years fewer schooling than nonindigenous people. The difference is even greater for indigenous girls, the most disadvantaged group in Bolivian society. The conclusion of the study was that indigenous people were more likely than any other social group of any Latin American country's population to be poor (Psacharopoulos and Patrinos 1994; see also Davis 2002).

48. A similar problem has developed with the oversight committees, the mechanism by which social organizations were to give voice to the democratic demands of civil society and to monitor the political process. In practice, however, these committees have not fulfilled this role because the law does not provide their members with resources, salaries, or, most important, political power (Calla Ortega 2000; Lema 2001; Ayo Saucedo 2003). In some urban zones, this system functions fairly well, but representatives from rural indigenous communities are often caught in a bind. They are not paid, they often live far away from the municipal section's capital, and they often lack understanding of the law and the budget process. The president of the oversight committee is usually from the city and tends to control the process. Mayor and council members are not required to give the committees information, and they often do not, thwarting their work through delays and obfuscation. The watchdog process takes a lot of work, but from the perspective of the community members, this work does not produce anything. As a result, the oversight committees end up being perceived by communities as another inefficient organ of the municipio, rather than as a body acting on behalf of the people (Blanes 2000: 51). This characterization is a reflection of the structural position of the OTBs and the oversight committees: they are civil society organizations, representing the community members, and at the same time organs of the state, which act to funnel government money to citizens. The result is that where the local Indian authorities take on the role of the oversight committees, not only is their work is duplicated, but in many cases their leadership is devalued as working for the government and abandoning the interests of the local people (CEADES 2003: 235).

An even more serious problem is that the LPP law does not give oversight committees sufficient sanctions to force the city to alter its actions or to comply with the demands of the OTBs. A 1998 study by the Secretary of Popular Participation showed that in 80 percent of the municipalities, the oversight committees did not participate in writing the five-year development plans, and in half the municipalities studied, neither the oversight committees nor the OTBs took part in the development of the annual operating plans. Instead, the plans were written by the mayor or city council (cited in Kohl 2003a: 159). Given this situation, it has proven hard for indigenous leaders to use the institutions of the LPP reform to bring resources or political power to their people. Instead, the political parties and the traditional dominant class have reinforced their stranglehold on municipal funding mechanisms.

49. The municipal remapping process accompanying the LPP can also provide opportunities for communities to reconsider their political alliances. Anthropologist John McNeish has described the case of Santuario de Quillacas in the Aymara highlands, where the remapping process inflamed a long-standing conflict between two ayllus over the control of regional resources. The community of Quillacas used the conflict to reassert its traditional authority in the region and to protect its integrity as a historical site. The community of Sevaruyo-Soraga, however, took the opportunity to shake off what it saw as inept government by the elite of Quillacas and to move to the neighboring municipality of Huari (McNeish 2001).

50. This homogenizing effect became even more pronounced under the government of former dictator and then president General Hugo Banzer Suárez. His government focused on a "war on poverty" that hardly mentions cultural differences. This prompted many jokes at the popular level all around the general theme of: "Have you heard about General Banzer's war on poverty? Yeah, he's going to kill all of us poor people!"

51. Aymara sociologist Mamerto Pérez Luna has suggested that this is a disturbing echo of the past. In some senses, he says, the LPP is a modern version of colonial administration, in which the Crown kept control of national-level decisions while allowing the administration of local affairs to be carried on by the Indians (Pérez Luna 2006).

52. Kohl has reached similar conclusions about the LPP: "The law has served fundamentally as a reform measure, ultimately serving the agendas of international financial institutions interested in lowering central government expenditures and incapable of changing the basic material conditions for the majority of Bolivians" (Kohl 2003a: 161). See also Medeiros 2001.

53. Ayo Saucedo has called this "municipal fundamentalism" (Ayo Saucedo 2003: 39).

CHAPTER 5: FORMING NEOLIBERAL SUBJECTS:
NGOS AND "RESPONSIBLE" SELF-GOVERNMENT

The chapter epigraph is drawn from Corrigan and Sayer 1985: 6.

1. Here we can see similarities between Foucault's idea of governmentality and Althusser's term "interpellation." While these theorists come from different traditions, and in fact have dissimilar views of how power works, both focus on the way subjects are created by forces outside the realm of the state. This might not be obvious from Althusser's terminology, but in fact his "ideological state apparatuses" include schools, the church, and the family (Althusser 1971). Thus if one amends interpellation to include other nonstate institutions, such as NGOs, as the interpellating mechanisms, I think it remains a useful term compatible with Foucault's theory.

2. Bolivia's FSE was the first social investment fund (SIF) in the Americas, but not the last. Since 1985, SIFs have been established in nearly every Latin American country as part of the World Bank's structural adjustment packages (Stahl 1996: 33).

3. In addition, NGOs found municipal government a site where their interventions could influence policy outcomes. Bolivian political scientist Diego Ayo Saucedo has lauded certain forms of international support, without which some of the most

important advances of the law could not have happened. He notes that without help and funding from Holland and Switzerland, the birth and functioning of the *mancomunidades municipales* (municipal commonwealths) would not have happened. Similarly, the funding from API-DANIDA (the Danish foreign aid agency) and the World Bank made possible the conformation of indigenous municipal districts (DMIs) as well as the first development plans for these districts (Ayo Saucedo 1999: 74–75).

4. I use pseudonyms for the NGO workers for the same reasons I do for the Guaranís.

5. Freire is most known for his 1970 book *The Pedagogy of the Oppressed*.

6. I do not know the amount of this grant.

7. The great majority of these ideas came from the previous project on which PROCESO had worked with the APG and had put into practice in the first municipality (which ultimately failed). It is not clear how much of the language was written by Guaranís in the first project or whether it was all written by the NGO. Certainly the 1997 agreement between CEADES and the capitanía was almost entirely the result of what CEADES had proposed. The capitanía held a few initial meetings with CEADES to explain the problems of the organization, so that the program could be tailored to it, but this is essentially the same project the CEADES staff had already tried before in the south. The agreement lays out several key objectives:

1. "To strengthen the base organizations of Zona Cruz and to promote the participation of the Guaranís in the OTBs (territorial-based organizations), vigilance committees, and school boards related to Zona Cruz." These are the local organizations named by the new indigenous reforms described in chapters 3 and 4, through which indigenous people are expected to participate in local government.

2. "To train the leadership of the territorial and functional organizations of the communities in the processes of *gestión* related to the series of state reforms." This means teaching Guaraní leaders to be able to negotiate the new laws, so they can get access to what the reforms, like Popular Participation, promised to make available.

3. "To train a technical team of the capitanía to transfer and continue programs and activities to the communities." Through this, CEADES was to help organize and train the ETZ, whose goal it was to work with the local communities to get them to exercise their rights under the new laws.

8. This is a version of the *rendir cuentas* (rendering accounts) model of social control discussed in chapter 4.

9. These new economic models of action have proliferated in many arenas that were formerly seen as social or even kin-based. The most visible of these is the *empresa indígena* (indigenous enterprise) model, which is being widely adopted by Bolivian indigenous organizations administering the forest resources of their newly titled territories.

10. Not all Guaranís are cowed by this terrain of power, however. Samuel Tapera told me proudly of how he went to open an account, after he got the first funding installment for a medicinal plants study sponsored by the British aid foun-

dation. After battling a similar scene, he finally told the teller his name. She was amazed that a Guaraní had that sort of money. He was able to use the occasion to educate a karai about indigenous people and their "modern" activities.

11. This split is more than a public relations problem. It also reflects, I think, a stereotyped splitting that is reproduced, often unconsciously, by NGOs in the national and international circuits. On the one hand, Indians are deemed childlike and less corruptible, incapable of serious corruption because of the very fact of their Indianness. On the other hand, Indians are seen as uncivilized and untrustworthy, likely to be thieves and drunks. See Gilman 1985. The concern about indigenous corruption also ignores the very real possibility of corruption by NGO staff.

12. Chris J. Shepherd has posed this question in a different way. Using the Actor-Network theories of Bruno Latour and Michel Callon, he argues that NGO workers are engaged in an unrelenting effort to persuade peasants of their "real needs," first by enrolling them into their development projects and then by making them "desire" the outcomes pushed by the NGOs. Rather than assuming that some agricultural practices are "internal" while others are affected by "external" change, Shepherd argues that these distinctions are not inherent but produced by contested negotiation and what he calls the "multiple translations of desire" (Shepherd 2005: 257).

CHAPTER 6: POPULAR PROTAGONISM SINCE 2000

The chapter epigraphs come from Olivera 2004: 29 and Durrell 1957: 13.

1. In December 2001, thousands of residents of Buenos Aires took to the streets banging pots and pans in protest of the economic crisis caused by adherence to neoliberal economic policies. This led to the resignation of two presidents and the largest debt default in international history (Malamud 2006).

2. My description of the public protests against neoliberal reforms should not suggest, however, that Indians have given up on local-level struggles. Far from it. Across the country Indian- and campesino-led territorial grassroots organizations continue to push municipal officials for resources and projects. The municipal elections in December 2004 were the site of concentrated attention for MAS, which won mayor and council positions in much greater numbers. Thus the shift to macro-level protests can be seen as arising from and dependent on increased power at the local level.

3. There were in fact two new laws: the Municipalities Law, which granted local governments the right to give water concessions for thirty years, and Law 2029 of Potable Water and Sewerage Services, which created a national water regulator that could grant concessions to national or transnational companies for forty years (Laurie, Andolina, and Radcliffe 2002: 258).

4. There are many interpretations of the water war. Bolivian political scientist Roberto Laserna, for instance, says the Coordinadora won this battle because its adversaries were scattered and weak. The consortium did not defend itself, except by some timid TV spots, and the municipal politicians, including the mayor, simply disappeared from the scene (Laserna 2002: 16).

5. Laserna has also argued that the agreement struck at the end of the war, when

the Coordinadora negotiated the cancellation of the contract with public officials, was inequitable and reactionary. According to him, it privileges urban users who already have service (Laserna 2002: 17). Coauthors Nina Laurie, Robert Andolina, and Sarah Radcliffe have also pointed out that the focus of the Coordinadora on the rural indigenous basis of opposition sidelined poor urban groups that did not share this belief system, as well as rural areas that would be adversely affected by the building of the Misicuni dam (Laurie, Andolina, and Radcliffe 2002: 268–69). Other scholars, however, have suggested these were substantial albeit partial accomplishments (see Vargas and Kruse 2000).

6. The Cochabamba case has received substantial notice among international antiglobalization advocates. For instance, Olivera has won two important international environmental prizes for his work, the Goldman Prize and the Letelier-Moffitt Prize. His book has a preface by Vandana Shiva, the Indian ecofeminist activist scholar. She says in her preface that Cochabamba "shows us that a world beyond corporate globalization is not just possible, but it is actually happening. As the Bolivian people remind us, there is one power stronger than the power of money — and that is the power of people" (Shiva 2004: xi).

7. Anthropologist Harry Sanabria (1993 and 2000) locates the massive growth of the cocaine industry in Bolivia within a new constellation of economic, political, and social processes on both local and global fronts. He notes that the shifting global division of labor and new capital flows brought profound economic transformations in North America. This was paralleled by escalating consumption of cocaine and derivatives such as crack. In Bolivia, by the late 1970s, the economy was in chaos. The "cocaine business as a form of primitive capital accumulation — from the poor peasant families who grow the coca leaf bushes, to the local makers of basic paste, to the big dealers who fly it out of the country to refine the final product" — offered Bolivians the chance to make enormous profits (Casanovas 1990: 49). So Bolivian peasants actively entered the business, expanding and intensifying coca cultivation despite antinarcotic state policies and efforts by the United States to eradicate it (Sanabria 1993: 201; see also Quiroga 1990). By the early 1980s, the wealthy and politically powerful eastern lowland agrarian capitalist class quickly entered and took control of coca paste production and cocaine trafficking, often with the help of the military and state apparatus. Thus Bolivia turned into an informal "narcocracy" (Casanovas 1990: 49). Huge profits were made, so much so that when, in 1983, drug baron Roberto Suárez Gómez offered to pay off the country's entire foreign debt of $3 billion in exchange for his freedom, his offer was taken seriously (but rejected).

8. Albro suggests at least sixty-seven cocaleros have been killed since 1987, with many more injured (Albro 2005).

9. Hindery has argued that the World Bank made the passage of the mining and hydrocarbons laws the conditions for a $30 million judicial reform loan (Hindery 2004: 289).

10. See Gustafson 2002 for a more detailed explanation of the divisions.

11. The Yuquí Indians are a small group of lowland indigenous people, living in a single small community, Bia Recuaté, in the tropical forest of the Chapare region. They lived as nomads in the forest until the 1960s, when they were contacted by the

New Tribes Missions (Stearman 1989; Tolan and Postero 1994). In 1992, the Yuquí received one of the first collective titles to their territory, which they share with several communities of Yuracarés (Lema 1998: 111–13).

12. The exact number killed varies across sources. Amnesty calculates thirty-three; Orduna, a reporter from the newspaper *El Pulso*, calculates thirty-one.

13. Accountability for state violence in Bolivia remains a thorny issue. The responsibilities for the deaths during February 2003 have still not been determined. Although four members of the army were charged with murder, their cases were transferred to military courts, prompting an outcry about the continuing impunity of military malfeasance (Amnesty International 2003). Their cases resulted in acquittals there, sparking international protests. In May 2004, Bolivia's highest court ruled that they must face prosecution in the civilian justice system. The military has filed objections to this ruling (Andean Information Network 2004). Crimes committed in February 2003 as well as during the October 2003 uprising remain the subject of political investigations and likely will not reach resolution for many years.

14. For an interesting profile of El Alto, see Arbona and Kohl 2004. Gill 2000 is an excellent ethnographical review of life and poverty in the urban barrios of El Alto.

15. Many El Alto residents disagreed with Quispe's strategy, however. Doña Beatriz Mamani, whom I discuss in the concluding chapter, told me she was opposed to the peasant strikes and felt they overly affected the poor urban residents who couldn't carry on their business or find food in the markets.

16. Radio Erbol, Radio San Gabriel (where Quispe held his hunger strike), and Radio Pachamama were particularly important. Radio Pachamama later issued a CD collecting the most dramatic of their radio shows (Radio Pachamama 2004).

17. Javier Gómez Aguilar, pers. comm. with the author, June 29, 2004, La Paz.

18. The details of these contracts were not made public by the Goni administration. This secrecy and the terms of the contracts became a source of intense public debate as Bolivians debated President Mesa's new hydrocarbons law and the national referendum on gas in June and July 2004.

19. I thank political sociologist David Mares, an expert on oil and gas development, for this analysis. Pers. comm. with the author, June 10, 2004, San Diego, Calif.

20. In his resignation speech, Mesa said that during his first seventeen months in office, he had faced 820 conflicts and 12,000 petitions, 4,250 of which he had attended (La Razón 2005b).

CONCLUSION: TOWARD A POSTMULTICULTURAL BOLIVIA

The chapter epigraph is cited in Thompson and McKinley 2005.

1. There is here a palpable sense of longing for the past, for a paternal state which would take care of the needs of the social sector, as the postrevolutionary state promised to do. Alteños I interviewed in 2004 said they wanted to nationalize the natural gas corporations so that the state could provide jobs, as it had in the past. Many remembered with nostalgia the days when miners were well paid, well organized, heroes of the nation, and education and health care were considered an investment in social welfare.

2. I am grateful to the community activists I interviewed in El Alto during July 2004 for this analysis. I also thank Forrest Hylton and Lina Brito for recounting their experiences covering the uprising for independent media.

3. García Linera uses this term in a different way than the famous Bolivian political scientist René Zavaleta. García Linera uses it to mean "a block of collective action through which the subaltern classes give rise to autonomous, organized structures, in relation to hegemonic discursive and symbolic structures. These anti-hegemonic structures may vary in origin among distinct segments of the subaltern classes" (García Linera 2004: 85).

4. The indigenous movement in Ecuador has taken advantage of this same sort of conjuncture (Zamosc 2004).

5. This quotation comes from a speech given at the Defense of Humanity Meetings, in the Polyforum Cultural Siquieros, Mexico City, October 24, 2003. Emphasis added.

6. There is a vast literature on citizenship. For reviews of historical models and philosophical debates about citizenship, see Beiner 1995, Janoski 1998, Stewart 1995, and Slawner and Denham 1998. For volumes concerning the conditions of modern citizenship and its relation to nation making, see Von Steenbergen 1994, Brubaker 1992, and Shafir 1998. For works discussing the forms citizenship takes in multicultural societies, see Soysal 1994, Kymlicka 1995a and 1995b, and Benhabib 2002. Ong 1999 and 2003 discuss transnational citizenship. For a feminist view of citizenship, see Yuval-Davis and Werbner 1999 as well as Bock and James 1992. For works centering on citizenship in Latin America, see Jelin and Hershberg 1998 and 2003, Caldeira and Holston,1999, Dagnino 2003, Oxhorn 2003, Taylor and Wilson 2004, and Yashar 2005.

7. Political scientist Philip Oxhorn has made a related argument, pointing out that in contrast to Europe's industrial trajectory, in Latin America economic growth exacerbated economic inequality at the same time that state distributive policies met with fierce opposition (Oxhorn 2003: 39). The resulting conflicts precluded real democracy, as elites controlled the demands of the poor through corporatist institutions or by resorting to authoritarian regimes. The result, he argues, is a fragmented and disarticulated civil society with limited abilities to challenge the exclusionary nature of society (Oxhorn 2003: 52–53; see also Yashar 1998 and 1999).

8. Political scientist Leonardo Avritzer has suggested that much more needs to be done to allow such civil society innovations to guide formal political decision making. Where civil society organizations are active in public fora of deliberation (such as election monitoring in Mexico and participatory municipal budgeting in Brazil), there have been some promising results (Avritzer 2002). The potential for this sort of "deliberative democracy," however, is in many cases overshadowed by practices and institutions that make political participation difficult for the poor and subaltern.

9. I use the term "race" to point out the racialized ordering of society in Bolivia. Its usage requires two points of clarification. First, biologists have clarified that race is a term with no scientific meaning in human populations. Thus most social scientists agree that race is a social construct rather than a biological one (see the American Anthropological Association's 1998 "Statement on Race"). Nevertheless, social constructs have important effects, the most salient of which is racism, discrimination

based on the idea of race. So my usage here is a reflection of the fact that Bolivian society, like most contemporary societies, has been ordered on the basis of race. Second, it is helpful to distinguish between race and ethnicity. Anthropologist Peter Wade has suggested that ethnicity tends to be used to refer to cultural or geographical differences, where race tends to refer to biological or phenotypical differences. He also notes that "ethnicity" is often used in place of "race" because of the bad reputation of race. I agree with his conclusion that although race is a troublesome concept, it is important to continue to highlight the history of race by calling it by its name (Wade 1997: 21). In Bolivia, the difference between Indians and non-Indians began as a racial distinction, and while many people now refer to Indians as ethnic groups, there is no doubt about the ongoing nature of the racism that divides the country. Thus I use "race" to point out the history by which the divisions were created and are maintained.

   10. Pers. comm. with the author, May 30, 2003, Santa Cruz.

References

Abercrombie, Thomas
1998   Pathways of Memory and Power: Ethnography and History Among an Andean People. Madison: University of Wisconsin Press.

Acción Andina
2001   Bolivia: Organizaciones sindicales de productores de coca compleja lucha de reinvindicación y estigmatización. Año 10, Nro. 1, Julio 2001. Available online at http://www.cedib.org/accionandina/?module=displaystory&story_id =12944&format=html, accessed April 1, 2005.

Aguirre Badani, Álvaro
2000   Deuda externa, HIPC, y reducción de la pobreza. La Paz: Centro de Estudios Para el Desarrollo Laboral y Agrario (CEDLA).

Albó, Xavier
1987   From MNRistas to Kataristas to Katari. *In* Resistance, Rebellion, and Consciousness in the Andean Peasant World, Eighteenth to Twentieth Centuries. Edited by Steve Stern. Madison: University of Wisconsin Press.
1990   Los Guaraní-Chiriguano: La comunidad hoy. La Paz: Centro de Investigación y Promoción del Campesinado (CIPCA).
1994   And from Kataristas to MNRistas? The Surprising and Bold Alliance Between Aymaras and Neoliberals in Bolivia. *In* Indigenous Peoples and Democracy in Latin America. Edited by Donna Lee Van Cott. New York: St. Martin's Press.
1995   ¡Ofadifa Ofaifa! Un pentecostés Chiriguano. *In* Chiriguano. Edited by Jürgen Riester. Santa Cruz, Bolivia: Apoyo Para el Campesino–Indígena del Oriente Boliviano (APCOB).
1996   La búsqueda desde adentro, calidoscopio de auto-imagenes en el debate étnico Boliviano. Artículo Primero, Año 1, Nro. 1, Enero/Marzo 1996. Santa Cruz de la Sierra, Bolivia: Centro de Estudios Jurídicos y Sociedad (CEJIS).
2000   El sector campesino-indígena, actor social clave. Opiniones y Analisis 52: 75–112. La Paz: Fundación Fundemos.
2002   Bolivia: From Indian and Campesino Leaders to Councillors and Parliamentary Deputies. *In* Multiculturalism in Latin America, Indigenous Rights, Diversity, and Democracy. Edited by Rachel Seider. London: Palgrave.

Albro, Robert
2004   The Indigenous in the Plural in Bolivian Oppositional Politics (draft version, later revised).

2005 Indigenous in the Plural in Bolivian Oppositional Politics. Bulletin of Latin American Research 24 (4): 433–53.

Albro, Robert, and Jeff Himpele
forthcoming Popularizing the Public and Publicizing the Popular in Latin America. *In* New Public Appearance of the Popular in Latin America: Regional Variations from North and South.

Almaraz, Alejandro
2003 La reforma constitucional desde la perspectiva indígena. Paper presented at the international seminar Movimientos Indígenas y Estado en América Latina, Cochabamba, Bolivia, May 22–24.

Almeida Vinueza, José
2005 The Ecuadorian Indigenous Movement and the Gutiérrez Regime: The Traps of Multiculturalism. Political and Legal Anthropological Review 28 (1): 93–111.

Althusser, Louis
1971 Ideology and Ideological State Apparatuses. *In* Lenin and Philosophy and Other Essays. Translated by B. Brewster. New York: Monthly Review Press.

Alvarez, Sonia, Evelina Dagnino, and Arturo Escobar
1998 Cultures of Politics, Politics of Cultures. Boulder, Colo.: Westview Press.

Amazon Watch
2003 Enron/Shell Cuiabá Gas Pipeline: News Clip. Available online at http://www.amazonwatch.org/amazon/BO/cuiaba/view_news.php?id=553, accessed March 10, 2005.

American Anthropology Association
1998 Statement on Race. American Anthropologist 100 (3): 712–13.

Amnesty International
2003 Annual Report, Bolivia. Available online at http://www.amnestyusa.org/countries/bolivia/document.do, accessed June 8, 2004.

Anaya, S. James
1997 Indigenous Peoples in International Law. Cultural Survival Quarterly (summer): 58–61.

Andean Information Network
2004 Impunity for Human Rights Violations through Military Trials in Bolivia. Available online at http://www.ain.org.bo/updates, accessed April 14, 2004.

Anderson, Benedict
1991 Imagined Communities. New York: Verso.

Arbona, Juan, and Benjamin Kohl
2004 La Paz–El Alto. Cities 21: 255–65.

Archondo, Rafael
1991 Compadres al micrófono, la resurrección metropolitana del ayllú. La Paz: Hisbol.

Arellano-López, Sonia, and James Petras
1994 Nongovernmental Organizations and Poverty Alleviation in Bolivia. Development and Change 25: 555–68.

Arrington, Vanessa
2003 Bolivia's Mesa Asks Patience from Indians. Associated Press/Miami Herald. Available online at http://www.miami.com/mld/miamiherald/news/world/americas/7054603.htm?template=co, accessed February 1, 2004.

Arze, Carlos, and Tom Kruse
2004 The Consequences of Neoliberal Reform. In NACLA Report on the Americas 38 (3): 23–28.

Assies, Willem
2000 Indigenous People and Reform of the State in Latin America. In The Challenge of Diversity, Indigenous Peoples, and Reform of the State in Latin America. Edited by Willem Assies, Gemma van der Haar, and Andre Hoekema. Amsterdam: Thela Thesis.
2003 David Versus Goliath in Cochabamba: Water Rights, Neoliberalism, and the Revival of Social Protest in Bolivia. Latin American Perspective 30 (3): 14.

Atack, Ian
1999 Four Criteria of Development NGO Legitimacy. In World Development 27 (5): 855–64.

Avritzer, Leonardo
2002 Democracy and the Public Sphere in Latin America. Princeton, N.J.: Princeton University Press.

Ayo Saucedo, Diego
1996 Indígenas en el poder local. In El Pulso de la democracia, participación ciudadana y descentralización en Bolivia. La Paz: Secretaría Nacional de Participación Popular (SNPP)/Nueva Sociedad.
1999 Los desafíos de la participación popular. La Paz: Centro Boliviano de Estudios Multidisciplinarios (CEBEM).
2003 Municipalismo, participación popular, apuntes de un proceso. La Paz: Muela del Diablo.

Bailey, Jennifer L., and Torbjorn L. Knutsen
1987 Surgery Without Anaesthesia: Bolivia's Response to Economic Chaos. World Today 43: 47–51.

Bakewell, Peter
1984 Miners of the Red Mountain: Indian Labor in Potosí, 1545–1650. Albuquerque: University of New Mexico Press.

Balslev, Anne
1997 Distritos municipales indígenas en Bolivia: Las primeras experiencias en el Chaco. La Paz: Subsecretaría de Asuntos Étnicos (SAE).

Barragán Romano, Rossana
1999 Indios, mujeres, y ciudadanos, legislación y ejercicio de la ciudadanía en Bolivia (Siglo XIX). La Paz: Fundación Dialogo.

Baskes, Jeremy
2000 Indians, Merchants, and Markets: A Reinterpretation of the Repartimiento and Spanish-Indian Economic Relations in Colonial Oaxaca, 1750–1821. Stanford, Calif.: Stanford University Press.

Bebbington, Anthony
1997 New States, New NGOs? Crises and Transitions Among Rural Development NGOs in the Andean Region. World Development 25 (11): 1,755–65.

Bebbington, Anthony, and John Farrington
1993 Governments, NGOs, and Agricultural Development: Perspectives on Changing Inter-Organizational Relationships. Journal of Development Studies 29 (2): 199–219.

Beiner, Ronald, ed.
1995 Theorizing Citizenship. Albany: State University of New York.

Benería, Lourdes, and B. Mendoza.
1995 Structural Adjustment and Social Emergency Funds: The Cases of Honduras, Mexico, and Nicaragua. European Journal of Development 7 (1): 53–76.

Benería-Surkin, Jordi
1998 From Warriors to Negotiators: An Analysis of the Sustainability of Izozeño-Guaraní Conservation and Development Strategies in Bolivia, unpublished paper.

Benhabib, Seyla
2002 The Claims of Culture, Equality, and Diversity in the Global Era. Princeton, N.J.: Princeton University Press.

Bennett, David
1998 Multicultural States: Rethinking Difference and Identity. London: Routledge.

Bierstecker, Thomas
1990 Reducing the Role of the State in the Economy: A Conceptual Exploration of IMF and World Bank Prescriptions. International Studies Quarterly 34 (4): 477–92.

Blanes, José
2000 Mallkus y alcaldes, la Ley de Participación Popular en comunidades rurales del altiplano Paceño. La Paz: Programa de Investigación Estratégíca en Bolivia (PIEB)/CEBEM.

Bock, Gisela, and Susan James, eds.
1992 Beyond Equality and Difference: Citizenship, Feminist Politics, and Female Subjectivity. London: Routledge.

Bonfil Batalla, Guillermo
1996 México Profundo: Reclaiming a Civilization. Translated by Philip Dennis. Austin: University of Texas Press.

Boron, Atilio
1995 State, Capitalism, and Democracy in Latin America. Boulder, Colo.: Lynne Rienner Publishers.

Brodie, Janine
1994   Shifting the Boundaries: Gender and the Politics of Restructuring. *In* The Strategic Silence: Gender and Economic Policy. Edited by Isabella Bakker. London, UK: Zed Books and the North-South Institute.

Brown, Wendy
1995   States of Injury: Power and Freedom in Late Modernity. Princeton, N.J.: Princeton University Press.

Brubaker, Rogers
1992   Citizenship and Nationhood in France and Germany. Cambridge, Mass.: Harvard University Press.

Brysk, Alison
2000   From Tribal Village to Global Village: Indian Rights and International Relations in Latin America. Stanford, Calif.: Stanford University Press.

Burchell, Graham
1996   Liberal Government and Techniques of the Self. *In* Foucault and Political Reason. Edited by Andrew Barry, Thomas Osborne, and Nikolas Rose. Chicago: University of Chicago Press.

Butler, Judith
1993   Introduction. *In* Bodies That Matter. New York: Routledge.

Caldeira, Teresa P. R.
2000   City of Walls: Crime, Segregation, and Citizenship in Sao Paulo. Berkeley: University of California Press.

Caldeira, Teresa P. R., and James Holston
1999   Democracy and Violence in Brazil. Society for Comparative Study of Society and History 41: 691–729.

Calhoun, Craig
1997   Habermas and the Public Sphere. *In* Habermas and the Public Sphere. Cambridge, Mass.: MIT Press.

Calla Ortega, Ricardo
2000   Indigenous Peoples, the Law of Popular Participation, and Changes in Government: Bolivia, 1994–1998. *In* The Challenge of Diversity: Indigenous Peoples and Reform of the State in Latin America. Edited by Willem Assies, Gemma van der Haar, and André J. Hoekema. Amsterdam: Thela Thesis.

Cárdenas, Víctor Hugo
1996   El rescate de viejos postulados. *In* El Pulso de la democracia, participación ciudadana y descentralización en Bolivia. La Paz: SNPP/Nueva Sociedad.

Carter, William E.
1971   Revolution and the Agrarian Sector. *In* Beyond the Revolution. Edited by James Malloy and Richard Thorn. Pittsburgh: University of Pittsburgh Press.

Casanovas, Winston Moore
1990   Capital Accumulation and Revolutionary Nationalism in Bolivia, 1952–85. *In* The State and Capital Accumulation in Latin America, vol. 2. Pittsburgh: University of Pittsburgh Press.

CEADES (Colectivo de Estudios Aplicados y Desarrollo Social), eds.
2003   Cultura democrática en municipios indígenas: Urubichá y Gutiérrez. Santa Cruz de la Sierra, Bolivia: CEADES/DIAKONIA.

CEDLA
2003   El Servicio de crecimiento y reducción de pobreza del FMI: Un callejón sin salida. La Paz: CEDLA.

CEJIS
1999   Titulación de territorios indígenas: Un balance a dos años de la promulgación de la ley INRA. Artículo Primero 3 (6).
2001   Ley INRA: El debate. Artículo Primero 5 (9).

Chance, John K.
1978   Race and Class in Colonial Oaxaca. Stanford, Calif.: Stanford University Press.

Chapin, Mac
2004   A Challenge to Conservationists. WorldWatch Magazine (November–December): 17–31.

Cherian, John
2003   The Bolivian Uprising. Frontline (India) 20 (23). Available online at http://www.frontlineon.net/fl2023/stories/20031121000206500.htm.

CIPCA
2004   Historia de los Hidrocarburos en Bolivia. De los usos ancestrales a los conflictos de Octubre. La Paz: Coordinadora de la Mujer/CIPCA.

Clifford, James
1986   Introduction: Partial Truths. In Writing Culture: The Poetics and Politics of Ethnography. Edited by James Clifford and George E. Marcus. Berkeley: University of California Press.

Collier, David
1995   Trajectory of a Concept: "Corporatism" in the Study of Latin American Politics. In Latin America in Comparative Perspective: New Approaches to Methods and Analysis. Edited by Peter Smith. Boulder, Colo.: Westview Press.

Comaroff, Jean, and John L. Comaroff
2000   Millennial Capitalism: First Thoughts on a Second Coming. Public Culture 12 (2): 291–343.

Comaroff, John
1996   Ethnicity, Nationalism, and the Politics of Difference in an Age of Revolution. In The Politics of Difference, Ethnic Premises in a World of Power. Edited by E. Wilmsen. Chicago: University of Chicago Press.

Conaghan, Catherine M., James Malloy, and Luis A. Abugattas
1990   Business and the "Boys": The Politics of Neoliberalism in the Central Andes. Latin American Research 25 (2): 3–31.

Conklin, Beth
2002   Shamans Versus Pirates in the Amazonian Treasure Chest. American Anthropologist 104 (4): 1050–61.

Conklin, Beth, and Laura Graham
1995   The Shifting Middle Ground: Amazonian Indians and Eco-politics. American Anthropologist, new series, 97 (4): 695–710.

Cope, R. Douglas
1994   The Limits of Racial Domination: Plebeian Society in Colonial Mexico City, 1660–1720. Madison: University of Wisconsin Press.

Cornblit, Oscar
1995   Power and Violence in the Colonial City: Oruro from the Mining Renaissance to the Rebellion of Tupac Amaru, 1740–1782. Translated by Elizabeth Ladd Glick. Cambridge: Cambridge University Press.

Cornejo Bouroncle, Jorge
1963   Túpac Amaru, la revolución precursora de la emancipación continental: Estudio documentado. Cuzco, Peru: Edit. H. G. Rozas.

Corrigan, Philip, and Derek Sayer
1985   The Great Arch: English State Formation as Cultural Revolution. Oxford: Basil Blackwell.

Cortés, Jorge, and Henry Tito
2004   Gasoducto Cuiabá: La resistencia indígena Chiquitana a las operadoras multinacionales ENRON y Shell. In El gas y el destino de Bolivia. Santa Cruz, Bolivia: CEJIS.

Crabtree, John, Gavan Duffy, and Jenny Pearce
1987   The Great Tin Crash: Bolivia and the World Tin Market. London: Latin American Bureau.

Dagnino, Evelina
2003   Citizenship in Latin America: An Introduction. Latin American Perspectives 30 (2): 3.

Dandler, Jorge, and Juan Torrico
1987   From the National Indigenous Congress to the Ayopaya Rebellion: Bolivia, 1945–1947. In Resistance, Rebellion, and Consciousness in the Andean Peasant World, Eighteenth to Twentieth Centuries. Edited by Steve Stern. Madison: University of Wisconsin Press.

Davis, Shelton
2002   Indigenous People, Poverty, and Participatory Development: The Experiences of the World Bank in Latin America. In Multiculturalism in Latin America: Indigenous Rights, Diversity, and Democracy. Edited by Rachel Seider. London: Palgrave.

Davison, C. P. P.
1987   Environments of Integration: Three Groups of Guaraní Migrants in Santa Cruz de la Sierra, Bolivia. Ph.D. diss., Institute for Social Anthropology, Oxford University, England.

DCONG (Departamento de Coordinación con ONGs)
1996   Departamento de Coordinación con ONGs. La Paz: Ministerio de Hacienda.

de la Cadena, Marisol
2000   Indigenous Mestizos: The Politics of Race and Culture in Cuzco, Peru, 1919–
        1991. Durham, N.C.: Duke University Press.
2001   Reconstructing Race, Culture, and Mestizaje in Latin America. *In* NACLA
        Report on the Americas 34 (6): 16–23.

Donham, Donald
1999   Marxist Modern: An Ethnographic History of the Ethiopian Revolution.
        Berkeley: University of California Press.

Doria Medina, Samuel
1986   La economía informal de Bolivia. La Paz: Editorial Offset.

Dougherty, Elizabeth
2003   "Corruption" and Civil Society: Formal and Informal Networks of an Envi-
        ronmental Trust Fund in Panama. Ph.D. diss., University of Pennsylvania.

Duran B., Jesus
1990   Las nuevas instituciones de la sociedad civil, impacto y tendencias de la co-
        operación internacional y las ONGs en el area rural de Bolivia. La Paz: Huel-
        las S.R.L.

Durrell, Lawrence
1957   Justine. New York: E. P. Dutton & Co., Inc.

Dworkin, Ronald
1981   What Is Equality? Part 2: Equality of Resources. Philosophy and Public
        Affairs 10 (4): 283–345.

Eckstein, Susan
1983   Transformation of a "Revolution from Below" — Bolivia and International
        Capital. Society and History 25 (1): 105–35.

Edwards, Michael, and David Hulme
1996   Too Close for Comfort? The Impact of Official Aid on Nongovernmental
        Organizations. *In* World Development 24 (6): 961–73.

Eley, Geoff
1997   Nations, Publics, and Political Cultures: Placing Habermas in the Nineteenth
        Century. *In* Habermas and the Public Sphere. Edited by Craig Calhoun.
        Cambridge, Mass.: MIT Press.

Elliston, Deborah
2000   Geographies of Gender and Politics: The Place of Difference in Polynesian
        Nationalism. Cultural Anthropology 15 (2): 171–216.

Escobar, Arturo
1995   Encountering Development: The Making and Unmaking of the Third World.
        Princeton, N.J.: Princeton University Press.

Farmer, John A., and Ilona Katzew, eds.
1996   New World Orders: Casta Painting and Colonial Latin America, Ilona
        Katzew, curator. New York: Americas Society.

Farthing, Linda, and Kathryn Ledebur
2004   The Beat Goes On: The U.S. War on Coca. NACLA Report on the Americas 38 (3): 34–39.

Ferguson, James
1994   The Anti-Politics Machine: "Development," Depoliticization, and Bureaucratic Power in Lesotho. Minneapolis: University of Minnesota Press.

Ferguson, James, and Akhil Gupta
2002   Spatializing States: Toward an Ethnography of Neoliberal Governmentality. American Ethnologist 29 (4): 981–1002.

Finnegan, William
2002   Leasing the Rain. The New Yorker (April 8): 43–53.

Fisher, Lillian Estelle
1966   The Last Inca Revolt, 1780–1783. Norman: University of Oklahoma Press.

Flores Galindo, Alberto, ed.
1976   Túpac Amaru II, 1780: Sociedad colonial y sublevaciones populares. Lima: Retablo de Papel Ediciones.

Forero, Juan
2005   Bolivia Elects a President Who Supports Coca Farming. New York Times, December 19.

Foucault, Michel
1991   On Governmentality. In The Foucault Effect: Studies in Government Rationality. Edited by Graham Burchell, Colin Gordon, and Peter Miller. Chicago: University of Chicago Press.

Fraser, Nancy
1993   Rethinking the Public Sphere. In The Phantom Public Sphere. Edited by Bruce Robbins. Minneapolis: University of Minnesota Press
1997   Justice Interruptus: Critical Reflections on the "Postsocialist" Condition. London: Routledge.

Freire, Paolo
1970   The Pedagogy of the Oppressed. Translated by Myra Bergman Ramos. New York: Seabury Press.

Friedlander, Judith
1975   Being Indian in Hueyapan: A Study of Forced Identity in Contemporary Mexico. New York: St. Martin's Press.

Galeano, Eduardo
1973   Open Veins of Latin America. New York: Monthly Review Press.

García, María Elena
2005   Making Indigenous Citizens: Identity, Development, and Multicultural Activism in Peru. Stanford, Calif.: Stanford University Press.

García Linera, Álvaro
2003   Autonomías indígenas. Descentralización y autonomía regional. Opiniones y Análisis 64: 11–50.

2004   The Multitude. *In* ¡Cochabamba! Water War in Bolivia. Oscar Olivera in col-
         laboration with Tom Lewis. Cambridge, Mass.: South End Press.

Gill, Lesley
1987   Peasants, Entrepreneurs, and Social Change: Frontier Development in Low-
         land Bolivia. Boulder, Colo.: Westview Press.
2000   Teetering on the Rim: Global Restructuring, Daily Life, and the Armed
         Retreat of the Bolivian State. New York: Colombia University Press.

Gilly, Adolfo
2003   Historias desde adentro: La tenaz persistencia de los tiempos. *In* Ya es otro
         tiempo el presente: cuatro momentos de insurgencia indígena. Forrest
         Hylton, Félix Patzi, Sergio Serulnikov, and Sinclair Thompson. La Paz:
         Muela del Diablo Editores.

Gilman, Sanders
1985   Difference and Pathology: Stereotypes of Sexuality, Race, and Madness.
         Ithaca, N.Y.: Cornell University Press.

Goldberg, David Theo
1994   Multiculturalism: A Critical Reader. Oxford: Blackwell.

Goldstein, Daniel
2004   The Spectacular City: Violence and Performance in Urban Bolivia. Durham,
         N.C.: Duke University Press.

Golte, Jürgen
1980   Repartos y rebeliones: Túpac Amaru y las contradicciones de la economía
         colonial. Translated by Carlos Degregori Caso. Lima: Instituto de Estudios
         Peruanos.

Gómez, Luis, and Al Giordano
2002   El Mallku Speaks: Indigenous Autonomy and Coca. Narco News. Available
         online at http://www.narconews.com/felipe1eng.html, accessed January 22,
         2004.

Gordillo, José M.
2000   Campesinos revolucionarios en Bolivia. La Paz: Editorial Plural.

Graham, Carol
1992   The Politics of Protecting the Poor During Adjustment: Bolivia's Emergency
         Social Fund. World Development 20 (9): 1,233–51.

Gramsci, Antonio
1971   Selections from the Prison Notebooks. Edited by Q. Hoare and G. N. Smith.
         New York: International Publishers.

Gray-Molina, George
2001   Exclusion, Participation, and Democratic State-Building. *In* Towards Demo-
         cratic Viability: The Bolivian Experience. Edited by John Crabtree and Lau-
         rence Whitehead. St. Anthony's, Oxford: Palgrave Press.

Guerrero, Andrés
2003   Administration of Dominated Populations Under a Regime of Customary
        Citizenship: The Case of Postcolonial Ecuador. *In* After Spanish Rule: Post-
        colonial Predicaments of the Americas. Edited by Mark Thurner and Andrés
        Guerrero. Durham, N.C.: Duke University Press.

Gustafson, Bret
2002   Paradoxes of Liberal Indigenism: Indigenous Movements, State Processes,
        and Intercultural Reform in Bolivia. *In* The Politics of Ethnicity: Indigenous
        Peoples in Latin American States. Edited by David Maybury-Lewis. Cam-
        bridge, Mass.: Harvard University Press.

Habermas, Jürgen
1989   The Structural Transformation of the Public Sphere. Translated by T. Burger
        and F. Lawrence. Cambridge, Mass.: Cambridge University Press.

Hale, Charles R.
1994   Between Che Guevarra and the Pachamama: Mestizos, Indians, and Identity
        Politics in the Antiquincentenary Campaign. Critique of Anthropology 14
        (1): 41–68.
2002   Does Multiculturalism Menace? Governance, Cultural Rights, and the Pol-
        itics of Identity in Guatemala. Journal of Latin American Studies 34: 485–
        524.
2004   Rethinking Indigenous Politics in the Era of the "Indio Permitido." NACLA
        Report on the Americas 38 (2):16–20.

Harris, Olivia
1995   Ethnic Identity and Market Relations: Indians and Mestizos in the Andes. *In*
        Ethnicity, Markets, and Migration in the Andes: At the Crossroads of His-
        tory and Anthropology. Edited by Brooke Larson and Olivia Harris.
        Durham, N.C.: Duke University Press.

Hayden, Tom
2002   In Chiapas. *In* The Zapatista Reader. New York: Thunder's Mouth Press/
        Nation Books.

Healy, Kevin
1984   Caciques y patrones. Cochabamba, Bolivia: Ediciones El Buitre.

Herrera Sarmiento, Enrique
2002   Tacanas y ayoreos frente a la ley IRNA, etnicidad y derechos territoriales
        indígenas (1996–2001). La Paz: PIEB.

Hindery, Derrick
2004   Social and Environmental Impacts of World Bank/IMF–Funded Economic
        Restructuring in Bolivia: An Analysis of Enron and Shell's Hydrocarbon Proj-
        ects. Singapore Journal of Tropical Geography 25 (3): 281–303.

Hirsch, Silvia María
2003   The Emergence of Political Organizations Among the Guaraní Indians of
        Bolivia and Argentina: A Comparative Perspective. *In* Contemporary Indige-
        nous Movements in Latin America. Edited by Erick D. Langer and Elena
        Muñoz. Wilmington, Dela.: Scholarly Resources, Inc.

Hispanicvista
2003 New Political Force—Bolivia's Indigenous Groups Instrumental in Power Shift. Available online at http://www.hispanicvista.com/html13/102403ca.htm, accessed February 11, 2004.

Honneth, Axel
1992 Integrity and Disrespect: Principles of Morality Based on the Theory of Recognition. Political Theory 20 (2): 188–89.

Hylton, Forrest
2003 Bolivia: Massacres Spark Mass Uprising. Available online at http://www.greenleft.org.au/back/2003/558/558p18.htm, accessed February 11, 2004.

Ignatieff, Michael
1995 The Myth of Citizenship. In Theorizing Citizenship. Edited by Ronald Beiner. Albany: State University of New York.

Irurozqui Victoriano, Marta
1994 La armonía de las desigualdades: Elites y conflictos de poder en Bolivia, 1880–1920. CUSCO: CSIC/CERA "Bartolomé de las casas."
2000 "A Bala, Piedra y Palo": La construcción de la ciudadanía política en Bolivia, 1826–1952. Seville, Spain: Diputación de Sevilla.

Jackson, Robert H.
1999 Race, Caste, and Status: Indians in Colonial Spanish America. Albuquerque: University of New Mexico Press.

Janoski, Thomas
1998 Citizenship and Civil Society. Cambridge: Cambridge University Press.

Jelin, Elizabeth
1998 Citizenship Revisited: Solidarity, Responsibility, and Rights. In Constructing Democracy: Human Rights, Citizenship, and Society in Latin America. Boulder, Colo.: Westview Press.
2003 Citizenship and Alterity: Tensions and Dilemmas. Latin American Perspectives 30 (2): 101–17.

Jelin, Elizabeth, and Eric Hershberg
1998 Constructing Democracy: Human Rights, Citizenship, and Society in Latin America. Boulder, Colo.: Westview Press.

Keck, Margaret, and Kathryn Sikkink
1998 Activists Beyond Borders: Advocacy Networks in International Politics. Ithaca, N.Y.: Cornell University Press.

Klein, Herbert S.
1992 Bolivia: The Evolution of a Multi-Ethnic Society. Second edition. New York: Oxford University Press.

Knight, Alan
1990 Racism, Revolution, and Indigenismo: Mexico, 1910–1940. In The Idea of Race in Latin America, 1870–1940. Edited by Richard Graham. Austin: University of Texas Press.

Kohl, Ben
1998   Market and Government Reform in Bolivia: Global Trends and Local Responses. Paper presented at the conference of the American Colleges and Schools of Planning (ACSP), Pasadena, Calif., November 5–8.
1999   The Role of NGOs in the Implementation of Political and Administrative Decentralization in Bolivia. Paper presented at the conference of ACSP, Chicago, October.
2003a Democratizing Decentralization in Bolivia: The Law of Popular Participation. Journal of Planning Education and Research 23 (2): 153–64.
2003b Restructuring Citizenship in Bolivia: El Plan de Todos. International Journal of Urban and Regional Research 27 (2): 337–51.

Kohl, Ben, and Linda Farthing
2001   The Price of Success: Bolivia's War Against Drugs and the Poor. NACLA 35 (1): 35–41.
2006   Impasse in Bolivia: Neoliberal Hegemony and Social Resistance. London: Zed Books.

Kruse, Thomas A.
1994   The Politics of Structural Adjustment and the NGOs: A Look at the Bolivian Case. Master's thesis, Cornell University.

Kymlicka, Will
1995a Multicultural Citizenship. Oxford: Oxford University Press.
1995b The Rights of Minority Cultures. Oxford: Oxford University Press.

Kymlicka, Will, and Wayne Norman
1996   Return of the Citizen: A Survey of Recent Work on Citizenship Theory. In Theorizing Citizenship. Edited by Ronald Beiner. Albany: State University of New York.

Lagos, Maria L.
1994   Autonomy and Power: The Dynamics of Class and Culture in Rural Bolivia. Philadelphia: University of Pennsylvania Press.

Langman, Jimmy
2002   Enron's Pipe Scheme. Available online at http://www.corpwatch.org, accessed March 10, 2005.

La Razón
2003a Mesa gobernará sin políticos y hará referéndum y Constituyente. La Paz: October 18.
2003b La luna de miel de Carlos Mesa empezó con muchos respaldos. La Paz: October 19.
2004   Bolivia ratifica que si Chile no habla del mar, no tendrá gas. La Paz: November 6.
2005a El Presidente renuncia, la decisión está en manos del Congreso. La Paz: March 7.
2005b Carlos Mesa levanta las manos y pide adelantar las elecciones. La Paz: March 16.

2005c Los sueños premonitorios y el pasado sindical marcan a Evo Morales Ayma. La Paz: November 15.

2005d Costas, vitoreado como gobernador en su reducto. La Paz: December 19.

2005e El próximo año empieza la nueva historia de Bolivia. La Paz: December 19.

2005f Los candidatos despiden la campaña con spots agresivos y con reflexiones por la unidad del país. La Paz: December 14.

2006 Los sectores aguardan a Evo Morales con grandes pedidos. La Paz: January 3.

Larson, Brooke

2004 Trials of Nation Making: Liberalism, Race, and Ethnicity in the Andes, 1810–1910. Cambridge: Cambridge University Press.

Laserna, Roberto

1994 Movimientos regionales y descentralización en Bolivia, una experiencia de concertación. In Reflexiones sobre la descentralización. La Paz: Instituto Latinoamericano de Investigaciones Sociales/Proyecto de Apoyo a la Descentralización (ILDIS/PROADE).

2002 Conflictos sociales y movimientos políticos en Bolivia. In Las Piedras en el Camino. La Paz: Ministerio de Desarrollo Sostenible y Planificación.

Laurie, Nina, Robert Andolina, and Sarah Radcliffe

2002 The Excluded "Indigenous"? The Implications for Multi-Ethnic Policies for Water Reform in Bolivia. In Multiculturalism in Latin America: Indigenous Rights, Diversity, and Democracy, edited by Rachel Seider. New York: Palgrave McMillan.

Lazar, Sian

2004 El Alto, Ciudad Rebelde: Organizational Bases for Revolt. Paper presented at the meeting of the Society for Latin American Studies (SLAS), Leiden, Holland, April 2–4.

2005 Citizens Despite the State: Everyday Corruption and Local Politics in El Alto, Bolivia. In Corruption: Anthropological Perspectives. Edited by Chris Shore and Dieter Haller. London: Pluto.

2006 El Alto, Cuidad Rebelde: Organisational Bases for Revolt. Bulletin of Latin American Research 25 (2): 183–99.

Lehm Ardaya, Zulema

1999 Milenarismo y movimientos sociales en la Amazonía Boliviana: La Búsqueda de la Loma Santa y La Marcha por el Territorio y la Dignidad. Santa Cruz de la Sierra, Bolivia: APCOB/Centro de Investigación y Documentación para el Desarrollo del Beni (CIDDEBENI)/OXFAM America.

Lema, Ana María

1998 Pueblos indígenas de la Amazonía Boliviana. La Paz: AIP FIDA-CAF.

2001 De la huella al impacto. La Paz: PIEB.

Lettieri, Michael

2005 Bolivia's Sunday Presidential Elections: Blindly into the Breach. Council on Hemispheric Affairs Press Release. Available online at http://www.coha.org/NEW_PRESS_RELEASES/New_Press_Releases_2005/05.118Bolivia_Morales_Election.html, accessed on December 15, 2005.

Lewin, Boleslao
1957   La rebelión de Tupac Amaru y los origenes de la emancipación americana. Buenos Aires: Hachette.

Li, Tania Murray
1996   Images of Community: Discourse and Strategy in Property Relations. Development and Change 27: 501.

López, Luis Enrique
1995   Intercultural Bilingual Education and the Training of Human Resources: Lessons for Bolivia from the Latin American Experience. *In* Teacher Training and Multiculturalism: National Studies. Edited by Raúl Gagliardi. Paris: International Bureau of Education/United Nations Educational, Scientific, and Cultural Organization (UNESCO).

Los Tiempos
2003   News article. Cochabamba: October 20.

Lucero, José Antonio
2006   Representing "Real Indians": The Challenges of Indigenous Authenticity and Strategic Constructivism in Ecuador and Bolivia. Latin American Research Review 41 (2): 31–56.

Macpherson, C. B.
1978   Property: Mainstream and Critical Positions. Oxford: Basil Blackwell.

Malamud, Andrés
2006   Social Revolution or Political Takeover? The Argentine Collapse of 2001 Reassessed. Paper presented at the Latin American Studies Association meetings, San Juan, Puerto Rico, March.

Malloy, James
1977   Authoritarianism and Corporatism: The Case of Bolivia. *In* Authoritarianism and Corporatism in Latin America. Edited by James Malloy. Pittsburgh: University of Pittsburgh Press.

Malloy, James, and Eduardo Gamarra
1988   Revolution and Reaction: Bolivia, 1964–1985. New Brunswick, N.J.: Transaction Books.

Mamdani, Mahmood
1996   Citizen and Subject: Contemporary Africa and the Legacy of Late Colonialism. Princeton, N.J.: Princeton University Press.

Marinissen, Judith
1998   Legislación Boliviana y pueblos indígenas, inventario y análisis en la perspectiva de las demandas indígenas. Santa Cruz, Bolivia: Servicio Holandés de Cooperación al Desarrollo (SNV)/CEJIS.

Marshall, T. H.
1949   Citizenship and Social Class. *In* Class, Citizenship, and Social Development. Garden City, N.Y.: Anchor Books.

Martínez, José
2001 Proceso de titulación de las tierras comunitarias de origen. *In* La tierras bajas de Bolivia a fines del siglo XX. Edited by Miguel Urioste F. de C. and Diego Pacheco B. La Paz: PIEB.

Martínez Cobo, José
1987 Study of the Problem of Discrimination Against Indigenous Populations. Vol. 5, Conclusions, Proposals, and Recommendations. New York: United Nations (E/CN.4/Sub.2/1986/7/Add.4/Sales No. E.86.XIV.3).

Martínez Montaño, Jose A.
1996 Municipios y participación popular: Un modelo de desarrollo en América Latina. La Paz: Semilla/Centro Boliviano de Investigación y Acción Educativas (CEBIAE).

Marx, Karl
1963 [1869] The Eighteenth Brumaire of Louis Bonaparte. New York: International Publishers.

Maybury Lewis, David, ed.
2002 The Politics of Ethnicity: Indigenous Peoples in Latin American States. Cambridge, Mass.: Harvard University Press.

McCullough, James, and Ronald Johnson
1989 Analyzing Decentralization Policies in Developing Countries: A Political-Economy Framework. Development and Change 20 (1) 57–87.

McEwen, William
1975 Changing Rural Society: A Study of Communities in Bolivia. New York: Oxford University Press.

McNeish, John
2001 Globalization and the Reinvention of Andean Tradition: The Politics of Community and Ethnicity in Highland Bolivia. Journal of Peasant Studies 29 (1): 228–69.

MDH (Ministerio de Desarrollo Humano)
1996 Guía de capacitación para comites de vigilancia. La Paz: MDH/SNPP.

MDH/SNPP
1997 Bolivia: La participación popular en Cifras: Resultados y proyecciones para analizar un proceso de cambio, Tomo II. La Paz: MDH/SNPP.

Medeiros, Carmen
2001 Civilizing the Popular: The Law of Popular Participation and the Design of a New Civil Society in 1990s Bolivia. Critique of Anthropology 21: 401–25.

Medina, Javier
1996 La participación popular como frutas de las luchas sociales. *In* El pulso de la democracia: Participación ciudadana y descentralización en Bolivia. La Paz: SNPP/Nueva Sociedad.
1997 Poderes locales: Implementando la Bolivia del próximo milenio. La Paz: Fondo Editorial FIA/Semilla/CEBIAE.

Mehta, Uday
1997   Liberal Strategies of Exclusion. *In* Tensions of Empire: Colonial Cultures in a Bourgeois World, edited by Frederick Cooper and Ann Laura Stoler. Berkeley: University of California Press.

Meliá, Bartomeu
1988   Ñande Reko, Nuestro Modo de Ser. Vol. 1, Los Guaraní-Chiriguano. La Paz: CIPCA.
1995   La Tierra Sin Mal de los Guaraní, economía y profecía. *In* Chiriguano: Pueblos indígenas de las tierras Baja de Bolivia. La Paz: APCOB.

Merry, Sally Engle
2001   Spatial Governmentality and the New Urban Social Order: Controlling Gender Violence Through Law. American Anthropologist 103 (1): 16–29.

Mirtenbaum, José
1995   Coca no es cocaina: Revista de humanidades y ciencias sociales. Santa Cruz de la Sierra, Bolivia: Universidad Autónoma Gabriel René Moreno.

Mohan, Gilles, and Kristian Stokke
2000   Participatory Development and Empowerment: The Dangers of Localism. Third World Quarterly 21 (2): 247–68.

Molina Monasterios, Fernando
1996   Historia de la Ley de Participación Popular. *In* El pulso de la democracia, participación ciudadana y descentralización en Bolivia. La Paz: SNPP/Nueva Sociedad.

Molina Saucedo, Carlos Hugo
1996   Participación popular y descentralización: Instrumentos para el desarrollo. *In* El pulso de la democracia, participación ciudadana y descentralización en Bolivia. La Paz: SNPP/Nueva Sociedad.

Moore, Donald S.
1998   Clear Waters and Muddied Histories: Environmental History and the Politics of Community in Zimbabwe's Eastern Highlands. Journal of Southern African Studies 24 (2): 377–403.

Morales, Evo
2003   Bolivia, el poder del pueblo. Available online at http://www.journada.unam .mx/2003/octo3/031025/019alpol.php?printver=1&fly=1. Accessed February 11, 2004.

Morris, Arthur, and Stella Lowder, eds.
1992   Decentralization in Latin America: An Evaluation. New York: Praeger.

Mosley, Samuel, Jane Harrigan, and John Toye
1991   Aid and Power: The World Bank and Policy-Based Lending. London: Routledge.

Nandy, Ashish
1983   The Intimate Enemy: Loss and Recovery of Self Under Colonialism. Delhi: Oxford India Press.

Nash, June
1992   Interpreting Social Movements: Bolivian Resistance to Economic Conditions Imposed by the International Monetary Fund. American Ethnologist 19 (2): 275–93.

Nelson, Diane
1999   Finger in the Wound: Body Politics in Quincentennial Guatemala. Berkeley: University of California Press.

O'Donnell, Guillermo, and Phillipe C. Schmitter
1986   Transitions from Authoritarian Rule: Tentative Conclusions About Uncertain Democracies. Baltimore, Md.: Johns Hopkins University Press.

Okin, Susan Moller
1999   Is Multiculturalism Bad for Women? Princeton, N.J.: Princeton University Press.

Olivera, Oscar
2004   ¡Cochabamba! Water War in Bolivia. With Tom Lewis. Boston: South End Press.

Ong, Aihwa
1999   Flexible Citizenship: The Cultural Logics of Transnationality. Durham, N.C.: Duke University Press.
2003   Buddha Is Hiding: Refugees, Citizenship, the New America. Berkeley: University of California Press.

O'Phelan Godoy, Scarlett
1985   Rebellions and Revolts in Eighteenth-century Peru and Upper Peru. Köln, Germany: Böhlau.

Opiniones y Analisis
2003   Tierra, campesinos, e indígenas. Opiniones y Analisis 65. La Paz: Fundemos.

Orduna, Víctor
2004   Los jóvenes, desde el 12 y 13 de febrero. In Para que no se olvide, 12–13 de febrero 2003. La Paz: Asamblea Pernamente de Derechos Humanos de Bolivia (APDHB)/Asociación de Familiares de Detenidos Deaparecidos de Bolivia (ASOFAMD)/DIAKONIA.

Orellana Halkyer, René
2000   Municipalization and Indigenous Peoples in Bolivia: Impacts and Perspectives. In The Challenge of Diversity: Indigenous Peoples and Reform of the State in Latin America. Edited by Willem Assies, Gemma van der Haar, and André J. Hoekema. Amsterdam: Thela Thesis.

Oxhorn, Philip
1998   Is the Century of Corporatism Over? Neoliberalism and the Rise of Neopluralism. In What Kind of Democracy? What Kind of Market? Latin America in the Age of Neoliberalism. Edited by Philip D. Oxhorn and Graciela Ducatenzeiler. University Park: Pennsylvania State University Press.

2003 Social Inequality, Civil Society, and the Limits of Citizenship in Latin America. *In* What Justice? Whose Justice? Fighting for Fairness in Latin America. Edited by Susan Eva Eckstein and Timothy Wickham-Crowley. Berkeley: University of California Press.

Painter, James
1994 Bolivia and Coca: A Study in Dependency. Boulder, Colo.: Lynne Rienner Publishers.

Patzi, Félix
2002 Movimiento Aymará: Una utopía razonada. *In* Las Piedras en el Camino. La Paz: Ministerio de Desarrollo Sostenible y Planificación.
2003 Rebelión indígena contra la colonialdad y la transnacionalización de la economía: Triunfos y vicisitudes del movimiento indígena desde 2000 a 2003. *In* Ya es otro tiempo el presente: cuatro momentos de insurgencia indígena. Forrest Hylton, Félix Patzi, Sergio Serulnikov, and Sinclair Thomson. La Paz: Muela del Diablo Editores.

Pérez Luna, Mamerto
2003 Apertura comercial y sector agrícola campesino, la otra cara de la pobreza del campesino Andino. La Paz: CEDLA.
2004 ¿El último capítulo? Posibles impactos del ALCA en las comunidades campesinas e indígenas de Bolivia. La Paz: CEDLA.
2006 La Ley de Participación Popular en una perspectiva indígena. *In* La Construcción de la Democracia en el Campo Latinoamericano. Edited by Hubert Carton de Grammont. Buenos Aires: Consejo Latinoamericao de Ciencias Sociales (CLACSO).

Pérez, Luna, Mamerto, B. Marcillo, and C. Alborta
2001 Escenarios virtuales y reales del sector agropecuario y rural del altiplano Boliviano. La Paz: CEDLA.

Petras, James
2004 Bolivia: Between Colonization and Revolution. Available online at http://www.canadiandimension.mb.ca/v38/v38_1jp.htm, accessed February 11, 2004.

Petras, James, and Morris Morley
1990 The Metamorphosis of Latin America's Intellectuals. *In* U.S. Hegemony Under Siege: Class Politics and Development in Latin America. London: Verso.

Pifarré, Francisco
1989 Historia de un pueblo. Vol. 2 of Los Guaraní-Chiriguano. La Paz: CIPCA.

Platt, Tristan
1982 Estado Boliviano y ayllu Andino. Tierra y tributo en el norte de Potosí. Lima: Instituto de Estudios Peruanos.
1993 Simón Bolívar, the Sun of Justice, and the Amerindian Virgin: Andean Conceptions of the *Patria* in Nineteenth-century Potosí. Journal of Latin American Studies 25: 161.

1999   La persistencia de los ayllus en el norte de Potosí, de la invasión Europea a la República de Bolivia. La Paz: Fundación Diálogo.

Polanyi, Karl
1944   The Great Transformation. Boston: Beacon Press.

Poole, Deborah
1997   Vision, Race, and Modernity: A Visual Economy of the Andean Image World. Princeton, N.J.: Princeton University Press.

Portes, Alejandro, and Kelly Hoffman
2003   Latin American Class Structures: Their Composition and Change During the Neoliberal Era. Latin American Research Review 38 (1): 41–82.

Postero, Nancy
2000   A Case Study of Land Loss and Leadership in a Guaraní Village. Paper presented at the meeting of the American Anthropology Association, San Francisco, Calif., November.
2001   Suburban Indians: Constructing Indigenous Identity and Citizenship in Lowland Bolivia. Ph.D. diss., University of California, Berkeley, UMI No. 30444632.
2004   Articulation and Fragmentation: Indigenous Politics in Bolivia. In The Struggle for Indian Rights in Latin America. Edited by Nancy Postero and Leon Zamosc. London: Sussex Academic Press.
2005   Indigenous Responses to Neoliberalism: A Look at the Bolivian Uprising of 2003. Political and Legal Anthropology Review 28 (1): 73–92.

Postero, Nancy, and Leon Zamosc, eds.
2004   Indigenous Movements and the Indian Question in Latin America. In The Struggle for Indian Rights in Latin America. Edited by Nancy Postero and Leon Zamosc. London: Sussex Academic Press.

Potter, George Ann
2004   Is the War on Drugs in Bolivia Bringing "Dignity" to Bolivia? Available online at http://www.coha.org/WRH_issues/WRH_19_21_Bolivia_War_on _Drugs.htm, accessed June 3, 2004.

Povinelli, Elizabeth A.
2002   The Cunning of Recognition. Durham, N.C.: Duke University Press.

Psacharopoulos, George, and Harry Patrinos
1994   Indigenous People and Poverty in Latin America. Washington, D.C.: World Bank.

Putnam, Robert
1993   The Prosperous Community: Social Capital and Public Life. American Prospect 13 (20): 35–42.
1995   Bowling Alone: America's Declining Social Capital. Journal of Democracy 6 (1): 65–78.

Quintana, Juan Ramón
2004   Policías y militares: Memorias y escenarios de conflicto. In Para que no se olvide, 12–13 de febrero 2003. La Paz: APDHB/ASOFAMD/DIAKONIA.

Quiroga, José Antonio
1990   Coca/cocaína: Una vision Boliviana. La Paz: AIPE-PROCOM/CEDLA/CID.
2004   Antecedentes y contexto de la crisis de febrero. *In* Para que no se olvide, 12–13 de febrero 2003. La Paz: APDHB/ASOFAMD/DIAKONIA.

Radcliffe, Sarah, and Sallie Westwood
1996   Remaking the Nation: Place, Identity, and Politics in Latin America. London: Routledge.

Radio Pachamama
2004   Para que el tiempo no borre la memoria . . . No a la impunidad. El Alto, Bolivia: Centro de Promoción de la Mujer Gregoria Apaza.

Ramírez, Susan E.
1986   Provincial Patriarchs: Land Tenure and the Economics of Power in Colonial Peru. Albuquerque: University of New Mexico Press.

Ramos, Alcida Rita
1998   Indigenism: Ethnic Politics in Brazil. Madison: University of Wisconsin Press.

Rappaport, Joanne
2005   Intercultural Utopias, Public Intellectuals, Cultural Experimentation, and Ethnic Pluralism in Colombia. Durham, N.C.: Duke University Press.

Rasnake, Roger
1988   Domination and Cultural Resistance: Authority and Power Among an Andean People. Durham, N.C.: Duke University Press.

Rawls, John
1971   A Theory of Justice. Cambridge, Mass.: Harvard University Press.

Richards, Patricia
1998   Finding the Loma Santa: NGOs and Civil Society in Bolivia. Paper presented at Mellon Conference of Latin American Sociology, Berkeley, Calif., February.

Riester, Jürgen
1985   CIDOB's Role in the Self-Determination of the Eastern Bolivian Indians. Cultural Survival, Occasional Papers, No. 16: 55–74. Cambridge, Mass., January.

Rivera Cusicanqui, Silvia
1987   Oppressed but Not Defeated, Peasant Struggles Among the Aymara and Qhechwa in Bolivia, 1900–1980. (English translation). Geneva: United Nations Research Institute for Social Development.
1993   La Raiz: Colonizadores y colonizados. *In* Violencias encubiertas en Bolivia. Edited by Xavier Albó and Raul Barrios. La Paz: CIPCA/Ediciones Aruwiyiri.
2003   Las fronteras de la Coca. La Paz: Instituto de Investigaciones Sociológicas "Mauricio LeFebvre"–Universidad Mayor de San Andrés (IDIS-UMSA) y Ediciones Aruwiyiri.
2004   Reclaiming the Nation. NACLA Report on the Americas 38 (3): 19–23.

Robins, Nicholas A.
2002   Genocide and Millennialism in Upper Peru. Westport, Conn.: Praeger.

Robinson, William
1996   Promoting Polyarchy: Globalization, U.S. Intervention, and Hegemony. Cambridge: Cambridge University Press.
2004   Global Crisis and Latin America. Bulletin of Latin American Research 23 (2): 135–53.

Romero Moreno, Fernando
1996   Desarrollo sostenible y participación popular ciudadana. In El pulso de la democracia: participación ciudadana y la descentralización de Bolivia. La Paz: MDH/SNPP/Nueva Sociedad.

Roper, J. Montgomery
2003   Bolivian Legal Reforms and Local Indigenous Organizations: Opportunities and Obstacles in a Lowland Municipality. Latin American Perspectives 30 (1): 139–61.

Rose, Nikolas
1996   Governing "Advanced" Liberal Democracies. In Foucault and Political Reason. Edited by Andrew Barry, Thomas Osborne, and Nikolas Rose. Chicago: University of Chicago Press.
1999   Powers of Freedom: Reframing Political Thought. Cambridge: Cambridge University Press.

Roseberry, William
1996   Hegemony, Power, and Languages of Contention. In The Politics of Difference. Edited by Edwin Wilmsen and Patrick McAllister. Chicago: University of Chicago Press.

Rus, Jan
1994   The "Comunidad Revolucionaria Institucional": The Subversion of Native Government in Highland Chiapas, 1936–1968. In Everyday Forms of State Formation. Edited by Gilbert Joseph and Daniel Nugent. Durham, N.C.: Duke University Press.

Rus, Jan, Rosalva Aída Hernández Castillo, and Shannon Mattiace
2003   Mayan Lives, Mayan Utopias: The Indigenous Peoples of Chiapas and the Zapatista Rebellion. Oxford: Rowman & Littlefield.

Sachs, Jeffrey
1987   The Bolivian Hyperinflation and Stabilization. American Economic Review 77 (2): 279–83.

Saignes, Thierry
1982   Guerres indiennes dans l'Amérique pionèrre: Le dilemme de la résistance chiriguano à la colonisation européenne (XVIeme–XIX siecles). Histoire, Économie et Société 1: 77–103.

Saignes, Thierry, and Isabel Combes
1995   Chiri-guana: Nacimiento de una identidad mestiza. In Chiriguano: Pueblos indígenas de las tierras bajas de Bolivia. Santa Cruz, Bolivia: APCOB.

Samoff, Joel
1990   Decentralization: The Politics of Interventionism. Development and Change 21: 513–30.

Sanabria, Harry
1993 The Coca Boom and Rural Social Change in Bolivia. Ann Arbor: University of Michigan Press.
2000 Resistance and the Arts of Domination: Miners and the Bolivian State. Latin American Perspectives 27 (1): 56–81.

Sanabria Fernandez, Hernando
1972 Apiaguaiqui-Tumpa, Biografía del pueblo Chiriguano y de su último caudillo. La Paz-Cochabamba: Amigos de Libro.

Sánchez C., Walter
1997 Fiesta y guerra, música, danzas, cantos e instrumentos musicales de los guaraní-chiriguano. In Música y canto de los Guaraní. La Paz: Fundación Simon I. Patiño.

Sánchez de Lozada, Gonzalo
1996 Bolivia debe cambiar. In El pulso de la democracia, participación ciudadana y descentralización en Bolivia. La Paz: SNPP/Nueva Sociedad.

Sandoval, Godofredo
1992 Gestión y organización de los ONGs. In Gestión y políticas institucionales en organismos no-gubermentales de desarrollo en América Latina. Lima: IRED/DESCO.

Sanjinés, Javier C.
2004 Mestizaje Upside Down: Aesthetic Politics in Modern Bolivia. Pittsburgh: University of Pittsburgh Press.

Sawyer, Suzana
2004 Crude Chronicles: Indigenous Politics, Multinational Oil, and Neoliberalism in Ecuador. Durham, N.C.: Duke University Press.

Schild, Veronica
1998 New Subject of Rights? Women's Movements and the Construction of Citizenship in the "New Democracies." In Cultures of Politics, Politics of Cultures. Edited by Sonia Alvarez, Evelina Dagnino, and Arturo Escobar. Boulder, Colo.: Westview Press.
2000 Neo-liberalism's New Gendered Market Citizens: The "Civilizing" Dimension of Social Programmes in Chile. Citizenship Studies 4 (3): 275–305.

Seider, Rachel, ed.
2002 Multiculturalism in Latin America: Indigenous Rights, Diversity, and Democracy. London: Palgrave.

Serulnikov, Sergio
2003 Subverting Colonial Authority: Challenges to Spanish Rule in Eighteenth-century Southern Andes. Durham, N.C.: Duke University Press.

Service, Elman R.
1954 Spanish-Guaraní Relations in Early Colonial Paraguay. Ann Arbor: University of Michigan Press.

Shafir, Gershon, ed.
1998 The Citizenship Debates: A Reader. Minneapolis: University of Minnesota Press.

Shepherd, Chris J.
2005 Agricultural Hybridity and the "Pathology" of Traditional Ways: The Translation of Desire and Need in Postcolonial Development. Journal of Latin American Anthropology 9 (2): 235–66.

Shiva, Vandana
2004   Water Democracy. In ¡Cochabamba! Water War in Bolivia. Oscar Olivera in collaboration with Tom Lewis. Boston: South End Press.

Shore, Cris, and Dieter Haller
2005   Sharp Practice: Anthropology and the Study of Corruption. In Corruption: Anthropological Perspectives. Edited by Shore and Haller. London: Pluto.

Slater, David
1989   Territorial Power and the Peripheral State: The Issue of Decentralization. Development and Change 20: 501–31.

Slawner, Karen, and Mark Denham, eds.
1998   Citizenship After Liberalism. New York: Peter Lang.

SNPP (Secretaría Nacional de Participación Popular)
1996   El pulso de la Democracia: Participación ciudadana y descentralización en Bolivia. La Paz: Editorial Nueva Sociedad.

Soruco, Ximena, Ximena Pabón, and Esteban Sanjinés
2000   Los Dueños del Micrófono: Tácticas y estrategias ciudadanas en los medios. La Paz: PIEB.

Soysal, Yasemin Nuhoglu
1994   Limits of Citizenship: Migrants and Postnational Membership in Europe. Chicago: University of Chicago Press.

Spedding, Alison, ed.
2003 En defensa de la hoja de coca. La Paz: PIEB.

Stahl, Karin
1996   Anti-Poverty Programs: Making Structural Adjustment More Palatable. NACLA Report on the Americas 29 (6): 32–37.

Stavig, Ward
1999   The World of Túpac Amaru: Conflict, Community, and Identity in Colonial Peru. Lincoln: University of Nebraska Press.

Stearman, Allyn MacLean
1985   Camba and Kolla: Migration and Development in Santa Cruz, Bolivia. Orlando: University of Central Florida Press.
1989   Yuquí: Forest Nomads in a Changing World. New York: Holt, Rinehart, and Winston.

Stern, Steve
1987   Resistance, Rebellion, and Consciousness in the Andean Peasant World, Eighteenth to Twentieth Centuries. Madison: University of Wisconsin Press.
1993 [1982]   Peru's Indian Peoples and the Challenge of Spanish Conquest. Second edition. Madison: University of Wisconsin Press.

Stewart, Angus
1995 Two Conceptions of Citizenship. British Journal of Sociology 46 (1): 63–78.

Stoll, David
1990 Is Latin America Turning Protestant?: The Politics of Evangelical Growth Berkeley: University of California Press.
1993 Rethinking Protestantism in Latin America. Philadelphia: Temple University Press.

Ströbele-Gregor, Juliana
1996 Culture and Political Practice of the Aymara and Quechua in Bolivia: Autonomous Forms of Modernity in the Andes. Latin American Perspectives 23 (2): 72–90.

Szeminski, Jan
1983 La utopía tupamarista. San Miguel, Lima: Pontificia Universidad Católica del Perú, Fondo Editorial.

Tandeter, Enrique
1993 Coercion and Market: Silver Mining in Colonial Potosí, 1692–1826. Albuquerque: University of New Mexico Press.

Tapia, Luis
2002 Movimientos sociales, movimientos societal, los no lugares de la política. In Democratizaciones plebeyas. La Paz: Muela del Diablo Editores.

Taylor, Charles
1992 Multiculturalism and "the Politics of Recognition." Princeton, N.J.: Princeton University Press.

Taylor, Lucy, and Fiona Wilson
2004 The Messiness of Everyday Life: Exploring Key Themes in Latin American Citizenship Studies, Introduction. Bulletin of Latin American Research 23 (2): 154–64.

Thompson, Ginger, and James C. McKinley
2005 Move Against Leftist Mayor Sets Off Protests in Mexico. New York Times, April 2.

Thomson, Sinclair
2002 We Alone Shall Rule: Native Andean Politics in the Age of Insurgency. Madison: University of Wisconsin Press.

Thorn, Richard
1971 The Economic Transformation. In Beyond the Revolution. Edited by James Malloy and Richard Thorn. Pittsburgh: University of Pittsburgh Press.

Thurner, Mark
1997 From Two Republics to One Divided: Contradictions of Postcolonial Nation-making in Andean Peru. Durham, N.C.: Duke University Press.

Ticona, Esteban, Gonzalo Rojas, and Xavier Albó
1995 Votos y Wiphalas: Campesinos y pueblos originarios en democracia. La Paz: Fundación Milenio/CIPCA.

Tolan, Sandy, and Nancy Postero
1992   Accidents of History. New York Times Magazine, February 22.

Trelles Aréstegui, Efraín
1982   Lucas Martínez Vegazo: Funcionamento de una encomienda peruana inicial. Lima: Pontificia Universidad Católica del Peru, Fondo Editorial.

Turner, Terence
1995   An Indigenous People's Struggle for Socially Equitable and Ecologically Sustainable Production: The Kayapo Revolt Against Extractionism. Journal of Latin American Anthropology 1 (1): 98–121.

UNDP (United Nations Development Program)
2004   Interculturalismo y globalización: La Bolivia Posible. La Paz: UNDP.

Unzueta, Fernando
2000   Periódicos y formación nacional: Bolivia en sus primeros años. Latin America Research Review 35 (2): 35–72.

Urioste Fernández de Córdova, Miguel
2002   Desarrollo rural con participación popular. La Paz: Fundación Tierra.

Valcárcel, Carlos Daniel
1970   El retrato de Túpac Amaru. Lima: Editorial Rocarme.

Van Cott, Donna Lee
1994   Indigenous Peoples and Democracy in Latin America. New York: St. Martin's Press.
2000   The Friendly Liquidation of the Past: The Politics of Diversity in Latin America. Pittsburgh: University of Pittsburgh Press.
2002   Constitutional Reform in the Andes: Redefining Indigenous-State Relations. *In* Multiculturalism in Latin America: Indigenous Rights, Diversity, and Democracy. Edited by Rachel Seider. London: Palgrave.
2003   From Exclusion to Inclusion: Bolivia's 2002 Elections. Journal of Latin American Studies 35 (4): 751–77.

Van Niekerk, Nico
1992   La cooperación internacional y la persistencia de la pobreza en los Andes Bolivianos. La Paz: Unión Nacional de Instituciones para el Trabajo de Acción Social (UNITAS)/ Misión de Cooperación Técnica Holandesa (MCTH).

Varese, Stefano
1996   Parroquialismo y globalización, las etnicidades indígenas ante el tercer milenio. *In* Pueblos indios, soberania, y globalismo. Quito, Ecuador: Ediciones Abya-Yala.

Vargas, Humberto, and Tom Kruse
2000   Las victorias de abril: Una historia que aún con concluye. CLACSO 2000: 7–14.

Vargas Llosa, Álvaro
2005   No Left Turn. New York Times, December 20.

Von Steenbergen, Bart
1994   The Condition of Citizenship. London: Sage Publications.

Wade, Peter
1997   Race and Ethnicity in Latin America. London: Pluto Press.

Walker, Charles
1999   Smoldering Ashes: Cuzco and the Creation of Republican Peru, 1780–1840. Durham, N.C.: Duke University Press.

Warren, Kay, and Jean Jackson, eds.
2002   Indigenous Movements, Self-Representation, and the State in Latin America. Austin: University of Texas Press.

Washington Office on Latin America
2003   Coca Conflict Turns Violent. Available online at http://www.wola.org/ddhr/ddhr_home.htm.

White, Sarah C.
1999   NGOs, Civil Society, and the State in Bangladesh: The Politics of Representing the Poor. Development and Change 30: 307–26.

Williams, Raymond
1977   Marxism and Literature. Oxford: Oxford University Press.

Wilmsen, Edwin
1996   The Politics of Difference: Ethnic Premises in a World of Power. Chicago: University of Chicago Press.

World Bank
2004   Community Driven Development Home Page. Available online at http://lnweb18.worldbank.org/ESSD/sdvext.nsf/66ParentDoc/Participationand CivicEngagement?Opendocument, accessed April 5, 2005.
2005   Indigenous Peoples, Poverty, and Human Development in Latin America: 1994–2004. Available online at http://web.worldbank.org/WEBSITE/EXTERNAL/COUNTRIES/LACEXT/0,,contentMDK:20505834~pagePK:146736~piPK:146830~theSitePK:258554,00.html, accessed May 19, 2005.

Wunsch, James
2001   Decentralization, Local Governance, and "Recentralization" in Africa. Public Administration and Development 21: 277–88.

Yashar, Deborah J.
1998   Contesting Citizenship: Indigenous Movements and Democracy in Latin America. Comparative Politics 3 (1): 23–42.
1999   Democracy, Indigenous Movements, and the Postliberal Challenge in Latin America. World Politics 52 (October 1999): 76–104.
2005   Contesting Citizenship in Latin America. Cambridge: Cambridge University Press.

Young, Iris Marion
1996   Polity and Group Difference: A Critique of the Ideal of Universal Citizenship. In Theorizing Citizenship. Edited by Ronald Beiner. Albany: State University of New York.

Yúdice, George
2003   The Expediency of Culture: Uses of Culture in the Global Era (Post Con-
       temporary Interventions). Durham, N.C.: Duke University Press.

Yuval-Davis, Nira, and Pnina Werbner, eds.
1999   Women, Citizenship, and Difference. London: Zed Books.

Zamosc, Leon
2004   The Indian Movement in Ecuador: From Politics of Influence to Politics of
       Power. In The Struggle for Indian Rights in Latin America. Edited by Nancy
       Postero and Leon Zamosc. London: Sussex Academic Press.

Zavaleta, René
1987   El poder dual: Problemas de la teoría del estado en América Latina.
       Cochabamba-La Paz: Editorial Los Amigos del Libro.

Žižek, Slavoj
1997   Multiculturalism, Or, the Cultural Logic of Multinationalism. New Left
       Review 225: 28–51.

Index